MIRRORS FOR PRINCES

MIRRORS FOR PRINCES

How "Tips for Tyrants" Became Clichés of Leadership

MICHAEL KEELEY

GEORGETOWN UNIVERSITY PRESS   WASHINGTON, DC

The publisher is not responsible for third-party websites or their content. URL links were active at time of publication.

Library of Congress Cataloging-in-Publication Data

Names: Keeley, Michael C., author.
Title: Mirrors for princes : how "tips for tyrants" became clichés of leadership / Michael Keeley.
Identifiers: LCCN 2023037214 (print) | LCCN 2023037215 (ebook) | ISBN 9781647124533 (hardcover) | ISBN 9781647125530 (paperback) | ISBN 9781647124540 (ebook)
Subjects: LCSH: Education of princes. | Political leadership. | Leadership. | Management. | Management literature.
Classification: LCC JC393 .K44 2024 (print) | LCC JC393 (ebook) | DDC 303.3/4—dc23/eng/20230812
LC record available at https://lccn.loc.gov/2023037214
LC ebook record available at https://lccn.loc.gov/2023037215

Interior Design: Classic City Composition, Athens, GA
Jacket Design: Spencer Fuller, Faceout Studio
∞ This paper meets the requirements of ANSI/NISO Z39.48-1992 (Permanence of Paper).
25 24   9 8 7 6 5 4 3 2 First printing
Printed in the United States of America

To Lorraine

CONTENTS

INTRODUCTION

For four thousand years kings and queens ruled the known world, and for four thousand years management experts told them how to do it. Some experts today will tell you management is a modern science, originating with assembly lines in Detroit or textile mills in England. But before there was ever a Detroit, before there was even an England, there were management gurus. Most were teachers, lawyers, clerics—the professions you'd expect—and they wrote books on leadership, strategy, ethics, the usual topics. Writers showed how an ideal ruler acted in textbook cases. They also showed how real rulers acted, which could be ugly and risky to tell a king to his face. Their books worked like a looking glass where a king could seek his own reflection and of course see the ideal. These books were called mirrors for princes.

Princes could not always read books themselves. Early on, tutors read mirrors for princes to them and to their courtiers. Long before the Bible, noble children learned to read and write by copying out proverbs from mirrors for princes. As literacy spread, authors wrote mirrors of general interest, whether princes read them or not. Popular mirrors got reproduced, revised, translated, and handed down to guide new rulers, ministers, and their subjects. Countless numbers of mirrors for princes—written in Greek and Latin, Norse and Arabic, Old Irish and English, French and Italian—survive in remote libraries around the world. You can go to your own library and read in your own language the classic of them all: *The Education of Cyrus*, composed by the military chronicler Xenophon in the fourth century BC.

Look, Xenophon writes, people are almost impossible to manage and they're getting worse. Take Persia, once a great empire. People there are less religious, less respectful of family values, less concerned for their

1

neighbors, and lazier than ever. Their leaders have grown soft, he says, putting soldiers to work as their "butlers and cooks and confectioners and cupbearers and bathmen and flunkeys." The police are corrupt; judges extort bribes; children play with poisons and kill one another just for fun. The trouble started with the death of Cyrus. Cyrus was the founding king of Persia. He learned how to grow an empire, how to manage people who lived far away, who never even saw him but who followed him anyway. Xenophon relates what Cyrus had to learn in order to be successful: He learned basic principles of management, how to divide labor and pay for results. He learned virtue, how to put the common good above his own. He learned leadership, how to unite people behind a shared vision of empire. Finally, he learned to get rid of individuals who thought they knew better. Now, Xenophon says, Cyrus is dead, now his empire has decayed, but future rulers can learn from Cyrus's example.[1]

For ages thereafter leaders and students of government looked at *The Education of Cyrus* to learn what he learned. Many people looked at the book simply because it reads like a romance novel. And, in fact, it is. Today teachers of literature, classics, philosophy, and political science all claim *The Education of Cyrus*—as a forerunner of the historical novel, the fictional biography, the ideal romance, and the constitutional treatise as well as mirrors for princes. Yes, there really was a King Cyrus. No, he didn't really do all the things Xenophon said. Still, Cyrus provided a leadership model for generations of kings and queens and sultans and other rulers, and Xenophon produced a model textbook for their mentors—for Cicero, Machiavelli, Erasmus, and a legion of lesser writers.[2]

While normally addressed to rulers, mirrors for princes appealed to a wider audience, just like trade books on leadership nowadays. They grew in popularity—selling almost as well as the Bible—up to the eighteenth century, when princes and royalist literature fell out of fashion. Since that time, only small groups of scholars have shown much interest in them, and then only in particular works. Political philosophers continued to read a few famous titles, such as Machiavelli's *Prince* and Aristotle's *Politics*. German specialists studied classical mirrors, termed *Fürstenspiegel*, for a while before World War II. But in general the genre was forgotten, and today well-read people have never heard of "mirrors for princes."[3]

Historians who *have* read them, like J. H. Hexter, dismiss mirrors for princes as "dreary, cliché-ridden books."[4] Anyone with the patience to sift through them can see why. They are fishy stories, transcribed homilies, old rulebooks, and textbooks after all. (Some, notes historian Jean-Philippe Genet, "are more like visiting cards left by the author to make himself known and to signal the potential granting of a favor."[5]) Even the classics, Hexter observes, drop rhetorical clinkers. The world's most brilliant thinkers on other subjects for some reason turned trite when they wrote to princes: Aristotle stooped to teaching "tips for tyrants" in the *Politics*; Machiavelli addressed *The Prince* to ruthless bosses, using language they'd understand, in a desperate bid for employment; Thomas Aquinas gave up writing a mirror, *On Kingship*—clearly no *Summa*—that his students labored to finish.

Yet one can learn something from mirrors for princes. It is mainly by reading cliché-ridden books that one learns to recognize clichés. After reading *The Education of Cyrus* and other ancient mirrors, one can see clichés in *The Prince* and the *Politics*—then in modern knockoffs of Machiavelli and Aristotle.[6] After reading nostalgic tales of grand empires ruled by visionary leaders in works by Xenophon and his successors, one can spot the clichés in memoirs by celebrity CEOs, in how-to books on management, and in academic articles on business ethics.

Ancient clichés show up especially in business ethics, for instance, in talk of community, virtue, and the common good. Ethics teachers sometimes wrench these terms from their historical settings and display them, like unearthed pottery shards, as fragments of a communal tradition that was built by the ancients but later shattered by rights-wielding liberals. Their hope is to restore the tradition through moral leadership. One leading communitarian, Alasdair MacIntyre, has longed to restore the virtues known to medieval kings and courtiers, such as King Henry II, Thomas Becket, and John of Salisbury, "because of what the medieval kingdom shares with the *polis*, as Aristotle conceived it": Both are "communities in which men in company pursue *the* common good and not merely," as modern liberals prefer, "the arena in which each individual seeks his or her own private good."[7]

Historians remain skeptical. Few think medieval kingdoms or ancient states actually were communities where people in company pursued the common good. Too many broken bones, pierced skulls, and other signs of violence turn up in archaeological sites. And mirrors for princes themselves cause skepticism. True, they say a lot about virtue, community, and the common good; but if you look closely you will see they mostly gripe about the *loss* of these things. In a twelfth-century mirror called the *Policraticus*, John of Salisbury complained just like MacIntyre about the individualism of his day, the lack of community, and disregard for the common good; he too supposed the ancients had the key to virtue. But the ancients, including Aristotle, had the same complaints. "The *polis*, as Aristotle conceived it" in the *Politics*, was an ideal he found nowhere on earth.[8]

In mirror after mirror for princes, writers imagined a better time or place where people were not so selfish, institutions not so corrupt, leaders not so bad. Certainly, readers can pick out memorable lines in such books and managers can identify some inspiring heroes. But when one reads the same laments and platitudes in mirrors going back century after century, one can see also the stereotypes, the half-truths, the old clichés standing in the way of fresh ideas.

See for yourself. This book is a guide to mirrors for princes you can find in English, either online or in larger libraries. It is necessarily selective. It focuses on a manageable number of representative mirrors, chiefly but not exclusively Western, starting with the appearance of mirrors for princes in ancient Egypt. It surveys mirrors of the Greco-Roman world and classical satires of the genre, which were already popular by the second century. It sketches the growth of mirrors for princes during the Middle Ages, from the courts of Charlemagne's family, through Muslim schools for sultans, to the palaces of Renaissance kings. It shows Machiavelli's famous mirror, *The Prince*, to be one among many such books on leadership—nothing very new, just more explicit. And it traces the transmission of the mirrors-for-princes tradition to colonial America in the form of Puritan election sermons, modeled on the jeremiads of biblical prophets.

Despite the variety of mirrors for princes, most preach the same lesson: They sense a problem—people are behaving badly. They diagnose a cause—people are too selfish, doing their own things. And they prescribe a cure—people should unite behind common goals, like members of one organic body. It is the job of the prince, king, queen, caliph, any leader, to articulate common goals and provide a transforming vision for everyone to follow. Over the centuries, this formula drew critics claiming it was impractical or immoral as a theory of governance. But it remained the official ideology of great empires until the age of revolutions. The American Revolution sped its demise in the United States; the obituary of mirrors for princes was written by political thinkers such as James Madison, who compared the diversity of personal goals and group interests in society to the diversity of religions. Such diversity stems not from pure selfishness but from legitimate differences of opinion. And trying to remove these differences by declaring common ends can be worse than the underlying problem (witness the Inquisition). For Madison, societies are more like social contracts than natural bodies; and the task of governance is to manage differences with fairness, not paper over them with mission statements or suppress them for reasons of state.

Although mirrors for princes are now passé, their clichés live on in modern mirrors for managers. Management theorists depict organizations as social bodies that exist to achieve shared goals. Actual organizations may not in fact have common goals, theorists concede, but they *should*. Lack of common goals is attributed to the ignorance, recalcitrance, or general selfishness of organizational members (as opposed to a flaw in theorists' goal-model of organizations). Therefore, organizations need transformational leaders, not mere transactional managers, to envision a shared purpose and inspire followers to place this common goal above their own. The aim of *this* book is to sensitize readers to these clichés, to raise awareness that they *are* clichés.

The rhetoric of common goals and transformational leadership has a pleasing resonance for top managers, affirming their authority, just as it did for kings and queens in mirrors for princes. I don't expect to persuade managers to abandon it. My intent is to help *readers* become more savvy consumers of management literature. After seeing the same clichés in one after another mirror for princes, readers can hopefully recognize and question them when they see them in management journals, leadership studies, the *Wall Street Journal*, or public relations campaigns like the Business Roundtable "Statement on the Purpose of a Corporation."

The book concludes with a chapter for writers of management literature, suggesting how organizational theorists and business ethicists might avoid the clichés of mirrors for princes and managers. My suggestion is to discard the old organic model of social bodies, which gives rise to the clichés of mirrors for princes, and instead develop a social contract model of organizations. Like the organic model, a social contract model has both descriptive and prescriptive features: It describes organizations as agreements on rules between a variety of stakeholders with diverse goals of their own for the organization, and it prescribes fairness among stakeholders rather than maximization of some(one's) so-called organizational goal as an overarching principle of governance. Practical implications include reform of ubiquitous but arguably unfair "contracts of adhesion," such as mandatory arbitration agreements that force stakeholders to accept corporate adjudication of their legal rights. To further such reforms, organization theorists and business ethicists may need to broaden their research and writing—away from focusing on managers' interests to addressing concerns of lawmakers and regulators.

Readers, of course, need not care about any final agenda for research to see the trouble with mirrors for princes.

ONE

Egyptian Mirrors

Doorkeepers say: "Let us go and plunder."... The laundryman refuses to carry his load.... [Farm hands] carry shields.... A man regards his son as his enemy.... A man of character goes in mourning because of what has happened in the land.... Foreigners [are] everywhere.... Robbery is everywhere. There is no man of yesterday.

This land is helter skelter.... Every mouth is full of "Love Me!," and everything good has disappeared.

Prophecies of Ipuwer and Neferti

In the twenty-first century BC, prophets looked around the kingdom of Egypt and saw chaos. They saw incivility in low places: "All maidservants make free with their tongues." They saw corruption in high places: "The storehouse of the king is a (mere) come-and-get-it for everybody." They saw "the land topsy-turvy": "Behold, nobles' ladies are (now) gleaners, and nobles are in the workhouse. (But) he who never (even) slept on a plank is (now) the owner of a bed" and "she who looked at her face in the water is (now) the owner of a mirror." They lamented, "The land is diminished, (but) its administrators are many; bare, (but) its taxes are great."[1]

What looked to the world like a great civilization looked to the prophets like a land in decline. The old guard pinned their hopes for revival on a family of kings who ruled at Heracleopolis, a city to the south of the Nile delta. One of these kings was named Merikare, and one of the earliest surviving mirror for princes was addressed to him.[2]

Titled the *Instruction for King Merikare*, it is written like many mirrors in the form of a king's advice to his son and successor. The author claims he is Merikare's father, "King of Upper and Lower Egypt," but that's doubtful. He says he once lost control, his mistake, which no pharaoh would admit. Some courtier to the royal family probably wrote it. He instructs Merikare to imitate his ancestors, the kings of old, and set an example of good character. He tells Merikare to mind the sages of blessed memory and keep the commandments found in sacred writings. He says don't steal widows' inheritances or cheat their sons; don't vandalize tombs for building stone but quarry your own; don't slaughter to punish petty crime—just kill partisans who create factions, hotheads who lure youth, and talkers who excite crowds. The author advises Merikare to divert the heat of the masses into worthy projects, where they work for him like a single team. And he reminds the prince to reward his top courtiers richly, for "great is a great man when his great men are great."[3]

Children of kings and courtiers recited instructions like these in palace schools many centuries before the education of Cyrus. While alluding to local issues, Egyptian mirrors reflect the universal teachings of later mirrors for princes. Commands such as *don't do this, don't do that*, for example, imply that people are behaving badly. The *Instruction for King Merikare* warns about factions, dissention, sedition, theft, deceit, extortion, violence, impiety, pride, envy, wrath, one vice after another. Egyptian mirrors suggest that the fundamental vice is greed, selfishness. They teach, "The virtue of a wise man is to gather without greed," and "Do not be greedy lest your name stink." From the outset, mirrors for princes prescribed a remedy for selfishness: a common goal. The Egyptians had a word for this goal; they called it *maat*.[4]

Maat

"Do maat that you may endure upon earth," says the *Instruction for King Merikare*. This dictum is literally etched in stone; you can see it on some of the oldest monuments in Egypt. Pioneering Egyptologist James Henry Breasted declared maat "one of the earliest abstract terms preserved in human speech." The term is hard to define—whatever maat was, it certainly was abstract. It's been translated as justice, righteousness, truth, authenticity, stability, balance, natural order, divine law, moral values, honesty, fair dealing, ethical conduct, social responsibility, peace, harmony, security, social solidarity, virtue, character, piety, goodness, the standard by which all deeds should be measured or judged, the reason for life, the purpose for speech, the source of happiness, statecraft, legitimacy, correct governance, the good of the cosmos, and the general welfare. There really is no one translation. That was the pharaoh's job, to translate *maat* into a shared vision of a good life.[5]

Abstract goals like maat were appealing to rulers, if not necessarily to their subjects. (Inscriptions left by lower-ranking Egyptians seldom mention maat.) Such goals justified authority, increasing job security for those charged with interpreting them. Pharaohs needed to do maat, they claimed, to save Egypt from chaos. Even better for rulers, abstract goals could mean almost anything in action. At one time or another, maat meant building a great pyramid for the king's burial; it meant branding foreigners as terrorists and critics as threats to national security; it meant giving tax breaks to religious leaders, government contractors, or other royal supporters. Doing maat meant whatever Pharaoh said it meant.[6]

It was the job of Pharaoh's subjects to make his vision happen. "Do maat for the king, for maat is what the king loves," was everyone's duty.[7] For ordinary Egyptians, this was hard work. For the privileged, doing maat was just good business. Courtiers, contractors, and consultants all got ahead by doing what Pharaoh defined as maat; the concept "furnished a sort of alibi for the most unbridled ambition," notes French Egyptologist Pascal Vernus.[8] Doing maat is portrayed in a ritual meeting between a king and his executive team, as deciphered by archaeologist Henri Frankfort: The king opens the meeting by saying, "'Behold My Majesty decrees a work and is thinking of a deed' [it's a new building]; and the councilors answer: 'Authoritative Utterance is (in) thy mouth, Understanding follows, thee. O Sovereign (Life! Prosperity! Health!), it is thy plans which come to pass.'"[9]

From age to age, royal counselors learned palace rituals and codes of conduct from specialized mirrors addressed to the courtiers of princes. Again, an Egyptian text from about 2200 BC is among the oldest examples; it is called the *Instruction of Ptahhotep*. The writer says he's the vizier or chief official of King Izezi. (Once more, he's probably not; ancient books were often attributed to famous persons, much like the Christian gospels.) "Ptahhotep" writes that he is retiring from office and wants to teach his son how to act in his place. Through a series of maxims, similar to modern management precepts, he teaches how to speak:

> If you are a man of worth
> Who sits in his master's council,
> Concentrate on excellence,
> Your silence is better than chatter.
> Speak when you know you have a solution,
> It is the skilled who should speak in council.

He teaches how to listen (in the human-relations style of the Hawthorne studies):

> If you are a man who leads,
> Listen calmly to the speech of one who pleads;
> Don't stop him from purging his body
> Of that which he planned to tell.
> A man in distress wants to pour out his heart
> More than that his case be won.

He teaches how to take orders:

> Don't oppose a great man's action. . . .
> He is the provider along with the god,
> What he wishes should be done for him. . . .
> Bend your back to your superior,
> Your overseer from the palace;
> Then your house will endure in its wealth.

Ptahhotep teaches how to behave around the boss:

> If you are one among guests
> At the table of one greater than you,
> Take what he gives as it is set before you. . . .
> He will give to him whom he favors. . . .
> A fool is who complains of it.

And as usual he teaches that the goal of maat trumps selfishness:

> If you want a perfect conduct,
> To be free from every evil,

Guard against the vice of greed:
A grievous sickness . . .
It embroils fathers, mothers,
And the brothers of the mother,
It parts wife from husband;
It is a compound of all evils,
A bundle of all hateful things.
That man endures whose [goal] is rightness.[10]

Whether addressed to kings or courtiers, mirrors for princes were typically written for a wider audience. The teachings of Ptahhotep, explains Miriam Lichtheim, the foremost editor of Egyptian literature, were "aimed at all aspiring officials and at Everyman."[11] All Egyptians were taught to be quiet in the presence of their betters, to bend to superiors at work, to accept their lot in life. Mirrors for princes helped to spread the message. They supplemented the outdoor advertising that pharaohs used to control their subjects: Egyptian architecture publicized Pharaoh's strength as a leader. Memorials depict him as commander-in-chief, suited up for battle, slaying enemies all by himself while his army lurks in the background as a decorative border. Egyptian mirrors for princes supported such fantasies with tales of heroic leadership: "I trod as far as . . . the limits of *the armed territory*, by my (own) strong arm," boasts the *Instruction of King Amenemhet.* "I OVERCAME LIONS; I CAUGHT CROCODILES. I subjugated [savages]. . . . I made the Asiatics do the dog-walk [crawl like a dog on a leash]."[12]

Egyptian mirrors showed the world how princes, any leaders, wished to be pictured.

Laments

The ancient Egyptians were not so easily led. Like citizens of later nations, many gave their rulers credit for good times and, fairly or not, blamed them for the bad. *The Instruction of King Amenemhet*, a mirror in the father-to-son format from the twentieth century BC, laments how the king's subjects turned against him: "No one hungered in my years," wails the king. "I gave to the destitute and brought up the orphan. I caused him who was nothing to reach (his goal), like him who was (somebody). (BUT) IT WAS HE WHO ATE MY FOOD THAT

RAISED TROOPS (against me) and he to whom I had given my hands that created terror thereby. They who were clothed in my fine linen looked upon me as *(did) those who lacked it.*" Now, "*much idle cant* is in the streets," King Amenemhet grieves. Yet, rather than give in to the mob, the king doubles down on his family's right to rule. He reminds his son that he is also the divine son of the sun god Re, and the kingdom of Egypt will stand if he acts like it.[13]

Egyptian mirrors for princes taught lessons that were preached anew for centuries to come. Into the eighteenth century AD, mirrors for princes taught that kings, if not gods themselves, were God's vicegerents on earth; they ruled by divine right. Long after their sages told Egyptians that foreigners, rebels, and riff-raff were taking over the country, turning society upside down, mirrors for princes taught Europeans to fear alien groups (the Irish, Muslims, Protestants, Catholics, Native Americans) and to seek their destruction. Just as Egyptian leaders fabricated a vision of maat to further their plans, future mirrors spun dreams of empire, reason of state, the national interest, and so on, to unite people in a purported common goal. These were old literary clichés even before the second millennium BC, duly scratched down on wooden tablets, limestone flakes, and pottery shards by generations of Egyptian schoolchildren. (Children's schoolwork, copied from long-lost texts and still surviving on ostraca, represents the primary record of much early Egyptian literature.) The clichés of mirrors for princes have remained popular exercises in schoolrooms ever since.[14]

TWO
Greek Mirrors

Into what utter confusion our city has fallen. . . . Our polity has been
corrupted, . . . year by year ever drifting on from bad to worse. . . . Under
the discipline of the old days the citizens were so schooled in virtue as
not to injure each other, but to fight and conquer all who attempted to
invade their territory. We, however, do the very opposite; for we never
let a day go by without bringing trouble on each other, and we have so
far neglected the business of war that we do not even deign to attend
reviews unless we are paid money for doing so.

Isocrates, *Areopagiticus*

Popular histories of the ancient world portray a golden age centered
around 400 BC in the Greek city-state of Athens. But scholars in Athens
back then saw a city in decline, an age of iniquity. Dismayed educators
saw citizens who were no longer "of the same mind regarding public
affairs," no longer "rightminded and partners in a common fatherland";
they saw able men retiring from politics, preferring to "sit around in our
shops denouncing the present order and complaining"; they saw young
people with no training for public service, choosing to "waste their time
in the gambling-dens or with the flute girls," drinking in taverns and
"playing the clown." So teachers called for higher, moral education. And
they founded schools to groom philosopher-kings.[1]

Isocrates

Isocrates was the most enterprising. For nearly fifty years he ran a
school for top executives, generals, and politicians from around the

Mediterranean. His school was a rival of Plato's Academy—only more practical, stressing leadership skills like rhetoric, and more exclusive. (Legend has it that Demosthenes, the great orator who trained by stuffing stones in his mouth, couldn't afford the tuition.)

Isocrates wrote his own teaching materials: He wrote mirrors for princes, addressing two books of advice to a king named Nicocles who ruled at Cyprus in the fourth century BC. The first book, *To Nicocles*, lists the duties of a good king and leadership principles for monarchs. A king's chief duties, Isocrates writes, are "to relieve the state when it is in distress, to maintain it in prosperity, and to make it great when it is small." The principles for monarchs are proverbs such as, "See to it that in proportion as you are above the others in rank so shall you surpass them in virtue." Do not act like the common people, Isocrates instructs Nicocles. They shirk their duties and make fun of authorities; they watch trashy shows and eat junk food; they trade insults in the streets, fight in neighborhood gangs, and plunge whole cities into civil wars. You must transcend the crowd and emulate your ancestors, Isocrates tells the king; think more of your family name than selfish pleasures. "Make it your practice to talk of things that are good and honorable, that your thoughts may through habit come to be like your words." Use legislation to "make industry profitable for your people and lawsuits detrimental." Be strong but compassionate, "causing your subjects one and all to defer to your judgment and to believe that your plans for their welfare are better than their own."[2]

Isocrates's second book of advice, *Nicocles*, is essentially a vision statement for the king to speak, articulating the goals and duties of his subjects. It's mostly about loyalty and teamwork. Nicocles should proclaim as public policy, for example, that "we reverence the gods and practise justice, and cultivate the other virtues" to bring to life "as many good things as possible"; we uphold monarchy because "one-man rule is more efficient than the other forms of government." To his subjects, the king should "declare it to be the duty of each one of you to perform whatever tasks you are assigned with diligence and justice, . . . knowing that the whole depends for its success and failure on each of the parts."[3]

Modern editors of Isocrates's books point out that he repackaged generic advice—nothing he says is specific to Nicocles's situation. Generic advice is a regular feature of mirrors for princes; it makes them adaptable texts for teaching both established and aspiring leaders. For such advice, students paid Isocrates fees on the scale of an executive MBA program. (His complete course cost one thousand drachmas, about three years' wages for an ordinary worker, payable in advance). Because "he was tiresome, long-winded and above all superficial," however, most Greeks were wary of Isocrates, writes George Kennedy in his history of rhetoric. Isocrates's critics charged that he taught despots how to talk like a leader, not how to think.[4]

Isocrates acknowledged there was hardly an original thought or saying in his advice to Nicocles. His innovation, his claim to fame, was pedagogical. "It was Isocrates who first brought history into the curriculum," notes educational historian Frederick Beck.[5] As in executive education today, Isocrates used history not just to teach facts but to shape character. He taught cases eulogizing the virtues of storied leaders like Nicocles's father, Evagoras—to whom he attributed the stereotypical virtues of courage, wisdom, justice, and moderation. Isocrates urged Nicocles to study not only his own ancestors but "men whose reputations you envy" and to "imitate their deeds"; he told Nicocles that his subjects would follow because "the manners of the whole state are copied from its rulers."[6]

The main idea Isocrates drew from textbook cases was the need for leaders to instill unity of purpose. The Greeks coined a word for unity of purpose; they termed it *homonoia*. Before Isocrates, homonoia was an ideal applied to families—the more unity the better. Isocrates extended the ideal to city-states and then to all of Greece. One pupil of his, an obese orator named Python, made the point while trying to quell civil unrest in Byzantium: "Gentlemen," he said, "you see my build. But I've actually got a wife much fatter than I am. When we're of one mind, any old bed does for us. If we quarrel, the whole house isn't big enough."[7]

Isocrates also drew on personal experience. His father was a wealthy flute manufacturer whose business was ruined by the Peloponnesian War between Athens and Sparta. Isocrates concluded that Greeks should stop fighting one another and unite in a common cause: a crusade against the barbarians of Asia Minor. Time and again he appealed to princes such as Philip of Macedon to lead it until finally his own students questioned his judgment. The trouble with princes, even princes with virtues, is that one cannot safely predict what they will do. In the end, Philip decided to lead his army not toward Asia but toward Athens, and, tradition says, Isocrates starved himself to death in despair.[8]

His fate was forgotten, but Isocrates's words endured. Educators ever after cited his books as model mirrors for princes. (Until the eighteenth century, Harvard College required applicants to display their knowledge of Greek by reading from Isocrates and the New Testament.[9]) Preachers through the ages taught Isocrates's strategy of a crusade to unify people behind a common vision. (The Harvard-educated Puritan Cotton Mather, for example, preached crusades with a vengeance against Native Americans.) It's a fraught legacy.

Aristotle

Scholars called Isocrates the educator of the Greek world; they called Aristotle the philosopher. In 335 BC Aristotle opened a school in Athens, not far from Isocrates's site. He taught theoretical subjects like metaphysics in addition to practical arts like rhetoric. He did basic research in natural science as well as applied research in political science and ethics. Aristotle and his students studied leadership, for example, by researching the governments of 158 city-states around the Mediterranean. In the *Politics*, Aristotle drew lessons of his research for rulers, and at least this part of the book was long viewed as a mirror for princes.

"Every state," he begins, "is a community of some kind."[10] That is a popular translation, but it is misleading to read much into it. Today, for instance, it suggests to teachers of business ethics that "we are communal creatures," which "is to say that we have shared interests"; it suggests that even business "corporations are first of all communities, social groups with shared purposes"; it suggests that communities, including states and corporations, are good things—moral bodies whose members help each other, practice virtue, and take part in governance. That is not what Aristotle meant.[11]

States, he clarifies, are "associations" (another standard translation) that can be good or bad. Good ones have shared purposes; they "aim at the common good." Bad ones do not; they "aim only at the good of the rulers." Good states are ethical ideals; bad ones are all too real.[12]

Of the 158 states Aristotle studied, there wasn't an ideal government in the lot—not at Athens, not at Sparta, not at Cyprus, not anywhere. "All the constitutions which now exist are faulty," he says. They appeal to personal interests, not the public good; they indulge the greed of both rulers and citizens, so actual city-states are rent by factions and dissensions, crime and violence. Aristotle cites case after case of cities whose governments were corrupted by selfishness. At Byzantium and at Sybaris, he says, majority leaders exploited racial divisions to expel minorities and seize their property. At Appolonia, public officials just helped themselves to the treasury. At Sparta, many "elders are good men and well trained in manly virtue"; but "elders are well known to have taken bribes and to have been guilty of partiality in public affairs." (Worse, Aristotle claims, are the women of Sparta: "The license of the women defeats the intention of the Spartan constitution, and is adverse to the happiness of the state." While Spartan men are hardy and disciplined, their women "live in every sort of intemperance and luxury." They have refused to take orders and undermined the state even in wartime when "they were utterly useless and caused more confusion than the enemy.")[13]

At Carthage, Aristotle goes on, rich men buy and sell even the top offices—jobs of kings and generals—and the richest hold multiple offices in order to retain their fortune. At Crete, a few noble families keep all the elective offices; "they get together a party among the common people and their own friends and then quarrel and fight with one another." Ruling families provoke wars over the silliest trifles, Aristotle observes: At Mytilene, "a wealthy citizen named Timophanes left two daughters; Dexander, another citizen, wanted to obtain them for his sons; but he was rejected in his suit, whereupon he stirred up a revolution." At Syracuse, the state fell because of "a love quarrel of two young men, who were in the government. The story is that while one of them was away from home his [lover] was gained over by his companion, and he to revenge himself seduced the other's wife. They then drew the members of the ruling class into their quarrel and so split all the people."[14]

Across the Greek world, Aristotle saw public officials driven by avarice and ambition: "Nowadays, for the sake of the advantage which is to be gained from the public revenues and from office, men want to be always in office," he says; "one might imagine that the rulers, being sickly, were only kept in health while they continued in office." Aristotle blames common people for acting selfishly as well. At Athens, he states, they control the law courts, where they are chosen by lot and then act like petty tyrants. "The avarice of mankind is insatiable," he complains; "at one time two obols was pay enough [for public aid in Athens]; but now when this sum has become customary, men always want more and more." The problem of government is "the poor and the rich quarrel with one another" and take turns ruling "for their own advantage."[15]

Aristotle prefers governance aimed at "the advantage of the whole community," but he is not clear on what an ideal government would look like or who, constitutionally, should rule. In bad states, he says, rulers can be one person (a tyranny), a few persons (an oligarchy), or many (a democracy). It doesn't much matter; they are all wrong since persons rule for their own benefit. In good states, too, rulers could be one person (a monarchy), a few (an aristocracy), or many (a polity). Again, it hardly matters; they are all right since persons rule for the common good. Aristotle does not say one form of government is always best.[16]

What matters is that rulers, whoever they are, are men of character. (Aristotle *is* clear that they must be men: he says the virtue "of a man is shown in commanding, of a woman in obeying.") Good states come from selfless leaders such as a virtuous prince. Aristotle claims the purpose of a state is a good life for its citizens—men of worth—and the best life is achieved when the best men rule the rest: "When a whole family, or some individual, happens to be so preeminent in excellence as to surpass all others," he says, "then it is just that they should be the royal family and supreme over all, or that this one citizen should be king." The king's job "is to be a protector of the rich against unjust treatment, of the people against insult and oppression." Rich citizens deserve protection of their property, other citizens deserve protection of their persons, and the king who rules for their common good deserves deference. One who rules merely for his own good deserves to be branded a tyrant.[17]

But these are, after all, ideals. (Aristotle's "common good" is almost as abstract as Pharaoh's "maat.") And, unlike some of his followers, Aristotle does not mistake ideals for reality. Knowing that the best will not necessarily rule, he has down-to-earth tips for tyrants: "The tyrant," Aristotle says, "should act or appear to act in the character of a king. In the first place he should pretend concern for the public revenues, and not waste money in making presents of a sort at which common people get excited when they see their hard-won earnings snatched from them and lavished on courtesans and foreigners and artists." It is better that "he should be seen to collect taxes and to require public services only for state purposes."[18]

"He should appear, not harsh, but dignified," and "whatever virtues he may neglect, at least he should maintain the character of a great soldier, and produce the impression that he is one."[19]

"Neither he nor any of his associates should ever assault the young of either sex who are his subjects." He should act "the opposite of our modern tyrants" and "not parade his vices to the world; for a drunken and drowsy tyrant is soon despised and attacked; not so he who is temperate and wide awake."[20]

"He ought to adorn and improve his city, as though he were not a tyrant, but the guardian of the state. Also he should appear to be particularly earnest in the service of the gods." If a tyrant can't be a philosopher-king, then he should learn to look like one. Character education, as taught in the Lyceum, could help.[21]

Although Aristotle was well connected, he left no imprint on the politics of his day. Before opening his school, he worked for King Philip of Macedon; he tutored Philip's son, the future Alexander the Great, but historians think the experience had little effect on either of them. Princes of antiquity looked to philosophers not for advice but for adornment, notes Frank Vatai in his history of Greek intellectuals. Philip surrounded himself with the usual courtiers—actors and musicians for entertainment, scholars for weight and respectability, speechwriters to publicize his vision and promote his policies. But, as the prince, Philip ran the show. He taught Alexander the business. And Aristotle knew, according to one classical chronicle, "to speak as seldom and as pleasantly as possible in the presence of a man who had at the tip of his tongue the power over life and death."[22]

No one disputes Aristotle's brilliance. It would be unfair to judge Aristotle, or any thinker, solely based on what they said or did not say to powerful princes. Aristotle produced the equivalent of fifty-some books on a vast array of subjects: *On Animals, On Plants, On Motion, On Astronomy, On Justice, On the Poets,* to name just a few. You can consult this work to get a fuller picture of Aristotle's thought. But the mind of Aristotle is not the topic here; it's mirrors for princes. And Aristotle's mirror has drawn criticism from even sympathetic specialists. Professor of ancient philosophy and Aristotle authority Jonathan Barnes, for instance, detects "the infant voice of totalitarianism" in the *Politics'* claim that citizens "all belong to the state" and the book's plan for teaching them all to believe it: "Since the whole city has one goal, it is evident that there must also be one and the same education for everyone."[23] Education to focus everyone's attention on a common goal is a classic, if problematic, tactic of governance that you will see again and again in mirrors for princes.

Aristotle's mirror inspired many imitators, especially in the High Middle Ages. While his mirror encouraged socially responsible kingship, it did not challenge princes' right to rule. (Greek mirrors in general emphasized self-control by kings, reinforcing their own self-importance.) Because Aristotle envisioned a common good more imperative than the mechanics of government, his theory was perfectly compatible with monarchy or aristocracy, so it gained acceptance among medieval rulers of both church and state (who took it upon themselves to define "the common good"). "The *Politics* was used to bolster monarchy," for example, "in France—perhaps the region where Aristotle's *Politics* was most widely read between 1260 and 1320," says Thomas Renna, a historian of political thought.[24] Whereas teachers today stress Aristotle's call for virtue and gloss over the philosopher's nods to one-man rule, the Scholastics of Paris seized on the latter to declare monarchy an ideal constitution.[25]

As Scholasticism waned, as the legacy of Aristotle collided with popular opinion in the West, the clerics and courtiers who wrote mirrors for princes looked elsewhere for inspiration. With characteristic nostalgia, they looked backward and found suitable ideals in the literature of ancient Rome.

THREE
Roman Mirrors

O for the admirable customs and principles which we received from our ancestors, if we could but keep them! but somehow or other they have slipped through our fingers.

If I were to give you a summary of what has happened [the immorality of youth, the bribery of officials, the corruption of juries], you would exclaim that it is impossible for the State of Rome to stand a day longer. . . . Meanwhile there is not a ghost of a statesman in sight. . . . [Pompey, Crassus, and] the rest [are] such fools, that they seem to think they can let the country go to rack and ruin and still keep their precious fishponds safe.

Cicero

In the first century BC, the entire Mediterranean world was ruled from Rome. Roman moralists said it was all going to hell.

Cicero

Rome itself was ruled by about twenty families whose members and henchmen, Cicero suggests, stole or ravished or killed almost anything they could lay their hands on. Cicero saw them do it. As a young lawyer he made a name for himself by prosecuting one of the biggest offenders, a governor of Sicily named Verres. "This avaricious lecher," Cicero told a Senate extortion court, "sacked the treasury" and "pillaged the province"; he robbed farmers, starved soldiers, and tortured citizens; he molested wives and children; he stripped temples and monuments: "Among the most sacred and revered Sicilian sanctuaries, there was not a single one which he failed to plunder," Cicero alleged; "not one . . . good work of art or valuable antique did he leave."[1]

Cicero charged that Verres—the name is Latin for "hog"—took "forty million sesterces" in his three-year term. (Ordinary workers and soldiers made about a thousand sesterces a year.) Verres was heard to boast that the first year's take was for himself, the second for paying his political protectors, and the third for bribing the judges who might later try him. Everyone knows "that in these courts, with their present membership, even the worst criminal will never be convicted provided he has the money," Cicero said. He ultimately shamed the judges into handing down a conviction—but only after they gave Verres time to skip town.[2]

The trial launched Cicero on a political career, and he soon rose to consul, the highest office in Rome. He campaigned on a platform to unite Rome's old and new families for the protection of law, order, and property; his slogan was "class harmony." Reality, however, overtook Cicero's rhetoric. He could not fix Rome any more than he could fix a crook like Verres. "The noblemen were too reactionary," observes historian Michael Grant, "the businessmen too grasping, the poor too poor," the politicians "too ambitious." Forced out of public service by critics who faulted his administration's hard line toward the landless masses and a few renegade aristocrats, Cicero turned to writing advice books for leaders who might have more control and better luck. His books, centuries later, became model mirrors for princes.[3]

Around 51 BC, when Cicero was fifty-five years old, he published the *Republic*. It resembles classical dialogues on governance, such as Plato's *Republic*, but it's written in the voice of a retired chief executive. The book is based on real-world experience, Cicero says, unlike Greek mirrors for princes, which reflect utopias no one's ever seen. It is practical, he claims, unlike Aristotle's mixed bag of ideals that offer no map of the best state. Cicero knows what's best; he gives tips, drops names, shares war stories, takes credit, blames enemies, and markets his skills and availability.[4]

The *Republic* is a nostalgic case study of Rome from the "glorious deeds" of its legendary founder to the now sorry scene of affairs. Romulus, Cicero writes, had the founding vision; he discovered "the principle that a State can be better governed and guided by the authority of one man, that is by the power of a king, if the influence of the State's most eminent men is joined to the ruler's absolute power." Romulus became the first king and—together with a group of great men (the first senate)—grew the state; "he waged many wars against his neighbors with the greatest good fortune, and, though he brought none of the booty to his own home, he never ceased enriching his people." According to Cicero, Romulus mobilized people by dividing "the plebeians up among the prominent citizens, who were to be their patrons." So king, nobles, and people cooperated from early on, Cicero says, because "our ancestors, rustics though they even then were, saw that kingly virtue and wisdom" advanced the common good.[5]

The kingship of Romulus is a myth, but it serves a point. Patriotic myths are often used in mirrors for princes to teach core values. Cicero teaches the values of unity, community, and moral authority. After Romulus, he says, successive kings smoothed Romans' rustic edges so they could work, play, and pray as a team. Progress was not painless. As the state grew bigger, some kings, some senators, or some people grabbed too much power, and the organization had to undergo restructuring. But eventually the princely, the aristocratic, and the popular institutions—the one, the few, and the many—all came together in perfect balance and harmony. Cicero can't say exactly when this happened but it was, he maintains, the golden age of the republic.

Cicero *can* say it's an age well past. Now the republic is just like a faded painting, he writes; you can barely make out the image, much less see the colors. Romans no longer practice or even remember the ancient customs on which Rome was founded, Cicero laments; instead, they go their own selfish ways. He links Rome's decay to a lack of virtuous men. He blames greedy men, such as Pompey and Julius Caesar, who "both want to reign" and who drag Romans into party politics and factional fights. Rome ought not be this bad, Cicero declares, even if the ideal republic is fading. You can still have a good community if you have good leadership.[6]

Cicero holds up a traditional picture of leadership. A good leader gives direction to the community, he says: "Just as the aim of the pilot is a successful voyage, of the physician, health, and of the general, victory, so this director of the commonwealth has as his aim for his fellow citizens a happy life, fortified by wealth, rich in material resources, great in glory and honored for virtue." A good leader brings harmony to the community the same way a music conductor brings harmony to the different sounds of harps and flutes and the voices of singers; he orchestrates "agreement among dissimilar elements, brought about by a fair and reasonable blending together of the upper, middle, and lower classes, just as if they were musical tones." A good leader sets an example for others to copy, "furnishing in himself as it were, a mirror to his fellow citizens by reason of the supreme excellence of his life and character." Cicero ends his own mirror with a dream in which a war hero from the golden age returns to life; he calls on leaders to serve the common good of the community, promising them that "all those who have preserved, aided, or enlarged their fatherland have a special place prepared for them in the heavens, where they may enjoy an eternal life of happiness."[7]

The *Republic* is long on vision, short on specifics. Much of the text has been lost, and what has survived does not describe how to manage a complex empire like Rome—where, for instance, public works and services were privatized, tax collections were outsourced, and leaders needed more than a vision to get things done with all the independent contractors. Cicero was content to give generic advice, following the custom of mirrors for princes, because his purpose was not strictly to inform but to inspire and exhort. He hoped to encourage leading citizens and senior statesmen such as Caesar and Pompey to restrain themselves, to curb their ambitions, for the common good. When they ignored him and led the country into civil war, he wrote a more generic mirror for the youth of Rome. It is his most famous book, *On Duties*.[8]

Cicero addresses *On Duties* to his son Marcus, but, as with most father-to-son books of advice, it is meant for any leader-to-be. Cicero tells Marcus: No matter what, be a man! The Romans' word for manliness was "*virtus*" (from *vir*, Latin for man); it's been rendered in English as "virtue." Cicero emphasizes the manly virtues of wisdom, justice, courage, and temperance. He explains to Marcus what duties these virtues demand.[9]

Wisdom means to seek the truth, up to a point. "Take time and care," he says, in making decisions, but don't waste time on "matters that are both abstruse and difficult, and unnecessary." It's fine to study things like astronomy, geometry, logic, or law; on the other hand, it's a dereliction of duty to let studies draw one "away from practical achievements: all the praise that belongs to virtue lies in action," Cicero writes.[10]

Justice means keeping law and order; it binds a community together. Justice implies two duties, he says: "No man should harm another unless he has been provoked by injustice" and "one should treat common goods as common and private goods as one's own." Here Cicero takes another swipe at Caesar, who "overturned all the laws of gods and men" to grab glory for himself. No vice "is more foul than avarice," he warns, "particularly among leading men and those who control public affairs. For to use public affairs for one's profit is not only dishonorable, but criminal and wicked too." It is not wrong to get rich, but wealth comes with social responsibilities. Give back to the community, he advises; honor your contracts; keep your word—unless your promises "harm you more than they benefit the person whom you have promised."[11]

Courage means fighting for what's right. Cicero says, "Do deeds which are great" and "yield to no man, nor to agitation of the spirit, nor to fortune." Do not chase after things "that appear to most men distinguished and even splendid," but "endure circumstances" even if they seem harsh and unfair. A brave leader is not broken by bad luck or fear or hard work, not softened by pleasure or desire for luxuries. If you want to lead others, "acquire the magnificent disdain for human affairs that I stress, and tranquility of mind and freedom from care." Begin by getting up off the couch.[12]

Temperance means showing decorum, due measure in all things. Cicero urges Marcus to use restraint, act seemly, feel shame, care what people think: "All action should be free from rashness and carelessness; nor should anyone do anything for which he cannot give a persuasive justification; that is practically a definition of duty." Remember, he goes on, your private words may be made public, so always watch what you say; "the light of an upright character should shine forth even from our jokes." Keep up your "appearance and standing as a gentleman": Whatever you do, don't demean yourself with dishonorable work; don't take after tax collectors or money lenders or those who buy and sell merchandise—"they would make no profit unless they told sufficient lies." Stay away from people who "minister to the pleasures: fishmongers, butchers, cooks, poulterers, fishermen . . . add to this, if you like, perfumers, dancers, and the whole variety show."[13]

One can imagine Marcus rolling his eyes at this point. He was then twenty-one years old, off at school in Athens enjoying the city's nightclubs. He was a big drinker, spender, and disappointment to his father. Do something useful with your life, Cicero tells him. Realize that you can do nothing great on your own; you must "entice and arouse other men to support what is beneficial" to Rome. You can lead and motivate others by fear or love, money or charisma. It is better to be loved than feared. Fear prods followers to get even, and that makes leaders fearful also. Once upon a time, a nasty ruler of Syracuse named "Dionysius had his hair singed with coals because he feared the barber's knife"—that's an awful way to live. So, too, it is better to lead through charisma than money. King Philip, for example, rightly rebuked his son Alexander for trying to buy goodwill: "'What reason,' he asked, 'led you—alas!—to entertain the thought that men you had corrupted with money would be faithful to you?'" Take my advice, Cicero says, give yourself to public service and excel others in virtue. If luck is on your side, people will put faith in you, admire you, and follow you. If not, then you've simply done your duty.[14]

Classicists point out there is not much original content in Cicero's works. His achievement was to translate the ideals as well as the clichés of Greek philosophy—the Stoic code of ethics, the list of cardinal virtues, the goal of the common good, the myth of the golden age, the fall of community and morality—into lucid Latin. This was more significant in later periods, when Latin became the language of Western scholarship, than it was in Cicero's day. As mirrors for princes, his books made little immediate impact. Cicero's moralizing offended contemporaries (especially Mark Antony, a frequent target of Cicero's rhetoric, who eventually ordered Cicero's death, then nailed his head and writing hand to the stage in the Roman Forum); his rehashing of Greek philosophy bored educated people in the first centuries who could still read Greek and the originals. As succeeding generations lost the ability to read Greek, scholars like St. Augustine found inspiration in Cicero. But no Christian thinker could forget he was a pagan—the church favored the Bible for inspiration—and Cicero's influence remained spotty until the later Middle Ages.[15]

In the twelfth century Europeans reawakened to Roman literature, and a minor renaissance occurred in the West. Educators took new interest in the classics, the Latin moralists, and particularly Cicero. Writers emulated his elegant style. They drew from Cicero not whole theories or arguments but saws and sayings that could fit with nearly any theology. "This method of selective borrowing," according to historians David Luscombe and G. R. Evans, helped "to avoid the difficulty of confrontation between Christian and pagan values and to bring out their points of similarity and agreement."[16]

For the next six centuries, mirrors for princes—by Aquinas, Machiavelli, Petrarch, and other theorists—cited the authority of Cicero on all sides of an issue. Royal tutors expanded the writings available to students of leadership; Queen Elizabeth I, they said, had read most of Cicero's works by the age of sixteen. The height of Cicero's popularity came in the eighteenth century, when *On Duties* became required reading for educated gentlemen. As the dominion of queens, kings, and noble gentlemen waned, people lost interest in mirrors for princes and, once more, in Cicero.[17]

Seneca

Next to Cicero, the Roman moralist quoted most often in mirrors for princes is Seneca. Like Cicero, Seneca came from privilege, trained in rhetoric, then pursued a political career. He climbed the ladder of public office and joined the Senate, becoming one of Rome's leading intellectual figures, before being forced into early retirement. Accused of adultery with the late emperor Caligula's sister, Julia Livilla, he was exiled to the island of Corsica where for eight years he read philosophy, wrote Stoic essays, and dreamed of finding useful employment again. His chance came when Julia Livilla's sister, Agrippina, married the emperor Claudius and asked him to recall Seneca. Agrippina had a job in mind for Seneca—tutoring her twelve-year-old son, the future emperor Nero.[18]

Seneca was the perfect courtier, gracing the imperial court with his literary prestige, schooling Nero in rhetoric, and serving as the young prince's speechwriter when he ascended to the throne. At the age of sixteen, Nero took over a vast empire—bigger than Alexander the Great's— but, as historians make clear, Nero was no Alexander. His meanness was apparent from the start. Rumor had it that Nero murdered his stepbrother (a rival for the throne), and Romans feared for their future. To instruct the emperor in virtue and help him sell his regime to the public, Seneca wrote a mirror for princes, *On Mercy*. "I have undertaken, Nero Caesar, to write on the subject of mercy," he says, "in order to serve in a way the purpose of a mirror, and thus reveal you to yourself as one destined to attain the greatest of all pleasures."[19]

The greatest pleasures are a clear conscience and a reputation for clemency, Seneca suggests. It is "a mighty burden" to manage people, he writes; Rome itself is a mob, "discordant, factious, and unruly, ready to run riot alike for the destruction of itself and others if it should break its yoke." The empire needs a mighty prince; otherwise, it will shatter into a multitude of parts. But a prince need not be a burden to the people of Rome. Seneca tells Nero that he should state as his policy: "I am the arbiter of life and death"; I can decree "what nations shall be utterly destroyed, which banished, which shall receive the gift of liberty, which have it taken from them, what kings shall become slaves and whose heads shall be crowned with royal honor, what cities shall fall and which shall rise." Yet, "with all things thus at my disposal, I have been moved neither by anger nor youthful impulse to unjust punishment." My sword is sheathed; "I am sparing to the utmost of even the meanest blood; no man fails to find favor at my hands though he lack all else but the name of man. Sternness I keep hidden, but mercy ever ready at hand." Then Nero could claim "the rarest praise, hitherto denied to all other princes," which is "innocence of wrong." And everyone would say, "no human being has ever been so dear to another as you are to the people of Rome—its great and lasting blessing."[20]

Seneca draws the old distinction between a king who rules for the common good and a tyrant who rules for his own benefit. Good kings (Nero's great-great-grandfather Augustus, for example) punish and kill, he says, "but only when the public good dictates it." Tyrants (such as Caligula) shed blood because they feel like it, because they are "corrupted by greed or natural impetuosity or examples set by earlier princes into testing how far one can go against one's fellow citizens." Kings, by showing mercy, bring out the best in people: Like members of one body, grateful citizens will give anything for the head of their fatherland—they know "he is the breath of life," the "mind of the empire," the "bond which holds the commonwealth together." Tyrants, by indulging in cruelty, bring out the worst: "In a five-year period," Seneca reminds Nero, "your father had more people sewn into the sack than there had been, or so we are told, in all the centuries before him." (Rome once punished patricide by sewing up the accused in a sack along with some live animals, then dumping the bag in the Tiber.) But the "penalty showed them the way to the misdeed. Filial piety in fact reached its lowest point after the sack had become a commoner sight than the cross." (Crucifixion was the standard capital punishment for noncitizens.)[21]

"Mercy," Seneca concludes, "enhances not only a ruler's honour, but his safety." A tyrant "invokes that accursed verse which has sent many to their ruin: 'let them hate, provided they fear,' in ignorance of the fury which arises, when hatred grows beyond measure." Tyrants fuel resentment in their subjects, their neighbors and nations abroad, their soldiers and servants, even the lackeys who work their tools of torture, Seneca says. With so many enemies, tyrants live short, wretched lives—while merciful kings "grow old and bequeath their kingdoms to their children and grandchildren."[22]

Nero could be such a merciful king, Seneca told the prince and the people of Rome. Seneca wrote Nero's first address to the Senate—a vision speech on mercy. He made *Mercy* a slogan of the new administration, its mission statement. He stayed on as Nero's public relations adviser, crafting rhetoric on virtue until it was clear to everyone that Nero didn't believe a word of it. Nero outdid his predecessors in cruelty; he went beyond sacks and crosses. According to the Roman historian Tacitus, who grew up under Nero, he had Christians torn apart by dogs for sport or burned like living torches to light his games. And he finally heard enough from Seneca. Ordered to commit suicide, the Stoic courtier accepted his fate and opened up his veins.[23]

Seneca elicited chilly reactions from his contemporaries. While upper-class Romans admired his plays and cultured Latin, scholars saw him as more evangelical than intellectual. "He was not very critical in philosophy," sneered the literary critic Quintilian, "though he was a remarkable denouncer of vice." Roman philosophers, who still wrote in Greek, ignored him. Historians called him everything from a pragmatic politician to a sermonizing hypocrite. The classical historian Dio said in hindsight that Seneca denounced tyranny while teaching a tyrant, criticized flatterers while fawning over patrons, faulted the rich while amassing a fortune, censured extravagance while living in luxury, and condemned infidelity while sleeping around.[24]

There is a ring of truth to some charges. Under Nero, Seneca became one of the richest investment bankers in the empire; "Italy and the provinces were sucked dry by his limitless usury," sniped Tacitus. However, Romans routinely accused anyone who disagreed with them of immorality. And hypocrisy was a stock charge against Stoics (many of whom actually did say one thing and do another). A more substantive complaint against the Stoics and Seneca in particular was that their teachings trivialized the problem of bad rulers.[25]

In his book *On Mercy*, Seneca idealized monarchy, discounted institutional checks on power, and relied on the king's personal virtue to unite people into one body with one will. Mercy itself was an imperial virtue—a gift bestowed by a superior on an inferior. Mercy, Seneca's modern editors note, "had been recognized since the time of Caesar as supremely the virtue of a conqueror or autocrat who, at least in theory, has everyone else in his power."[26] Indeed, mercy has been a slogan of authoritarian states from Roman times to the present. Such states issue sweeping decrees against treason, for instance, and draft detailed laws about public conduct that no one could help but violate at some time. In ancient Rome, where sumptuary laws regulated everything from food to apparel, and where vigilant informers reaped profits from prosecutions, even a quiet dinner with friends might be reported as a subversive act. Most violations are overlooked in an authoritarian state; most citizens are shown mercy, or society could not function at all. But anyone can be denounced at any time—to settle a score, silence a critic, seize another's house, or curry favor with authorities—and mercy can suddenly cease. If you are accused and hauled before a magistrate, you have little defense. You broke the law, didn't you? It's no excuse that everyone does it. You can be found guilty and sentenced to a fine, loss of property, exile, or death—again depending on the mercy of the ruler. This is not a system of justice but of oppression. No wonder Seneca's rhetoric left Romans cold.[27]

Like Cicero, Seneca had his greatest influence long after he died. For the first five centuries, writers mentioned him sporadically. In the sixth and ninth centuries, teachers of princes borrowed a bit more from him. Only in the twelfth century, with the revival of classical literature, did scholars begin to take Seneca seriously. Once more, they mostly quoted short sayings to lend the weight of age to their own opinions. Seneca "is loud in the praise of virtue and ethics; and his aphoristic style is succinct, yet decorative," declared John of Salisbury; "among the pagans no ethical writer is to be found (or at least hardly any) whose words or sayings can be more appropriately used on any question."[28] Renaissance mirrors for princes are filled with Seneca's adages. His popularity peaked in the seventeenth century, then fell along with people's faith in merciful princes.

Lucian

Although Roman moralists displayed little originality in repackaging Greek rhetoric, the sheer volume of moralizing spawned a genre of literature that Romans claimed as their own invention. They called it *satura*—satire. One of Rome's sharpest satirists was a writer named Lucian.

Lucian was born in the second century to a working-class family in Syria. His career options in this outer province were few. (Lucian thought he might have become a stonemason but lacked the talent.) So he left home to study classical literature, then traveled around the empire making his living as a public speaker and entertainer. He learned how to cut through the bunkum of official rhetoric. He poked fun at philosophers, orators, the talking heads of his day. He performed satirical sketches and political comedy. "I try to amuse," he wrote, "and that is all there is to it."[29] He still gets good reviews from classicists for lampooning "the hypocrites, grandstanders, fakers, and boobs of the ancient world."[30]

Lucian wrote (in Greek) for an educated audience. His essays include a parody of mirrors for princes titled "On Salaried Posts in Great Houses." It is addressed to a philosopher named Timocles (or Master Ambitious), who is contemplating a job in the household of some regal family; it speaks more generally to intellectuals who think they can teach princes to govern responsibly. Lucian describes what it's like to work as a teacher, or any courtier-for-hire, in a great man's house.

People imagine they'll get a glamorous position with good benefits, he says, "having the noblest of the Romans for their friends, eating expensive dinners without paying any[thing], living in a handsome establishment, and travelling in all comfort and luxury, behind a span of white horses, perhaps, with their noses in the air." Job seekers envision high pay, light duties, nice managers. Once hired, they are soon disappointed. "They fall into the hands of shrewd, experienced minions who treat them superciliously," Lucian says. A boss smiles at them, promises to be generous, seems always on the verge of giving but never quite delivers. They work like slaves, beg for wages, live in want and fear for the rest of their lives. "Then before they know it, they . . . are old. . . . They have done nothing in all their life except to hope."[31]

It starts the moment you set out to join their company, Lucian explains. You must first buy clothing beyond your means, in the right cut and colors to fit in with the entourage. Dressed up for work you hang around, shoved about by servants, for days on end but the great man of the house does not even look at you. Eventually, he asks you a question to test you and you are caught off guard: "Your head swims confusedly, you tremble inopportunely, and the company laughs at you for your embarrassment." From then on, you are alert to his every mood. Meanwhile, agents pry into your whole past life. "If a fellow countryman out of jealousy or a neighbor offended for some insignificant reason says, when questioned, that you are a follower of women or boys, there they have it!" You are out.[32]

If by luck you make this cut, Lucian says, you will receive an invitation to dinner at the great house. You tip the messenger, you buy more clothes, and you go in wide-eyed "as though you had entered the mansion of Zeus." Everyone knows you're new and stares at you to see if you will make a mistake. You've never seen such a variety of foods; you don't know which dishes to eat in what order, so you steal glances at your neighbors and copy what they do. Your host may offer a toast of welcome to you, addressing you as "the professor" or whatever. That only makes his old friends jealous of the attention, and they begin to crack jokes about your manners and plot against you. You join in other toasts, you're not used to the wine, and you drink too much; you feel sick but you can't leave. It's bad form. Then the entertainment begins. You don't listen to the singers or the musicians but you applaud with the rest "while you pray that an earthquake may tumble the whole establishment into a heap or that a great fire may be reported, so that the party may break up at last." And that is the best night you'll ever spend in the place.[33]

If the great man finds your conversation interesting and if his wife, attorney, steward, and other top advisers have no objections, he will meet with you the next morning to negotiate salary. As Lucian tells it, the great man will call you to his room where you will find him with two or three of his friends. He will invite you to sit down. Then he'll say something like this:

"You have already seen what our establishment is like, and that there is not a bit of pomp and circumstance in it. . . . You must feel that we shall have everything in common; for it would be ridiculous if I trusted you with what is most important, my own soul or that of my children"— suppose he has children who need instruction—"and did not consider you equally free to command everything else. But there should be some stipulation. . . . Say yourself what you wish, bearing in mind, my dear fellow, what we shall probably give you on the annual feast-days. We shall not forget such matters, either, even though we do not now reckon them in, and there are many such occasions in the year, as you know. So if you take all that into consideration, you will of course charge us with a more moderate stipend. Besides, it would well become you men of education to be superior to money."[34]

You're stunned, Lucian writes. Maybe you were dreaming of figures in the thousands and millions, whole farms and apartment buildings, and now the great man's meanness starts to dawn on you. But you seize on his promise that *We shall have everything in common* and you sit hopefully, like a puppy, leaving the reward up to your master. Still, he refuses to state an amount. He tells one of his friends who are present to settle the business and name a sum that would neither break their budget nor insult a teacher with your credentials. The friend, a sly toady, says to you: "'You cannot say, sir, that you are not the luckiest man in the whole city,'" to be honored with entry into the first household in the Roman Empire. "'I cannot sufficiently congratulate you on your good luck, since you are actually to receive pay for such felicity. I think, then, that unless you are very prodigal, about so and so much is enough.'" Your jaw drops because he names a paltry sum, stingier than you could have imagined. But you're stuck now. You accept it with grace, consoled by all the perks you have been promised, dimly aware that you've just been duped and set up for bigger humiliations to come.[35]

Gradually you realize that you have sold your freedom and your pride to the great man, Lucian says. Forget the fine sermons of Plato and Aristotle about virtue and wisdom, you have sold *yourself.* You find "the purpose for which he engaged you, saying that he wanted knowledge, matters little to him." The truth is, "he does not want you for that purpose at all, but as you have a long beard, present a distinguished appearance, are neatly dressed in a Greek mantle, and everybody knows you for a grammarian or a rhetorician or a philosopher, it seems to him the proper thing to have a man of that sort among those who go before him and form his escort; it will make people think him a devoted student of Greek learning and in general a person of taste in literary matters." So you need to be available all hours of the day and night. Early in the morning you are roused by a bell. You shake off sleepiness and the wine from the night before. You rush to be counted in attendance among the flatterers, spongers, and jesters who surround the great man. You stay by your post until he shows up. Then you "run about town with the pack, up hill and down dale, with yesterday's mud still on your legs." It's hot; you sweat to keep up. "Putting his hand upon your shoulder now and then, he talks nonsense at random, showing those who meet him that even when he takes a walk he is not inattentive to the Muses but makes good use of his leisure during the stroll." Sometimes he stops to visit a friend but you are not invited in; "as you have no place to sit down, you stand up, and for lack of employment read the book with which you armed yourself."[36]

Days like this are bad enough. Nights, the way Lucian describes them, are worse. The common baths are wretched; you wash as best you can in the evening. By then you are hungry and thirsty, but you wait until the middle of the night when the great man summons the company to dinner. At your first dinner party you were a novelty; he tried to impress you by seating you at a place of honor, setting choice dishes before you, and engaging you in conversation. Very quickly your novelty wears off, Lucian says, and "you are pushed off into the most unregarded corner and take your place merely to witness the dishes that are passed, gnawing the bones like a dog if they get as far as you." You must tip the carver for a decent slice of pork or venison, but "if there is a shortage when another guest appears of a sudden, the waiter takes up what you have before you and quickly puts it before him, muttering: 'You are one of us, you know.'" The great man has lost interest in anything you might have to say. He prefers the spectacle of cheap entertainers—magicians, fortune-tellers, lewd dancers, Egyptian dwarfs who recite erotic ditties. You must not only sit there through the whole floorshow but pretend to enjoy it: "If a whispering servant accuse you of being the only one who did not praise the mistress's page when he danced or played, there is no little risk in the thing."[37]

So it goes, on and on. After the dinner party you grab a wink of sleep until the rooster crows, the bell rings, and you are on call again. You are "not the slave of one man but of many"—including the women of the house. Rich women trust servants to care for their bodies; they ask you to look after their pet Maltese dogs. They think it is a symbol of status "to have men of education living in their households on a salary and following their litters." For all this, you get paid a few obols at a time,

Lucian says, "and when you ask for it you are a bore and a nuisance." You must flatter the master and pester the steward and court his counselor, and when you finally get something, you turn around and pay your bill to the clothier or shoemaker or doctor, and you've nothing left. You are not cut out for this job, you fear. You don't know how to be a success, you haven't the charm to be a favorite, you can't compete with men who relish political intrigue.[38]

While your mind dwells on these things, eventually your body starts to fail. Some days you feel too sick to get out of bed. "But this is not permitted. They think illness a pretext, and a way of shirking your duties." So you rub your knees with liniment, you delude yourself that things will get better, and you slave on until you are too old for it. Then all hopes of promotion, pension, and peace are finally dashed by malicious rumors— slander about overtures you made to a page or the wife's maid, the usual household gossip. By now the great man "is glad to receive charges against you, for he sees that you are used up by your unbroken exertions and pay lame and exhausted court to him, and that the gout is growing upon you," Lucian says. "After garnering all that was most profitable in you, after consuming the most fruitful years of your life and the greatest vigour of your body, after reducing you to a thing of rags and tatters, he is looking about for a rubbish-heap on which to cast you aside unceremoniously, and for another man to engage who can stand the work."[39]

Just like that, you are sacked. Too ashamed to show your face, you slink away in the night. You've nowhere to go; because of your age, your beggarly appearance, and your dismissal under a cloud of scandal, no one else will have you. Your fate should be a warning to otherwise learned men: Don't be tempted into the service of a great prince.

Some years after publishing this piece, Lucian himself went to work for the emperor in an administrative job, and he wrote a halfhearted "Apology for the 'Salaried Posts in Great Houses.'" By taking the kind of employment he once ridiculed, he feared he might "seem just like that drug-seller who was advertising cough medicine and promising immediate relief to sufferers, while he himself was racked by a cough as he talked for all to see." His excuse was, "there is a very great difference between entering a rich man's house as a hireling, where one is a slave and endures what my essay describes, and entering public service, where one administers affairs as well as possible and is paid by the Emperor for doing it." The big difference is a cause worth working for. Through public service, Lucian wrote, "I take a share and play my part in the mightiest of empires." Just like any employee, sure he gets paid, sure he's under a master's orders, sure he hopes for a promotion (maybe "the supervision of a province"); but that's not why he serves a prince. He does it because they share the same goal—securing "the common weal and its improvement." As usual, he's pulling your leg.[40]

Classicists do not know what became of Lucian. They can't tell you how or when he died. They can only guess at the effect he had on contemporaries. Lucian says in his "Apology" that "On Salaried Posts in Great Houses" was widely read and praised by insiders for its "knowledge of the world," but ancient authors often said things like that. His literary influence followed a path much like that of Cicero and Seneca. For centuries after he wrote, few other writers cited him. Church Fathers took a dim view of him because he made fun of religious zealots, including some early Christians.[41]

Lucian's popularity ticked up during the ninth century in the eastern branch of the Roman Empire known as Byzantium. Byzantine educators collected lines from his essays in books of maxims and epigrams. They copied vivid scenes from his sketches to spice up their mirrors for princes. Greek scholars brought Lucian's writings from Byzantium to Italy around the fifteenth century. Lucian soon joined Xenophon and Isocrates in the educational curriculum of Europe's ruling families. Scholars like Erasmus and Thomas More made names for themselves as translators of Lucian, then incorporated his ideas into mirrors of their own (Erasmus's *Education of a Christian Prince* and More's *Utopia*). "On Salaried Posts in Great Houses," Erasmus claimed, revealed as much about court life in his day as in Lucian's. This piece became a favorite of Renaissance humanists, inspiring numerous works of anti-courtier literature. Lucian had a broad influence on letters—through Shakespeare, Marlowe, Cervantes, and others—well into the eighteenth century.[42]

Lucian's satire is clearly an outlier among mirrors for princes, exaggerating the clichés of the genre for comedic effect. Most mirrors for princes, throughout antiquity, were deadly serious. Almost all stressed the same points and followed the same formula. The formula begins with an observation: *People are behaving badly.* It diagnoses a cause: *Individuals have grown too selfish.* And it prescribes a cure: *Self-interest must be refocused on some common goal.* The job of a ruler is to articulate such a goal in a vision that all can share.

The formula was always controversial. It provoked not just satire but reasoned doubts about its fairness and usefulness in the real world. Nevertheless, as long as teachers wrote mirrors for princes, they taught the formula—in the Middle Ages and the Renaissance, in Christendom and the Islamic empires, in Confucian China and Puritan New England. Writers quibbled over details (whether it is better for princes to be loved or feared, for example), but they stuck to the formula in mirror after mirror for princes, not because it was wise advice for the ages but because it was prudent rhetoric for the sages.

FOUR
Frankish Mirrors

In the times of Charles the Great of good memory, who died almost thirty years ago, peace and concord ruled everywhere because our people were treading the one proper way, the way of the common welfare, and thus the way of God. But now since each goes his separate way, dissension and struggle abound. Once there was abundance and happiness everywhere, now everywhere there is want and sadness.

Nithard's *Histories*

After the Roman Empire collapsed in the fifth century, Germanic people called Franks took over the ancient province of Gaul. By 800, the Franks under King Charles the Great, Charlemagne, had grown an empire of their own stretching across western Europe. Later in the ninth century, Charlemagne's descendants felt *that* empire crumbling.

Charlemagne, his grandson Nithard recalled, "was a man who so much excelled all others in wisdom and virtue that to everyone on earth he appeared both terrible and worthy of love and admiration." With "tempered severity," he brought the Franks and barbarians "in harmony with the public welfare"—no easy job since "not even Roman might had been able to tame these people"—and when he died "he left the whole of Europe flourishing." After Charlemagne's death, Nithard said, "the state of the empire grew worse from day to day, since all were driven by greed and sought only their own advantage." The empire was torn apart by civil war and finally partitioned among three other (legitimate) grandsons: Lothar, Charles the Bald, and Louis the German. Louis got most of present Germany, Charles much of France, and Lothar a strip in between from the Low Countries south to Rome.[1]

The rise and restructuring of Charlemagne's empire created work for persons who could read orders, write reports, and direct others—skills common to churchmen. "The Carolingian Age witnessed a phenomenon that would manifest itself more fully in the twelfth century," notes historian Mayke de Jong: "Royal courts were using the written word, to such an extent that a class of professional literate clergy could readily find employment in the king's service, thus giving opportunities to social climbers."[2] Aspiring clerics and courtiers learned to read and write in schools attached to cathedrals and monasteries. Literacy was generally taught from the Bible, but bishops, abbots, and masters of these schools composed material for further instruction. Some wrote mirrors for princes. They wrote the customary precepts about princely virtues, but they found new authority for them in the scriptures and the works of church Fathers. Mirrors of old told a prince to be good to save his job, his head, or his name. Newer mirrors told a prince to be good, moreover, to save his soul. Carolingian mirrors also enlarged the prince's job description: He was responsible not just for the kingdom's well-being but now, with hell breaking loose, for everyone's salvation.[3]

Rhetoric

The first known Carolingian mirror for princes was written for Charlemagne by an English schoolmaster named Alcuin. Alcuin was born to a landed family near the town of York around 740. As a young boy he entered the York cathedral school, where he stayed for the next forty years, rising from student to teacher to headmaster. He earned a reputation as a keen educator of adolescents, and he built a world-class library with a team of monks who copied every antique text they could get hold of. After a mission to Charlemagne for his bishop, Alcuin was invited to join the king's court. At the time, Charlemagne's court was the typical traveling pageant that surrounded early medieval princes. The royal household moved around, from one country estate or monastery to another, to showcase the king's authority and to spread the cost of his upkeep among his landholders. Charlemagne brought with him good cooks, entertaining companions, and a series of wives and mistresses. His entourage also included a group of serious scholars—from Spain, Italy, Britain, and Frankland—who advised the king, taught the children, and raised the culture of the whole enterprise. Alcuin, then almost fifty years old, joined the group sometime in the 780s.[4]

While at court, Alcuin addressed a mirror to Charlemagne called the *Rhetoric*. Borrowed mostly from a book by Cicero on the topic, Alcuin's *Rhetoric* takes the form of an imaginary dialogue between a teacher—Alcuin—and a student-prince—Charlemagne. Alcuin offers to instruct Charlemagne in the art of dealing with public questions that arise "in the course of the duties of government." Again, however, the book is meant for anyone "who well would know the custom of the State."[5]

Alcuin first explains the ancient importance of rhetoric. Once upon a time, he writes, "mankind wandered here and there over the plains very much as do wild beasts, and men did nothing through the reasoning power of the mind, but everything by sheer brute strength." They did not revere God, they did not respect their neighbors, they just followed their passions. Then one day some great and wise man had a vision. He saw that people had the capacity for higher things. And he found within himself the capacity to articulate his vision. By the pure force of his words, "he collected men into one place from being scattered as they were over the plains, and hidden in dwellings in the forests; and he assembled them together, and led them into each useful and honorable pursuit; they, at first protesting against the strangeness of it, yet finally with eagerness listening because of his reason and eloquence, were made gentle and mild from being savage and brutal." Ever since, Alcuin tells Charlemagne, wise kings have used rhetoric to lead men away from selfish habits and toward common goals.[6]

Alcuin proceeds to teach King Charles how to communicate a purposeful, godly vision to unify his empire. He advises Charlemagne to use logic in public speeches, say, by arguing from the intelligent design of the universe—where sun and moon, days and seasons are all perfectly regulated by God's conscious plan—to the sovereignty of an earthly king to govern the affairs of mankind. Logic alone may not convince wayward subjects to fall in line. To win them over, Alcuin encourages Charlemagne to use emotional appeals in his speeches. Gain the sympathy of your listeners, he says, by voicing laments: "Show what benefits we may have lost, and with what misfortunes we are now beset." Focus on calamities like poverty or physical disabilities, acts of disloyalty by servants or trusted citizens, separation from family and friends, the death of a son, things that people can feel personally.[7]

Next, Alcuin counsels, try to arouse indignation, antipathy toward a possible opponent: Begin by suggesting that a view "upheld by our opponent appears to be degrading in the eyes of the immortal gods, the wisest men, the Senate, the people." Define the opponent as "cruel, unjust, miserly, dishonest, insolent." Particularize your opponent: "Condemn his past life and habits." Ask if he took advantage of strangers, guests, neighbors, friends. Look for any willful or unusual crime, especially acts against children, women, old men, or invalids. "Demonstrate what would have happened if a crime like this should have been perpetrated upon those near and dear to the listeners." Call attention to the opponent's pride and arrogance. "Show what evil will befall if he is not punished." Conclude with outrage at the injustice if unspeakable, bloodthirsty, wicked, tyrannical deeds are not avenged.[8]

Alcuin goes on to teach Charlemagne about style—how to choose his words and manage the impression he makes. One's speech should be eloquent, for instance; "It will be eloquent if it observes the rules of grammar, and is supported by the authority of the ancients." Alcuin tells Charles to familiarize himself with the ancients' books, to commit their ideas to memory so they habitually find expression in his own speech. From ancient philosophers like Cicero, one can learn not merely how to talk but how to model a life of virtue. Alcuin recommends to Charlemagne the four cardinal virtues: prudence, justice, temperance, and especially courage—which involves high-mindedness, "the capacity to conceive and to carry out lofty and splendid designs," and confidence, "the ability of the mind to believe infallibly in itself and in the conduct of enterprises of great pith and moment." (What pagans like Cicero understood by these virtues is fine as far as it goes, Alcuin says, but more is expected of a Christian. Prudence, for example, requires knowledge and fear of the one true God. Justice means keeping God's commandments. Courage demands that one stand up to the devil and bear the trials of this world. Temperance implies that a man "governs his lust and controls his greed and calms and moderates all the passions of his soul.")[9]

Alcuin ends with a personal lament. The virtues, he concedes, may be unrealistic ideals for most people, even for Christians: "So very many of us cannot be made to acknowledge the inherent worth of a virtuous life, either by the fear of punishment or the hope of reward." Still, a great and blessed leader could set a good example for everyone. Alcuin addresses Charlemagne with a final prayer: "May God make you great and truly blessed, my Lord King," and through your virtuous leadership "may He grant that this evil generation mount to the summit of the heavenly kingdom."[10]

Like classic mirrors for princes, Alcuin's *Rhetoric* provided generic advice such as the need for leaders to communicate a vaguely inspirational vision. Alcuin followed up with letters of instruction—miniature mirrors for princes—that spelled out what his king's vision should be. This is your mission, he wrote to Charlemagne, "your glory, praise and reward in the judgment of the great day and in the eternal company of the saints, that you diligently strive to correct those entrusted to you by God and lead souls long blinded by the darkness of ignorance to the light of the true faith." If that wasn't plain enough, Alcuin explained to Charlemagne: "This is your special gift from God, that with equal devotion you work to purge and defend the churches of Christ from the teaching of traitors within, and to protect them without from the ravagings of the heathen. So is your power armed with two swords, on the right and on the left." These two metaphorical swords, symbolizing religious and civil authority, would become grounds of contention between future popes and princes, but Alcuin preached a shared vision of *imperium christianum*, a "Christian Empire," and he set the tone for centuries of crusades to realize that vision.[11]

Past popes—Zacharias, Stephen II, Paul I—had told Charlemagne's father, Pippin, that the Franks were now God's chosen people and the king of the Franks was a new David, defender of the true faith, the one church, the holy nation. Alcuin addressed his own letters to Charlemagne, "To the King David" because "it is precisely with this name, inspired by the same virtue and the same faith, that our leader and guide reigns today: a chief in whose shadow the Christian people repose in peace and who on all sides strikes terror into the pagan nations" and "against the followers of heresy." Alcuin urged Charles to use his "God-given power," his arms, to spread the vision of a Christian empire. Indeed, almost every year of his reign from 768 to 814, Charlemagne did launch crusades against pagans and heretics. He pushed north into Germany against the Saxons, south into Italy against the Lombards, east into Hungary against the Avars, and west into Spain against the Arabs, conquering more territory than any Western general between Alexander the Great and Napoleon. There came a point, however, when the swords in the king's hands alarmed even Alcuin.[12]

The non-Christians who gave Charles the most trouble were the Saxons who lived in the woods of northern Germany and worshiped forest gods. Time and again Charles subdued them, forced them to accept baptism, and placed missionaries among them. Whenever Charles left, the Saxons would return to their pagan rites, attack Frankish outposts, and burn and pillage the missions. When they rebelled in 782, Charles put down the uprising, then took vengeance by beheading some four thousand Saxon prisoners. (Charlemagne's biographer Alessandro Barbero finds a precedent in King David's defeat and execution of the Moabites.[13]) Charles subsequently issued laws that went well beyond what Alcuin envisioned. Known as the Ordinances Concerning Saxony, they decreed:

> Whoever enters a church by violence, and by force or by theft takes away any object or sets fire to the building, shall be put to death. Whoever out of scorn for the Christian religion refuses to respect the holy fast of Lent and at that time eats meat, shall be put to death. Whoever kills a bishop, priest, or deacon, shall be put to death. Whoever burns the body of a deceased person and reduces its bones to ashes according to the pagan rite, shall be put to death. Any unbaptized Saxon who tries to hide among his compatriots and refuses to be baptized, shall be put to death. Whoever plots with the pagans against the Christians or persists in supporting them in their struggle against the Christians, shall be put to death. Whoever falls short in the loyalty that he owes to the king, shall be put to death.[14]

Alcuin worried about a backlash to Charles's ordinances and to his missionaries, who exacted tithes from the Saxons before teaching them the tenets of the faith. "Had they preached to the hardened Saxons the gentle yoke of Christ and his sweet burden with the same zeal they applied to the collection of tithes and legal fines for the most paltry lapses, perhaps they would not abhor the sacrament of Baptism," Alcuin wrote to Charles's treasurer, Megenfrid—"Did the apostles, taught and sent forth by Christ to teach the world, levy tithes and demand gifts?"[15] Alcuin urged Megenfrid to use his influence and restrain Charles, but even senior courtiers feared offending Charlemagne, and it was not until an extraordinary episcopal conference condemned his policies that he finally relaxed them.[16]

Alcuin's own deference to his boss shows through in his personal letters. As time wore on, he confided to colleagues back in England that he wished he could just come home, but "the King has gone to lay waste Saxony, and I could not leave without his permission. A friend such as he is not to be scorned by one like me."[17] Alcuin always excused himself from Charlemagne's military campaigns, observes historian Donald Bullough, which limited his contact and influence with the king. When Charles returned home from his wars, he preferred the company of family and less sober friends at court. Biographers describe boisterous banquets with drinking songs, lewd stories, mimes. and minstrels, attended by fawning courtiers and Charlemagne's ever-present wives, concubines, daughters, and grandchildren. Alcuin's letters, reminiscent of Lucian's writings, suggest that he found life at court trying, and his eventual departure may not have been altogether voluntary. Still, Alcuin was rewarded with a golden retirement; Charles made him abbot of the rich monastery of St. Martin, where he lived out his years once more teaching schoolboys about virtues and vices. He continued writing to princes on professional ethics and social responsibilities. And despite the Saxon troubles, he kept preaching a vision of "the 'Christian empire' whose government God had bestowed on Charles and his sons."[18]

Alcuin's works were not known for originality of content, even among sympathetic readers, but they reverently conserved the thought of past ages. After his death in 804, and especially after the shock to the empire of Charlemagne's death in 814, Alcuin's writings gained value as Carolingian memorabilia. "In the tenth and eleventh centuries, they were part of the general Carolingian heritage in the libraries of the older religious communities," notes Bullough, but "with the rise of new forms of thinking and teaching in the late eleventh and twelfth centuries, much of what Alcuin had written came to be read, if at all, only through the filter of other men's writings, in usually anonymous excerpts."[19] Alcuin's pedagogical works enjoyed a brief revival among humanists in the late fifteenth century, and the *Rhetoric* was printed in 1529 for use "in the teaching of *pueri*."[20] By the eighteenth century Alcuin was a vague memory, cited merely as a supporting character in romance novels idealizing the life of Charles the Great.[21]

Jeremiads

Charlemagne was succeeded as emperor by his son Louis. Louis had a priestly education and a monkish mindset. Insiders nicknamed him Monk, sources say, "to tease him mildly with his tendency to wish to subject the whole world, including his court, to a kind of monastic discipline." He is known to history as Louis the Pious.[22]

Louis set out to reform the court, now settled at Aachen in the Rhine Valley, by replacing his father's worldly advisers with clerics who shared his values. The advisers of Louis the Pious included an abbot by the name of Smaragdus, who wrote a mirror for princes titled the *Via Regia*, the *King's Highway*. It tells the king to go the way of God who "raised you to the temporal throne" and "invested you with the royal purple." Follow the way of virtue and work smart, be just, act brave, stay sober. Lead others; show mercy, but keep them on the road to truth and righteousness. The *Via Regia's* argument, states professor of medieval history Karl Ubl, is this: "The zeal for righteousness is legitimate if the ruler detects acts of unchristian behavior in his subjects, such as lewdness, avarice, or drunkenness. Such conduct must be punished by the king as a representative of Christ." Louis the Pious said, Amen.[23]

Louis cleansed the imperial palace of vice. He evicted women of loose morals, including Charlemagne's daughters, who were sent to convents. He rid the court of their illegitimate children. He closed houses of ill repute in the surrounding town. He ordered ladies of pleasure to be hauled off and whipped in the market. Some historians see ulterior motives behind Louis's purge. Vice "charges were a code for political opposition," Janet Nelson points out—Charlemagne's daughters were potential enemies; branding them Jezebels "was the oldest accusation in the book, and it was the pretext that enabled Louis the Pious and his supporters to pose as moral reformers with puritan values, bent on cleaning up the . . . *ancien régime.*"[24]

Louis's zeal for reform reached well beyond Aachen. He tightened rules in religious houses, shored up homeland defense, and rooted out inefficiencies in government throughout his realm. Louis has been portrayed as obsessive, even paranoid, but he faced big problems and real enemies. During the final years of Charlemagne's reign the economy slowed, and cracks appeared in the veneer of Frankish unity. Louis "inherited an empty treasury, a corrupt and rebellious following, an ill-knit empire, a countryside often ruled by vendetta, famine-stricken and plague-ridden," according to Carolingian scholar John Michael Wallace-Hadrill.[25] While Louis attempted to control his kingdom, Viking raiders attacked his borders, pillaging towns and churches. But the worst threat came from his sons.[26]

Louis the Pious fathered four sons: Lothar, Pippin, Louis (the German), and Charles (the Bald). The trouble stemmed from resentment over *their* inheritance. Frankish kings treated the empire like a family farm, passing it on from father to son. For almost a century, successions had gone smoothly because there was a sole surviving son who inherited the whole thing. Anticipating no such luck at his own death, Louis the Pious tried to plan his estate. With more than one legitimate son, Frankish custom called for him to divide his lands equally between them. But Louis's religious advisers warned him that God willed a united empire. So he gave his sons regional kingdoms to rule, and he named the eldest (Lothar) emperor-to-be, boss over all. Unhappy with their shares, the sons of Louis the Pious deposed him, restored him, then deposed him again, fighting among themselves and splitting the empire into warring camps.[27]

Reflecting on these matters, one of Louis's advisers, Bishop Jonas of Orleans, addressed a mirror to the emperor's son Pippin, king of Aquitaine. It dates from the 830s and goes by the title, *De institutione regia*, or *Concerning the Instruction of a King*. "Your Excellency knows only too well," Jonas writes to Pippin, "what expense, what sorrow, what oppression, and what misery and discord have been inflicted upon the people of God in this wretched kingdom during the past year." If God has so far spared the realm from all out civil war, it is only "because the Lord was touched by the prayers of His servants and His favor turned toward your father by his pious and religious deeds." But for peace and prosperity to prevail, Jonas says, Louis the Pious's sons must "stand immovably firm in mutual affection, and, according to the reverence due to a father and to the divine ordinance and command, must with one mind submit to your father in harmony."[28]

Jonas cautions Pippin that the tribulations of this world are generally deserved; they are God's punishment for our sins. "If we are ruled by hatred and jealousy and avarice and discord and deceit and self-indulgence and all the other wicked things which are hateful to the Christian purpose," he says, "then it is not surprising if the divine censure should strike us within and without with the most manifold evils, and inspire the attacks of our enemies against us." Throughout history, people have invited the wrath of God by ignoring His laws and the preaching of His prophets, Jonas asserts; he gives the examples of Adam's Fall, Noah's Flood, the destruction of Sodom and Gomorrah, the plagues of Egypt, and the exile of the Israelites who "perished in the wilderness for their greed and contempt and wicked practices." The moral is clear: "There is no doubt that, through disobedience and contempt for the commandments of God, danger comes to the kingdom and damnation to souls."[29]

The Franks are now in such danger due to their sinfulness, Jonas says: "They believe that they can live blamelessly merely by doing what pleases them." Christians of the day don't practice the faith like the Christians of old, he laments. "In the early days of God's Holy Church, the ardour of faith was so strong amongst those who believed that they persevered in the teaching of the apostles," Jonas states. Back then, people came together to break bread and pray, to share and praise God. "But most people are now very far from any display of Christian devotion: love of earthly affairs is preferred to the teaching of the apostles, and meanness to the sharing in the breaking of bread. Their love has grown cold; they would rather covet the property of another than be generous with their own; and their minds are distracted from their prayers by carnal loves, idle curiosity, worldly anxieties and many other things." Once men praised the Lord for their daily bread, Jonas says, now they praise the cooks for sumptuous feasts; once they prayed at table, now they boast, lie, slander, tell obscene jokes, and talk to hear themselves talk. Small wonder God is vexed with the Franks.[30]

To save the kingdom from God's wrath, Bishop Jonas appeals for a transforming leader who will turn people away from selfish ends toward a common goal. A king like Pippin could be such a leader by refocusing subjects on the common good and guiding them on the path to salvation. Jonas elaborates using quotations from biblical, patristic, and pseudo-authorities. Carolingian writers borrowed freely from a work called *The Twelve Abuses of the World*, an anonymous Irish tract from the seventh century that was sometimes attributed to Augustine or St. Patrick but mostly to the third-century bishop and martyr Cyprian. Jonas quotes this pseudo-Cyprian at length so that any king "may see in his words, as it were in a mirror, what you should be, what you should do, and what you should avoid."[31]

The abuses of the world are grave evils, such as a feckless king. What a king *should not be* is "an unjust man," Jonas tells Pippin, "but the corrector of unjust men." What a king *should do* is

> to restrain men from robbery; to punish adulteries; not to exalt the wicked; not to encourage the unchaste and boastful; to destroy the impious from the face of the earth; not to permit parricides and perjurers to live; to defend the churches; to sustain the poor with alms; to appoint just men over the affairs of the kingdom; to have as his counselors men of mature years who are wise and sober; to pay no attention to the superstitions of magicians and fortune-tellers and oracles; to keep his anger in check; to defend the fatherland bravely and justly against its adversaries; to live in all things for God ... according to the Catholic faith.[32]

This, Jonas suggests, is how kings advance the common good.

When kings think only of their own good, Jonas warns, "the peace of the people is often disrupted." As Cyprian prophesied, under unjust kings "many sorrows taint the prosperity of the kingdom." From every side, "the invasions of enemies lay waste the provinces; the domestic animals and herds of cattle are scattered; storms in spring and winter hinder the fertility of the earth and the employments of the sea; and the standing corn, flowering trees and the shoots of the vines are sometimes stripped bare by bolts of lightning." Ultimately, people bring disasters on themselves, Jonas maintains. Just as bad princes bring bad weather, bad subjects are to blame for bad princes. "When kings are good men, this is a gift of God; but when they are evil, this is due to the wickedness of the people," he says, invoking church Fathers: "When God is angry, peoples receive such a ruler as they deserve for their sins."[33]

While more explicit than most, Jonas's book is a wholly conventional mirror for princes—with stock lessons for kings and subjects alike. Because both good and bad rulers are sent by God, Jonas concludes, one must obey them all. "Every subject should faithfully and beneficially and obediently submit to [royal] power," he argues, for according to scripture "he who resists the power ordained of God certainly resists the ordinance of God." Jonas cites "the admonition of the Lord in the Gospel, where he says: 'Render to Caesar the things that are Caesar's and to God the things that are God's.'" Jonas quotes the Apostles Peter

("Fear God; honour the king") and Paul ("Let every soul be subject to the higher powers; for there are no powers except from God") to show that from the outset Christians are taught to "be subject to the princes."[34]

This does not mean princes are unaccountable. Princes are subject to God in heaven, and on earth they should submit to priests, especially to bishops like Jonas who can instruct them in social responsibilities and restrain them with "humble admonition and wholesome guidance." Brandishing the old "two swords" metaphor, Jonas says there are two main authorities in Christendom: priests and kings. In Jonas's hierarchy of authority, priests are superior "since it is they who are to render to God an account even of kings." Because they are closer to God, "even though the priests of our own day may be in many respects negligent, they still are not to be condemned and despised," Jonas writes—for Jesus Himself said to His apostles, "Whoever hears you, hears me; and whoever despises you despises me." Speaking for many Frankish bishops, Jonas pleads for a larger role in ruling the post-Charlemagne empire: "We therefore suppliantly call upon Your Excellency to see to it that, through you, your nobles and other faithful subjects come to understand the title, power, strength and authority, and also the dignity, of the priesthood, lest, being ignorant, they place their souls in any kind of danger."[35]

Jonas took pains to uphold the authority and dignity of the priesthood in reaction to the subordinate place of clergy under the Carolingian kings. From the start of the dynasty, Charlemagne's grandfather Charles Martell hired and fired bishops, abbots, and others, using their offices and property to reward followers. Popes were powerless to interfere, and by going along they gained royal protection. Boniface, the papal missionary to Germany in the eighth century, acknowledged that "without the patronage of the prince of the Franks, I could neither govern the faithful nor defend the priests, clerics, monks, and nuns"; but, he griped, "the Franks have not convened a synod [of senior clergy] in more than 80 years; they have no archbishops . . . and in most cases, the bishoprics have been handed over to greedy laymen, or to adulterous, uneducated clerical carousers who profit from them in a worldly way."[36]

Under Charlemagne, clerics received more education, but even scholars like Alcuin never forgot they were patronage workers, mere courtiers. The king still named bishops and abbots. Local landlords built their own proprietary churches and employed their own priests. Under Louis

the Pious, reform-minded bishops campaigned against these practices. "Almost no one can be found," complained Jonas's fellow bishop,
Agobard of Lyon, "who does not have a domestic priest, whom he doesn't
obey but from whom he ceaselessly demands both due and undue obedience, not only in divine offices but in human ones too; so you can find
plenty of priests who serve at table, or mix the wine, or take the dogs out,
or act as grooms for horses on which women are mounted, or look after
plots of land."[37] According to Agobard, landlords

> treat these clerics with scorn: when they want them ordained priests, they
> ask us [bishops]—or rather, order us—in these sorts of terms: "I've got a
> cleric here—picked him out from my serfs and brought him up for my
> own service: now I want you to ordain him priest for me." And when
> that's been done, they think afterwards that they never have any need
> for clergy in higher orders, and they very often give up attending public
> worship or preaching.[38]

To address relations between civil and religious authorities, Frankish
bishops pressed Louis the Pious to summon an episcopal synod, held at
Paris in 829. Bishop Jonas recorded the Acts of this synod and he copied
key sections of the Acts into his mirror for princes. The synod fathers
viewed church and empire as an organic whole. This implied that kings
and bishops were not rival factions, as in a constitutional state, but were
complementary jobs, as in a corporation. So the issue for the synod was
not political, it was organizational. It was not how to divide *power* among
groups with separate goals; it was how to divide *labor* "within one unified
and raceless community or body, having its collective goal the glory of
God and the salvation of His people," notes Robert Dyson, the editor of
Jonas's *Instruction*.[39] In his mirror, Jonas reveals the optimal division of
labor: The job of priests and bishops, he says, is to watch over people and
teach them how to live. The king's job is to make sure people listen and correct those who go astray. There would be no need for kings, Jonas argues,
"were it not for the fact that, by the discipline of terror, they reinforce
what the priest accomplishes by the instruction of preaching." Kings
have a special duty, he adds, "diligently to secure the well-being of the
priests and their ministry and to protect the Church by force of arms."[40]

Civil authorities gave lip service to the organizational theories of
Jonas and the bishops in Paris. "Louis the Pious let them talk away," says

historian Louis Halphen; one contemporary cleric fretted, however, that "no positive results emerged from all this." Another complained to the emperor that "We remember that in previous meetings several articles were, at your request, discussed and worked out in view of the common good and welfare of the two orders, ecclesiastical and lay; but we do not know why these articles were relegated to oblivion."[41]

Jonas of Orleans had no more success with his *Instruction* for Prince Pippin, who continued battling his father and brothers. Over the years many Frankish churchmen wrote similar mirrors for princes, with similarly disappointing results. They looked back with nostalgia to the reign of Charlemagne. They preached the old vision of imperium christianum, a Christian empire united to do God's will. They warned that without such a vision, without shared faith in a higher purpose, the empire would cease to exist. Kings paid scant attention. Like modern CEOs, Frankish kings tolerated talk about their social responsibilities in books and conferences because it flattered them and confirmed their right to command, but they ignored it at work when it seemed out of touch with the real problems of governing.

In reality, kings, bishops, and nobles *were* rival powers—the empire never was very united. What held it together at all, Louis the Pious came to realize, was not simply faith but patronage. And patronage was running out. Charlemagne had grown the empire like most warrior kings by distributing conquered territory and treasure among the great families who joined forces with him. Many of the people he conquered—for example, the Avars, descendants of Attila the Hun—were themselves ruthless plunderers, and their loot fueled the expansion. (One chronicler reported that fifteen wagons, each drawn by four oxen, were needed to haul away the gold and silver from the Avars' stronghold to Aachen.) "So long as the Frankish empire was still growing and bringing in the money," says medievalist Timothy Reuter, internal divisions could be overlooked.[42] But expansion stalled in the early ninth century, perhaps because the most profitable victims were already subdued, and further military campaigns promised less return on investment. As the king's money and patronage dried up, noble families fell back on defense to protect their wealth from the Vikings and other marauders who came looking for it. Frankish magnates raised local forces and fortifications to defend their own neighborhoods, shielding themselves from intrigues surrounding the emperor in the process. Eventually local lords took over the administration of justice and other tasks of government, decentralizing authority across western Europe.[43]

Any realistic hope for Frankish unity ended in 843. With their father (and Pippin) now dead, the three surviving sons of Louis the Pious met at Verdun and partitioned the empire along lines that exist in places to this day. History books once portrayed the breakup of the empire as a failure of vision or leadership, but recent scholarship suggests it was only a matter of time. Many contemporaries accepted the partition as a revival of Frankish tradition. Many stood to benefit from decentralization of authority. "The truth is that most people," concludes Wallace-Hadrill, "thought that European unity was an over-rated ideal, like that of its parent, the *Imperium Christianum*."[44]

A small but vocal clerical party lamented the division of Charlemagne's empire, claiming the Franks were turning their backs on authority, morality, and God.[45] When "there was a single prince and one people as his subjects," wrote Florus of Lyon, "our citizens lived in peace, our might frightened the enemy away. Priests performed their holy charges with energy." They taught young men the holy writings, they baptized conquered peoples, they stamped out heresies. "Far and wide, high and low, the word of salvation resounded." But now, Florus despaired, no one fears prince *or* priest, or even hell-fire; "there is no respect for sacred things." Instead, there is flagrant adultery, crime, and wickedness since "the united kingdom has fallen to three lots." Today "a petty king supplants a monarch, the fragments of a kingdom replace a realm. Councils meet frequently to decide upon theft and aggression, salvation's laws are destroyed in bustling assemblies, the common good comes to naught, each man looks to his own, private concerns are everything, only God is forgotten."[46]

The aim of such jeremiads, of course, was to remind people about God and the ideal of imperium christianum. The message would take root and bear fruit in the twelfth century when the vision of a united Christendom inspired crusaders to march across Europe. Mirrors for princes again showed the way.

Christian Mirrors

As you read medieval mirrors for princes, keep in mind a point made earlier concerning Aristotle. What you are reading is not the whole story of any particular thinker, and it is certainly not the whole of political thought within a rich religious tradition like Christianity. From the beginning, Christians disagreed about their duties to civil authorities, observes political historian Joseph Canning. Some Christians, recalling their persecution by Nero and other Roman emperors, challenged authorities. Some, following Christ's words, "My kingdom is not of this world," were apolitical, indifferent to authorities. Some, heeding St. Paul's instruction to "obey the governing authorities" since "all government comes from God," cooperated with authorities. It was mainly this last, cooperative group who wrote mirrors for princes.[47]

FIVE

Storybook Mirrors

Our fathers, though less in number, so often bravely withstood in battle the far larger forces of the enemy . . . that the very name of Christian became a terror to nations ignorant of God, and thus the Lord was glorified in the works of our fathers. In contrast to this, the men of our times too often have been conquered by inferior forces. . . . Because of their sins, the Lord justly withdraws His favor, as if provoked to wrath. Such are the men of the present age . . . [that] one who would undertake with careful pen to portray their morals, or rather their monstrous vices, would succumb under the vast amount of material; in short, he would seem to be writing satire rather than compiling history.

William of Tyre, *A History of Deeds Done Beyond the Sea*

As the twelfth century dawned, churchmen saw Christendom mired in darkness. Prelates blamed selfish lifestyles, irresponsible leadership, priestly scandals, pick-and-choose Catholicism. "In nearly all the circle of the earth, belief had failed, especially among those who were called the faithful, and the fear of the Lord no longer prevailed among men," wrote Archbishop William of Tyre. "Justice had perished from the world, and . . . violence held sway among the nations. Fraud, treachery, and chicanery overshadowed all things. All virtue had departed" and "evil reigned in its stead."[1]

With Charlemagne's Christian empire a fading memory, the great princes of Europe "disregarded their treaties of peace and quarrelled with each other for the most trivial reasons," William said. "They burned and plundered lands, seized booty everywhere, and exposed the goods of the poor to be plundered by their wicked followers."[2] They respected neither life nor property. They dragged innocent people from basilicas, highways, cities, and towns to be tortured and killed. They ransacked churches and monasteries, stealing altar cloths, precious robes, and sacred vessels.

People in turn lost all respect for authority. Echoing the prophets of old Egypt, William complained that "class distinctions were disregarded, and the world seemed to wish to return to its primal condition of chaos." People scorned traditional values, he said: "Luxury, drunkenness, and night-long games of chance . . . [left] no room for thrift and sobriety." People debased bonds of marriage and family: "Every kind of fornication was practiced openly and without shame." Priests behaved no better: Even "bishops had become remiss in their duty, 'dumb dogs, they cannot bark'; they received anyone [with money] and their heads were sleek with the oil of the sinner; like hirelings, they left the sheepfolds committed to their care to the attacks of wolves."[3]

While Christians went their sinful ways in the West, Muslims occupied their holy places in the East. In 1095 Pope Urban II responded by preaching a vision to unite and cleanse the Christian nations. He called for a crusade to liberate Jerusalem. "Let the deeds of your ancestors move you and incite your minds to manly achievements," he told the Franks; think of "the glory and greatness of King Charlemagne, and of his son Louis, and of your other kings, who have destroyed the kingdoms of the pagans, and extended in these lands the territory of the holy church." As reported by a monk named Robert, Urban urged the Franks to "let your quarrels end, let wars cease, and let all dissensions and controversies slumber. Enter upon the road to the Holy Sepulchre, wrest that land from the wicked races, and subject it to yourselves. That land which as the Scripture says 'floweth with milk and honey,' was given by God into the possession of the children of Israel."[4]

To those who undertook this crusade, Pope Urban promised remission of all their sins. Nobles, knights, and poor alike turned from their selfish aims and answered the call, according to a chronicle by Guibert of Nogent: "The change of heart they soon underwent was remarkable and scarcely believable because of the heedless state of their souls, as they all begged the bishops and priests to give the sign prescribed by the above-mentioned pope, that is, the crosses" (cloth badges worn by crusaders signifying their vows and salvation). To arm themselves for crusading, persons sold "whatever items of value they had piled up," wrote Guibert. As they rushed to depart, "each tried to get whatever money he could scrape together by any means; each seemed to be offering whatever he had, not at the seller's, but at the buyer's price, lest he be late in setting out on the path of God. It was a miraculous sight: everyone bought high and sold low." On the roads, Guibert said, "you would have seen remarkable, even comical things; poor people, for example, tied their cattle to two-wheel carts, armed as though they were horses, carrying their few possessions, together with their small children, in the wagon. The little children, whenever they came upon a castle or a city, asked whether this was the Jerusalem to which they were going."[5]

Despite Guibert's glib portrayal of children chanting "Are we there yet?," the reality of crusading was anything but comical. Crusading was deadly dangerous work. It was temporary work besides, not the most attractive career path for someone with an education. Educated men gravitated toward vocations that involved more opportunities for advancement, more writing than fighting. Many trained as clerics, then took jobs as clerks in one of the burgeoning bureaucracies—the court of some bishop, abbot, prince, or noble—and worked their way up the organization. Like Guibert and William of Tyre, these scholarly bureaucrats wrote marvelous stories about events of the age. They also wrote mirrors for princes.

Twelfth-century mirrors are more fun to read than the classics. As before, authors wrote for a wide professional audience, not just for princes. But now, to engage readers, they used literary tricks to freshen up dry theology and philosophy. They embellished for popular consumption the old teachings with vivid imagery, anecdotal history, witty satire, and above all good stories. Language scholars call these tricks exempla. They are used to this day to make works of instruction—sermons, self-improvement courses, ethics and management books—sound less preachy, more compelling. Since Isocrates, educators have known that academic theorizing about virtue attracts fewer readers and listeners than tell-all tales showing how courage, mercy, and other classical virtues worked for Alexander the Great or the latest leadership hero.

Gerald of Wales

The medieval master of this craft was Gerald of Wales. Gerald was born in 1146 to a family of knightly Normans in colonial Wales. The youngest of four sons, Gerald was "brought up for the Church and given the best clerical education that his age could offer," says his biographer Robert Bartlett. (His father referred affectionately to young Gerald as "my bishop," a title he aspired to all his life but never achieved.) He studied law in Paris, served under his uncle, the bishop of St. David's, then clerked for King Henry II of England. He was known to be a black-and-white bureaucrat—a stickler for rules, a moral reformer—but he was best remembered as a colorful storyteller.[6]

In his autobiography, Gerald tells how he preached the crusade while touring Wales with the archbishop of Canterbury. The archbishop, Baldwin, had no success in recruiting the locals. But Gerald moved throngs to tears with his words and persuaded countless Welshmen to take the cross—even though, he says, he could not speak their language but addressed them in French and Latin.[7]

Along with personal stories, Gerald wrote about the countries he visited on diplomatic trips for the Crown. He stressed the vices of the native people and the virtues of their English conquerors. In his *Topography of Ireland*, he praised Henry II as the model of a lettered prince, who conquered lands from the Pyrenees to the Irish Sea, like "our Western Alexander," but who in victory showed clemency, with Seneca's *On Mercy* always at hand. Gerald thought the Irish lived like animals, only lazier. "They do not devote their lives to the processing of flax or wool, or to any kind of merchandise or mechanical art," he wrote, but care only about making music. "They think that the greatest pleasure is not to work, and the greatest wealth is to enjoy liberty." The Irish are "a filthy people, wallowing in vice," according to Gerald. "They do not avoid incest. They do not attend God's church with due reverence." "They do not yet pay tithes." Not even Saint Patrick could break their barbarian habits. (Gerald says he is reluctant to describe the bestiality they practice up in Ulster; but he does so anyway, in lurid detail.)[8]

Gerald's books earned him notoriety but not the promotions he felt he deserved. Gerald wrote in his autobiography that he traded the noble life of a scholar for the detestable life of a courtier because of King Henry's urgings and promises. After years of faithful service as Henry's clerk, however, "he received of the King, who enriched and promoted so many unworthy persons, nothing save empty promises void of all truth."[9] The king praised Gerald in private but remarked it was too bad he had been born in the backwater of Wales; otherwise, the king said, he would have exalted him with ecclesiastical titles and rich rewards "and would have made him a great man in his kingdom."[10] Gerald put up with disappointments and backstabbers at court—"that image of death and model of Hell"—until 1194, when he chose or was forced to take early retirement.[11] At age forty-eight he resumed the life of a scholar and composed a mirror for princes.

Gerald's mirror is titled *De principis instructione, On the Instruction of Princes*. Gerald dedicates the book not to the memory of Henry II or his sons, Prince John or Richard the Lionheart (for whom Gerald also worked), but to their enemy—Louis of France—because he above all others might have the education and virtue to appreciate it. Gerald starts with maxims culled from *florilegia*, medieval works of collected sayings from Cicero, Seneca, church Fathers, and other authorities. Gerald's maxims express traditional virtues. A prince should be mild in attitude, modest in speech, dignified in appearance: "In every time of life one must be careful to keep his actions appropriate and his conduct of life fitting and becoming," Gerald writes. A prince should be chaste in morals and set a good example for his subjects. A prince should be just, "assigning and preserving for each man his own position." A prince should be generous without squandering his patrimony or draining the treasury. He should be a student of religion, letters, history, and strategy. He should make prudent decisions, especially in emergencies; "fortune favors the brave," but a prince should not make war rashly. He should be patient, merciful, and slow to anger. Rage is bad for one's health and "a prince should never punish when he is angry." Gerald follows Seneca in stressing the virtue of clemency. "It is a glorious thing to hold punishment well within the maximum bounds," he says. Capital punishment should be used only as a last resort: "A good prince who is concerned in bringing force upon the wrongdoings of certain men will now imprison them, now inflict bodily pain upon them, and sometimes even cut off a bit of their flesh. Only when he has exhausted all other remedies will the prince have recourse to the supreme penalty." In general, it is better for a prince "to be loved than to be feared."[12]

Gerald adds stories and exempla to illustrate his precepts. He tells how Christ was patient with people and how virtuous Roman emperors copied his example. He relates how Charlemagne benefited from the moral education provided by "his teacher" Alcuin. He pays tribute to legendary princes like King Arthur, whose grave and bones he claims to have seen in Glastonbury. Gerald goes on to extol natural leaders such as the kings of France who rule graciously, he says, instead of roaring about like bears and lions.[13]

The last and longest part of Gerald's mirror is a case study tracing the rise and fall of King Henry II. Henry ruled England for almost thirty-five years. For the first thirty, until 1185, Gerald suggests, he was successful at it. Born to a French family with a low reputation and the nick-name Plantagenet (possibly for the broom plant they wore in their hats), Henry attained the English throne through good luck and divine providence. With God's help, Gerald says, he grew the kingdom beyond any of "his predecessors from the coming of the Normans." His domain, sometimes called the "Angevin Empire," stretched across the island of Britain, west to Ireland, north to Scotland, south through France, and his influence spread east into Italy down to the holy city of Rome. Over time, Gerald writes, Henry became "above all the kings and princes of the earth, a glory to the faithful, and a terror to the infidels"; and "the fame of his name was celebrated throughout the whole world."[14]

Like many creative writers, Gerald supplies intimate details to make his stories more interesting. He describes Henry as a charismatic leader with a rough voice, red hair, and bright gray eyes that turned bloodshot when he got angry. Henry had strong arms but a flabby body and a big belly for someone so active. He had a leadership style that could be termed "Management by Moving Around." Henry never sat down, Gerald says, but rode around the country all day, hunting and doing business; he stood all night, working and wearing out his whole court. Truth be told, Gerald reveals, Henry had problems in the area of virtue. He took a wife, Eleanor of Aquitaine, away from her husband, King Louis of France. He later betrayed Eleanor with multiple mistresses. In addition, "he was a seller of justice," Gerald writes, "considering things right or wrong according to his own convenience or advantage." He named his friend and chancellor Thomas Becket the archbishop of Canterbury. (Becket was not a priest, so Henry had him ordained one Saturday and consecrated as archbishop on Sunday.) Then Henry stood by while his men murdered Thomas after he challenged the king's authority. But Henry did penance for his sins, trudging barefoot through the streets of Canterbury to kneel at Thomas's tomb. By God's grace, Gerald reports, Henry kept his crown and went on to gain even more glory.

In 1185 Henry fell from grace when he turned his back on God—in the person of Patriarch Heraclius of Jerusalem, who had come to ask for his help with the crusades. As Gerald tells it, the patriarch announced that infidels were about to retake the Holy Land, which was, for the time being, in Christian hands. On behalf of defenders of the faith and the military order of the temple, he offered Henry the keys to Jerusalem and the Lord's very sepulcher if he would lead an army to save them. Gerald encouraged the king, reminding Henry what an honor it was that the patriarch would come from the farthest corner of the world to him, not to any other prince, with such a great mission. Henry felt pressured, and he didn't like it. "If the Patriarch or anyone else comes to us," he scoffed, "they are seeking their own advantage here, not ours." Gerald begged Henry to consider the patriarch's request, but the king had heard enough. "These clerks," he said with contempt, "can incite us boldly to arms and danger, since they themselves will receive no blows in the struggle, nor will they undertake any burdens which they can avoid." Then Henry told the patriarch he had his own land to protect and offered him a donation for his trouble. "We are looking for a leader," the patriarch replied, "not money"; if you won't lead a crusade yourself, he asked, why not send your son John to Jerusalem? Henry refused, and the patriarch realized "he could not force honey from a stone." So he went home, but not before he called the king worse than an infidel and prophesied his downfall.[15]

Sure enough, Henry's successes turned to defeats. The king's last five years brought him one affliction and punishment after another, Gerald says. "Henry's first enterprise within that period, one that he had prepared for with such care, namely the dispatch of his son John to [take control of] Ireland, came to nothing and was totally unsuccessful, so that all his careful preparation and expenditure of money was wasted."[16] (Gerald, who accompanied John as an adviser on this doomed expedition, claims "the Irish people have deserved to suffer . . . invasion and conquest by foreigners, since their misdemeanours and vile practices demanded this punishment";[17] but John failed because his father displeased God even more.) The next year, Henry, who had never before surrendered any of his territories, lost Auvergne—the birthplace of the First Crusade—to the young King Philip of France. During the following years Henry lost nearly the whole region of Berry, the city of Tours, his hometown of Le Mans, and many castles until finally, Gerald says, "he lost himself."[18] In the end, Henry's flesh and blood—his own sons—turned on him, and he died a miserable death. Let that be a lesson, Gerald concludes, to princes everywhere. Great leaders unify people for great causes, like crusades; princes bent on their own security perish alone.[19]

Readers have recognized Gerald's talent for telling a story. Many, however, have questioned his reporting of history. Gerald's fellow chroniclers were less sympathetic to Patriarch Heraclius, for example. Oxford historian Christopher Tyerman points out that contemporaries viewed the patriarch as a bit of a con man who peddled his keys all over Europe, offering the kingdom of Jerusalem to just about any prince he met. As the patriarch toured London and Paris with an entourage sporting gold jewelry, fine clothes, and expensive perfume, Henry was not the only one to take offense and turn him down.[20]

Speaking for modern historians, Lewis Warren states that Gerald's account of Henry's reign "is so blinkered and wildly partisan that it is worthless for the purpose of interpreting events." But Gerald supposed that in telling tales and shading facts he was teaching bigger truths. His case study of Henry II was meant to inspire leaders, not just to impart information. Henry was a typical feudal king, what management books label a *transactional* leader; he rewarded and punished, wheeled and dealed, to get what he wanted. Henry acted as if subjects, allies, churchmen, everyone had a price, and he tried to buy their cooperation as cheaply as he could. Gerald disliked this kind of leadership. He resented how cheaply Henry bought and rewarded his own services. He longed instead for a *transformational* leader who would unite people behind a common goal.[21]

Gerald had never actually seen such leadership—even the crusaders, he complained, "lacked unity and concord."[22] But he believed it could be taught through education that stressed virtue over self-interest. He believed the ancients learned it, the Carolingians as well, and he wrote his *Instruction of Princes* to carry on the tradition. Gerald had few illusions about the princes of his day, whom he compared to untutored "asses wearing crowns."[23] (Look around, he wrote in the preface to his mirror. "Which modern prince does not nonchalantly abuse his prerogatives, indulging each and every capricious thought, each and every license and luxury of the flesh, each and every atrocity of depraved tyranny?"[24]) Although learned princes "have for some time now been a dead breed, banished from the face of the earth," Gerald imagined his work might inspire socially responsible leaders, like the new French prince to whom he dedicated his *Instruction*.[25]

That was an illusion too. The French prince of Gerald's imagination became King Louis VIII, a religious warrior who took to crusading not against infidels in the Holy Land but against heretical Christians in southern France. Louis is still infamous there for leading an army to "cleanse" the town of Marmande, where his soldiers massacred everybody—butchering men, women, and children alike. Gerald may not have approved of the French crusaders' cruelty (even Louis seemed upset by it), but his mirror for princes prescribed nothing but homilies to protect persons from abuses of power. And his stories fueled the flames of intolerance for centuries.[26]

Four hundred years after King Henry II sent his son John to control Ireland, for example, the Irish remained uncontrollable. This fact vexed English monarchs who envisioned a great British empire. The regime of Queen Elizabeth I set out to crush Irish resistance, but wars of conquest now required more justification. Politicians needed to overcome the scruples of God-fearing English men and women against exploiting other human beings. With new technologies in printing, the talk-radio of the age, propagandists eased English consciences with a flood of anti-Irish tracts. Prominent writers like Edmund Campion and Edmund Spenser as well as a pack of strident pamphleteers portrayed the Irish as animals—filthy barbarians wallowing in vice—and they relied for these clichés on Gerald of Wales. In 1662 an Irish scholar named John Lynch protested that "the wild dreams of Gerald have been taken up by a herd of scribblers" who repeat his lies again and again and embellish his stories of Irish vice with such venom that "he has made our name a byword of reproach, in the mouths of mountebanks, in taverns, in club-meetings, in private societies," around the world. Far from teaching big truths, Gerald "lighted the way for Machiavelli in teaching princes the art of treachery," according to Lynch: "The excesses of a foreign soldiery in Ireland, the devastation of her provinces, the plunder and conflagration of her houses, and the massacre of her sons, must all be laid at Gerald's door." Modern experts in British colonial propaganda have sustained Lynch's verdict.[27]

John of Salisbury

Gerald's rise from village schoolboy to royal courtier paralleled the careers of others in the twelfth century. Social mobility was increasing because of new opportunities for education as well as employment. In cities across

Europe, schools attached to cathedrals grew into universities, offering advanced study in the liberal arts. At Oxford and other places, business schools sprang up, teaching accounting, legal practice, and language skills. Such opportunities enabled men of middling birth—a Gerald of Wales, John of Salisbury, or Thomas Becket—to climb up the social ladder. Becket climbed the highest, from merchant's son to king's chancellor, but his colleague John of Salisbury gained the most literary renown.[28]

Born between 1115 and 1120 to a family of churchmen, John grew up around the cathedrals of Salisbury and Exeter, then studied philosophy and theology at Paris. He went on to clerk for the archbishops of Canterbury, Theobald and Becket, under King Henry II. Like his coworkers, John had his troubles with the king, but he rose through the Canterbury organization and represented it in diplomatic missions to popes, princes, and powerbrokers of Europe. To impart his experience, he wrote a mirror for princes of state and church titled *Policraticus*. The title is a pseudo-Greek invention—John made up the word to sound scholarly—but medievalists have called it the first extensive book on government and the most important mirror for princes written in the Latin Middle Ages. It contains conventional wisdom, illustrated throughout with edifying analogies, stories, and anecdotes.[29]

John tells a story he heard from Pope Adrian IV, a fellow Englishman and personal friend. John visited the unpopular pope at his refuge in Benevento, and they shared private thoughts, as friends do. Adrian asked what the people in the street were saying about their leaders. Frankly, John replied, "even the Roman pontiff himself is burdensome and almost intolerable to everyone, since all assert that, despite the ruins and rubble of churches (which were constructed by the devotion of the Fathers) and also the neglect of altars, he erects palaces and parades himself about not only in purple vestments but in gilded clothes."[30]

Adrian just laughed, John said, and told him this parable. One day the members of the body decided to rebel against the stomach. The other members all had a job—the eyes to see, the ears to hear, the hands to hold, the feet to walk, the tongue to talk—but the stomach just sat there, consuming everything. So the members agreed they would stop working and punish the stomach by starving that parasite. The first day, they muddled through; they next day, they got irritable; the third, they grew faint. Weakened and feeble, they learned that their common good required them to feed the stomach, not fight with it, so it could in turn nourish them. Consequently, "persuaded by reason, the stomach was replenished, the members were revived, and the peace of all was reestablished." Then "they absolved the stomach, which, although it is voracious and covetous of unsuitable things, still asks not for itself but for others which are unable to be sustained by its emptiness."[31]

The moral of the story, John explains, is that "the stomach in the body and the prince in the republic [or church] are the same office." Their health benefits all the members, while their injury weakens the whole. Therefore, "even if the ruler is too loose in the virtues of his office, still he has to be honoured," and "even if he is afflicted with the vices, he is to be endured as the one with whom rests the hopes of the provincials for their security."[32]

It's an old story. The ancient Egyptians left a version of it on school tablets. The Greeks knew it from Aesop's fable, *The Belly and the Members*. Romans heard it from a speech attributed to Menenius Agrippa, who told the story—with patricians as the belly—to quell a rebellion by the plebs in 494 BC. (Modern critics picture the plebs replying, *Right, Agrippa; if the state needs a belly, let us be the belly from now on!*) Such stories stressed the virtues of cooperation and community, but they were first and foremost rhetorical tools that could be used to rationalize the rule of the prince and to justify almost any policy he proposed. John's tale, for example, was used during the Middle Ages to support new taxes.[33]

John's best-known exemplum is an expanded organic analogy comparing political and human bodies. It takes up almost a quarter of the *Policraticus*, over two hundred pages of text. John claims he copied it from an "Instruction for Trajan," a mirror for princes written by Plutarch for the Roman emperor Trajan. No such mirror has ever been found, and scholars now believe John made this up too, perhaps to lend the weight of antiquity to his own views.[34]

As John tells it, Plutarch likened a republic to the human body, their members having comparable functions. In a republic, in any state, the prince is the head, thinking for the whole body "subject only to God and to those who act in His place on earth." Priests are the soul of the body politic, sent by God to tell right from wrong. The senate is the heart, keeping the prince on a steady course with strategic advice. Judges and governors of the provinces are the ears, eyes, and mouth—the public face of the regime. Lesser officials and soldiers are the hands, courtiers the flanks, extending the prince's reach in the business of state. Treasurers and bookkeepers are now the stomach and intestines (here, derogatory metaphors similar to bean-counters), nourishing the body but prone to infection. Peasants are the feet, "perpetually bound to the soil," serving the needs of those above them. This corporate analogy, as it's often called, idealizes the features of classical monarchy—centralized authority, hierarchical organization, specialized labor, interdependent members with a common goal.[35]

You might expect John to go on with the analogy, explaining how in his experience states and their members actually work like human bodies. But that's not what John does. Instead, he tells you how states, communities, and institutions of his day are thoroughly *unlike* healthy bodies. While head, heart, hands, feet, and all the members of a sound body work together for their common good, the members of John's society seem bent on doing their own things, seeking their own goods.

John sees, for example, judges who are "ignorant of the science of law and devoid of a good will," demanding "presents and compensation," and misusing their power "in the service of greediness, ostentation, or their own flesh and blood." He sees magistrates "chasing after their own desires in the pursuit of avarice and the plundering of the people." He sees governors so corrupted by bribes that they market their "duty to king and queen, to whom [they] owe fealty, like merchandise in a doorway." John sees the hands of the republic—soldiers, peace officers, tax collectors—grabbing whatever they can. All "are notoriously accustomed to being wicked," he writes, "inasmuch as they can plunder and molest private persons under the pretext of official business." Tax collectors especially, "from the greatest down to the lowest, only have time these days for extortion rather than justice." They are more frightful than thieves, John claims. A thief steals things furtively, afraid of getting caught and punished for breaking the law; a tax collector steals money, farms, whole estates brazenly, believing "that law is whatever he does."[36]

John sees the flanks and internal organs of the body politic—courtiers, treasurers, other civil servants—serving neither the prince nor the public but only themselves. Court procedures look to John like farces out of classical satire. "If requests are to be presented, if a case is to be examined, if the execution of a sentence is to be ordered, if bail is to be rendered—in all cases money talks, truth is blind," he says. If you approach the prince's gatekeepers, you are told you don't have the proper papers. You can buy the right documents for a price, but you must pay dearly if you want your case presented in the best possible words. Naturally, you have to tip the person who handles your paperwork. "If perhaps a beautiful belt is yours, or a suitable knife, or anything in the way of a decent small possession, number it among his goods." Once you get past that first bureaucrat, you will encounter another—more greedy and condescending than the last. He will look at you with a pinched face and glance at your papers with disgust. He will find that your documents are "inappropriately drafted, or that the style reflects lack of cultivation, or that the notary or scribe departs (through benign or negligent disregard for the law) from the standard form; and some problem always requires money for its resolution." This goes on and on while you wait around for the next courtier to squeeze you, for a fee, into his busy schedule. "Believe an expert," John says, "I have fallen into their hands on innumerable occasions"; they are not like the ferrymen of old satires who transport people into the netherworld for small change; they command pounds "multiplied over and over again."[37]

Courtiers take bribes, John observes, because their superiors take from them. "Never is an office," he says, "free of charge; no general or judge, no commander or courtly official, not even a herald or huckster, is appointed except for a price." Church authorities are in on the take, transforming the house of God "into a house of business affairs; and the temple founded upon the rock . . . into a den of robbers." John bemoans that "at the moment everything is purchased openly"—church offices, benefices, property rights to the holy altars themselves.[38]

John sees selfishness metastasizing deep into the head and soul of twelfth-century institutions. If there were any enterprise that ought to have characteristics of a healthy human body, it should be the crusade to Jerusalem, with its clearly articulated vision and inducements to sacrifice self-interest for the common good. Yet John, in his papal memoir, depicts the crusade as a disaster due to "the jealousy of princes and the wrangling of priests." He points to the bishops, Arnulf of Lisieux and Godfrey of Langres, who accompanied French forces to the Holy Land: "Few if any have brought more harm on the Christian army and whole community," John writes. "Both received large sums of money from the sick and dying whom they attended and absolved in the name of the pope, claiming to be his representatives. Indeed they are believed to have accumulated more wealth during the expedition than they paid out of their own pockets." As John describes it, the crusade was nothing like the corporate body pictured in the *Policraticus*. The Catholic bishops fought over which of them was the true soul of the venture. The Christian princes fought about who should head the thing and direct operations. The French, German, Flemish, and other crusading knights fought among themselves because they had no use for foreigners. It was a miracle of God they got as far as Jerusalem, and eventually even he gave up on them.[39]

Although crusaders and clerics, courtiers and tax collectors, sheriffs and judges are the most visible faces of avarice, John says all members of the community are corrupted by it. Now "everyone struggles after wealth," he laments. "In the present world, whoever does not have riches is stupid, asinine, a dummy, a blockhead"—while "one who is wealthy and prosperous in his external trappings is judged wise and happy." No one tries to do good anymore; "the appetite for wealth excludes wisdom and drives off virtue." No one cares for ancient moral truths; "the thoughts and ideas of philosophers have entirely vanished."[40]

John hoped to revive ancient moral truths with his fiction of Plutarch's corporate analogy. The purpose of this organic analogy is not to describe how the world really works but to prescribe how it's supposed to. It is a sad fact that contemporary societies don't look much like living bodies, John suggests, but the moral truth is *they should*. They should have wise heads, brave hearts, clean hands, and all their members should work together for the common good. If everyone did his proper job, "the circumstances of each and every person would be absolutely optimal, and virtue would flourish and reason would prevail, mutual charity reigning everywhere." To show that such ideals are feasible, not mere figments of his imagination, John looks backward to the ancients for examples.[41]

The most important job, the ancients knew, belongs to the prince. Just as any body needs a head to direct it, John argues, any society needs a prince to control the other members, to restrain their impulses and focus their efforts on patriotic goals. To illustrate the character of an ideal prince, John tells stories of legendary leaders, like Codrus, king of Athens back when the city was facing war with the Dorians. The Dorians were a fierce but superstitious people. In preparing for battle, they consulted an oracle who prophesied they would win the war—so long as they did not kill the Athenian king. Before taking the field, the Dorian army was ordered to watch out for King Codrus and spare his life. Codrus learned of this and set out on his own to foil the enemy. He disguised himself as a peasant, he strolled into the Dorian camp, then he purposely bumped into a soldier with his pruning hook and was slain for his clumsiness. When the Dorians recognized the body of the Athenian king, they conceded defeat and went home without a fight. It's just a legend, but it makes the point: A good prince would lay down his life for his country. A prince who sets an example of selflessness inspires more love than fear, John adds, which is a competitive advantage because love motivates followers to act selflessly as well, to sacrifice their own skins for the prince.[42]

The task of any leader is to create "a tenacious unity of wills," according to John. His favorite exemplars are the ancient Romans. "In fact, if all the histories of peoples are reviewed," he says, "nothing shines more brightly than the magnificence and virtue of the Romans." He tells stories of Cato, Caesar, Augustus, and others who showed such justice, reverence, maturity, and dignity "that they subjected the entire world to their commands." John tells, for instance, how Julius Caesar gained success through servant leadership: He "never said to his troops, 'Go here,' but 'Come with me'"; he knew that "labour in which the commander shares will seem less laborious to the soldier." Caesar learned that virtuous leadership also means avoiding lust and luxury, that "in war the human body is injured by the sword, whereas in peace it is injured by pleasure." Likewise, John says, the ideal "prince must be chaste and shun avarice." He should not consort with "actors and mimes, clowns and prostitutes, pimps and similar prodigal men whom the prince ought rather to exterminate than to encourage." (John illustrates the fullness of the prince's power over other members with a tortured example from the Gospel of Matthew: "If your eye or your foot offend you, root it out and cast it away from you." Applied to the body politic, John writes, "I think that this is to be observed by the prince in regard to all of the members to the extent that not only are they to be rooted out, broken off and thrown far away, if they give offence to the faith or public security, but they are to be destroyed utterly so that the security of the corporate community may be procured by the extermination of the one member.")[43]

John names Trajan the best of the Roman emperors because he "built the majesty of his reign solely upon the practice of virtue." Personifying the virtues of clemency and justice, Trajan "was merciful towards everyone, yet tough with those few whom it was wrong to spare," Johns submits. Embodying wisdom, Trajan combined the vision of a guiding father with the ear of an orchestra director, demonstrating how "subjects are made to be of a single mind as in a household and the works of peace and charity create one perfect and great harmony out of pursuits which appear discordant." Outshining his predecessors in fortitude, Trajan restored the glory of Rome and "he spread in all directions the boundaries of the Roman Empire."[44]

John must have realized that some churchmen would frown on Trajan as a role model. It was common knowledge that Trajan deemed Christians a subversive cult and sanctioned their execution. But John exonerates him on grounds that Trajan was milder than prior emperors, such as Nero. He goes on to place Trajan in heaven for showing mercy to widows and orphans, as in this story: Trajan was riding off to war, John says, when a weeping widow grabbed hold of his foot. She pleaded with the emperor to meet out justice to the evildoers who murdered her son. *I will do it when I return from battle*, Trajan said. *But what if you don't come back?* the widow wailed. *Then my successor will take care of it*, Trajan said. *That's not fair*, replied the widow; *this injustice is your responsibility; your successor will have his own cases to deal with.* Moved by the widow's plea, Trajan got off his horse and ordered justice done to her on the spot. "The Lord in His rich mercy rewarded the justice which Trajan had displayed toward the crying widow," John claims. Trajan's kindness so touched Pope Gregory the Great that he wept for Trajan until he saw in a dream that the emperor was freed from hell and admitted to heaven—the only pagan to be so glorified. (The story was repeated by Thomas Aquinas, Dante, Machiavelli, and others, remaining a chestnut of faith-based poetry down to the Victorians.)[45]

Through such stories, John aims to instruct princes in their social responsibilities, just as Plutarch instructed Trajan. Princes' social responsibilities derive from the power vested in them by God. The prince is not only "the public power," John asserts, but "the image on earth of the divine majesty." To the prince, "men bow their heads and generally offer their necks to the axe in sacrifice, and by divine impulse everyone fears him who is fear itself. I do not believe that this could have happened unless it happened at the divine command. For all power is from the Lord God," John writes. "Whatever the prince can do, therefore, is from God"; the prince's power is "a substitute for His hand, making all things learn His justice and mercy."[46] Princes ought not misuse this power for their own ends, John insists. Their responsibilities are "to repress the wicked, to reward the good, and so to uphold the law of God on earth."[47]

To guide princes in fulfilling their responsibilities, God sends priests and prophets as a conscience of the body politic. John mixes in another conventional metaphor—the two swords representing the dual authorities in the world, priests and princes. Priests exercise spiritual authority, preaching the law of God. Princes exercise "the power of bodily coercion," a necessary but subordinate duty to punish wrongdoers symbolized by the profane sword of an executioner. "The prince is therefore a sort of minister of the priests," John says, answerable to them in matters of faith and morals—the end goals of public policy. John cites the example of Constantine, "the most faithful emperor of the Romans," who convened the Nicaean Council of priests but deferred to them by taking the hindmost seat. When their work was done, he honored the council's decisions "just as if he supposed them to emanate from the court of the divine majesty." Princes should take a back seat to priests even if some don't practice what they preach. When Constantine received accusations of crimes against priests, John says, he placed them unopened in his pocket. "He himself said that inasmuch as he was a human who was subject to the verdict of priests, it was not allowed for him to examine divine cases which none except God alone could adjudicate." The complaints he received "he consigned to the flames uninspected, fearful to publicize the crimes or abuses of the Fathers."[48]

Like the social responsibilities of modern managers, the social responsibilities of medieval princes were of course voluntary. Churchmen could preach them; princes could, and did, ignore them. Twelfth-century princes treated priests as *their* ministers. In England, kings named their friends to ecclesiastical offices; they routinely exiled their archbishops for one offense or another. John's king, Henry II, fought running battles with priests, bishops, and popes over church appointments, revenues, and the right to hear criminal charges against clerics. John himself had been accused of crimes and banished from Henry's court. (The exact charges are unclear; historians speculate that John lobbied behind the king's back for the invasion of Ireland in order to bring the Irish church under the control of Canterbury.) Henry bristled at even voluntary restraints. He lost his temper when churchmen pressured him, especially on foreign policy. Henry's problem was he had no time for philosophy; he was busy running a multinational empire that, historians point out, had "no common government, no common financial or judicial system, and no common linguistic, ethnic, or cultural tradition" but was held together by feudal strategic alliances.[49] John's problem, on the other hand, was that, despite his flair for political theory, he had a tin ear for politics.[50]

This was a chronic affliction of academic courtiers, limiting their influence and career prospects. They saw a life of letters as noble; they saw politics, particularly court politics, as self-serving. They imagined they were writing truth to power; they griped when they were not rewarded for it. John complained that lesser men got ahead by flattery, that princes surrounded themselves with toadies telling them what they wanted to hear, addressing them as "'my light,' 'my salvation,' 'my refuge,' 'my heart and my life,' 'invincible commander,' 'the wisest of those alive,' 'the most generous and benevolent of all,' 'mirror of the virtues,' and other such inappropriate ascriptions." According to John, "among all courtly fools" the worst "are those who are accustomed to glossing over their wretched frivolities under the pretext of honour and liberality, who move about in bright apparel, who feast splendidly, who often urge strangers to join them at the dinner table, who are courteous at home, benign when abroad, affable in speech, liberal in judgment, generous in the treatment of kin, and distinguished for the imitation of all virtues." John declared that these walking abominations should be expelled from the prince's court, replaced by priests and philosophers.[51]

Sadly, he concluded, it is men of real virtue and wisdom who wind up expelled. It was soon after his own expulsion from court that John wrote the *Policraticus*—subtitled *Of the Frivolities of Courtiers and the Footprints of Philosophers*. If Henry ever read it, there is no evidence that he paid any attention to it. John eventually returned to court as an aide to the archbishop of Canterbury; he got expelled again during the king's clash with Thomas Becket, and he moved to France where he finally secured a position as bishop of Chartres under King Louis VII. John's later years and writings were devoted to promoting Becket's sainthood, and it was as St. Thomas's hagiographer that John was best known in the twelfth century.[52] (British historian Frank Barlow notes the irony: John had always shown more affection for Canterbury than for the archbishop; late in life an old friend, Abbot Peter of Celle, reminded him "of how, during the exile, they had often joked together about Thomas and groaned over the impossibility of ever being able to obtain a shrine big enough to contain him," and "now everyone in England as in France was flocking to his tomb."[53])

It was not until the second half of the thirteenth century that John's *Policraticus* attracted serious interest. Around 1280 the book was referenced in Giles of Rome's mirror for Prince Philip the Fair of France and, about 1300, in Bartholomew of Lucca's completion of Thomas Aquinas's mirror for the king of Sicily. Researchers find more influence of the *Policraticus* in fourteenth-century literature, for instance, in Dante's *Divine Comedy* and Chaucer's *Canterbury Tales*. Most surviving manuscripts were produced in the fourteenth and fifteenth centuries, mainly for university students and faculty of law and theology. A popular excerpt from the *Policraticus* was John's spurious "Instruction for Trajan," which publishers distributed under the authorship of Plutarch. John's central exemplum—his metaphor of the corporate organism—became a staple of political theory, supporting monarchy as a governing ideal well beyond the Middle Ages.[54]

To this day, college students read the *Policraticus* as a representative mirror for princes in courses on the history of political thought. Modern reviews of the book are mixed. For the range of ideas in the *Policraticus*, admirers have called John "the foremost political theorist of his age."[55] But few would call him an original thinker. "John stayed completely within the tradition of the Carolingian *specula regnum* [mirrors for princes]," says professor of medieval history Tilman Struve.[56] In the *Policraticus*, John "tried to set forth with a fair degree of order what everyone believed and, so far as was known in the twelfth century, had always believed," writes George Sabine in his classic history of political theory.[57] Critics fault John for fudging facts and faking sources. John defended himself as a teacher of his time, a storyteller: "I am not promising that all which has been written here is true," he said in prefacing the *Policraticus*, "but that, whether it is true or false, it will serve the reader as useful. I am not so silly as to ascribe truth to the tale that the winged bird was once spoken to by the tortoise or that the country mouse accepted into his poor house the city mouse, and so on; but I do not doubt that these fictions of ours are of service to instruction."[58] Like many teachers of princes, John stretched the truth to make a point; at least he was honest enough to admit it.

Trifles

General histories of Europe allude to a cultural renaissance in the twelfth century, a flowering of scholarship, art, and literature reflecting a lofty optimistic age. Yet experts point out that this renaissance is a reconstruction by historians far removed from the experiences of twelfth-century men and women. If you look at literature of the period, you're more likely to find the language of "decline," "decay," "collapse," and "corruption" than any reference to a "renaissance," notes medievalist Stephen Jaeger: Actual "observers of secular culture in the twelfth century were unanimously of the disillusioned and cynical bent."[59] No one expressed this better than Walter Map.

Born around 1135 in the Anglo-Welsh borderland, Map followed the career path of his colleague Gerald of Wales. He studied theology in Paris, then clerked for the bishop of London and King Henry II. While the king and bishops fought over who could try clerks for crimes, Map kept his head down and his wits about him. He rose only to archdeacon of Oxford, but he gained a measure of fame for his skill at telling stories. Map collected his stories in *Courtiers' Trifles*, a book in the mirror-for-princes mode, which readers recognized as a spoof of the *Policraticus*.[60]

By the twelfth century, mirrors for princes were so hackneyed that the genre was ripe for parody. Map writes in the style of great satirists from Lucian to Monty Python. He tells stories about heroic leaders such as "Conan the fearless, so called because he never flinched"; faced with danger, he just ran away. Map pens proverbs that mimic the dos and don'ts of old-fashioned mirrors for princes. "Do not trust a red-haired man of low birth," for instance, and "Do not marry the daughter of an adulteress." (Coincidentally, King Henry's hair was red, his ancestry and marriage the subject of scurrilous gossip.)[61]

Map ridicules the crusaders. Are they crazy, he asks, trying to serve Christ with arms and violence? "It was by the word of the Lord and not the edge of the sword that the Apostles conquered Damascus, Alexandria, and a great part of the world, which the sword has lost." Of course, he adds, if the Holy Land were at peace, there'd be no jobs for thugs like the Templars. Map also pokes fun at the royal family. King Henry had an illegitimate son named Geoffrey—born, Map says, to "a common whore." Promoted to bishop of Lincoln, he'd rant and rave and throw his father's name around to show his authority. One day Map urged him to display some humility for a change and "swear by the profession of your mother." Geoffrey had a fit.[62]

Written to amuse court personnel, *Courtiers' Trifles* features stories of lecherous monks, clumsy knights, venal bureaucrats, stingy accountants, clueless consultants, evil employment managers, and even a vampire or two. But as in modern satires of corporate life, Map mostly exaggerates for comic effect the familiar rituals of workplace management. Tramping in the footprints of John of Salisbury, Map writes from personal experience: Look, he says, "I myself am the ruler of but a small establishment, and yet I cannot hold the reins of my little team. I try to be good to them all so far as I can, that they may suffer no lack either in food, drink or raiment: *their* object, on the other hand, is to scrape together out of my subsistence by any and every means something to increase their own. All that I have they call 'ours,' all that they have, 'their own.'" If the boss tries to cut costs or "take some prudent step which inconveniences them," the staff get upset. "Up comes one with a long face, an air of depression, and with a pumped-up sigh he says: 'Don't take it to heart, dear master. People are talking about your having done this; as far as I am concerned, God knows I'm perfectly satisfied; it seems to me the right thing to do; but you should hear the language they're using.'" Then comes another and another and everyone with the same old song.[63]

But that's all theater. The court of a prince, in contrast, is pure hell—"the prison of body and soul alike" where no good deed goes unpunished. The devils who run the place tempt courtiers with promises of wealth, perks, and promotion, and at first it's exciting. Then "covetousness, the Lady of the Court, urges us on with so many prickings that our mirth gives way to anxiety." Whatever courtiers attain, it never satisfies them for long because there's always some promise unmet, some ambition unfulfilled, someone less deserving who has more. So courtiers "climb to glory and fall to wretchedness," Map says. "When at the top they exult, when at the bottom they mourn; when on the right hand they are in hope, when on the left they are in fear." What they fear is the sheer capriciousness of the court; no matter how hard they work or how good they are, their food and drink and the clothes on their backs come at the whims of managers above them. Managers in the court hierarchy "oppress their inferiors and deceive their superiors that from each side they may make gain anyway. But all their villainies they hide from the king in order not to be corrected and make less profit. . . . They craftily urge him out of doors to sport with hounds and hawks" while they do business indoors, ruling in his name to fill their purse. "When the king returns from hunting or hawking he shows them his bag and shares it with them, but they do not show theirs to him." At the end of the day, however, the king is still the king; he takes what he wants and shares his favors with whomever he chooses. "We courtiers," Map sighs, are "all striving to please one individual."[64]

Accordingly, Map is careful to exempt his own king from overt criticism. He portrays the king as a victim of his corrupt courtiers, like "a husband who is the last to learn of the unfaithfulness of his wife." Influence peddling goes on everywhere, Map says, but the court of Henry II exhibits more virtue than others because of its leader. Henry, he claims, "is wellnigh alone in this vale of misery in being an acceptable minister of justice." Even the kings of Spain ask him to arbitrate their disputes. "Whoever has a good case is anxious to try it before him; whoever has a bad one will not come to him unless he is dragged." Wrongdoers fear him more than God, Map declares, "for God is a late avenger, the king a swift one."[65]

It is telling that a writer as irreverent as Walter Map concludes his mirror in this traditional way, with a flattering portrait of the king as a paragon of justice. In gently reminding kings how they should act and particularly in stressing virtues like justice, mirrors for princes reflect a fact that's almost too big to be seen, says historian Peter Brown: "We are in a world characterized by a chilling absence of legal restraints on violence in the exercise of power."[66] A feudal king such as Henry II not only commanded more patronage—jobs, estates, marriages, inheritances, benefices, tax breaks, and so on—than any robber baron, but he held the power of life and death. And a king with a temper like Henry's was doubly dangerous. Everybody knew the fate of Thomas Becket, then archbishop of Canterbury, who angered Henry and was murdered at the mere suggestion of the king. According to John of Salisbury, to curry favor with the king, four of his knights grabbed Becket in his cathedral, sliced open his head, scooped out his brains with a sword and spread them on the church floor.[67]

Eventually English lords would wrest legal restraints on this sort of violence from Henry's son, King John, in the Great Charter (Magna Carta) of 1215. Mirrors for princes meanwhile stuck to the traditional remedy—preaching to kings and their staffs on the virtue of mercy.

Walter Map, naturally, told them a story. Once there was a French knight named Waleran, a beloved servant of King Louis VII. Waleran was not a great scholar, but he had the gift of speech and a keen eye. He saw that the king's top ministers were stealing most of the profits of the French Crown, bankrupting the country. So he composed a satirical song for the king, exposing their crimes. One of the ministers' consorts, a lady close to Louis, accused Waleran of insulting the court with ribald rhymes. She pleaded with Louis, "'Lord king, leave his punishment to me; I will suit him. I know well enough how clowns ought to be corrected; I will find three harlots to whip him as he deserves.' 'Madam,' said Waleran, 'You have little more to do; you only have two to get.'"[68] To appease his court, the king banished Waleran, who fled to England and found refuge with King Henry II. Some time later the two kings, Henry and Louis, were conferring in an open field surrounded by their knights when Waleran appeared, "riding on a little black horse, thin and ugly, himself in a very mean guise—clothes ragged with age, unshaven, unwashed, spurs hanging down from his heels, boots stiff and split, in all points like the poorest of mankind."[69] Louis took pity on him, recalled him to France, and restored all his property. In this parable on mercy, Waleran of course is a thinly disguised image of Walter Map himself. And the lesson—as in mirrors for princes since the *Instruction for King Merikare*—is that virtue means taking care of loyal courtiers.[70]

There's no evidence that Map's mirror had much influence on court conduct. *Courtiers' Trifles* is aptly described by its modern editor as the material of a great after-dinner speaker, all the more enjoyable if one is not entirely sober. After he died, Walter Map's name was remembered not for what he wrote but for what readers thought he wrote. For centuries, he was misidentified as the author of popular French romances, such as the legend of Lancelot and the Holy Grail—an ironic tribute to his Monty Python–style of humor.[71]

Fables

People have always loved stories. But for most of recorded history, cultured people distrusted storytellers, lumping them together with actors, clowns, and other riffraff. As lowbrow entertainment, storytelling remained mostly an oral tradition until the twelfth century, when learned civil servants like Gerald of Wales, John of Salisbury, and Walter Map made story-*writing* respectable. Soon the written word, long dedicated to scripture and scholarship, was adopted for stories by poets who added their own twists to traditional folk tales and who wrote to people in their own language. First among these poets was Marie de France, called the James Joyce of the twelfth century by Howard Bloch, Sterling Professor of French at Yale University.[72]

No one knows much about Marie's identity. She was from France but probably lived in England. Scholars have speculated that she was the half sister of King Henry II, or the daughter of Louis VII and Eleanor of Aquitaine, or a nun or the abbess of Reading. But it is all guesswork. "Marie de France comes as close as one can imagine to being anonymous," Bloch writes. Her fame came from narrative poetry and a collection of fables she composed as a mirror for princes.[73]

Written toward the end of the twelfth century, Marie's book of *Fables* is addressed to a count named William but is aimed at any leader "for the purpose of moral edification, in order that those who set their mind upon the good might improve themselves." Just as the emperor Romulus taught his son with the fables of Aesop, Marie proposes to teach William about courtly behavior with tales of the animal kingdom and human nature.[74]

Marie shows the central theme of court life in a fable titled "The Lion's Share." "Long ago it was the custom and the law that the lion should be king over all the beasts," she writes. The lion-king made the wild ox his seneschal (business manager) and the wolf his provost (operations manager). One day the three went into the woods and hunted down a deer. After they skinned it, the wolf asked how they should divide the carcass. The lion spoke up: Since he was king, he would take the first part as his due. Since he was a member of the hunting party, he would take the second part as his profit. And, because he had killed the deer, he would take the remaining part unless anyone else wished to claim it and become his mortal enemy. "Thus no one dared touch it, and they had to relinquish the whole deer." The moral of the story is to be careful in associating with powerful princes; if there's a gain to be made, they'll want it all.[75]

Whatever Marie's true station in life, she shares with Walter Map the outlook of an experienced court observer. Marie warns kings to be careful how they use the power of their office. She tells another fable of a lion-king who grew old and feeble. All the animals gathered around him at court, some to express grief, some to inquire about his will, some just to see if he was really dying. The ox came and butted him with his horns, the ass kicked him with his hoof, the fox bit him on the ear. Thinking back to all he had given his friends and the fear he instilled when he was in his prime, the lion was shocked by the abuse and ashamed of his weakness. The king never realized, Marie writes, that "he who falls from power and loses his strength and his wealth is regarded with great contempt, even by the many who have loved him."[76] A modern translator of Marie's work, Mary Lou Martin, comments that this fable could well apply to Henry II, whose sons pained the old king with treachery on his deathbed and whose servants, according to court gossip, even stole the clothes off his body.[77]

Marie's collection of *Fables* mirrors traditional values as well as the political realities of her day. To show the interdependence of prince and people, she tells the old tale of the stomach and the members. To reveal the shallowness of wealth, she tells the story of the city mouse who lives in fear amid the baits and traps of town while the country mouse lives more simply and securely out in the woods. To illustrate the virtue of patriotism, she tells of upstart rabbits who leave home and get into trouble thinking the grass is greener outside their own country.[78]

Marie's book contains 102 fables. The first 40 derive from a translation of Aesop's fables that Marie traces to the emperor Romulus. The rest are based on oral and written folk tales from France, Germany, Italy, Russia, and an Arabic book of fables known as *Kalilah and Dimnah*. Named for a pair of jackals who counsel their lion-king, *Kalilah and Dimnah* is a translation of an older Indian collection called the *Pañcatantra*, dating from about AD 300. The *Pañcatantra*—Sanskrit for "five books"—is itself a mirror for princes written to teach leaders the art of practical living. (The author was a Brahmin guru tasked with tutoring young princes who were "supreme blockheads." Since they were "hostile to education," the princes were told to memorize fables even a child could understand. In fact, the fables are elaborate stories with mature lessons for kings, courtiers, and commoners alike.)[79]

Reflecting the folk wisdom of the ages, Marie's *Fables* offers a breadth of thought that is rare in mirrors for princes. If classic mirrors often read like professors' lecture notes or preachers' sermons, Marie's story collection sounds like a conversation among different cultures, generations, and social classes. All these voices speak from life experience, defying moral absolutes. Blended together by Marie's own take on the stories, they teach a nuanced, situational ethics where lying, for example, is neither virtue nor vice but right or wrong depending on the circumstances.[80]

Marie tells the story of a goat who got cornered in the woods by a hungry wolf. The goat pleaded with the wolf to spare his life just long enough for him to say a mass for both their souls. When the wolf granted this last request, the goat raised his voice as if to pray but instead cried out for help to nearby goatherds who came and tore the wolf to pieces. So lying to bullies in self-defense is all right. On the other hand, lying to take advantage of another is wrong. Marie tells of a fox who tried to lure a dove into his clutches during a windstorm. "Come down and sit beside me in this shelter," said the fox, "You've no reason to be afraid of me." The fox insisted that he had just come from a council of the king, who decreed that no animal should harm any other—all should live and play together in peace. "Then I'll come down," said the dove, adding that she saw two knights riding their way with hunting dogs. At that, the fox ran off, claiming he wasn't sure the dogs had heard of the king's decree. Like the fox, scoundrels lie to others for profit, Marie warns; so don't be fooled.[81]

Marie's *Fables* follows the usual formula of mirrors for princes—up to a point. As in traditional mirrors, Marie portrays people behaving badly. In casting them as animals focused on eating or being eaten, she highlights the selfishness of human beings. "The question that Marie poses most persistently in the *Fables* is not whether man acts like an animal (this much is obvious)," says Bloch, "but whether that which makes him human, that is his capacity for reason, might overcome his fundamentally predatory animal nature."[82] Marie suggests how hard it is for princes to change their predatory ways. One fable has a priest trying to teach a wolf the alphabet; the wolf learns the letters but all he can spell is "lamb"—a not so subtle dig at clerical courtiers who relied on moral education to curb abuses of power.[83] No doubt Marie was concerned about the absence of restraints on feudal power, and she hoped that the moral education entailed in her fables might limit some of the violence. "The *Fables* are about nothing if not about the taming of the feudal beast," Bloch remarks, "the institutionalization of the violence of the feudal world, in which, as in the animal kingdom, the law of the strongest prevailed."[84] But Marie seemed to recognize that the strongest will not restrain themselves, even with the expert instruction and voluntary codes of ethics prescribed in traditional mirrors for princes. Civil laws are required.

In several stories, Marie shows rulers rejecting war and brutality in deference to legal procedure. She shows predators and prey transcending the law of the jungle by making their case in court. Marie reworks an old Aesop fable of the lion and the mouse. In the original, a mouse accidentally wakes a sleeping lion who gets angry and prepares to eat her. In Marie's fable, the mouse wakes a lion who again gets angry but this time threatens to sue her. In both versions, the lion quickly realizes the mouse meant no harm and lets her go; she later returns the favor by freeing the lion from a hunter's snare. The message remains the same—rulers should be merciful—but, merciful ruler or not, Marie's mouse still has the right to defend herself in court.[85]

In story after story, Marie brings her characters together in deliberative assemblies to shape public policies. She gives a populist twist to another Aesop fable. It so happened that the sun wished to take a wife and asked all the animals for advice. The animals held a council and decided to take their concerns to Destiny, the goddess over them all. A speaker for the group said to the goddess, "In the summertime when the sun is high, it is so hot that nothing can flourish, and it makes the ground and the grass dry up. If it had help and a companion to its liking, nothing would be able to bear up or to live or prosper under it." The goddess Destiny agreed this was true, so she forbade the sun to wed. Let that be a lesson to people, Marie concludes; "they should not strengthen their lords or join them to anyone wiser or wealthier than themselves, but rather should do all in their power to prevent such a union. The stronger the lord becomes, the worse he treats them." Marie's *Fables* are hardly proto–*Federalist Papers*, arguing for a radical division of powers. Yet her book is remarkably progressive for a twelfth-century mirror for princes.[86]

Marie's stories resonated with general readers. Unlike most mirrors, her *Fables* became a best seller (by medieval standards) soon after initial publication. At least twenty-three manuscripts survive dating from the thirteenth to the fifteenth centuries. By comparison, only one manuscript survives of Gerald's *Instruction of Princes* and Map's *Courtiers' Trifles*. Marie had a major impact on vernacular literature, inspiring fables and romances in many European languages. Students of literature point to Marie's influence on Geoffrey Chaucer's *Canterbury Tales*, John Lydgate's *Isopes Fabules*, and other popular works.[87]

In contrast, Marie had little effect on mirrors for princes. Fables were fiction, after all, scorned by scholars as frivolous entertainment.

Storytellers, despite their popularity, were suspected of earning their living by misleading the gullible. Over the next century, writers of mirrors for princes ignored Marie and flocked to the rediscovered works of Aristotle, whose name lent weight to their own works. They turned from storytelling to Scholasticism, from the local language back to Latin, from progressive ideas of legal rights to classical visions of empire.

SIX

Scholastic Mirrors

The people of today are not like the people of old times. On the contrary, this is an age when men are shameless, mannerless, and merciless. If, God forbid, the Sultan in their midst were weak, universal ruin would befall the religion and the (whole) lower world.

Al-Ghazali's Book of Counsel for Kings

The word "prince," meaning a royal family member, is a historian's term. According to Oxford historian Jean Dunbabin, the word initially meant nothing that specific. People used it as a catchall title for any leader—king or crook, well-born or not. Princes were "by definition the successful."[1]

The most successful were hailed as emperors. Cicero tells the story of a pirate captured by Alexander the Great. *How dare you prey upon the sea*, Alexander said to him. The pirate replied, *I take trinkets with a petty ship and I'm called a robber, but you take the whole world with a big fleet and they call you emperor*. Mirrors for princes encouraged this notion of success. Writers since Isocrates told princes to dream big visions of empire. But princes, by definition, didn't need to be told. Lack of vision was not their problem.[2]

Visions cost money, and big visions cost lots of it. The prince's problem was how to get enough money and work from others to make his vision come true. Ancient princes like Alexander just demanded it. They seized lands, enslaved enemies, intimidated friends, and taxed everyone to the absolute extent of their power. But even absolute power reached only so far, as Alexander learned when his vision of world empire drove his troops to mutiny. Feudal princes like Henry II of England tried to contract for what they needed. They offered income, positions, and protection in return for services, trading favor for favor with landlords and under-bosses. But feudalism had limits too.

For one thing, few princes were strong enough to make offers that could not be refused. In the thirteenth century, for example, no king—not even the charismatic Saint Louis—could impose his vision on the great families of France. French kings waged costly wars, went on crusades, and got along with their magnates largely because they were richer than other princes and could pay their own way. Absent such wealth, English kings required help from their barons to advance their visions, and English barons insisted on being consulted before giving it. Henry II's son John (nicknamed Lackland) was so desperate for venture capital that he had to agree in Magna Carta that no tax "shall be imposed in our kingdom except by the common council of our kingdom."[3] King John had to further promise his barons that he would limit extortion, follow due process, and obey the law of the land.[4]

For another thing, wars and government were growing so expensive that kings needed aid not only from their feudal barons but from rank-and-file subjects as well. While kings might contract personally with their barons, they could not possibly negotiate with individual merchants, tradespeople, and everyone else. So they appealed to representative groups, in parleys or parliaments, which levied taxes but in turn put checks on authority. In the process, feudal princes faced demands of commoners for customary rights (freedoms to do what they were used to doing) plus demands of guilds for special rights (protections for masons and millers and brewers and who-knows-what labor union). It was good to be king in the Middle Ages, but it was hard to realize a vision of one's own.[5]

Mirrors for princes said there was another, better way to rule. A Dutch priest named Erasmus introduced his book, *The Education of a Christian Prince*, by offering his prince, Charles, "something beyond human nature, something wholly divine," the secret of "absolute rule over free and willing subjects." The secret was to tell people that the prince's vision was, in fact, their *shared* vision.[6]

Mirrors for princes, especially in the Near East, had taught this "secret" since the time of Aristotle. It became a favorite bromide of writers who popularized Aristotle's works toward the end of the High Middle Ages.

Secret of Secrets

If storytellers dominated the twelfth century, Aristotle towered over the thirteenth. Up until then his books on ethics and politics were known only indirectly in the West. But crusaders, merchants, and pilgrims to Muslim lands brought back Arabic copies, which were translated into Latin around 1250, engaging European scholars for the rest of the century. The flood of Aristotelian manuscripts into western Europe included spurious as well as genuine writings of the philosopher. The most popular book was a mirror for princes, supposedly written by Aristotle for Alexander the Great, titled the *Secret of Secrets*.

The book blends mystery and suspense, self-help tips and positive thinking, old-fashioned platitudes and new-age spiritualism—a timeless recipe for a bestseller. An anonymous prologue dedicates the book to an unnamed caliph, describing it as a "work of direction for the management of state" compiled by Aristotle for his pupil, Alexander, after the philosopher had grown too old to accompany the prince on his wars. The book begins with Aristotle (as the author calls himself and is so called here) promising to reveal secrets to Alexander that he has not shared with anyone lest the knowledge "fall into the hands of wicked and tyrannical men, who might discover what God did not deem them worthy to understand." Master these secrets, Aristotle tells Alexander, and "you will thereby achieve your highest desires and fulfill your loftiest expectations."[7]

Before revealing any secrets, Aristotle goes through a list of conventional steps to becoming a good leader. He says princes should practice the virtues of justice, prudence, courage, temperance, and more, for they reign in God's place: "The king whom God has chosen to rule over His people, and to whom He has granted the government of their affairs and power over their lives and properties and all other matters, is like a god, and it is necessary for him to resemble Him in the attributes of mercy, wisdom, etc." The attributes of God are numberless, and so are the virtues of a good prince. Besides practicing the four cardinal virtues, a king should show clemency, honesty, modesty, piety, magnanimity, and liberality (charity). It's generic advice, but Aristotle embellishes it with instructions on how a virtuous king can inspire people to support his goals.[8]

For example, a king should express concern for his people but not get too close to them. Aristotle says that when people see and hear authorities too often, they grow contemptuous. "Therefore, a king should show himself to them only from afar, and always when surrounded by a retinue and guards"—ideally, once a year. He should not address subjects in person but have an eloquent minister speak to them, following a script like this: Standing between the king and people, the minister first "praises God and thanks Him for [everyone's] allegiance to their sovereign. Then he says how well pleasing they are, and how much care is taken on their behalf, and exhorts them to be obedient and warns them against disobedience. Then he reads their petitions, hears their complaints, dispenses justice, and grants gifts to them. He pardons their sins and makes them feel how near he is to the highest and lowest among them." In this way the king makes a good impression on his people. Subjects come to celebrate the annual spectacle; they reminisce with their families about it "so that their little ones grow up to obey and love him." And the king inhibits the growth of opposition parties, intrigues, and seditions.[9]

Eventually people get tired of speeches, however infrequent or eloquent, and the king has to actually do something for his subjects. Aristotle says, "it is necessary that he should lower all the taxes, especially in the case of those who come into his presence as merchants and traders." A king might find this indulgent, but there's an economic rationale: By lowering taxes on businesses, "their number will increase, and his country will be greatly benefited by the variety of goods and men and beasts. And this is the means of the civilization of the country, increase of its revenue, flourishing of its condition, and humiliation of its enemies." Tax-wise, a shrewd king observes the supply-side precept that "he who abstains from little gains much."[10]

Not the least of what a king gains is the loyalty of subjects who have to pay for his policies. In growing and defending the state, kings necessarily impose burdens on people, much like forces of nature. A king resembles the rain sent by God to nourish the earth, Aristotle says. "It may bring inconvenience to travellers, demolish houses, cause lightening and floods which destroy men and animals, and make the sea to rage and bring about severe calamity. But this does not prevent mankind, when they consider the effects of the grace of God whereby vegetation is revived and sustenance comes forth and mercy is shed abroad, from appreciating the favour of God and thanking Him for it." Similarly, people thank God for kings, even harsh ones, who may deliver them from want and destroy evildoers. Certainly, kings should never act out of impulse or anger. They should refrain from shedding blood without cause and try to avoid capital punishment; severe physical penalties and long prison terms are adequate to control wrongdoers, Aristotle says, except "if any one is guilty of an offence willfully done in contempt of the royal presence, his punishment should be death."[11]

Aristotle continues with advice on managing staff: "Choose such men of thy court who are perfect in wisdom, judgment, dignity, appearance, and honesty, and who are beyond all suspicion," he tells Alexander. But, he warns, don't expect a lot, "for human nature is very much subject to influence and temptation."[12] He compares the moral qualities of humans to those of animals: rarely noble, generally beastly:

> Man is courageous as a lion, timid as a hare, generous as a cock, avaricious as a dog, licentious as a crow, wild as a leopard, sociable as a pigeon, sly as a fox, tame as a sheep, swift as a deer, slow as a bear, proud as an elephant, humble as a donkey, thievish as a magpie, vain as a peacock, unerring as a partridge, stupid as an ostrich, fugitive as a ram, importunate as an ox, refractory as a mule, mute as a fish, talkative as an owl, useful as a horse, harmful as a rat.[13]

All this implies that leaders need to keep a tight rein on subordinates.

A king should maintain a narrow span of control over military officers, for instance; if "one has to look after ten men only, there is less confusion in the forces, and their duties are simplified." A king should monitor especially bookkeepers and tax collectors, who will otherwise line their own pockets. To deter corruption, a king should keep a close eye even on his most trusted aides; one should "not allow a minister to leave thy presence" nor "to hold any communication with any other king." If you must send an ambassador abroad, Aristotle suggests, try to select an intelligent and honest man to whom you can delegate some authority; confide your desires to him "and give him no further orders, . . . for probably he will discover the right course by himself." If you don't have an envoy that reliable, then choose one who can remember instructions; and if you can't find anyone like that, send someone who can at least find his destination and his way back home.[14]

To manage a nation of such people, a leader needs all the help he can get. Aristotle has tips for Alexander, derived, he says, from secret sciences known to the ancients. He has a chapter on physiognomy, telling how to identify troublemakers based on physical features. ("He whose eyes are slanting is wicked. He whose eyes are motionless, like those of animals, is rough natured and ignorant. And he whose eyes are constantly moving and revolving is cunning and of treacherous and thieving propensities.") The author has a section on numerology, showing how to predict victory in war based on "the numbers of the letters in the names of the commanders of both the armies." He has pages on astrology, explaining how to make decisions using horoscopes and the movement of planets in their houses.[15]

At last, Aristotle reveals "the greatest secret" to Alexander: the secret of secrets, which he has never shared with anyone else. It turns out to be "a Talisman that endows one with sovereignty and dignity," that "secures the submission and obedience of the people and inspires enemies with fear and trembling." To make it, Aristotle says, "take the substance of Saturn, Jupiter, Mars, Venus, Mercury, and the moon," add a proportionate quantity of gold, and melt it all together when the stars are in perfect alignment—"on Thursday morning in the hour of Jupiter. Then make out of it a signet ring. Inlay it with a square piece of red ruby and engrave upon it the image of a lion with a black man riding on it. Let there be a standard in his hand, and let him have two wings, and a crown on his head." Put the ring on your finger, Aristotle says, and it wards off evil and harm, "it creates love and hatred, and does many other wonders too numerous to relate." Best of all, it signifies to everyone that the king's goals are their goals too.[16]

Modern managers might flinch at this mysticism, but medieval readers loved it. More manuscripts of the *Secret of Secrets* have survived than any other Aristotelian work, genuine or fake. One student of the book, history professor Steven J. Williams, has counted 130 extant manuscripts in Latin (plus translations into Anglo-Norman, Old French, Italian, Dutch, German, Castilian, and Hebrew) dating from the High Middle Ages and another 500 manuscripts from the Late Middle Ages, making the *Secret of Secrets* one of the most copied books of the whole medieval period. Marketed by entrepreneurial booksellers serving college towns in the thirteenth century, some of the earliest Western copies circulated among teachers and university students at Paris and Oxford. By the early fourteenth century, Williams notes, the *Secret of Secrets* had won a modest but respectable place within the academic community. It was widely available in libraries as well as bookshops. It was cited in lectures, debates, and sermons. And it influenced a number of later mirrors for princes, mostly second-tier writings, for example, by Guibert of Tournai for King Louis IX of France and by Engelbert of Admont for dukes Albrecht and Otto of Austria.[17]

Like current trade books on management, the *Secret of Secrets* raised eyebrows among serious scholars. Early on, philosophers expressed doubts about its authenticity. Theologians ridiculed the occult-science sections. Skeptical scribes omitted the talisman pages entirely. Yet many Schoolmen still accepted parts of the *Secret of Secrets* as the work of Aristotle. And editions containing the classic clichés of mirrors for princes remained popular until the turn of the sixteenth century, when the title was finally shelved, in the words of one Renaissance writer, with the endless "books of nonsense" ascribed "to ancient, illustrious men."[18]

Aquinas

Whether academics believed in the *Secret of Secrets* or not, they embraced its quest for the secret of leadership. Scholastics found inspiration in more reliable Aristotelian texts, especially the *Politics*, which began to circulate around European universities in the mid-1200s. Foremost among these Scholastics was Thomas Aquinas.

Thomas was born about 1225 to noble parents at the family castle of Roccasecca, between Rome and Naples. At the age of five he was sent to the Benedictine Abbey of Monte Cassino for basic education and formation in monastic life. If Thomas grew up like a child monk, secluded from the world, he faced as a young man some of the major conflicts of his century. Two great powers, the Holy Roman Empire and the Roman Catholic Church, controlled much of Europe while their leaders fought to control one another. In one such fight, Emperor Frederick II ordered his army to take Monte Cassino for use as a strategic fortress, and Thomas's education there came to an end. Around the age of fifteen he was sent to Frederick's secular university at Naples where he studied the liberal arts and first encountered the works of Aristotle. At nineteen or twenty he joined the Order of Friars Preachers—the Dominicans, a controversial religious community that polarized the faithful.[19]

"A thirteenth-century aristocrat distinguished sharply between monks, who followed a stable calling of ancient respectability on well-endowed estates, and friars, who were new-fangled itinerant evangelists mingling with the urban poor and living by begging," explains Aquinas scholar Anthony Kenny.[20] Like some evangelicals today, Dominicans were known for the preaching of orthodoxy and the policing of heresy, particularly since their commission in 1231 as papal "inquisitors." To escape family censure, Thomas left home and continued his education at the University of Paris where he studied theology under Albert the Great, one of the leading Aristotelians of the day. At the age of twenty-seven Thomas was assigned to lecture under another Dominican professor at the university. His appointment ran afoul of a faculty statute—only one Dominican teacher was allowed—and when Thomas was given his own chair in theology three years later (against the wishes of university faculty but with the backing of Pope Alexander IV), anti-Dominican sentiment grew so fierce that King Louis IX sent troops to stand guard day and night outside the order's house in Paris.[21]

Thomas left Paris in 1259 for Italy, where he taught, wrote, and mingled with the papal court. During this period he began work on a mirror for princes, dedicated to the king of Cyprus and titled *On Kingship*. Aquinas specialists are not sure why he wrote it. Reading the book, you can sense Thomas reacting to the power politics he experienced himself.[22]

He begins with a line from Aristotle's *Politics*: "Man is by nature a social and political animal, who lives in a community." For Thomas, communities are natural means of providing the necessities of life, allowing for division and specialization of labor to better meet human needs. But communities do not abrogate human nature. People are selfish—they choose perverse goals, they neglect their duties, they disturb the peace—and if they do as they please, communities will break up. So members must find some way for a community to be ruled. Thomas says someone must have the "responsibility for the good of the community as a whole, just as the body of a man and of any other animal would fall apart if there were not some general ruling force to sustain the body and secure the common good of all its parts."[23]

Thomas borrows Aristotle's six-way table of governance. In any community, rulers may be one person, a few, or many; and in each case rulers may seek the common good or their own private goods. Governments devoted to private goods are wrong, whether ruled by one (a tyranny), by a few (an oligarchy), or by many (a democracy). Governments devoted to the common good are right, whether ruled by one (a kingship), by a few (an aristocracy), or by many (a polity).

Aristotle suggested that a few aristocrats or many citizens could rule as well as one king. But Thomas claims that "government by a king is best"; he says, "the welfare of any organized group is based on the preservation of its unity" and one person can promote unity better than a number of persons. It takes a crew of many to sail a ship, for example, but unless one person steers, it will never reach its destination; therefore, "government by one person is better than by many." Just look around, Thomas says: "Provinces and cities that are not ruled by one person are torn by dissension and disputes," while "provinces and cities under a single king enjoy peace, justice flourishes, and they delight in the abundance of wealth." Look at nature: "Nature always operates for the best," and "in nature government is always by one. Among the members of the body, the heart moves all the other parts; among the parts of the soul one power, reason, predominates. Among the bees there is one king bee, and in the whole universe one God is the Maker and Ruler of all." Look at the Bible: Through Jeremiah, the Lord promised His people a favor—"that he will place them under one hand and that there will be 'one prince in the midst of them.'"[24]

While unity of command is an efficient, natural, God-given principle, it is not arbitrary; it carries social responsibilities. The social responsibility of a prince, by definition, is to manage for the common good. A prince who shirks this responsibility is not a true king but a tyrant. People confuse the two, Thomas says; they wrongly hate kings when they should really hate tyrants. "The tyrant despises the common good" and seeks selfish pleasures; he steals the property of his subjects, he gives in to anger and sheds blood for nothing. Tyrants don't unite people but divide them to make themselves feel more secure. They suppress public assemblies and social gatherings—"marriage celebrations and feasts and the like that foster familiarity and mutual trust"—and they crush the spirit of community. They block people from becoming powerful or rich because they fear others will "use their power and wealth to harm them." They are wickedly jealous of virtue in anyone else and "hinder it as much as they can." Invoking the authority of Aristotle and Cicero, King Solomon and the Apostle Paul, Thomas says the ruler sets the moral tone of the community—that is why so "few virtuous men are found under tyrants." Kings, however, inspire virtue and, by taking responsibility for the common good, they lead their subjects to act likewise.[25]

It is this transformative goal of the common good, not some mystical talisman, that is the real secret to commanding obedience from free and willing subjects. By promoting the common good, Thomas contends, responsible kings also inspire love, the kind of love that unites true friends. Everyone needs the love of friends, for "it is friendship which brings the greatest pleasures" that make life worth living. And every community needs the bonds of friendship, for "it is friendship which [brings] virtuous men together as one." Thomas says, "no matter how much they may desire it, tyrants cannot secure this good of friendship. For when they do not seek the common good but their own, there is little or no communion between them and their subjects." Tyrants despise their subjects, their subjects despise them in return, and their kingdoms are shaky because they are sustained by fear alone, which is a weak foundation. In contrast, kings dedicated to the common good "are loved by most of their subjects because they themselves have shown love for them." And "from this love comes the fact that the kingdoms of good kings are stable; for their subjects do not refuse to expose themselves to any peril whatsoever for their sake." Thomas gives the example of Julius Caesar, whose "regard for his soldiers was so great that, hearing of the death of some of them, he cut neither his hair nor his beard until he had avenged them. Such gestures made the soldiers so exceptionally devoted to him and so strenuous in his service that when some of them were made prisoners and it was put to them that they might save their lives by taking up arms against Caesar, they refused to do so."[26]

Like a Roman general's love, a king's love must sometimes be tough, Thomas hastens to add. To permanently preserve the spirit of community, the king "should restrain the men subject to him from iniquity by means of laws and commands, penalties and rewards."[27] Even a good king may hurt one person "if it contributes to the good of the community, as when a thief is put to death in order to secure the community's peace," Thomas says.[28] And "even a good king may take away the sons of his subjects and make them tribunes and centurions, and may take many other things for the sake of the common welfare, without thereby becoming a tyrant."[29] Like loyal soldiers, patriotic citizens willingly bear conscription, taxation, and other sacrifices for a king who leads them toward the common good: "In times of necessity," Thomas states, "they will give freely to kings more than tyrants would be able to exact."[30]

As with Aristotle and the ancients, Thomas does not spell out exactly what "the common good" *is*. He does not tell how it translates into public policies. He does not say whether good people can disagree about it in specific cases. While the common good has been a focus of Thomistic philosophers, Thomas in fact says little about it at all.[31] He seems to be aware that it is a troublesome concept, elastic enough to mask abuses of power and therefore more appealing to princes than to ordinary people. "It often happens that men who are ruled by a monarch are slow to interest themselves in the common welfare," he notes, "since they are of the opinion that whatever they do for the common good will in no way benefit themselves, but only serve to enrich whoever appears to control the public interest."[32] Still, he argues, it is better to have one ruler in charge of the common good than many pursuing their own ends—for even a selfish king only takes things from certain individuals, whereas many people acting on their own desires destroy the peace of the whole community in a war of all against all.

Although Thomas acknowledges the danger of tyranny, he offers no method of escaping it but says it must simply be tolerated to avoid "perils more grievous than the tyranny itself." These perils include "dissentions in the populace," factions in the community, and the possibility of even greater tyranny. Thomas tells a story of the Greek tyrant Dionysius, who was astonished to find an old woman praying for his health. Asked to explain herself, she said that when she was a little girl she lived under a mean tyrant and prayed he would die. He did, and a meaner king took his place. She wished for his death too, and he died only to be replaced by a still meaner man—namely, Dionysius. So she prayed for Dionysius to live, fearing that his successor would be even worse. Thomas suggests that, similarly, people should pray to God not to smite tyrants but to convert them "for it is within His power to turn the heart of the cruel tyrant towards gentleness."[33]

In the end, Thomas sloughs off the practical problem of tyranny and falls back on abstract ideals, pleading with kings to fulfill their social responsibilities: A king "should establish the good life of the community under him; second, he should defend it once it is established; and third, once secured he should foster its improvement." In other words, it is the king's duty to lay out a unifying vision of a good life and see that the community has the means to attain this common good. If that seems vague, it's all right, for kings are not the final authorities anyway. "Under the law of Christ," Thomas says, "kings should be subject to priests"— the presumption being, they know the common good when they see it, and they can teach kings to achieve it.[34]

These days students of Aquinas are a diverse lot. If there is anything they might agree on, it's that *On Kingship* is not his finest work. A few question whether Thomas even wrote it, but experts accept his authorship up to a chapter in book 2 where he leaves off writing about the temptations of city life. Thomas's biographers can only guess why he never finished the book. The simplest answer is that he had better things to do.

By the 1260s, when many Scholastics began writing mirrors for princes, the genre was so circumscribed that even Thomas had to trace within the lines. Scholars now conclude that *On Kingship* is a thoroughly conventional mirror, reflecting little that's original to Thomas—or to Aristotle, for that matter. It looks "like a quick collation of commonplaces" appropriated from "inherited texts, their patterns and authorities," says Mark Jordan, Harvard's Niebuhr Professor of Divinity.[35] Besides the Carolingian themes of corporate unity and the social responsibilities of a prince, there are the axioms that good kings are good for trade, that it's better to be loved than feared. There is the old doctrine that the king is a minister of God: "The king should recognize that he has a duty to act in his kingdom like the soul in the body and God in the world," Thomas writes. He should remember that "he has been appointed to exercise judgment over the kingdom in God's place" and that God will one day judge—punish or reward—his performance:[36] To "good kings who rule the people of God with pious intent, and repulse His enemies," Thomas preaches, "He promises them not an earthly reward merely, but an eternal one."[37] (Just as a boss earns more than a worker, a good king earns a greater reward in heaven than a good subject. A devout king who "gladdens a whole country with peace, restrains the violent, preserves righteousness, and orders the actions of men by means of his laws and precepts" merits the greatest reward.)[38]

All this rhetoric sounded better in the age of Charlemagne than in the century of Magna Carta, suggesting to Jordan that "the incompletion of *On Kingship* could be a wise choice rather than a lamentable accident" on Thomas's part.[39]

Thomists

Followers of Aquinas picked up where Thomas left off. His student Ptolemy of Lucca completed *On Kingship*, adding chapters about service to God and country, fiscal policy, and public administration. Another disciple, Giles of Rome, expanded on Thomas's interpretation of Aristotle to produce one of the most popular mirrors for princes of the Middle Ages. Giles's mirror, *On the Rule of Princes*, is also among the longest, over 150,000 words. While Thomas was Doctor Angelicus, the Angelic Teacher, contemporaries called Giles Doctor Verbosus—the Verbose Teacher. That trait is actually helpful for shedding light on the genre.

Giles was born around 1243 to an aristocratic family in Rome. At the age of fourteen he joined the Augustinians, a mendicant order of friars. After a year or two of novitiate, he was sent to Paris to study the liberal arts, and he remained at the university for theology, likely as a student of Thomas Aquinas (who began a second stint there in 1269). At Paris Giles got swept up in a crackdown by church leaders on the teaching of heretical ideas attributed to Aristotle. For holding suspect beliefs, he was expelled from the university by the bishop of Paris, Stephen Tempier. Over the next few years, Giles tended to the business of his religious order and wrote commentaries on the books of Aristotle. It was during this period that he wrote *On the Rule of Princes* for the heir to the French throne, Philip the Fair.[40]

Giles addresses his mirror "to the Lord Philip, descended from royal and most holy stock, first born and heir of the most distinguished Lord Philip, by the grace of God most illustrious King of the Franks." He aims to show "how his Royal Majesty may become virtuous and how he may bring those whom he has as his subjects to be morally honorable and virtuous." He promises that anyone who follows his advice will gain not only virtue but self-control, control over others, and eternal happiness in heaven.[41]

Giles tells Philip nothing new in his book, but his verbosity makes explicit what many took for granted. He describes, for instance, how mirrors for princes are meant for everyone. "Although this book is entitled *On the Instruction of Rulers*," he writes, "it is nevertheless also a means by which the whole populace is to be instructed. For while not everyone can be king or ruler, everyone still ought to devote the greatest attention toward being the sort of person who is worthy to rule or govern, which they cannot be unless they know and observe the contents of this work." Like authors of mirrors for princes since antiquity, Giles intends to show not just how to be a good ruler but how to be a good subject. Citing Aristotle, he says, "the subject needs to know how to do those things which the lord needs to know how to command." Therefore, "if this book instructs rulers how they ought to conduct themselves and how they should command their subjects, then this teaching must be extended to the populace so that they may know how they ought to obey their rulers."[42]

Gearing his book toward a public audience would have seemed as natural to Giles as to any management guru today. Along with sermons, mirrors for princes were the channels used by medieval theologians to popularize their philosophies. Scholastics of course watered down their philosophies for popular consumption. Since "the whole populace is the audience for this art," and "since the whole populace cannot comprehend refined argumentation," Giles says, his mirror is purposely superficial and general.[43] This is appropriate, he claims, because "superficial and general arguments have a greater capacity to move and kindle the emotions"—which is what mirrors for princes are *for*.[44] They are motivational books, written not to teach truths but to spur action, read "not for the sake of contemplation or in order to know, but to become good."[45] Giles recommends that his book *On the Rule of Princes* be read out loud during meals, after the monastic custom of listening to sacred readings instead of talking at table, "so that princes themselves might be instructed in how they should rule, and that others might be taught how to be obedient to princes."[46]

If Prince Philip ever ate quietly while Giles's mirror was read to him, he would have heard that he needed all the classical virtues and then some. He must be prudent concerning the affairs of his realm, courageous without being rash, moderate in all things, and just above all. He must be merciful, kind, honorable, truthful, dignified, and generous to win the love and respect of his people. He must be energetic, magnanimous, and munificent in undertaking great things. Echoing the sages of ancient Egypt, Giles stresses the value of big building projects. A great prince, he says, "should do great works and build houses and structures to last his lifetime, and make them strong and durable and not merely outwardly impressive."[47] Giles tells Philip that magnificent buildings inspire wonder in subjects, distracting them from hardships and making them less likely to rise up against princes in their midst. The same goes for majestic ceremonies, such as royal weddings and coronations.

Despite Giles's vow to give practical lessons, he fills his book with stock theory. He teaches the old textbook formula: People have bad attitudes; they are selfish; they need a common goal and a ruler to unite them. He invokes Aristotle, identifying "the common good of virtue as the goal of all good government."[48] And he joins Aquinas in specifying monarchy as the best form of government to achieve the common good. In some respects, Giles's *On the Rule of Princes* goes beyond Thomas in upholding the ultimate authority of the monarch. The prince is portrayed as "the minister of God," tasked with removing impediments to the common good—seditions by the citizens, disturbances of the peace, and other violations of the law—and he is answerable to God, not men.[49]

To dissidents who would try to call the king to account and limit his power, Giles insists that rule by one man (monarchy) is more natural, more efficient, and less disruptive than rule by a few (aristocracy) or by many (democracy). A good king knows what's good for his people. "It is this that gives legitimacy to royal rule and permits the king's subjects to serve him willingly, to obey him freely." In well-run states, "the king is the archer, the people the arrow he directs to its appropriate end." Some may miss the mark, human nature being what it is. To keep people on target, Giles suggests, a king should hire plenty of police and not let anyone build fortified castles in his realm.[50]

To advocates of laws like Magna Carta, Giles says "it is far better for a people to be governed by the best king than by the best laws."[51] He argues that man-made laws can be abused: If the rich make the rules, "the very rich will not know how to conduct themselves toward the very poor"; they "will injure them and do them harm for no reason" because "they do not know how to be subjects."[52] On the other hand, "if the poor have power over the rich, they will treat the rich and mighty badly"; they will "rob them and deprive the rich of their goods" because "they do not know how to rule."[53] Giles concludes that "human laws, however detailed they may be, will necessarily be deficient in particular cases. It is therefore better for a kingdom to be ruled by a king than a law, since deficiencies in the law can be corrected by a king."[54]

The problem obviously is that authority can be abused as well as laws. How can any society hope to crown the best king, or even a tolerably good one, given the long history of tyrants who cared nothing for the common good but only for their own? Some of Giles contemporaries called for an elective monarchy, similar to regimes in the Italian city-states, as a defense against tyranny. Election would seem to raise the odds of a virtuous prince; everyone knew that some of the worst—say, King John of England—inherited their jobs. Like most Schoolmen, however, Giles endorsed hereditary succession, claiming that elections cause political strife, sedition, and civil war. A hereditary monarchy is more stable, he says, because "if the people through long-enduring custom has obeyed the fathers, it is quasi-naturally inclined voluntarily to obey the sons and the sons' sons."[55] Plus, he adds, if a king knows his son will succeed him, the king will try harder to maintain a healthy treasury, and his son will not be so impressed with the trappings of power.[56]

Eventually, Giles falls back on the same hedge against tyranny relied on by Aquinas and his predecessors—moral education of the prince. From a young age, the prince must be exposed to good habits and especially to teachings of the Christian faith. He should be entrusted to devout caregivers and kept from bad influences, Giles says, for just "as soft wax takes the impression of a seal, so the child's soft and pliable nature easily receives and absorbs impressions from without." As the prince matures, he should take instruction in the classical liberal arts—Latin grammar, logic, rhetoric, arithmetic, geometry, music, and astronomy. In addition, he should study moral and political principles under the direction of a teacher of exemplary virtue, lest the prince "fall into the danger of becoming tyrannical." Once upon the throne, he should continue his moral education by surrounding himself with wise and ethical counselors.[57]

Such an education, not a constitutional government, is the surest way to avoid tyranny according to Scholastic mirrors for princes. "Autocracy tempered by conscience is the doctrine emphatically taught both by St. Thomas in his *De regno* [*On Kingship*] and by Giles of Rome in his *De regimine principum* [*On the Rule of Princes*]," states Jean Dunbabin. Almost all thirteenth-century scholars, she points out, downplay legal restraints on the king and emphasize instead "that a royal son must be so trained and conditioned from his earliest youth that the misuse of power becomes an abomination against the whole grain of his nature."[58] In the formation of a Christian prince, Giles teaches: "As the health of the whole body depends on the sound condition and action of the heart, so the virtue and safety of a kingdom depend on the ruler's life and character." The ruler's character, in turn, stems from his moral education; and his education, finally, rests on the virtue of his teachers and counselors. In effect, the good society originates with the authors of mirrors for princes.[59]

If rulers ignore mirrors for princes, if they fail in their education and oppress their people, it is the people's problem. People enjoy the benefits of community—for instance, the division of labor where one person digs ditches, one makes shoes, one rules, and most are better off for what they create together. So people must bear the costs of a well-ordered community, such as the risk of an occasional tyrant. Giles writes, "If it is considered how much good comes from kingship, not only when kings rule rightly, but even if in some ways they behave tyrannically, the people should endeavour to obey. Some tyranny on the part of the prince is more tolerable than the evils which arise from disobedience to the prince."[60] People may pray, certainly, that God will remove a tyrant from their midst, but they should be careful what they wish for. As Thomas Aquinas warned, the next ruler could be even worse.[61]

Giles surely got worse than he wished for in Philip the Fair. Nicknamed for his fair hair, not his virtue, Philip inherited the French crown from his father in 1285, five years after Giles wrote *On the Rule of Princes*. Whether or not Philip ever read Giles's mirror (he wasn't much for books), he learned at his father's court that he was the greatest prince in Christendom, the vicar of God on earth. As king, he promoted a vision of the French monarchy "far grander and more militant than had ever before been advanced," says historian Elizabeth Brown, a longtime student of his reign.[62] Philip's aim was to unite the different regions of France into one kingdom under his authority. His twenty-nine-year reign was marked by long wars against the English (who ruled Aquitaine) and the Flemings (who ruled Flanders); by big building programs in Paris, including work on the Louvre; and by an epic struggle with Pope Boniface VIII that redefined church-state relations and caused Giles to clarify his views on monarchy. At issue between Philip and Boniface was taxation. The story is a bit involved, but it demonstrates the risky consequences of what mirrors for princes were teaching; it reveals how the rhetoric of common goals could threaten anyone, even religious authorities who preached the common good.[63]

By the end of the thirteenth century the French treasury had been depleted by the policies of successive kings and the increasing cost of war.

Philip the Fair needed money for his many projects, and he took it from whomever he could. He expelled the Jews from France and confiscated their property. He ordered the arrest and execution of all the Templars in France (big bankers by now), confiscating their wealth as well. He judged entire towns, such as Carcassonne, guilty of crimes against the crown and imposed heavy fines on their citizens. He squeezed his subjects to pay a large tax for the marriage of his daughter. But, for potential tax revenue, he eyed above all the rich estates and incomes of the French clergy.[64]

National taxation had been developing in the West along with the crusades. Popes encouraged kings to tax their subjects for the defense of Christendom—first for crusades against Muslim enemies of the Church, later against fellow Christians suspected of heresy. Envious of the revenue generated, kings soon began taxing subjects for their own wars, arguing that the defense of Christendom encompassed the defense of their realms. Kings then extended the defense-of-the-realm goal to legitimize other plans in need of funding. Of course, people complained; taxes were never popular. So kings sought justification from moral experts like Thomas Aquinas, who wrote: "Sometimes it happens that princes do not have revenues sufficient to protect their lands or to perform other tasks which might reasonably be expected of princes; and in such a case it is just that their subjects should be called upon to furnish whatever is necessary to secure the common welfare." To further the common good, to defend the realm, simply "to preserve the honourable standing of the prince," Aquinas held, a king can "make a charge upon the business of the community either through the established forms of taxation or, if these are not in place, or if they are not sufficient, by levying a charge on individuals."[65] Philip the Fair did just that in his war with England, but he went even further. Clergy were customarily exempt from royal taxes for private wars; Philip ended their privilege—not without a fight.[66]

Clergy were used to paying taxes levied by the pope for one crusade or another, but they were forbidden to pay taxes to lay rulers without papal authorization. On his own, Philip the Fair imposed a war tax on the French clergy, using the Scholastic argument that they were members of the community of France, not isolated individuals, and they had a duty to support the community in time of need just like everyone else. The French clergy appealed to Pope Boniface VIII. Calling Philip's tax a terrible abuse of secular power, comparable to slavery, Boniface issued a decree excommunicating any rulers ("emperors, kings, or princes, dukes, earls, or barons, powers, captains, or officials, or rectors, by whatsoever names they are called") who would tax clergy without his permission and any clergy who would pay such a tax.[67] Philip retaliated, prohibiting transfers of money from France, thus cutting off a key source of papal income. Boniface backed down, conceding that Philip could indeed tax prelates and bishops for "the general or particular defense of the realm" without consulting the Roman pontiff—the necessity for such taxes in defense of the realm being "left to the consciences of the aforesaid king and his successors."[68]

Constrained only by his conscience, Philip the Fair set off to defend the common good as he envisioned it, and he continued to tangle with Boniface over royal prerogatives. Philip's arrest and arraignment of a French bishop in a lay court triggered a new round of recriminations. Boniface accused the king of oppressing the clergy; Philip accused the pope of subverting the civil authorities of France. Giles of Rome, now archbishop of Bourges, sided with the pope and qualified his earlier remarks on the sovereignty of the prince. In his treatise *On Ecclesiastical Power*, written at the height of the dispute, Giles reworked the venerable theory of the two swords, making the spiritual sword of the pope superior to the temporal sword of the prince. "Every earthly power," he wrote, "is under the ecclesiastical power, and especially under the Supreme Pontiff," under whom all men—kings included—are subject.[69] Using similar language, Boniface issued another decree (*Unam sanctam*) in which he brandished his sword at Philip: "Therefore we declare, state, define, and pronounce that it is altogether necessary to salvation for every human creature to be subject to the Roman Pontiff."[70] Boniface's sword was metaphorical, however; the king's was real. Philip sent soldiers to Italy to arrest the pope for abusing his own power. Locals intervened to protect Boniface, but he died soon after, it was said, from the shock.[71]

In the end, Philip the Fair saw to the election of a French pope, Clement V, who moved the papal court to Avignon, where the king was able to keep closer watch on it. Clement eased whatever conscience Philip had, absolving him of fault for his tax policies and his disputes with Boniface. Giles of Rome followed the papacy to Avignon, where he died in 1316. His *On the Rule of Princes* became an instant classic despite its unfounded faith in monarchy to do good and in moral education to ward off tyranny. Many copies survive from the thirteenth century, even more from the early fourteenth century, when it was used as a textbook in the arts curriculum at Paris. Some 350 manuscripts are extent, compared, for example, to 27 for Aquinas's *On Kingship*, according to professor Charles Briggs who has studied the book's transmission. Giles's text was translated into French, English, Italian, Castilian, Portuguese, Flemish, a half-dozen dialects of German, and other vernacular languages, and his revisionist reading of Aristotle on kingship was widely imitated. From Philip the Fair forward, nearly every king of France had a mirror written for him, observes Nicholas Orme, a specialist in medieval education; any number of these mirrors were derived from Giles's *On the Rule of Princes*. The book remained popular among educators until the late fifteenth century, when scholars turned away from such derivative Aristotelian works.[72]

Giles has few followers among modern scholars. "Tiresome to the last degree," is the verdict on his mirror by the noted constitutional historian Charles Howard McIlwain. *On the Rule of Princes* and books like it, McIlwain contends, parrot "the same general ideas, the same vague counsels, the same impersonal observations; in this medley of commonplaces, copied one from another it is difficult to single out one work which shows any trace of interest or originality."[73] Difficult but not impossible.

Purveyance

Once in a great while you will see a mirror for princes that seems different from all the rest—less slavish, not so abstract, more reflective of the practical concerns of real people. Such a mirror was written for King Edward III of England in the early 1330s. It's actually two mirrors, both written by a rural parish priest named William of Pagula, both stressing the same point, both usually printed together as the *Mirror of King Edward III*.

William begins his mirror with a brief statement of the king's responsibilities. The king should honor God, defend the fatherland, bring peace to his people and freedom to the masses, and care for orphans and paupers in particular. The king's primary responsibility is to do justice to each individual, William says. Then he gets right to the point: "So that justice may be done to each one, nothing may be taken for a lesser price than the seller wishes to sell it for." William repeats this point in one context after another, ignoring the typical clichés of mirrors for princes through most of the book.[74]

The central focus of William's mirror is a practice called purveyance, involving the right of kings to confiscate supplies from their subjects or demand their sale at a low fixed price. The practice originated as a means for kings to provide for themselves and their households when touring their realms. But under Edward I, Edward II, and especially Edward III, it had grown into a significant source of funding for the kings' many wars. The initial use of purveyance to requisition a few items like fish and wine for the king's table led over time to demands for enough food to feed his army (plus the horses, carts, and labor to haul it all away). Payment to farmers at a nonnegotiable price led to payment with non-negotiable IOUs, or no payment at all. Use of confiscated goods to feed solders led to use of stolen property to compensate soldiers in lieu of wages. Ultimately, purveyance amounted to a massive scheme for shifting the cost of the king's military visions onto working people. Or so says William of Pagula.[75]

How it works, William explains, is that agents of the king scout the countryside:

> If they find oats anywhere, they say that they wish to pay for one bushel of oats only three pennies, even if it is worth five pennies; and if they do not find oats, but barley, they seize from the unwilling owner one bushel of barley for three pennies, even if it is worth nine pennies. If, however, they do not find barley, but beans, they seize one bushel of beans for three pennies, even if one bushel is worth twelve pennies.[76]

In his own neighborhood around Windsor, William reports, the king's men "even steal from widows, orphans, and poor little women . . . the chickens from which they have their sustenance, and they promise to pay one penny per chicken, although each is worth two pennies, and also they even make them swear how many chickens they have" so the authorities won't miss any.[77]

William likens the king to a leader of robbers who take grain, bread, beer, fowl, fattened pigs, sheep, and oxen, whatever they want for next to nothing. "Because of extortions of this kind, many poor people will not have what they need to sow their fields," he says. And many stand to lose their homes because they can't pay their creditors. "A poor man comes to the market with one ox at a price of one mark and he has to pay one mark on a certain day or lose his own land," William informs the king, but "his ox is seized by your ministers and nothing is paid to him, because of which he loses his land."[78] Under the king's leadership, the poorest of the poor have suffered the worst, William tells Edward:

> Those from your household have seized from the forests of Windsor, and places of the area, the persons, wagons, and horses of paupers, and they compelled them to return to their own homes, through ten miles and back, to carry firewood, not only for three or four days, but for many, and they promised to pay them for the labor, but they paid nothing. And on account of this diabolical deed, the lands of the paupers were not cultivated, not planted, nor did the paupers have any goods by which they were able to sustain burdens of this sort.[79]

No king can win the cooperation of people this way, William says. When villagers hear Edward's agents approaching, they cower in fear; "they act as if they think thieves and plunderers or such sorts of men are coming to their village"; and "they hide geese, hens, and other goods, or they get rid of them, or they consume them by eating and drinking, lest they lose them."[80] How shameful for the king, how futile for his projects, how unfair for his subjects. William pleads with Edward

> on behalf of the English people, and for the health and salvation of your soul, that you should cause to be legislated and ordained that no one, under severe penalty, should take anyone's goods against his will. But one should buy things only if one is able to agree with the seller, and one should immediately pay the money to the seller himself, in no way delaying payment against the will of the seller. And one should hire carts, horses, and the labor of men in a manner in which one can contract for them more honestly.[81]

If you do this, William assures Edward, "then men will come from everywhere and bring everything you need, even to your door."[82]

William restates the old adage that a king should be loved, not feared. He advises Edward that the secret to gaining the love of his people is "to buy like some foreigner and pay the fair price." Otherwise, if the king goes on to seize his subjects' goods against their will, William warns, they will reject Edward's visions, they will be "not of one mind with you" and they will "rise against you, just as they did against your father" (an inept and unpopular monarch who was deposed, imprisoned, and likely murdered, to the relief of the English people).[83]

This admonition against tyranny is routine in mirrors for princes. What's unusual is William's suggestion that oppressed people are not just empirically hard to manage but are morally right to rebel. Since purveyance amounts to theft, William asserts, "it is against the precept of God to seize anything against the will of the seller," and "in these things that are against the precept of God, one must not obey, but rather resist, the king." Even the king's retainers have a duty to resist him. Addressing prelates, priests, counts, barons, soldiers, anyone commissioned by the king, William tells them, "If the king orders anyone to seize the goods of another man unjustly, one must not obey"; further, "whoever in this case does not obey the king acquires a great reward for himself" from the King of Kings.[84] What is most striking in the *Mirror of King Edward III*, observes professor Cary Nederman, a specialist in medieval texts, is the book's "very strict insistence on the absolute inviolability of the rights of subjects"—something you'd expect to find in a seventeenth-century treatise on government, not a fourteenth-century mirror for princes.[85]

Other mirrors of the day were still offering Edward advice from the *Secret of Secrets*, still pretending it was Aristotle's teaching to Alexander the Great. For example, Walter of Milemete's *On the Nobility, Wisdom, and Prudence of Kings* instructed Edward to "live virtuously in accord with all forms of virtue"; "to please God" and "subdue enemies"; to "reward the merits of the meritorious; to punish the mistakes of transgressors"; to win the "affection of the counts, barons, and all the nobles of the land"; to "gain money, possessions, and treasure"; to "win battles; to defeat castles and cities; to subject diverse kingdoms and foreign peoples to your authority"; to "achieve conquest wherever it pleases you"; and "finally, after exiting this life, to wear the crown of glory in the celestial kingdom." Walter urged Edward to draft peasants for fighting his wars, alleging that "the rural masses are best adapted to arms, since they are nourished in constant labor [and] strenuous activity, enduring the sun, neglecting shade, unfamiliar with baths, ignorant of luxury, simple of mind, content with little food, their limbs tolerant of endurance in all labors. They turn away less from death." With respect to rights, Walter's message was to "maintain unharmed the rights and liberties of the church." The contrast with William of Pagula's mirror could not be any starker.[86]

Of course, William was a man of his age. Classically educated, with a doctorate in canon law from Oxford, he was conversant with the conventions of Scholastic literature. Like his contemporaries, he advised his king to serve the common good, practice the virtues, respect the church, and all the rest. However, he did not trust such abstractions to guide the behavior of powerful princes who invoked patriotic goals to justify their own ambitions. Princes would say they needed to field big armies and expensive warhorses for the defense of the realm, but William replied, "it is not for defense of the land, but more for vanity and the destruction of the earth."[87] He challenged Edward to get rid of some warhorses rather than burden his subjects with their care and feeding. Calculating the cost of each horse just for hay, oats, and a groom—over six pounds annually—he figured the king could feed four or five paupers instead.[88]

Unlike the bishops and academics who wrote most mirrors for princes, William was a rural vicar with pastoral priorities. (Besides his mirror for King Edward, he wrote several handbooks of pastoral theology—dealing with confessional practice, sermon topics, and basic church rules—that became standard references for parish priests.) Perhaps because William stayed closer to the common people he served, he reflected more of their daily concerns in his mirror for princes. Accordingly, he preached that even kings must respect freedom of contract, that "to buy something for a lesser price than the seller wishes to sell them for" is "contrary to consent," and "when there is no consent, there is no selling but extortion, no justice but seizure."[89] No matter the king's cause, William sanctioned no excuses, notes Nederman, "no special circumstances in which the personal rights of subjects might be breached on grounds of the common welfare."[90]

As a practical preacher, William avoided gimmicks—mythic talismans and grand visions—for transforming individuals into free and willing subjects. He seems to have understood a simple truth about organizations that management experts still find hard to grasp. What binds people together and enables groups to function is not necessarily a shared goal but shared behaviors, mutually agreeable means to members' separate goals and their own visions of the common good. A prince can pursue his objectives, his subjects can pursue their ends, and people in general can cooperate productively, so long as they agree on rules of the game, such as *No purveyance allowed.*

William's preaching had no noticeable effect on Edward III, if he heard it at all. William died soon after finishing his mirror; Edward went on to wage one war after another—against the Scots in 1333 and against the French in 1337, beginning the Hundred Years War that would last until 1453. To support these ventures, Edward employed purveyance on a vast scale, writes historian W. R. Jones; "complaints against royal purveyance multiplied during the late 1330's, with the result that it became a major issue of English politics."[91] It was during this time that the folk ballads of Robin Hood appeared, likely in protest of purveyance, adds fellow historian J. R. Maddicott.[92] Despite efforts to control it, purveyance remained a prerogative of English kings until it was finally abolished by Parliament in 1660.

William's *Mirror of King Edward III* proved fruitless on a deeper level as well. Literature scholar David Matthews suggests that it was not actually written for Edward but for other preachers, for William's colleagues among the clergy. Addressing his work to the king may have been William's way of drawing attention to it. It's a classic rhetorical ploy. Today management books often address CEOs in their titles but their real audience is other teachers or business students; the implication that a chief executive might someday read a particular book lends it real-world authority that it might otherwise lack. Likewise, "William of Pagula transmits a sense of privilege to readers by letting them feel that they are reading something addressed to someone very important," says Matthews. If he were writing mainly for other clergy, this could account for William's unusually blunt tone. It might have been his aim to contest their vision of a Christian empire and their view of war as a divine mission to spread the faith. In any case, his book had no known influence on clerics of his time nor on humanist writers who carried on the classical tradition of mirrors for princes.[93]

Muslim Mirrors

William of Pagula is the exception that proves the rule-bound nature of mirrors for princes. What is remarkable about the genre is the monotony of mirrors across different cultures—not only among Christian writers but among their declared enemies. "The affinities among the mirror literatures produced in Muslim and Christian settings, and to a degree over an even wider canvas, are striking," states Louise Marlow, a specialist in the history of medieval Islamic literature.[94] Islamic mirrors teach the same old formula, the same clichés, the same nostalgia for empire building and holy war as their Christian counterparts. Examples from the High Middle Ages include *The Book of Government* of Nizam al-Mulk, a Seljuq prime minister; *The Sea of Precious Virtues*, written by an anonymous Syrian scholar; and the *Book of Counsel for Kings*, attributed to al-Ghazali, a Persian theologian who has been called "the Muslim Aquinas."[95]

Islamic mirrors for princes feature the customary jeremiads. "This present age is one in which the people's outlook has been corrupted, and in which they have all grown wicked in both deed and intention," says al-Ghazali.[96] *The Sea of Precious Virtues* bemoans that "today the world has been turned upside down," as revealed by the gains of the crusaders. "In the early days of Islam two Muslims would stand fast against a hundred infidels, while today a hundred Muslims cannot stand against two Franks." The reason is that "today there is no concern for the faith." The people of Islam have become just like the infidel—drawn to "wine, taverns, drinking parties, boon companions, musicians, illegal taxes and imposts, neglect of prayers." All these evils weaken Muslims, so the Christians win jihad.[97]

Because people are perverse, they need a strong leader to keep them in line. "As long as they are not intimidated and disciplined by the Sultan, they do not obey God and do not practise virtue," writes al-Ghazali.[98] Even a bad prince is better than none, or one incapable of controlling his subjects. "If there were no kings the people would devour one another," says *The Sea of Precious Virtues*.[99] And if the sultan were weak, the whole world would fall into chaos, claims al-Ghazali. To be sure, sultans do not always practice virtue themselves, but "a century, say, of unjust rule by Sultans will not cause so much damage as one hour of the injustice of subjects to one another."[100] God will hold unjust sultans to account on Judgment Day; it is not for men to judge them, for their power does not derive from the people but from Allah. Good or bad, "the Sultan is God's shadow on earth," chosen by God to be his deputy; therefore, he must be obeyed, loved, and followed by his subjects.[101] Just as Christian mirrors cite St. Paul's instruction to honor earthly rulers, so Muslim writers invoke the Qur'anic commandment to "obey God and the prophet and those in authority among you."[102]

Augmenting his authority, a king's character and virtue shape his entire country, for better or worse. A virtuous king brings honest businesses, safe roads, bountiful crops, fair weather, and other blessings from

God, whereas a bad king brings crime, famine, and calamity. "The ruler's virtue underlies the well-being of his subjects and the prosperity of the world," declares Nizam al-Mulk.[103] The virtues of a good king include justice, integrity, manliness, bravery, piety, knowledge, compassion, mercy, truthfulness, and steadfastness. The king should manifest such virtues by praying to God, giving alms to widows and orphans, showing kindness to subordinates, respecting religious authorities, honoring men of learning, and relieving his people from overbearing officials. In his personal demeanor, he must present a comely appearance and a kindly disposition. He should look good on a horse and display skill in the use of arms. He should impress his subjects with public works—by digging deep canals, erecting big bridges, raising strong fortifications, founding new cities, constructing lofty buildings and magnificent dwellings. Stately architecture demonstrates to everyone the magisterial character of their prince.[104]

Like most mirrors for princes, Muslim writings promote special virtues to deter kings from losing their tempers and doing violence. *The Sea of Precious Virtues* urges kings to practice the virtues of clemency, patience, and forbearance: "When they hear something against someone they [should] not make haste to punish him, but pause and wait, for it may be that a lie has been told, some fraud perpetrated, or some enmity manifested." After all, the king can kill someone whenever he wants, "but once that person is killed, regret is of no avail."[105] Al-Mulk tells a story about a corrupt courtier who informed the sultan that a court scholar was drinking wine and worshiping an idol in his bedroom. The sultan summoned the scholar to have him killed, but, having second thoughts, he stayed his order and instead interrogated the informant, who confessed that he lied in hopes of acquiring the scholar's house after his death. The moral of the story is that the sultan understood the falseness of men and the truth of God's word: "O you who believe, if a wicked man brings you tidings, verify it lest you smite some people in ignorance and then repent of what you did" (Qur'an 49:6).[106] Still, people have little defense against a tyrant who regrets nothing. *The Sea of Precious Virtues* suggests that the best protection from a bad king is prayer: One should "repeat '*Lord, Your Hand is above all others; avert me from the evil of So-and-so*' twenty-five times. God will empower him against harm from the ruler and make the king favorably inclined toward him."[107] If that doesn't work, it means the tyrant is God's punishment for one's sins.

Just as in Christian mirrors for princes, Islamic texts stress moral education to train kings in virtue and prevent tyranny. (As ever, character education was a preferred alternative to institutional checks and balances—self-regulation was deemed better for business than the real thing.) Surveying Muslim mirrors since the *Secret of Secrets*, Islamic history professor Neguin Yavari finds each one assumes that a just society depends on a just prince, that "the justice of a prince is the end result of his education," and that his education "reflects the quality of his educator, the counselor."[108]

A king's education begins in the nursery, states *The Sea of Precious Virtues*: Wet-nurses should be chaste and pious, never loose or Christian women who will nourish a child to their tastes. The young prince should be shielded from luxury—from satin robes, silver cups, gold rings, and the like—so he won't grow up spoiled, grasping, and demanding. Early on, tutors should read to him not from popular books but from the Qur'an, so that its words become part of him. Then, as he learns the Arabic language, he should be taught Islamic prayers, laws, and rituals as well as rules of proper conduct. The prince must learn to be careful of the company he keeps. He should not be allowed to associate with astrologers, naturalists, drinkers, gamblers, musicians, dandies, fools, and women—the typical tempters who lead people into sin and on to hell. Rather, he should be surrounded by devout scholars who can continue his training in religion and ethics even after he ascends the throne.[109]

A ruler should be thirsting to meet religious teachers and ask for their guidance, says al-Ghazali. If the king separates his regime from religion or is lax in defending the faith, Nizam al-Mulk argues, "there is confusion in the country; evil-doers gain power and render the king impotent and despondent; heresy grows rife and rebels make themselves felt."[110] Therefore, several times a week the king should invite holy men to teach him the commandments of God, lessons of the Qur'an, tales of good princes, and lives of the prophets. In this way, "his judgment will be strengthened and he will increase in justice and equity; vanity and heresy will vanish from his kingdom."[111] Nizam al-Mulk promises that throughout the empire of a faithful king the righteous will prosper "and the wicked shall be no more. In this world he shall have fame, and in the next world he shall find salvation, high degree and inestimable reward."[112] In return for such assurances, the king should of course honor his religious teachers with earthly rewards and "pay their salaries out of the treasury."[113] *The Sea of Precious Virtues* calls on Muslim kings to treat their holy men the same way the Franks treat their priests: "They seat monks in their presence with honor, and do whatever the monks command. They give life and wealth for love of them. . . . Praise be to God!"[114]

To be successful, a leader must be worthy of love by his subjects. A good king puts the interests of his kingdom and his people before his own. Nizam al-Mulk points to the example of Sultan Mahmud Ghazi (The Raider), who took the throne after the death of his father, Sabuktigin. The young sultan had a pinched face, big nose, long neck, and sallow complexion. One day he said to his prime minister, "I am afraid that people don't love me because I am not handsome; they always prefer handsome kings." The minister, a wazir named Ahmad ibn Hasan, replied, "Master, do just one thing, and they will love you more than their wives and children and their very selves, and at your command they will go through water and fire." Seek the common good instead of personal wealth, the wazir told him: "Take gold as your enemy and men will regard you as their friend." The sultan followed his advice, renounced selfish goals, and "all the world adored him and praised him, and many noble works and great victories sprang from his hands."[115]

As in the West, Muslim calls for common goals sound nobler in the abstract than in specifics. According to *The Sea of Precious Virtues*, the sultan should present a unifying vision for the Islamic world similar to the Christian empire of the Franks, and jihad or holy war toward that end is a collective responsibility of the Muslim community. The author cites the Qur'an instruction to "Employ your substance and your persons for the advancement of God's religion," which means to believers, "wage jihad against the infidel with both your wealth and your bodies." *The Sea of Precious Virtues* teaches that even if infidels pose no direct threats and remain in their own regions, the leader of the Muslim community "is required to wage holy war every year, or send out an army (against them), so that jihad will not be suspended and the enemy will not become attracted to Muslim lands." Rules of engagement are explicit: Upon meeting infidels, the Muslim army should invite them to embrace Islam. If they refuse, they may be killed—"It is permitted to attack the foe by night, to cast fire and mangonel [catapult-propelled] stones at them, and to pour water upon them so that they drown, no matter how many women and children among their followers perish." Their property becomes war booty, to be distributed among the army with shares set aside for poor and orphaned Muslims and the Prophet's kinfolk. Holy martyrs who die in battle are promised forgiveness of their sins, a place in Paradise, a robe of honor and crown of nobility (plus the "seventy-two houris" or heavenly maidens of tradition). Mustering forces for such spiritual visions need not cost sultans a lot of money, since "holy war becomes obligatory upon [Muslims], and wages should not be received for discharging an obligation."[116]

To restate the obvious, there is nothing inherently violent about major religions like Islam or Christianity. What inspired men to go off crusading or to drown women and children wasn't the tenets of their faith but the rhetoric of their leaders, as reflected in mirrors for princes. Muslim writers produced a vast number of mirrors for princes—in Arabic, Persian, Turkish, all the Islamic languages—describing the ideal ruler in much the same terms. Louise Marlow points out that many of these mirrors survive only in a single manuscript, suggesting that they were offered with the aim of gaining patronage or employment. Sultans, like kings everywhere, retained scholars and commissioned mirrors for princes to enhance their moral standing and legitimacy. "A ruler's generous reception of such a work was a sign of his subscription to the catalogue of royal virtues it contained, and reflected positively on his personal merit and that of his court," says Marlow.[117] As always, however, Islamic rulers heard what they wanted to hear. "Kings listen to advice," concludes *The Sea of Precious Virtues* in an outburst of candor, "but they do not apply it; they know what is right, but do not act accordingly," damn their black hearts.[118]

You can understand why medieval kings might collect mirrors for princes but not rely on their advice. What king wouldn't appreciate books that affirmed his traditional right to rule over others, accountable to no one but God? On the other hand, as people claimed rights of their own, what king could hope to solve political problems of state with the simple precepts set out in mirrors for princes? Historian Linda Darling remarks that Muslim mirrors for princes, much like their Western counterparts, finally lost their political currency in the eighteenth century, when "no longer was it sufficient to address a single holder of concentrated power with personal advice."[119]

"Modern readers sometimes marvel at the popularity of this genre," observes Islamicist Patricia Crone, because so "many mirrors are banal and formulaic. But the same can be said of modern advice literature, which is also widely read ('how to succeed at business,' 'how to achieve happiness,' 'how to preserve your marriage,' and so on). A steady stream of banalities seems to be what one gets when there is a strong market for concrete advice without anyone actually having any to give."[120]

As the Middle Ages waned, the market for leadership advice grew stronger. The Italian Renaissance spurred freedom of thought and brought new challenges to rulers. Court literature and print technology developed to meet the demand, ushering in a golden age of mirrors for princes.

SEVEN

Renaissance Mirrors

The state is being undermined by party rivalries and afflicted by wars,
robbery is everywhere, the common people are reduced to starvation
and the gallows by rampant extortion, the weak are oppressed by the
injustice of those in high places, and corrupt magistrates do what they
please instead of what the law says; and in the middle of this, the prince
is playing dice as if he were on holiday?

Erasmus, *The Education of a Christian Prince*

Since the age of Charlemagne, Germanic princes had a vision. They
dreamed of a great empire stretching from the North Sea to the Mediterranean. They saw it as a rebirth of the ancient empire of Rome. They
imagined it sanctified by God. They called it the Holy Roman Empire.

The vision appealed more to princes than to ordinary people. Most
subjects of the Holy Roman Empire never even heard of it, and many who
had ignored it. People in northern Italy, for instance, went their separate
ways and built great cities of their own—at Pisa, Milan, Bologna, Padua,
Genoa, Venice, Florence, and other places—where, in the view of Otto
of Freising, a twelfth-century German historian, individuals behaved "in
hostile fashion" toward the emperor, "whom they ought to accept as their
own gentle prince."[1] Time and again German princes sent soldiers south
to impose their vision of the Holy Roman Empire on the cities of Italy.
Time and again they failed. Still, sympathetic writers urged them on—
with the old clichés of mirrors for princes. Two such writers were Dante
and Petrarch, Italy's foremost poets, who looked back with nostalgia to
the glories of ancient Rome.

Born in Florence in 1265, Dante experienced from childhood the warfare between rival political parties that reduced local neighborhoods to rubble in the late 1200s. He also witnessed the renewal of the city into a European financial capital by Florentine banks and trading companies. (The gold florin became the standard coinage of international commerce, similar to today's dollar, and money flowed back to Florence for urban development.) Dante deplored the civil wars, but he disliked even more the business wheeling and dealing—and perceived moral corruption— that ensued. His biographer Marco Santagata remarks that Dante felt "the new men of power, who had become powerful through business, had put profit in place of the civic and military virtues" of the past. To inspire his countrymen to look beyond themselves and the values of the market, Dante wrote a traditional book on political leadership titled *Monarchy*.[2]

Composed around 1313, *Monarchy* follows the classical formula. Dante first observes that people are behaving badly: "Humanity," he says, is "a many-headed beast lusting after a multiplicity of things!" Dante diagnoses the problem as selfishness: Men have lost all sense of justice; and, as Aristotle taught, "the greatest obstacle to justice is greed." Dante prescribes a cure—namely, a common purpose: "Mankind at its best depends upon unity in the wills of its members." As the ancients knew, it is the monarch's job to set a common goal. Harmony in a household, a city, a kingdom, anywhere "is impossible unless there is one will which dominates all the others and holds them in unity," Dante says. Individuals would run wild and push one another around "if men, like horses stampeding to satisfy their bestiality, were not held to the right path by the bit and the rein." Thus, "mankind is in its best condition under a Monarch; from which it follows that monarchy is necessary for the well-being of the world."[3]

The best monarch ever, Dante suggests, was the Roman emperor Augustus, who ruled over a world free of civil strife. "Mankind at that time was resting happily in universal peace," Dante claims, because in conquering the whole world the Roman people had the common good as their goal. Indeed, "they seem to have sacrificed their own advantage in order to secure the general well-being of mankind." Plus they had God on their side—"When all the peoples were racing to secure control over the world, the people who won did so by divine decree." Since then, Dante laments, the world has been in decline, awaiting a second Augustus to restore the empire.[4]

Dante had a candidate in mind. He wrote to the Holy Roman emperor, Henry of Luxembourg, urging him to reclaim his rightful empire by force of arms. He also wrote to the "crazy and contrary" people of Florence who were resisting Henry's rule, accusing them of rejecting reason and the will of God. But Henry died leading an expedition to Italy, the Florentines turned back his soldiers, and Dante's dream of world monarchy came to naught.[5]

Petrarch

Dante's younger contemporary Petrarch took up the cause but scaled down the vision—from a worldwide empire to a united Italy.

Petrarch was born in 1304 at Arezzo, a town near Florence that attracted refugees from Florentine politics. (His father was a friend of Dante's; both were active in the White Guelf party, and both had been expelled from Florence when the rival Black Guelfs seized power.) Petrarch studied law at Montpelier and Bologna, but his true love was the classic literature of ancient Rome, especially the works of Cicero and Virgil. He began writing poetry during his college days at Bologna; afterward he pursued a literary career, becoming the first poet laureate crowned in Rome since antiquity. His celebrity stemmed not just from his poems but from his scholarly essays and orations, his historical and political writings, as well as his letters to princes, popes, and other famous people of the day. Petrarch's work as a whole revived the ideals and literary forms of the ancient world, for which he has been dubbed the "father of Renaissance humanism." His writings on politics espoused Italian patriotism, urging an end to partisan strife and the unification of Italy under an emperor, pope, or other great leader. Among his works, you will find a mirror for princes.[6]

Titled *How a Ruler Ought to Govern His State*, Petrarch's mirror is addressed to one of his patrons, Francesco da Carrara, the ruler of Padua. Petrarch begins in the style of the ancients. He praises Francesco profusely for his mastery of the classical virtues—for his justice, fortitude, wisdom, temperance, modesty, dignity, magnanimity, humanity, tranquility, and his love of public order and peace. For the security, freedom, and prosperity brought to Padua, he writes, "you have been viewed as vastly superior to all other rulers of your state and to all rulers of other cities, not only in the judgment of your own subjects but indeed in the opinion of the whole world as well." Petrarch proposes to teach the prince how to do even better. "I want you to look at yourself," he tells Francesco, "as though you were gazing in a mirror. If you see yourself in what I am describing (as no doubt you will quite often), enjoy it." On the other hand, "if sometimes you feel that it is difficult for you to meet the standards I describe, I advise you to put your hands to your face and polish the countenance of your great reputation written there."[7]

The overall theme of the book is that rulers do well by doing good, or, as Cicero put it, the honorable deed is also the useful. Above all else, Petrarch says, a prince should seek the love and goodwill of his subjects. One "should be friendly, never terrifying, to the good citizens, even though it is inevitable that he be terrifying to evil citizens if he is to be a friend to justice." It is much better to be loved than feared, he contends, because only love brings longevity in office and security in life. Petrarch looks back to the Romans for affirmation. He cites Cicero: "Fear is but a poor safeguard of lasting power," while affection "may be trusted to keep it safe forever." He quotes the words of Laberius to Julius Caesar: "He who is feared by many must himself fear many in turn." He holds up Caesar as a role model: Despite his enormous appetite for empire and glory, Petrarch claims, Caesar kept no treasure for himself and took no pleasure in vengeance, but "he did everything with mildness and mercy, with munificence and incredible generosity, so that he would be loved rather than feared." Hence, he instructs Francesco to "put away arms, bodyguards, mercenaries, bugles, and trumpets, and use all these things only against the enemy because with your citizens love is sufficient." (At least it is sufficient to manage patriots. Mirroring the emperor Augustus, Petrarch discounts the rest: "I reckon as citizens those who desire the preservation of the state and not those who are always trying to change things, for these should be thought of not as citizens but as rebels and public enemies.")[8]

Petrarch covers cases of beloved emperors such as Marcus Aurelius who met happy ends. He presents contrasting cases of Roman princes who ruled through fear and earned the hatred of citizens—Caligula, Nero, Domitian, Galba, and Vitellius: He details their miserable deaths, the dismemberment of their bodies, the desecration of their remains, the destruction of their statues, and the obliteration of their names. To avoid such a fate, a prince must demonstrate his commitment to justice, mercy, the familiar virtues. Besides setting a good example, Petrarch suggests, the best way for a prince to win affection is through public generosity. Again he points to emperors like Augustus, who built and restored the city of Rome. Francesco cannot hope to match Augustus's boast that "he found a city of brick and left one of marble," Petrarch writes; but he could at least fix Padua's streets, long neglected and broken up from all the traffic. (While he's at it, Francisco should get rid of the herds of pigs that freely roam the city. They're everywhere, digging with their snouts and grunting—"A filthy spectacle, a sad noise!" Petrarch exclaims. It's the fault of irresponsible pig owners, who let their animals loose to forage in the streets, flouting the municipal ordinance that forbids it. The prince ought to enforce the law, send out officers to remove the swine, and clean up the city, he counsels, so that citizens and visitors don't imagine they are living in a pigsty.) What's more, Francesco should drain the marshes and bogs lying just outside Padua that foul the air and spoil the view. This is a bigger project but good for the community and even better for the prince's reputation.[9]

Petrarch concedes that these things take money. He offers to donate a little of his own, even though he isn't a citizen of Padua. For the most part, he recommends using public funds, but he advises Francesco to be cautious in levying new taxes on his people. A ruler should first cut "useless and superfluous expenditures," he says. Funds wasted on public games and spectacles, for example, would be better spent on works bringing beauty and order to the city. Sometimes a prince must raise taxes, of course, to further his goals for the realm. Here Petrarch gives instructions resembling Aristotle's tips for tyrants: "When a ruler has decreed that his people are to be burdened with some new tax, which he will never want to do unless in times of public need, he should make all understand that he is struggling with necessity and does it against his will." Specifically, "he should argue that, except for the fact that events compelled him to levy the tax, he would gladly have done without it." Petrarch comments it would look even better if the ruler contributed some of his own money to any new tax. By pleading need and sharing in the cost, "however high it is, the exaction will always be judged lighter and milder." Remember, Petrarch warns rulers, do not be greedy. He endorses the sentiment of the Roman emperor Tiberius: "Good shepherds ought to shear their sheep but not skin them."[10]

In addition to all the classical clichés, Petrarch includes the stock images of medieval mirrors for princes. He describes the prince wielding his sword as "a minister of God." He tells Francesco, "The state is one body and you are its heart." He condemns the passion for wealth that consumes princes and courtiers, declaring that instead of lusting after riches, "you must lust after the treasure of virtue and win the fame of outstanding glory. This is a property that moths and rust cannot corrupt, nor can thieves steal it in the night." Don't reward followers for fawning and flattering, he urges the prince, but "be generous and kind to scholars" for "it is only learned men who can provide the right advice at the right moment, and thus ensure the fame of your name."[11]

Finally, Petrarch thanks Francesco for his past patronage and makes a last request. Can't the prince of Padua do something about the emotional women who disturb the peace by making so much noise at funerals? "Some old dowager dies," he gripes, and "they carry her body into the streets and through the public squares accompanied by loud and indecent wailing so that someone who did not know what was happening could easily think that here was a madman on the loose or that the city was under enemy attack." When the funeral cortege finally reaches the church, the terrible keening gets worse. Where one should hear solemn prayers for the deceased, "the walls resound with the lamentations of the mourners and the holy alters shake with the wailing of women." Petrarch implores Francesco to order excitable women to just stay home.[12]

It is easy to imagine that Petrarch was trying to be funny, but it's easier to suppose he was serious. Elsewhere he lamented the bad manners and sheer selfishness of his contemporaries: "Alas, what besides groans and complaints is left for a miserable man, when even our kings love nothing but pleasures and our popes nothing but riches, when the people either weep in their bondage or rage in their freedom, and everybody seeks his own interest?" He deplored the quarrels between Christian rulers, their "insatiable lust and flaming hatred," that caused the failure of the crusades and the surrender of the Holy Land to "the Egyptian dog." He regretted the decline of faith and the loss of believers across the Christian empire that once spanned East and West. He grieved to see the Italian peninsula devastated by wars, her sea infested with pirates, neighborhoods terrorized by gangs and violence, cities in ruins from plagues and earthquakes—God's punishments for sin. "Remember this one thing," he said, "nothing is more miserable than humanity, nothing weaker, nothing poorer and more needy of outside assistance."[13]

And so Petrarch asked God to send help. He prayed for a new Charlemagne, a charismatic leader to instill a shared vision for God's people. Before writing to Francesco da Carrara, he begged the Holy Roman emperor, Charles of Bohemia, to rush to Italy's rescue and "reunite all these precious fragments into a single body." He assured the emperor that, because no one else can heal her wounds, "Italy has never awaited the coming of any foreign prince with more joy."[14] He tried to inspire Charles with examples of great leaders from antiquity— Alexander the Great, who extended his kingdom "over alien races" to the gates of India;[15] Hannibal, conqueror of Italy, Gaul, and Spain; Scipio Africanus, who defeated Hannibal and freed Rome from the yoke of Carthage; and, of course, Julius Caesar, the glorious "founder of the Empire."[16] Charles was now one of them, a Caesar too, Petrarch proclaimed. March bravely forward with God's blessing, he wrote to Charles, and "the armed cohorts of the good and upright will gather about thee, demanding to regain under thy leadership their lost liberty."[17]

Despite a dozen such letters to the emperor and similar appeals to the rulers of Milan and Venice, no prince took Petrarch's advice seriously. Charles remained aloof, and the lords of Italy's city-states continued fighting one another. Soon after composing his mirror for Francesco da Carrara, Petrarch died, and Francesco led Padua in repeated wars— finally losing his territories to Venice and Milan and his life in a Venetian prison.[18]

For his love poems, Petrarch was, at this death in 1374, "the most famous and influential intellectual of his time," notes professor of Italian studies Martin McLaughlin.[19] For his paeans to princes, Petrarch was maligned as "the familiar friend of tyrants," he himself acknowledged.[20] In succeeding centuries his poems spread his fame; his mirror for princes was forgotten. One of the few scholars to study *How a Ruler Ought to Govern*, language professor Arpad Steiner, concludes that Petrarch merely restated in Ciceronian terms the teachings of Aquinas and the Scholastics; even a wordsmith like Petrarch could not break free of the "stereotyped rhetoric" of the mirrors-for-princes genre.[21]

Christine de Pizan

Steiner submits that no one could write a thorough history of mirrors for princes—the number of such books "produced by all ages and all lands since the dawn of history is appalling and defies all imagination." Nor would anyone want to *read* a history of the genre, he suggests, since the static "set of ideas passed on from one author to another" simply repeats "the nearly identical hoard of wisdom by which the Good Prince was to be governed in public and private life." Yet, some authors managed to discover a new angle and add a fresh voice; their mirrors still stand out.[22]

A few years after Petrarch's death, a noblewoman named Christine de Pizan expressed her own concerns about mirrors for princes. Christine had read every mirror she could find; she'd read Aristotle, Cicero, Seneca, John of Salisbury, Giles of Rome—too many others to name. As she browsed these books, she wondered "how it happened that so many different men—and learned men among them—have . . . express[ed] in their treatises and writings so many wicked insults about women." It seemed to her that all the philosophers and poets and orators repeated the same thing: "that the behavior of women is inclined to and full of every vice." Honestly, she said, "I could hardly find a book on morals where, even before I had read it in its entirety, I did not find several chapters or certain sections attacking women, no matter who the author was."[23]

She knew from personal experience with all sorts of women that these esteemed men were wrong. So she wrote her own mirror. In fact, she wrote five mirrors for princes, two for princesses, and a couple more for courtiers. The most distinctive is *The Treasury of the City of Ladies*, dedicated to Marguerite of Nevers—the young wife of Louis of Guyenne, heir to the French throne. The book addresses women of many different classes but mostly princesses, empresses, queens, duchesses, and other great ladies. Such women are born to luxury, Christine writes. They sleep between soft, smooth sheets. They sigh and ladies-in-waiting run to pamper them. They wear the newest fashions, adorn themselves with gold and precious jewels. They feast on delicacies and fine wines. They amass great wealth, which they use to buy friends and punish enemies. To working women, it looks wonderful, like a storybook life.[24]

But it's not, Christine says, in the eyes of God and His people. All the pleasures, status, and wealth in the world will not bring a lady honor, but only contempt. A lifetime of luxury, she warns princesses, "makes you so disdainful and so difficult to please that almost no jewel, no costume, nor any ornament really satisfies you. You always find some detail to complain about. Furthermore, no person pleases you. You are so overbearing and presumptuous, you think not even God can cross you." Don't become such a silly woman, Christine tells Marguerite; don't let pride and greed cause your fall from fortune and damnation for all eternity. Determine to be a good princess.[25]

A good princess will humble herself before she is humbled by God, and she will seek out a path to virtue. There are two possible paths, Christine says. The first is the contemplative life, where the princess turns away from the world and its fleeting joys: "She remains solitary, apart from others, knees to the ground, joined hands pointing heavenward, heart raised up in such elevated thought that in contemplation she ascends to the presence of God." This is the better way of life, but religious orders are not for everyone. The other path to virtue is the active life, where the princess serves the world. She helps in hospitals, for example, aiding the sick and the poor with her energies and wealth. Devoting herself to charitable works, "she seeks her neighbor's good as if it were her own." An active life of virtue also offers women a voice in society.[26]

Besides doing good works, a virtuous princess is an advocate for her people before the prince. If her husband or son, as ruler, should succumb to bad advice and harm his subjects, she should show them clemency and intercede for them in gaining justice. She is a spokesperson for peace when the prince and his council rush to war. Men are foolhardy and headstrong, Christine says, "and their overwhelming desire to avenge themselves prevents them from foreseeing the resulting dangers and terrors of war." A good princess is a check on kings who fight first and regret it later.[27]

A wise queen or princess learns how to govern on her own in her lord's absence. In governing, she will have to attend meetings of the king's council and carry herself with such presence that "she will indeed appear to be the ruler of them all." She should find out in advance what will be proposed at the council so she can prepare and speak with authority on pressing matters. She should listen to diverse opinions, seek out worthy advisers, host meals with important people, hold court for honored guests, and make herself available to petitioners. Christine sets out the particular virtues a princess should cultivate to do her job—reason, rectitude, justice, prudence, chastity, and sobriety—followed by a list of corresponding behaviors. For instance, a prudent princess will remain gracious to her in-laws, "speaking well even of those who don't deserve it." Should she find herself suddenly widowed, she will defend her rights boldly against the inevitable legal challenges—and get herself a good lawyer. She will keep tabs on the kingdom's finances: "Forbidding the taking of anything from people against their will, she will buy at a fair price, and pay promptly." From her surplus, she will make gifts to religious houses, ensuring that her benevolence is publicized to enhance her reputation among those she must rule. (This "expedient hypocrisy" is justifiable for princesses, Christine says, "as long as they practice it for worthy ends"; after all, "long-ago princes requiring their subjects' reverence and respect pretended that they were related to the gods.")[28]

Obviously, Christine was no stranger to the palace. *The Treasury of the City of Ladies* drew lessons from her own experiences. Born in Venice in 1364, Christine lived most of her life around Paris. Her father was a physician and astrologer to Charles V, king of France, and Christine received a basic education at the French court where she learned how to express herself in a chorus of male voices. "One day," she recalled, "a man criticized my desire for knowledge, saying that it was inappropriate for a woman to be learned, as it was so rare, to which I replied that it was even less fitting for a man to be ignorant, as it was so common." Christine knew well the ups and downs of court life. Early on, fortune lifted her high. Raised in the household of a favored courtier and married at the age of fifteen to a royal secretary, she lacked for nothing. By twenty-five, the wheel of fortune had turned on her. First, the king died and her father lost his regular salary and pensions. Next her father died, then her husband, leaving Christine to support her three children plus her widowed mother and exposing her to multiple lawsuits over their inheritance. Her memories of those days echo the bitter stories of court corruption told by John of Salisbury: "Alas," she wrote, "How vividly I remember many a chilly winter morning spent in that palace, shivering from the cold while waiting for those representing me so I could remind them of my case and urge them to action, only to hear at the end of the session decisions that made me burst with outrage, or else puzzled me; but what hurt even more was the expense I could ill afford."[29]

Like single mothers today, Christine tried to continue her education and look for work. She studied history, philosophy, and literature. She probably copied letters and manuscripts for clients to make ends meet.

And she began to write poetry. Inspired by Dante, Petrarch, and other early humanists, Christine emulated the ideals and rhetorical styles of ancient Greece and Rome. Starting with courtly verse, such as poems for St. Valentine's Day, she went on to write deeper poetic stories, then books of advice for princes and women in their circle. She promoted her work by sending copies to various princes in hopes of landing a patron. Many of these gift copies were richly illustrated manuscripts produced under Christine's supervision by professional scribes and artists. But wars, plagues, and famines had made money tight, even among princes, and she got in return some small thank-you gifts (silver goblets and tankards) and invitations to the courts of unstable rulers (Henry IV of England and Gian Galeazzo Visconti of Milan). Eventually the duke of Burgundy, after receiving one of Christine's manuscripts, commissioned her to write a biography of his late brother, King Charles V, and more patronage jobs ensued. The duke's son, John the Fearless, paid Christine for several works (possibly including *The Treasury of the City of Ladies*), followed by payments from other family members. John further arranged a position for Christine's son and a dowry for her orphaned niece. In line with the interests of the Burgundian court, Christine now focused her writing on mirrors for princes.[30]

The most traditional of Christine's mirrors is *The Book of the Body Politic*, composed around 1406 for Louis of Guyenne (the dauphin of France, husband to Marguerite, and son-in-law of John the Fearless). As always, the book caters to a wider audience; Christine specifically addresses (1) princes, (2) knights and nobles, and (3) the universal people. These three estates, she writes, "ought to be one polity like a living body." Borrowing from John of Salisbury's organic metaphor, Christine compares the prince to the head of the body politic, willing the other members into action. "The knights and nobles take the place of the hands and arms," she says, "defending the law of the prince" and the polity from harm. The universal people, representing the belly, the feet, and the legs, sustain the body politic.[31]

Christine restates the usual maxims of mirrors for princes. The good prince, like a good shepherd, protects those in his care and safeguards their land. His goal is the common good, not selfish interests. Because he cares for them, the good prince is loved by his people, while he is feared by wrongdoers. He controls his anger, avoids cruelty, and shows mercy; but, Christine says, "his kindness ought to be considered a thing of grace," not an entitlement. He speaks with eloquence, maintains a dignified bearing, and abstains from lechery. He listens to the downtrodden, widows, and orphans. He is generous to his counselors, staff, and soldiers. (If the prince's agents were well compensated, Christine adds, "one could restrict them on pain of punishment to take nothing without paying for it.")[32]

Christine goes on to advise knights and nobles, the militant limbs of the body politic. She tells them to practice the classical virtues, particularly courage, so they may bravely face death for the good of the prince and their country. Christine supplies examples of how the Romans built their empire by showing courage in battle. Most are copied from Valerius Maximus's *Memorable Words and Deeds*, such as her incredible story of the Roman knight who was badly wounded and lost the use of his hands, "so he did as much as he could with his feet to attack one of his enemies, and then, standing on top of him, he seized his nose with his teeth and tore up his whole face!"[33]

Finally, Christine turns to the common people whose work sustains the body politic. These people serve specialized functions in a community, just like members in a human body: For instance, artisans or craftsmen produce different goods so that citizens do not have to make everything themselves, and merchants bring these goods from far-off producers to buyers all over the country. Workers are prone to drunkenness, gluttony, and lust, Christine says, but they need to be well treated to keep them productive and the body politic healthy. For their part, the common people should stick to their jobs and quit complaining about their masters. They should not concern themselves with politics, and "they should not meddle in the ordinances established by princes." Christine invokes St. Paul's instruction that "all living creatures ought to be subject to powerful rulers, for those powers that princes have are commanded by God." Because they are divinely ordained to punish evildoers, even bad princes must be obeyed; anyone who resists their power rebels against the Almighty. Fortunately, "there are no more benign and humane princes than in France," Christine claims, "and thus they ought all the more to be obeyed."[34]

Like most mirrors for princes, Christine's *Book of the Body Politic* teaches that good government comes from the traits of a perfect prince, not from impersonal laws and institutions, notes Kate Langdon Forhan, who has edited the book for modern readers.[35] Christine's biographer,

Charity Cannon Willard, points out that her "concept of the perfect prince varies only in detail from the long series of treatises on the subject, beginning with Xenophon's *Cyropedia* (*The Education of Cyrus*)."[36] As in the classics, Christine counts on moral education to produce good if not perfect princes and protect people from tyrants. A young prince should be assigned a virtuous tutor who will show him cases of good and bad rulers so that he learns the glory that comes from acting honorably and the evil that befalls those who act wrongly. A mature prince's continuing education should include lectures on relevant issues by experts such as theologians on laws of the church, merchants on how they make their profits, and diplomats on conditions in different countries. Formal learning should be supplemented by the appointment of wise counselors to remind the prince of his social responsibilities.[37]

For over a century Christine's mirrors for princes circulated around the royal houses of Europe, although they had no traceable influence on rulers of the period or on writers of similar books. Now, six hundred years after she wrote, Christine gets mixed reviews. "She is sometimes dismissed as a mere compiler or as a conservative apologist for the ruling classes," observes Forhan.[38] But it's the nature of the genre to compile what princes were willing to hear: "If she insulted her patrons there would be no bread on her table."[39] Christine was no more slavish than the great men who wrote mirrors for princes—John of Salisbury, Thomas Aquinas, Petrarch, and all the rest who copied clichés from the classics and told princes they were God's gift to mankind. At least Christine added something original, reflecting in her mirrors for princesses the concerns of women who were invisible, if not objects of scorn, to her predecessors.

Erasmus

Until the mid-fifteenth century, a "book" meant to readers a manuscript, hand copied on papyrus or parchment or paper. Such books were expensive. If you were well-off, you could buy copies in varying grades of legibility (priced accordingly). If not, you could borrow books and copy pages yourself, a common practice among university students.

Then in 1454 a visitor to the Frankfurt Book Fair spotted a new mechanically produced Bible. "The script is extremely neat and legible," reported Aeneas Silvius Piccolomini, the future Pope Pius II: You "would be able to read it without effort, and indeed without glasses." What Piccolomini saw at the Frankfurt Fair were proof sheets of the first printed Bible made by Johannes Gutenberg, a merchant from Mainz, Germany. Gutenberg's Bible caused an immediate sensation, and his technology was rapidly copied by other printers who cranked out an array of religious and secular works—liturgical missals and lectionaries, prayerbooks and schoolbooks, Greek and Latin classics, fables and other popular fiction as well as mirrors for princes. Within a couple of decades, publishers had grown so numerous that authorities were being petitioned to curb the industry's influence. In 1474 a Benedictine scribe named Filippo de Strata called for the banning of printers in Florence, warning that the flood of cheap books was corrupting the morals of readers.[40]

Most of the early printers were forced out of business, not for endangering community morals but because they couldn't pay their bills. Gutenberg's Bible, although it sold out before the Frankfurt Fair, ruined him financially. Still, his invention proved irresistible to entrepreneurs, creating jobs for everyone from metalworkers making type, to typographers composing text, to salesmen showing samples, to wagoners delivering orders, to venture capitalists funding them all. With the advent of printing, there also arose professional writers eager to exploit the new medium. Foremost among them was Desiderius Erasmus, one of the first authors to earn a comfortable living by writing books. Professor Andrew Pettegree, a specialist in the history of the book, estimates that "more than one million copies of Erasmus's writings were in circulation during his lifetime."[41]

Erasmus was born in Rotterdam around 1467. His parents—a local priest and a single mother—enrolled him in one of the best grammar schools in the Netherlands, but they died of the plague when he was about fourteen, and he was entrusted to guardians who (he claims) just wanted him off their hands. He was sent to the Augustinian monastery at Steyn for further education and was eventually ordained a priest. He left monastic life as soon as he could, landing a job as secretary to the bishop of Cambrai, then finding his way to Paris to study theology. At Paris he became drawn to classical literature and began writing poetry. To support himself, he tutored young students as he looked for better-paying patrons. He gained modest support from a few aristocrats. He had some success editing Greek and Latin classics for publication. And he started writing books of his own, making a name for himself with a popular collection of moral adages and emerging as the leading literary figure of his day.[42]

While fame came steadily to Erasmus, wealth did not. In 1517, still searching for a reliable patron, he followed the strategy used by Christine de Pizan to advertise her work. He produced a hand-illustrated copy of one of his books, which he sent to England's King Henry VIII in an attempt to secure a place at Henry's court. The book was a mirror for princes titled *The Education of a Christian Prince*. The gesture was wasted on Henry; the king gave Erasmus no job, just a £20 tip for the gift. Nevertheless, among students of such mirrors, *The Education of a Christian Prince* went on to sell well, going through ten editions and multiple translations during Erasmus's career.[43]

The book was originally written for another prospective patron— Prince Charles, soon-to-be king of Castile and Aragon. (The grandson of Ferdinand and Isabella, he would eventually rule much of Europe as Holy Roman Emperor Charles V.) Erasmus told Charles that he was "the greatest of princes" and even "more blessed than Alexander," who violently seized an empire that was destined to crumble. For Charles was "born to a splendid empire" and he can make it even greater, without violence and without end, because he has the genius of the ages to draw on—Isocrates's principles of kingship, Plutarch's instruction to princes, and now Erasmus's "ideal of the perfect prince for the general good."[44]

Erasmus offers to teach Charles the wisdom of the ancients—the secret to "absolute rule over free and willing subjects." Distancing himself from peddlers of self-help books like the *Secret of Secrets*, Erasmus writes that the key to leadership is not foolish "incantations and magic rings." It is the love and allegiance that a virtuous prince instills in his subjects through his focus on the common good.[45]

A prince who wants to be loved by his people must deserve to be loved. He can't simply "court the affections of the common people with handouts, feasts, and shameful indulgence," says Erasmus. These things might make a prince popular for a while, but people get used to them; "meanwhile, the vicious greed of the populace is fostered, and they come to think . . . that nothing is enough, and they become unruly if their selfish demands are not met at every point." So a prince who tries to buy the loyalty of his subjects just corrupts them. To really win the love of his people, a prince must exhibit the classic virtues—good judgment, fairness, mercy, compassion, friendliness, honesty, restraint, sobriety—and he must avoid vices known to cause hatred—greed, brutality, violence, arrogance, drunkenness, gluttony, gaming, negligence, keeping company with fools and parasites. More broadly, a prince should heed the ancients' advice to put the common good above his own.[46]

Erasmus counsels against practices that encourage contempt for princes. Rulers should limit public pomp and extravagance, for instance. Subjects who see their prince parading around in gold and jewels think of all their tax money going to waste. Similarly, a prince should curtail trips abroad; otherwise citizens doubt his affection for them and question his spending on foreigners. The prince should be especially careful about raising taxes. He should extract as little as possible from his people, Erasmus says. Instead, to raise revenue he should cut excess expenditures, disband redundant offices, avoid expensive wars, and curb graft on the part of his officials. If he still finds it necessary to raise taxes, the prince should make sure the burden does not fall too heavily on the poor. "When he is thinking of increasing his retinue, when he is anxious to make a brilliant marriage for his grand-daughter or sister, or to raise all his sons to his own status, or to make his nobles wealthy, or to display his substance to other countries while on foreign tours then the conscientious ruler must continually remind himself how cruel it is that on these accounts so many thousands of men with their wives and children should be starving to death at home, getting into debt, and being driven to complete desperation." Desperate people, of course, pose a risk of rebellion.[47]

Erasmus includes typical tips for rulers to keep their subjects' goodwill. A prince should surround himself with people of good repute who inspire public confidence; he should select as judges and administrators "those most upright in character and best suited to perform the appointed tasks"—"not the highest bidder, the most brazen lobbyist, his closest relatives, or those most adept at pandering." He should use motivational techniques that enhance his image; for example, "gratitude for a favor given is doubled by giving it quickly, with enthusiasm"; punishment, on the other hand, should be "carried out in such a way that the prince gives the impression of having been driven to it against his will." He should avoid sudden changes to government policies, business customs, or long-established laws; change upsets people, even if it improves their lot, so innovations should be introduced subtly and gradually over time. The prince should never be seen off-duty or on holiday but only performing some public service; he should carry out personally those programs the people support "and delegate to others the tasks which the people resent." He should improve his cities by building bridges, colonnades, churches, embankments, and aqueducts; he should clean up plague spots by clearing swamps and rubble; he should alleviate floods by damming rivers and erecting sea walls; he should increase crop yields by modernizing agriculture. "There are a thousand similar tasks, whose supervision is an admirable job for the prince," Erasmus says. By directing these works instead of leading his kingdom to war, the good prince shows his love for his people, who will love and follow him in return. Just like members of a happy family, subjects rally around a caring king as the father of their country, "for he has them so devoted and dedicated to himself that they do not shrink from anything, even from laying down their lives, not just their money, for their prince."[48]

In place of the bigger realm envisioned in most mirrors for princes, *The Education of a Christian Prince* calls for a better one. Erasmus faults his predecessors for glorifying the expansion of empire through war. His preferred vision is a world at peace. "The good and wise prince," he says, "will try to be at peace with all nations but particularly with his neighbours, who can do much harm if they are hostile and much good if they are friendly." Just as in business dealings, Erasmus argues, peaceful relations between states depend on mutual trust, not on "niggling bits of paper" that provide raw material for lawyers. He warns the prince against foreign treaties, which are negotiated among Christians "as if everyone were the enemy of everyone else." Treaties are supposed to prevent conflict; but wars often result from alleged violations of some obscure clause in these contracts, and the parties would have been better off without them. Likewise, Erasmus cautions against marriage alliances. Princes arrange marriages in an attempt to strengthen bonds between states, but instead they too result in war—when some article in the marriage contract is thought to be breached, or when the bride's family feels slighted, or the birth of children disturbs lines of succession, or whatever. Finally, Erasmus is critical of crusades to spread the Christian faith. "Wars of this kind," he says, "have too frequently been made an excuse to fleece the Christian people." Remember, "the kingdom of Christ was created, spread, and secured by very different means"—"by the suffering of martyrs, not by military force." Judging by the men currently fighting these wars, Erasmus snipes, crusaders are more apt to turn into infidels than to make infidels into Christians.[49]

Although his vision is more pacifist than most, Erasmus's *Education of a Christian Prince* reflects the same governance formula as classic mirrors for princes. The formula posits a problem: People are behaving badly. Erasmus claims that "the nature of man inclines toward evil." He points to the riffraff tolerated at the courts of princes—"whores, degenerate comrades, the most shameful flatterers, buffoons, street-players, drinkers, gamblers, and pleasure-mongers" who exhibit nothing but "pride, arrogance, greed, irascibility, and bullying." He gives examples of all the idlers who live off the state—"tax farmers, pedlars, usurers, brokers, panders, estate managers, game wardens, the whole gang of agents and retainers." He singles out soldiers, who practice "a very energetic kind of idleness," which "causes the total destruction of everything worthwhile." He adds priests who "fritter away lethargic lives" in monasteries or "hawk certain sacred relics from town to town," who "live in idleness and luxury under the guise of religion."[50]

Continuing with the formula of mirrors for princes, Erasmus identifies a cause for bad behavior: People are too selfish; they've lost the sense of community that keeps societies from turmoil. The whole world is unstable "nowadays when everyone pursues his rights to the letter," Erasmus complains. "At present, while each man looks out for himself, while popes and bishops are preoccupied with power and wealth, while princes are made reckless by ambition," he says, "we are running headlong into the storm with folly as our guide."[51] Elsewhere he laments the selfishness of his generation, calling it "the most corrupt there has ever been. . . . All we appeal to, all we read, all we hear, all our decisions—what do they taste of except of ambition and greed?" In business, mere usurious money-lending is not enough for a "sordid class of merchants" who cheat the public by "buying in one market to sell for twice the price in another." Even the new printing press—his own meal ticket—degrades the culture, Erasmus frets, because money-hungry publishers spew out "useless rubbish," swamping "honorable fields of study."[52]

Per the classic formula, Erasmus's mirror for princes prescribes the old remedy for selfishness: Societal failure can be avoided if we recognize our mutual interests, put aside our personal motives, and work for a common cause. "If we acted with common purpose in our common affairs," Erasmus suggests, "even our private business would prosper." But people can't pull together on their own; they need a leader, someone more selfless and visionary than all the rest to give them direction. Because "the people are unruly by nature, and the magistrates are easily corrupted by avarice," Erasmus says, "the prince remains, as it were, the sheet-anchor for the ship of the state." The prince's job is to refocus people's attention on the common good. No one else has such capacity for transformative leadership. "No comet, no fateful power affects the progress of human affairs in the way that the life of the prince grips and transforms the moral attitudes and character of his subjects," Erasmus asserts. People may listen to priests or bishops, for example, but few want to emulate them (the good ones are too good, the bad ones too bad). On the other hand, everyone wants to be like the prince. "Under a gambler," Erasmus says, "gambling is rife; under a fighter, everyone gets into fights; under a gourmandiser, they wallow in extravagance." But under a virtuous prince, people embrace his goals for the state as their own and they work as one for the common good.[53]

Erasmus concedes that virtuous princes are rare, tyrants all too plentiful. He grants that aristocratic and democratic elements in a state can be helpful in checking tyranny; however, he glosses over this point and comes down in favor of monarchy as the best form of government. As usual, the main corrective to despotic regimes, the source of a perfect prince and good government, is moral education. "The chief hope for the state," Erasmus writes, "is founded in the proper training of its children—something which Xenophon wisely taught in his *Cyropaedia* (*Education of Cyrus*)." The prince should be taught to think "healthy thoughts" from birth under the guidance of a good tutor, who can subsequently model proper behavior. Later, "while his pupil is still a little child he can introduce into entertaining stories, amusing fables, and clever parables the things he will teach directly when the boy is older." Eventually the prince's tutor can teach cases of great kings and instill higher philosophical truths, such as "virtue is its own great reward." Just as good governance depends on traits of the prince, the perfect prince depends on hiring the right teacher—someone of integrity, purity, dignity, and learning—in fact, someone just like Erasmus.[54]

Throughout his writings, there is no theme Erasmus returns to more often than "the need for a well-trained, well-paid, competent, compassionate, and yet inventive teacher," notes J. Kelley Sowards, a modern editor of his works. "To be a schoolmaster is an office second in importance to a king," Erasmus says.[55] And a king is next in importance to God. "As God set up a beautiful likeness of himself in the heavens, the sun, so he established among men a tangible and living image of himself, the king," Erasmus contends.[56] It is the task of teachers to bring this glorious image to life through mirrors for princes:

> Let the teacher therefore depict a sort of celestial creature, more like a divinity than a mortal, complete with every single virtue; born for the common good, sent indeed by the powers to alleviate the human condition by looking out for and caring for everyone; to whom nothing is more important or more dear than the state; who has more than a fatherly disposition towards everyone; who holds the life of each individual dearer than his own; who works and strives night and day for nothing else than that conditions should be the best possible for everyone; with whom rewards are ready for all good men and pardon for the wicked if only they will mend their ways.[57]

In short, "the happiness of the whole people depend[s] upon the moral quality of this one man," Erasmus concludes, "let the tutor point this out as the picture of a true prince!"[58]

As ever, if education fails in forming a perfect prince, it is the people's problem. According to Erasmus, if kings ignore the teachings of wise men like himself, they must nevertheless be obeyed. Kings maintain order in the world; "they are the ministers of God and in a way rule for him"; "they must be honoured where they perform their duty and put up with perhaps where they use power for their own advantage, lest something worse arise in their place." Something worse, Erasmus believed, is the chaos and anarchy that would result if people tried to rule themselves. Reasoning from the old organic analogies, he argued that if public policies were determined by "the foolishness of the people" instead of the authority of the prince, it would be as destructive and unnatural as if one's body told the mind what to do.[59]

Erasmus's mirror was the culmination of classical and medieval thinking on the education of the perfect prince. Five centuries on, however, even sympathetic biographers such as Sowards have questioned the "unrealistic idealism of his approach to princely power."[60] Anthony Levi, a cultural historian and editor of *The Education of a Christian Prince*, observed: "Erasmus prefers a grandiose and rhetorical appeal for some ideologically desirable aim like peace to discussion of the practical politics for achieving it." "Erasmus must have known" that his picture of the perfect prince was "abstract, theoretical, and ideological, and that real life was bound to call for compromise." But "he was simply not interested enough in politics either to sustain a long and complex inquiry or to develop a coherent general theory."[61] Erasmus anticipated this type of criticism, bemoaning that "some idiot courtier, who is both more stupid and more misguided than any woman ever was, will protest: 'You are making a philosopher for us, not a prince.'" Well, "I am indeed making a prince," Erasmus declared, "Unless you are a philosopher you cannot be a prince, only a tyrant."[62]

By his own standards, Erasmus failed to educate any perfect princes. The rulers to whom he addressed *The Education of a Christian Prince*—King Henry VIII and Emperor Charles V—became more feared than admired by their subjects. ("If all the pictures and patterns of a merciless prince were lost in the world," Sir Walter Raleigh wrote of Henry, "they might all again be painted to the life, out of the story of this king."[63] While not as reviled, Charles has been dubbed the "impresario of war" for the ongoing fights with his European neighbors and the violent colonization of the Americas by his Spanish conquistadors.) Erasmus in later years seemed to recognize that he had "sung to deaf ears this long while." By the time Erasmus died in 1536, people's faith in a perfect prince was dying as well. *The Education of a Christian Prince* remained in print for the next hundred years, but it was eclipsed almost immediately by mirrors for princes and courtiers that aimed to be more relevant—books that seemed to readers more realistic, less preachy, not so trite and formulaic.[64]

The Courtier

One such book stressed practical rather than philosophical education of the prince, reversing Erasmus's preference for an academic teacher over "some idiot courtier." It was titled *The Book of the Courtier*, and it was one of the most popular of all Renaissance mirrors. Within fifty years of its publication in 1528, there were nearly one hundred editions; one could read it in Italian, Spanish, French, German, Latin, English, and a replica in Polish. (Even Emperor Charles V, some said, kept a copy at his bedside.)[65]

The author, Baldesar Castiglione, worked as a diplomat for the dukes of Urbino. Urbino, Castiglione says, was a little jewel among Italian cities, long admired for the excellence of its rulers and the beauty of their palace. Other places, he notes, were not so blessed, "since the princes of today are so corrupted by evil customs and by ignorance and a false esteem of themselves." There is nothing worse than a bad prince, and "there is no good more universally beneficial than a good prince." A good prince has the usual virtues; Castiglione says he must be "very just, continent, temperate, strong, and wise, full of liberality, magnificence, religion, and clemency." A good prince not only displays virtues but leads others toward them, "like the square used by architects, which not only is straight and true itself, but also makes straight and true all things to which it is applied." A good prince corrects the wicked, cares for the peaceful, and reflects, as in a mirror, an image of God himself.[66]

This classic picture of the perfect prince is a nostalgic illusion, however, and Castiglione does not dwell on it. Except for his old bosses at Urbino, actual princes don't come anywhere near perfect. That's why Castiglione writes *The Courtier*, not *The Prince*. There's no point addressing a book to princes; most won't read it. It's no use telling philosophers or theologians what to teach princes, most won't pay attention. It is up to clever courtiers like Castiglione to steer princes from evil ways—by devising a more personal and productive approach to moral education.[67]

"Among the many faults that we see in many of our princes nowadays," he says, "the greatest are ignorance and self-conceit." These faults exist because no one will tell princes the truth about what is right. Everyone flatters the prince. His friends, to profit from their friendship, lie to him about how good he is. His enemies, to spite him, encourage him to do as he pleases. "From this it results that, besides never hearing the truth about anything at all, princes are made drunk by the great license that rule gives," Castiglione says; they "have their minds so corrupted—seeing themselves always obeyed and almost adored with so much reverence and praise, without ever the least contradiction, let alone censure—that from this ignorance they pass to an extreme self-conceit, so that they become intolerant of any advice or opinion from others." Because princes don't listen, "they think that to know how to rule is a very easy thing, and that to succeed therein they need no other art or discipline save sheer force." They "seize states boldly, by fair means or foul, whenever the possibility presents itself." They "hate reason or justice, thinking it would be a kind of bridle and a way of reducing them to servitude"—as if one who submits to scruples is not a true leader. Their arrogant visions and clumsy mistakes eventually bring them to ruin, but still they dress up in gold and gaudy gems, they put on imperious airs and stern faces, until they finally isolate themselves from everyone but a few toadies.[68]

Nothing can turn a very bad prince into a good king. But, Castiglione says, a very good courtier can make even a bad prince better. The perfect courtier has this aim: to win for himself, through charm and talent, "the favor and mind of the prince whom he serves that he may be able to tell him, and always will tell him, the truth about everything he needs to know." It takes extraordinary qualities to so captivate the mind of a prince, speak to him freely without giving annoyance, and show him right from wrong. Among other things, Castiglione says, the perfect courtier should have noble ancestry, handsome features, a beautiful body, and smooth movements. He should possess the manners of a gentleman, the courage of a warrior, and the skill of an athlete with every kind of weapon. He should be an expert at horse-riding, bullfighting, casting spears and darts, swimming, jumping, running, throwing stones, wrestling, and playing tennis. He should stand for honor and integrity; "included in this are prudence, goodness, fortitude, and temperance of soul." He should know how to apply these virtues in any situation, and he should "be of such good judgment that he will not let himself be persuaded that black is white." He should inspire confidence, without seeming pompous. "Let him laugh, jest, banter, frolic, and dance, yet in such a manner as to show always that he is genial and discreet; and let him be full of grace in all that he does or says." He should speak with a clear, sonorous voice, with fitting posture and gestures. He should be able to explain his thoughts precisely, without being tiresome; he ought not be afraid to use appropriate figures of speech or to coin new words. He should read Latin and Greek, know the great poets, orators, and historians such as Cicero and Xenophon. He should write good verse and poetry himself. He should read music and play various instruments. He should be trained to draw and paint, with an eye for color, light, shading and perspective.[69]

Whatever he does, however, the perfect courtier should make it look easy. He should, Castiglione says, "avoid affectation in every way possible as though it were some very rough and dangerous reef; and (to pronounce a new word perhaps) to practice in all things a certain *spezzatura* [nonchalance], so as to conceal all art and make whatever is done or said appear to be without effort and almost without any thought about it." Such a perfect courtier will be "at first sight pleasing and lovable to all who see him" and "worthy of the company and the favor of every great lord." Having true goodness in himself "together with readiness of wit, charm, prudence, knowledge of letters and of many other things—the Courtier will in every instance be able adroitly to show the prince how much honor and profit will come to him and to his from justice, liberality, magnanimity, gentleness, and the other virtues that befit a good prince."[70]

Modern managers might view Castiglione's book as farfetched. But *The Courtier* captured the imagination of Renaissance bureaucrats. (Thomas Cromwell, arch courtier and chief minister to King Henry VIII, was known to have a copy.) If you worked for a prince, you worked for an autocrat by definition; and if you hoped to keep working for the prince, you had to please him. *The Courtier*, literature professor Daniel Javitch reminds readers, is a guidebook for prince pleasers. It contains the kind of material you'll find in any popular business book—entertaining stories, gritty dialog, gossip about celebrity leaders, inspirational figures to imitate.[71] But it has as well practical tips for managing a boss who rules by divine right. Castiglione teaches: Don't just kiss up to the prince like ordinary flatterers who feed off courts. That's the way to corruption. Don't talk down to the prince like scholarly courtiers who write mirrors for princes. That's the way to irrelevance. (Castiglione's own lackluster career was proof of it.) Instead, beguile the prince "with salutory deception[,] like shrewd doctors who often spread the edge of the cup with some sweet cordial when they wish to give a bitter tasting medicine to sick and over-delicate children." Please the prince, "now with music, now with arms and horses, now with verses, now with discourses of love." Try to "keep his mind continually occupied in worthy pleasures, yet always impressing upon him some virtuous habit along with these enticements." In this way, Castiglione concludes, "the Courtier will be able to lead his prince by the austere path of virtue, adorning it with shady fronds and strewing it with pretty flowers to lessen the tedium of the toilsome journey."[72]

And this way, even if a courtier fails to reform the prince, he helps himself. A prominent courtier of the day, Francesco Guicciardini, recalled, "When I was young I used to scoff at knowing how to play, dance, and sing, and other such frivolities." But he said he learned from experience how important these things can be, "because skill in this sort of entertainment opens the way to the favor of princes, and sometimes the beginning or the reason for great profit and high honors. For the world and princes are no longer made as they should be, but as they are."[73]

Scholars suppose that Guicciardini and Castiglione were reacting to political realities of the Late Renaissance. Italy, once dotted with self-governing city-republics, had over the centuries succumbed to despotic rule—in Milan, Ferrara, Ravenna, and Verona; then in Bologna, Padua, Modena, Parma, Pavia, Genoa, and elsewhere. Political theorist Frank Lovett has suggested that, where republican government is unattainable, the *Courtier*'s aim to instruct the prince in virtue represents a patriotic "politics of the second best." A courtier's attempt to make his prince a better person and presumably a better ruler is "a pragmatic response to tragically diminished opportunities for civic participation."[74] In other words, public service as a courtier is a potentially honorable calling for one who wants to actually do something for his country. Still, the gap between a "second best" politics, which relies on charismatic courtiers to tame their masters, and a system of institutional checks on princes' power is wide indeed. A courtier or teacher might in theory become a model public servant and improve a bad prince. But, as Castiglione's critics point out, perfect servants are as elusive in the real world as perfect princes. They are figures of art posing as pragmatic responses to tyranny. Flesh-and-blood courtiers accountable not to the public but to the prince for their sustenance and their very lives are in a poor position to speak truth to power (and not in the best position to know the truth to begin with). Since antiquity, mirrors for princes—by Lucian, Walter Map, Christine de Pizan, and others—have attested to this fact. Castiglione recognized it too, that under bad princes "courtiers are like caged birds."[75]

Many of Castiglione's contemporaries wrote books addressing the tension between princely rule and republican government. Authors of mirrors for princes naturally came down in favor of the former. A notable exception was Machiavelli, who favored neither (but thought each had its place). His mirror for princes would dominate the genre forevermore.

EIGHT

Machiavellian Mirrors

The Florentines lived in prosperous tranquility until the death of Lorenzo de' Medici in 1492; for after having established peace by his good judgment and authority, Lorenzo devoted his attention to the aggrandisement of the city and of his own family. . . . He aimed to maintain abundance in the city, to keep the people united and the nobility honoured. . . . All Florence, then, as well as all the princes of Italy, lamented the death of Lorenzo. . . . They had just cause for their regrets; for Italy being deprived of Lorenzo's counsels, no means could be found to satisfy or check the ambition of [selfish men]. From this, soon after Lorenzo's death, there began to spring up those evil seeds of trouble, which ruined and continue to cause the ruin of Italy, as there was no one capable of destroying them.

Machiavelli, *History of Florence*

In December of 1513, an out-of-work civil servant named Niccolò Machiavelli was running out of money and fearing for his future. Desperate for a job, he wrote for help to Francesco Vettori, the Florentine ambassador to Pope Leo X. The pope was a member of the powerful Medici family, and Niccolò asked Vettori how to approach the family for work. "The wolf is at the door," he wrote, and "I would like their lordships, the Medici, to start putting me to use, even if they only assign me some menial task, for if, once I was in their employment, I did not win their favor, I would have only myself to blame."[1]

Niccolò does not have an impressive resume to offer. Once a senior bureaucrat in Florence, lately he's been getting by on a small firewood business that he runs out of his home in the country. His days are unremarkable, he tells Vettori. He gets up at daybreak and goes off to the woods where he is harvesting trees for sale. He settles quarrels among the woodcutters, he chases neighbors who cart off wood without paying, he deals with customers who want a cord for the price of a half cord, he explains why he can't deliver whatever people demand. Late morning, he checks the traps he's set for birds; he reads a little poetry, maybe Dante; he daydreams about women and stops by the inn to hear any news travelers might bring. At lunchtime, he says, "I sit down with my family to eat such food as I can grow on my wretched farm."[2] Then

> I go back to the inn. The landlord will be there, and, usually, the butcher, the miller, and a couple of kiln owners. With them I muck about all day, playing card games. We get into endless arguments and are constantly calling each other names. Usually we only wager a quarter, and yet you could hear us shouting if you were in San Casciano [a nearby town]. So, in the company of these bumpkins, I keep my brain from turning moldy.[3]

But, when evening comes, Niccolò goes back home and heads to his study. "On the threshold," he says, "I take off my work clothes, covered in mud and filth, and put on the clothes an ambassador would wear. Decently dressed, I enter the ancient courts of rulers who have long since died." There, in books, the princes of history still rule. "I am not ashamed to talk to them," he continues, "and to ask them to explain their actions. And they, out of kindness, answer me. Four hours go by without my feeling any anxiety. I forget every worry. I am no longer afraid of poverty, or frightened of death." What Niccolò does in those evening hours is record his talk with the dead in a book he's writing *On Princedoms*. It's a guidebook about how one acquires a principality, holds onto it, or loses it, he writes Vettori; and "a ruler, especially a new ruler ought to be delighted by it. Consequently, I have addressed it to His Highness Giuliano" (the pope's brother). Any boss who reads the book, Niccolò hopes, will see he knows leadership and will want to hire him.[4]

Principalities

Machiavelli's book is the most famous of all mirrors for princes, known to everyone as *The Prince*. It begins with an important—but easily overlooked—distinction. All states, all governments, all regimes, Machiavelli writes, are either principalities ruled by a single individual or republics ruled by many. He says that only principalities are the subject of *The Prince* (he deals with republics elsewhere). He does not say principalities are better than republics; so *The Prince* does not teach the one best way to rule—just how to govern a state where one rules alone.[5]

Machiavelli suggests that different leaders can succeed in different situations. He observes that there are various ways a prince can come to power, making for situations where it harder or easier to govern. A prince can, for example, inherit the job, a relatively easy situation for managing people and events. "It is simply a matter of not upsetting ancient customs, and of accommodating oneself to meet new circumstances," Machiavelli says. "If a prince is just ordinarily industrious" and "if he has no extravagant vices to make him hateful," he can survive. Machiavelli points to the duke of Ferrara, an undistinguished prince who managed to get by for no better reason than his family had ruled the place for a long time.[6]

Another way a prince can come to power is to take over a state, say, by annexing territory to an established kingdom. This is a harder situation to manage, Machiavelli says, since the prince must overcome resistance to change. Some people will welcome a new leader in the hope of bettering their lot but will soon feel remorse, fearing they are even worse off, and make trouble. Other people will oppose any new leader from the outset. So the prince must win dissidents' cooperation by means of soldiers and associated hardships. This job takes some skill; one must be careful in applying force because "however strong your armies may be, you always need the backing of local people to take over a province."[7]

A third way a prince can gain power is to found a completely new kingdom. This is the most difficult situation; "nothing is harder to manage, more risky in the undertaking, or more doubtful of success than to set up . . . a new order," Machiavelli declares. Opponents of change are more obstinate, clinging to whatever has profited them in the past, and supporters of the new order are harder to attract because people are skeptical of unproven ventures. Such a situation requires extraordinary leadership; the personal virtues of the prince, his talents and capabilities, are critical for success.[8]

Good fortune, pure luck, helps of course. So does vision. But luck and vision only offer opportunities to exercise leadership. Leadership itself comes from strength of character, backed if necessary by strength of arms, Machiavelli argues. He cites examples of legendary leaders like Moses, Cyrus, and Romulus, who founded great kingdoms. Luck may have helped them rise to prominence, and vision may have helped persuade followers to believe in them. But it was strong leadership that caused people to stand fast in their belief. Machiavelli adds that "things must be arranged so that when [people] no longer believe they can be compelled to believe by force." He claims that if Moses, Cyrus, and Romulus "had had no weapons, they could never have imposed their institutions on their peoples for so long."[9]

Machiavelli accentuates the virile, martial virtues attributed to leaders in Greek and Roman literature; he downplays the abstract, ethical virtues featured in Scholastic mirrors for princes. The ideal prince is a student of war. He reads history, paying special attention to the actions of heroic generals. "He can see how they carried themselves during their wars, and study what made them win, what made them lose, so that he can imitate their successes and avoid their defeats." He goes out and learns to read terrain as well as books. "He will see how the mountains rise, how the valleys open out, and how the plains lie; he will know about rivers and swamps," all so that he can better defend his own land and size up foreign territory. He trains with officers in the field, learning "how to find the enemy, pick a campsite, draw up an army, prepare it for battle, and organize sieges for his own advantage." Machiavelli gives the example of Philopoemen, prince of the Achaeans, who traveled around the country with friends, stopping now and then to ask them, "Suppose there were enemies up in those hills, and we were here with our army, who would have the advantage? How could we get at them, without breaking ranks? If we wanted to get away, how would we do it? If they tried to get away, how could we cut them off?" By debating strategies with fellow leaders, by constantly rehearsing tactics, Philopoemen was ready for any eventuality. A prince who ignores the art of war, Machiavelli concludes, gambles on the mercy of fortune—putting his job, his state, and his people at risk.[10]

Machiavelli addresses the usual questions posed in mirrors for princes. Is it better, for instance, for the prince to be loved or feared? "If you have to make a choice," he says, "to be feared is much safer than to be loved." This seems contrary to traditional advice; but Machiavelli reasons from an old maxim of mirrors for princes: Human beings, he submits, "are ungrateful, fickle, liars, and deceivers, fearful of danger and greedy for gain." Such people will walk all over—and, in time of need, run away from—a leader who tries to be loved. While Scholastics like Thomas Aquinas presumed that love creates a sense of gratitude and obligation toward a good prince, Machiavelli says that "love is a link of obligation which men, because they are rotten, will break anytime they think doing so serves their advantage." Fear, in contrast, "involves dread of punishment, from which they can never escape."[11]

"Still," Machiavelli goes on, "a prince should make himself feared in such a way that, even if he gets no love, he gets no hate either." It is perfectly possible, he says "to be feared and not hated, and this will be the result if only the prince will keep his hands off the property of his subjects or citizens, and off their women." Most people will go along with a leader who respects their property and honor, even one with a fearsome reputation for dealing with troublemakers.[12]

A prince "should maintain such a reputation that nobody will even dream of trying to trick or manage him," Machiavelli says. One does this by ensuring "that his actions bespeak greatness, courage, seriousness of purpose, and strength." The purpose of a great prince must be preservation of his state. He should stop at nothing to achieve this goal. So long as he does not shed blood without cause, a prince needn't worry if he gets a reputation for cruelty. In fact, Machiavelli says, "no prince should mind being called cruel for what he does to keep his subjects united and loyal." A prince who makes examples of a few public enemies does more for his people than indecisive rulers "who, in their tenderness, allow disorders to occur, with their attendant murders and lootings. Such turbulence brings harm to an entire community, while the executions ordered by a prince affect only one individual at a time."[13]

As in mirrors of old, Machiavelli tells the prince to be cautious—to temper punishment with humanity, to think before reacting to rumors or letting anger get the best of him. But Machiavelli takes issue with "all the imaginary things that are said about princes," especially the saintly virtues prescribed in most mirrors for princes. "A great many men have imagined states and princedoms such as nobody ever saw or knew in the real world," Machiavelli says. From Aristotle on, pundits have dreamed of perfect worlds where princes could act pure and good. Machiavelli, however, insists on "getting down to the truth." And the truth is that "any man who tries to be good all the time is bound to come to ruin among the great number who are not good. Hence a prince who wants to keep his authority must learn how not to be good, and use that knowledge, or refrain from using it, as necessity requires."[14]

Philosophers are forever telling princes to keep their promises, for instance; but Machiavelli says, "a prudent prince cannot and should not keep his word when to do so would go against his interest." Again, in a community of saints where everyone was truthful, the prince could be honest; in the real world where men are deceitful, "you must be a great liar and hypocrite." (As an exemplar, Machiavelli points to the Borgia pope Alexander VI.) Promises, oaths, treaties, all can be ignored when necessary to preserve the state. Naturally, the prince should not flaunt immoral behavior, which might turn the public against him; he should seem to practice the accepted virtues. "It is good to appear merciful, truthful, humane, sincere, and religious; it is good to be so in reality," Machiavelli says. "But you must keep your mind so disposed that, in case of need, you can turn to the exact contrary."[15]

In the end, the public will judge the prince on results. If a prince achieves his goals and upholds his state, Machiavelli claims, "his methods will always be considered worthy, and everyone will praise them, because the masses are always impressed by the superficial appearance of things, and by the outcome of an enterprise." Keeping himself in favor with the many, however shallow their values, is the prince's best hedge against challenges to his rule from the few.[16]

The rest of Machiavelli's book contains generic advice. He instructs the prince to delegate unpleasant jobs to other people and reserve the pleasant duties for himself. He tells the prince to entertain his subjects, choose loyal managers, avoid flatterers, and reward talented public servants. (In the case of an able adviser, like Machiavelli, the prince should "think of his welfare, honor him, enrich him, load him with distinctions and offices.") Machiavelli urges the prince to envision "great enterprises" and field big armies to grow his realm. At the same time, he counsels the prince to create a friendly climate for business and keep taxes low. He complains about factions, political parties, and other divisions in the state. He finishes with a typical plea for national unity.[17]

Machiavelli calls for a new prince to rescue Italy from the ravages of civil war, invasions, and barbarians that have kept her "headless, orderless, beaten, stripped, scarred, overrun, and plagued by every sort of disaster." He is being dramatic, but he's reflecting the views of his audience. Italy in Machiavelli's day was the battleground of five regional powers—the cities of Florence, Milan, and Venice, the kingdom of Naples, and the Papal States. One would make war on another and try to leverage its power with foreign troops, either making allies of militant nations like France and Spain or hiring mercenary soldiers from Switzerland and Germany. As popes and princes got replaced, allies and mercenaries switched sides; meanwhile hostile forces marched all over the Italian peninsula. Now, Machiavelli says, "Italy, left almost lifeless, waits for a leader who will heal her wounds." He yearns for someone like Cesare Borgia, who could have united the country had not fortune turned against him. He appeals finally to the house of Medici for a redeemer—to Giuliano (to whom *The Prince* was dedicated) or Lorenzo (to whom the dedication was changed after Giuliano's death). The Medici are blessed with both luck and strength of character, he asserts; "all things point to your greatness." With Machiavelli's little book to guide him, a new Medici leader could expel the foreigners and be received like a rightful prince, secure in his throne and welcomed with joy throughout Italy.[18]

It's the same old nostalgic vision, with predictable results. No great man on horseback would ride to Italy's rescue or unite her people. Nobody in the Medici family wanted anything to do with Machiavelli's unsolicited book on princedoms. And no one offered Machiavelli a job. So he went back to his place in the country, whiled away the days, and worked on another book—a companion piece to *The Prince* called the *Discourses on Livy*.

Republics

The *Discourses* is not a mirror for princes. It is a treatise on republican government, written as a commentary on Livy's *History of Rome*. It too is nostalgic, idealizing a golden age of the Roman republic when free men governed themselves. Instead of a brief for monarchy, it makes the case for democracy.

"There are and have been plenty of rulers but there are few who have been good and wise," Machiavelli writes. Since the earliest kings and tyrants, "one finds far more examples of unreliable behavior and of shifts of policy and attitude among them than among any populace." Therefore, the common opinion that democracies are undependable and unpatriotic is all wrong, he says. In fact, a populace in power is generally preferable to a single ruler, even a wise one, for "all men are alike, and if any type of person is better than the rest, it is the common man." Admittedly, men are not what they were in the glory days of Rome; they are not now as respectful or disciplined. But the worst are despots who cling to power, act like gods, and order everyone else around. Machiavelli hopes that "any young men who read what I write will be encouraged to reject the world they live in and will want to try to imitate the ancients" who believed in self-government.[19]

Disputing the benefits of one-man rule alleged by the Scholastics, Machiavelli argues that a community of persons is apt to be more prudent, be more logical, and show better judgment than a monarch. It is rare, he says, that a group of people will hear two speeches favoring different policies and not pick the right course of action. It is hard to convince a populace to promote a public official with a bad reputation or temper, although monarchs do it all the time. In other matters, a "populace makes fewer mistakes than a monarch, and the ones it makes are less significant and easier to put right." This is because "a populace that is licentious and disorderly needs only to be talked to by someone who is good, and he will find it easy to set it on the right path. A bad monarch will not listen to anyone, and the only way to correct him is to kill him." In a republic, people are free to develop their talents and enjoy the fruits of their labor; they are not only happier but more productive, more cooperative, and more invested in their community. As the Romans learned, government by the people better serves the common good than government by princes who care more for their own good.[20]

Some readers have struggled to reconcile Machiavelli's advice in *The Prince* and the *Discourses*, imagining the first as a textbook for dictators and the second a primer for populists. But Machiavelli supposed that leadership and organization, to be effective, depend on the situation. He held what management experts today call a "contingency theory." While he expressed a general preference for republics, he thought principalities are appropriate under certain circumstances. Princes are necessary to establish new states from scratch and to construct new political institutions in hopelessly corrupt states. In other situations, republics are better.[21]

You'll find a similar contingency idea applied to modern organizations by sociologist Tom Burns and psychologist G. M. Stalker. In *The Management of Innovation*, Burns and Stalker describe two types of organization they call "mechanistic" and "organic." Much like monarchies and principalities, mechanistic organizations have hierarchical chains of command, narrowly defined roles and responsibilities, and centralized decision-making. Authorities insist on loyalty to the enterprise and obedience to superiors as a condition of membership. Each member is told "what he has to attend to, and how, he is also told what he does not have to bother with, what is not his affair." Classic examples are government bureaucracies and mass-production assembly lines.[22]

In contrast, more like republics, organic organizations have fluid lines of command, broadly defined rights and responsibilities, and decentralized decision-making. Authority stems from competence and consensus. Members are held to professional standards; they use their own discretion and coordinate their own behavior to achieve common goals, without close supervision. Typical examples include research and health organizations composed of teams of doctors or scientists.

According to Burns and Stalker, there is no one best form of organization; it all depends on the situation. Mechanistic organizations are appropriate under stable conditions, where events can be foreseen and procedures can be engineered in advance. Organic organizations are more appropriate under changing conditions, where unforeseen problems require new procedures and adjustment to new circumstances.

This, in essence, is Machiavelli's approach in *The Prince* and the *Discourses*: Different governing systems are better for different conditions (although Machiavelli's systems and contingencies are not quite the same as Burns and Stalker's). "One can see," he writes in the *Discourses*, that "a republic should survive longer and should more frequently have fortune on its side, than a monarchy, for a republic can adapt itself more easily to changing circumstances because it can call on citizens of differing characters." However, in a very corrupt state, "if one had the opportunity to carry out reform or revolution, one would have to introduce a constitution that was more monarchical than democratic. For men who were so ill-behaved that they could not be kept in order by the laws would need to be kept in check by a more or less arbitrary authority"—that is, a prince. Machiavelli concludes it is not only difficult but cruel "to set up a monarchy where a republic is wanted, or a republic where a monarchy is required."[23]

A contingency approach is not all that novel. It goes back at least to Aristotle, who suggested that different people are suited to different kinds of rule. But it's not what Machiavelli's contemporaries were used to reading. A few years before he wrote *The Prince* and the *Discourses*, for example, another Florentine by the name of Aurelio Brandolini offered the Medici a mirror for princes titled *Republics and Kingdoms Compared*. It consists of a dialogue between a king, Mattias, and his son, Prince Janos. Mattias asks Janos, "Would you prefer to live in an excellent republic or an excellent kingdom?" Young Janos replies that if he were not a prince, he'd rather live in a republic "because everything is better governed by many than by one." *Everything?* Mattias asks, *Even heaven?* No, not heaven, Janos concedes. *Then how about an army? Or a ship?* Mattias asks. Again and again, Janos is forced to admit that one person is a better ruler than many. The conversation winds up defending monarchy no matter the circumstances and reaffirming the traditional virtues of a good king. Nothing so categorical can be found in Machiavelli's mirror for princes.[24]

While not as simplistic as prior books on kingship, Machiavelli's contingency approach may still seem dubious to readers today. Since the eighteenth century, citizens in nation after nation have rejected monarchy as an appropriate form of government in *any* situation. The trouble with contingency theories is that they require people to agree on a goal for comparing alternatives; this is often impractical in private organizations, more so in whole nations (where the very survival of an institution or regime may be a contested goal). Nonetheless, a presumed common goal for government is ultimately what ties *The Prince* and the *Discourses* together. For Machiavelli, monarchies and republics are alternative means to the same end, preservation of the state. He highlights this goal in closing the *Discourses*: Whether you are a prince or citizen of a republic, for the safety of the homeland "you should pay no attention to what is just or what is unjust, or to what is kind or cruel, or to what is praiseworthy or shameful. You should put every other consideration aside, and you should adopt wholeheartedly the policy most likely to save your homeland's life and preserve her liberty."[25]

Public and scholarly opinions of Machiavelli have varied over the centuries. Early reactions were hostile, focusing on the apparent amorality of *The Prince*. Critics charged Machiavelli with teaching cruelty, duplicity, and tyranny. They claimed he glorified thugs like Cesare Borgia, made a virtue of unprincipled opportunism, and undermined Christian values. They called *The Prince* a work of the devil. Despite all that, or else because of it, the book sold well. *The Prince* was first printed in 1532, five years after Machiavelli died. By 1541, seven editions had been published in Rome, Florence, and Venice. In England, Cardinal Reginald Pole bemoaned Machiavelli's corrupting influence: "This poison is spread through the courts of princes in this man's books which are circulating almost everywhere."[26]

Religious authorities led the attack on Machiavelli. In 1542 Portuguese bishop Jerónimo Osório published a mirror for Christian nobles to exorcise the "spirit and ghost of this wicked person."[27] Spanish, Flemish, and German Jesuits followed with a string of anti-Machiavellian mirrors for princes. In 1559 Machiavelli's works were all put on the Index of Prohibited Books by the Sacred Congregation of the Roman Inquisition. Repeated attacks, though, created ever more publicity for Machiavelli. By the late sixteenth century, people didn't have to actually read *The Prince* to know what it said, notes literature professor Victoria Kahn.[28] The evil "Machiavel" was part of the culture, a stock figure of sermons and popular entertainment—as in Shakespeare's *Henry VI, Part 3*, where a scheming prince boasts:

I can add colours to the chameleon;
Change shapes with Proteus for advantages;
And set the murdrous Machiavel to school.[29]

From the outset, Machiavelli had admirers as well as critics. In the 1530s, for example, Richard Morison—a publicist for Henry VIII—cited Machiavelli as a wise political analyst. In the 1550s French translators of *The Prince* and the *Discourses* praised Machiavelli's realistic depiction of statecraft. In 1584 English publisher John Wolfe portrayed Machiavelli as an honest reporter who showed readers what a bad prince looked like. Such positive opinions gained wider acceptance during the next century. In England, observes historian Felix Raab, Machiavelli became respectable in two phases—first when antiroyalist pamphleteers held his mirror of *The Prince* up to their own king, Charles I, to reveal the face of a tyrant and, second, when essay writers invoked the *Discourses* to call for republican government.[30]

The second, republican image of Machiavelli has secured his reputation among scholars to this day. Modern historians have traced the influence of Machiavelli's *Discourses* on seventeenth-century republicans like James Harrington, to eighteenth-century patriots like John Trenchard and Thomas Gordon, all the way to American revolutionaries like John Adams. Among serious students of government, Machiavelli is best remembered as a staunch defender of liberty, not the shifty place-seeker who granted monarchs a rightful place the world. It is ironic that the author of *The Prince* could have helped to shape, with his *Discourses*, a New World free of princes and mirrors to instruct them.[31]

Of course, the stereotype of the evil Machiavel remains embedded in popular culture and trade books on management. What exactly makes *The Prince* so fascinating?[32]

Inside Advice

One could find, in the library or the inbox of almost any Renaissance ruler, a mirror for princes. Powerful families like the Medici, no less than chief executives today, received any number of books telling them how to run their organizations and manage their people. The heyday of such advice books came just before Machiavelli wrote *The Prince*, according to Quentin Skinner, a leading historian of political thought. In 1468, for example, Giovanni Pontano penned a book on *The Prince* for King Ferdinand of Naples. In the 1470s Bartolomeo Sacchi wrote his version of *The Prince* for the duke of Mantua, and Francesco Patrizi dedicated *The Kingdom and the Education of the King* to the regal Pope Sixtus IV. In the 1480s Diomede Carafa presented King Ferdinand with yet more advice on *The Office of a Good Prince*.[33]

Then as now, most advice books for leaders just repackaged the conventional wisdom of the day and had a fleeting existence, states literature scholar Robert Adams: "Rulers rarely read them, and even more rarely [made] use of their precepts; the typical manual for rulers [seemed] to be chiefly of interest to other writers of manuals, and after a while only to students of manual writing."[34] Machiavelli's *Prince* is the exception. It is still in print five centuries after it was written. ("It's the most translated book from the Italian language, beating even Dante's 'Divine Comedy,'" adds Alessandro Campi, the curator of an exhibition in Rome celebrating the book's five-hundredth anniversary.[35]) The reasons for its dominance of the advice genre, however, are not perfectly obvious.

On the one hand, *The Prince* is a representative mirror for princes. It too repackages conventional wisdom. Allan Gilbert, a specialist in Renaissance literature, has dissected *The Prince* chapter by chapter, documenting similarities with earlier mirrors for princes. Machiavelli follows the old formula: People behave badly, he gripes; they're self-centered, they need a common goal and a leader to unite them. Machiavelli recycles the ancient exemplars of leadership: He tells the prince to imitate the actions of great men just as "Alexander the Great imitated Achilles, Caesar imitated Alexander, and Scipio imitated Cyrus."[36] Machiavelli pays homage to the classic texts: He copies Aristotle's *Politics*, Xenophon's *Education of Cyrus*, Isocrates's *To Nicocles*. Machiavelli covers the same syllabus of topics as neoclassical authors such as Aquinas and Giles of Rome.[37]

Even the cruelty endorsed in *The Prince* harkens back to earlier books of advice. From the beginning, mirrors for princes taught rulers that their duties included the punishment of wrongdoers, and punishments could be cruel indeed. Some writers shared specifics; Gerald of Wales instructed the prince to "inflict bodily pain" upon wrongdoers and "even cut off a bit of their flesh." Some writers proscribed particular offenses; Christine de Pizan urged her prince to "forbid on pain of severe punishment anyone swearing on or denying his Creator." Most writers remained vague; Walter of Milemete told his king simply "to punish the mistakes of transgressors."[38] Yet everyone knew the grisly details of criminal punishments. The whole point was to make them public to deter bad behavior, and from the Middle Ages to the Renaissance, cruelty was the norm. Public punishments included cutting off offenders' hands for theft, their tongues for blasphemy, ears and noses for other minor crimes. Executions involved hanging, burning, and dismemberment in ways that maximized suffering. Hangings were interrupted while the victims were still alive so their bodies could be cut into quarters and disemboweled. Burnings took place not only at the stake but inside cast-iron roasters shaped like a bull, which would bellow the victims' screams. Dismemberment used horses, racks, wheels, and other devices to tear people limb from limb. Psychologist Steven Pinker, who studies social violence, notes that medieval executioners and torturers were the state's foremost experts on anatomy and physiology, "using their knowledge to maximize agony, avoid nerve damage that might deaden the pain, and prolong consciousness for as long as possible before death."[39] Authorities sentenced men and women to slow, painful deaths for all sorts of "crimes" that are no longer punishable, such as heresy, witchcraft, and criticism of the government.

In this culture of violence, no one would have been shocked to read that a prince could use cruelty to keep subjects in line. Machiavelli (who suffered torture himself for alleged crimes against the rulers of Florence) just made explicit in his mirror for princes what others had long suggested. In fact, "few of the ideas expressed in *The Prince* are altogether novel," concludes Allan Gilbert; "most of them are to be found in medieval and renaissance works belonging to the type of books of advice to kings."[40]

On the other hand, *The Prince* pushed the genre in a new direction. To distinguish his book from all the rest, Machiavelli added advice that senior counselors often gave to rulers in private but rarely divulged in public mirrors for princes. This advice was familiar to Machiavelli from his days as a staffer in the diplomatic corps of Florence; and it would certify to prospective employers his credentials as a knowledgeable insider. The advice concerns what Machiavelli called, in his correspondence with Francesco Vettori, "the art of the state."[41]

Machiavelli would have made a lousy businessman, he confided to Vettori: "I do not know how to talk about either the silk or the wool trade, or profits or losses," he wrote, so "I have to talk about the state."[42] The state, he said, makes good behavior possible. Law and order, religion and justice, all the virtues prized in classic mirrors for princes presuppose a state. In a stable state, Machiavelli believed, a ruler should practice the traditional virtues and observe Christian ethics in making policy. But when a state is facing attack, takeover, collapse, any threat to its existence, then the normal virtues and ethics don't apply; every other reason for policymaking must be secondary to survival, to reason of state. This was common opinion within the ruling circles of Florence, explains Machiavelli's biographer, Maurizio Viroli. Machiavelli knew well, for instance, the maxim of Cosimo de' Medici, "the Father of his Country," that "states were not held with prayer books in hand."[43] Machiavelli knew the kind of arguments made by advisory board (*Pratiche*) members to Florentine leaders, for example, that in foreign affairs honesty is not always the best policy, that reasons of state trump the honoring of promises and treaties. He knew about the private memos circulating within the halls of power, which advocated state security measures such as a secret service of vigilant and well-paid spies. He knew Medici underbosses like

Francesco Guicciardini, who saw the need for force and fear in starting a new state—but who cautioned such views were not for publication. Machiavelli put this "inside" advice out for all the world to see.[44]

Reason of State

The Prince, in theorists' jargon, "endowed the state with a moral personality of its own." In other words, the state was not just an artificial person, as in the organic analogies of past mirrors for princes; it was a moral person with goals, rights, and interests that could outweigh the goals, rights, and interests of natural persons. (Related theories today extend goals, rights, and interests to *corporations* as people.) After *The Prince*, reason of state became a central concern of mirrors for princes. Even writers critical of Machiavelli accepted the reality of the concept while preaching a more Catholic or Puritan or otherwise ethical reason of state. Typical of these writers was Giovanni Botero.[45]

Botero was born in 1544 in the Italian principality of Piedmont. His family and early years are lost to history, but by the age of fifteen he was enrolled at the Jesuit college in Palermo, Sicily, where his uncle was a priest in the Society of Jesus. At sixteen he moved to the society's college in Rome and entered the Jesuit novitiate. He went on to teach philosophy and rhetoric at small Jesuit schools in Italy and France. Ordained a priest in 1572, Botero seemed ardent but temperamental and prone to political gaffes, limiting his career prospects. His religious superiors turned down his requests to preach the faith in protestant Germany or the missions of America, and they questioned his fitness for final vows. After two decades as a Jesuit, he was allowed, if not asked, to leave the order (although he stayed in touch and was eventually interred in the society's chapel at Turin).[46]

In the early 1580s Botero found a job with the archbishop of Milan, Charles Borromeo, who appointed him to a parish and then made him his personal secretary. Borromeo, the nephew of a Medici pope, Pius IV, represented the Church in dealings with the Catholic monarchs of Europe, and he introduced Botero to ecclesiastical and princely courts. Botero took the opportunity to present a sketchy mirror for princes (*On Kingly Wisdom*) to Duke Charles Emmanuel of Savoy. When the archbishop died in 1584, Botero went to work for the duke as an aide to his ambassador in France, a hotspot of religious warfare. He was subsequently hired to assist young Cardinal Federico Borromeo (Charles's cousin) in Rome, where Botero witnessed the high-level politics of four papal conclaves and the reorganization of the curia into departmental congregations of cardinals. (Botero was assigned to the Congregation of the Index.) In 1589 he published a more professional mirror for princes, reflecting his political experiences, titled *Reason of State*.

The book is addressed to princes of both Church and state. Botero dedicates the work to Wolf Dietrich von Raitenau, a relative of Charles Borromeo, who was prince of Salzburg as well as its archbishop. Botero tells Wolf Dietrich that in his travels through France and Italy, in all the courts of kings and princes, he has heard two things discussed repeatedly—one, the term "Reason of State," and, two, the opinions of Machiavelli about it. Botero commends Reason of State as a valid goal of princes, but he faults Machiavelli for teaching princes to ignore their consciences in its implementation. Botero aims to restore morality as a basis for Reason of State and true leadership.[47]

A "state is a stable rule over a people," Botero begins, "and Reason of State is the knowledge of the means by which such a dominion may be founded, preserved and extended." Botero skips over how states are founded, taking their legitimacy for granted. He focuses on how they can be preserved and enlarged.[48]

States decline and fall, he proposes, because of external enemies or fateful events, but more often from internal corruption—from the ambitions and licentiousness of rulers, from envy and rivalry among the nobles, from fickleness and passions of the people. As states mature, they grow richer and everyone is consumed by selfishness, "the root of all evil." Even in great states, "high purposes and honorable enterprises fall away and their place is taken by pride, arrogance, avarice among those in office, and insolence among the populace." Eventually, "clowns find more favour than captains, chatterers than soldiers, adulation than truth; wealth is held in honor above virtue, gifts above justice; simplicity gives way to deceit, goodness to malice, so that as the State grows the foundations of its strength are sapped." How, then, to revive belief in high purposes?[49]

The foundation of any state, Botero says, "is the obedience of the subjects to their prince, and this in turn is founded upon his outstanding excellence." To preserve a state against the forces of decline is an almost superhuman task, but it can be managed by a virtuous prince. People freely submit to rulers of exceptional wisdom and courage, Botero argues: Just "as the elements and the bodies formed from them obey unresistingly the movements of the heavenly spheres because of their exalted nature and in the heavens themselves the lesser bodies are ruled by the motion of the greater, so a people submits willingly to a ruler adorned by splendid talents." As evidence, Botero offers a list of exemplary leaders whose virtue and dedication to the common good inspired followers to preserve their rule; he cites Christian princes from Constantine to Charlemagne to Ferdinand the Catholic, plus no less than forty popes from Sylvester to Urban II to Nicholas V. (Botero includes pious but venal leaders such as Emperor Constans and Pope Nicholas III, implying that he associates the common good with religious conformity.)[50]

To Botero, these exemplars show that Machiavelli was wrong to think that leaders must ignore Christian morality for reason of state. Botero claims that princes, prelates, any leaders can be both virtuous and successful in preserving their dominions. The key to leadership is to practice those virtues that inspire love and, more importantly, admiration from followers. Love comes mainly from the practice of justice and generosity (liberality). In pursuit of these virtues, Botero tells the prince to reward merit and punish evil, to avoid flatterers and watch out for favorites. He says to hire trustworthy judges and administrators, not to sell jobs or give them away to family members. He advocates charity for the poor and afflicted, support of arts and commerce, aid to schools and universities, respect for scholars and clerics, although he warns the prince about raising taxes and wasting money—the typical advice you'd find in any mirror for princes.[51]

While a prince who is loved for his generosity and justice can *command* people, Botero suggests, a prince who is admired for his strength of character can *transform* them. Admiration comes from two special virtues, prudence and valor. These virtues are the "twin pillars" of effective government, he says: "Prudence is the eye of the ruler, valour is his arm; without the one he would be blind, without the other, powerless." (Machiavelli makes a similar point, instructing the prince to imitate both the fox and the lion.[52]) Prudence sharpens a leader's judgment. It requires knowledge of many things—moral philosophy and political science, human feelings and behavior, characteristics of the planets, winds, tides, rivers, lakes, animals, minerals, herbs, crops, any natural phenomena effecting the works of mankind. Knowledge of such things enables the prince to speak with authority, "to calm a nation, win round the multi-tude, or soothe their passions." The virtue of valor helps to fortify the prince's heart in overcoming obstacles (say, dissidents in the multitude who are not won round to the prince's thinking). Valor involves bold-ness and daring, a desire for honor and glory, and the will to emulate the deeds of great men—Alexander, Scipio, Hannibal, Caesar, and so on.[53]

The virtues of prudence and valor together create the chief charac-teristic of a perfect prince, what Botero calls "reputation." Reputation is the quality of greatness that is apparent to anyone. It distinguishes "the heroes and the personages who for loftiness of virtue and perfection have almost passed beyond the ordinary limits of human nature [and so] are honored and beatified." It evokes a feeling of "esteem, but with the addition of grandeur," a vision of wonder with faith in its reality, an outpouring of love overshadowed by fear—as if one were beholding God almighty. If men were angels, Botero posits, all a perfect prince would need is love to lead them. But since men are self-interested and hard to please, a prince needs fear to control them. The power of an awe-some reputation is that it elicits fear from people without incurring their hatred; and thus it enables the prince to transform recalcitrant individ-uals into willing subjects.[54]

Machiavelli said much the same, and Botero copies many recom-mendations from *The Prince*. In controlling the multitude, he writes, "some examples should be made, by punishing very severely those who have acted unjustly, because for one who is punished thousands are deterred."[55] As in *The Prince*, for reason of state, a ruler should not worry about appearing cruel. Machiavelli illustrated appropriate cruelty by pointing to Cesare Borgia's execution of a despotic boss of Cesena, whose body was discovered in the town square one morning, lying in two pieces beside a chopping block and a bloody knife.[56] Botero tops that story with the tale of King Cambyses of Assyria, who "found one of his judges at fault and ordered that he should be flayed alive and his skin used to cover the tribunal from which his son dispensed justice."[57] Botero portrays such cruelty as effective in restraining people who might challenge the prince's authority.

While punishments can deter common criminals, other methods are required to deal with organized resistance. "The hand, the rod, the curb and the halter may all be needed," depending on the situation, Botero says; "the great need here is for a fertile imagination, capable of thinking up expedients to inspire in the populace feelings in turn of pleasure, fear, suspicion, and hope, so they can be held in check and then reduced to obedience." Botero recommends the prohibition of popular assemblies, parties, factions, sects, and the elimination of suspected ringleaders before they can cause trouble. He recommends the use of eloquent spokesmen to charm audiences with patriotic myths like the fable of the human body and its members, told by Agrippa to pacify the people of Rome. He recommends more elaborate deceptions to divert the mind of the populace from domestic grievances: "Just as a doctor can relieve the disordered humours of the human body by diverting them elsewhere with cauterizing and blood letting, so a wise prince can placate an enraged people by leading it to war against an external enemy."[58] (Botero proposes a suitable enemy to attack: the Turks who hold former Catholic lands.)

To secure his reputation, a prince must project strength at every opportunity. He should hide his weaknesses and only show himself in public on state occasions, amid great ceremony. He should avoid effeminate activities, like playing music or writing poetry, and shun projects that carry risks of failure. Above all, he should not share power with anyone; "he must allow none to participate with him in what pertains to his greatness, majesty, and supremacy." The prince alone should make law, declare war, appoint officials, award honors, bestow pardons, issue currency, regulate trade, impose taxes, and make any other important decisions. If all else fails and the prince has to make concessions to his subjects, Botero says he can improve his reputation through face-saving devices, such as taking credit for popular programs that he can't forestall and benevolently granting rights that he's forced by fate to respect.[59]

To many readers, Botero's advice looks patently Machiavellian. *Reason of State* seems to justify the same tactics of fear, deception, and expediency you find in *The Prince*. How, then, could Botero claim to offer a moral alternative to Machiavelli? The answer is that he had a different end in view for the state: Machiavelli's goal for the state was the preservation of a secular principality (a bad reason of state). Botero's goal for the state was the old ideal of a Christian empire (a good reason of state); such a Christian goal unites people for a moral good and validates the means necessary for its attainment. Or so Botero tells his prince.[60]

"As we learn from Aristotle," Botero writes, "in the heroic age the rulers were also the custodians of whatever was held holy"—the ancients viewed religion as the basis of government. So today, Botero asserts, "a ruler must do all he can to introduce and foster religion and piety in his country, to the glory and service of the Divine Majesty." A religious state is not only a moral goal but a productive goal, with practical benefits for the prince and the nation. Religion is important for the tranquil and successful government of a state, Botero says, because "a people devoted to religion and piety is much more obedient than one without a guiding principle." Religion makes individuals good to others, generous toward the community, brave at war, eager to serve God and His minister, the prince.[61]

Of course, the prince should not encourage just any religions, but only one: "Of all religions none is more favorable to rulers than the Christian law, according to which not merely the bodies and possessions but even the souls and consciences of his people are subject to [the prince]." Christians are taught that all authority comes from God; "they are enjoined to obey wicked rulers as well as moderate ones, and to suffer all rather than disturb the peace." Botero raises the example of the early Christians, who suffered tyrants and tortures, sword and fire and wheel; yet for the sake of public peace they never "rebelled against the Empire, or turned against their own rulers," choosing instead "to pray daily for the well-being of the Roman Empire." Catholics of Botero's day, he maintains, could show the same allegiance to a Christian empire, if only a leader would unite them.[62]

Sadly, Botero points out, Catholics in Scotland, England, France, Flanders, Germany, and elsewhere are beset by enemies of the faith. Christendom is in disarray because "Luther and Calvin and the rest have strayed from the truth of the Gospels, sowing everywhere the seeds of heresy, revolution and the overthrow of kingdoms." Protestant firebrands seduce the people, inciting them to indulge their lusts and ambitions, defame Catholics and clergy, loot churches and ecclesiastical property, battle their betters and civil authorities—all "under the pretext of freedom of conscience, or of speech or action or life," Botero says. To preserve the state, therefore, the prince must root out heresy and restore unity to the Catholic religion. He should support religious teachers and missionaries like the Jesuits who indoctrinate youth, reform heretics, and convert unbelievers throughout Europe and its colonies. The prince should deprive Protestants of their preachers, books, and papers; he should "burn the works of Calvin and all such disseminators of schism and impiety."

He should employ secret agents and spies to disrupt the ability of radicals to "league together." Botero recommends the same means used by Charlemagne "to hold down the people of Westphalia who, although they had received baptism, lived most dissolutely and were strongly suspected of being infidels." Charlemagne, Botero recounts, instituted a special secret judgeship, which sent out spies into the community to elicit reports of any lapses in piety; these judges "were given authority to put to death without trial, by their own decision, any man whom they found to be a perjuror or a bad Christian." Botero praises this "wonderfully effective" magistry, which "was carried out with so much secrecy and severity that no one dared to confide even in his friends, and there seemed to be no defence against it except to lead a good life."[63]

Political historian Harro Höpfl concludes that Botero's religiosity "only thinly disguised a readiness to set aside moral and legal constraints which was as icy as Machiavelli's."[64] Like Machiavelli, Botero put princes' claims for reason of state above peoples' claims to human rights. Even in the sixteenth century, this was controversial. (Botero testified, for example, that "there is no scarcity of men, as impious as they are foolish, who counsel princes that heresies have nothing to do with politics" and should be tolerated.[65]) But, again like Machiavelli, Botero only made public what had long been said in the private suites of prelates and princes. And the candid revelations of *Reason of State* made it a political best-seller. Robert Bireley, a student of counter-Reformation literature, counts ten Italian editions, six Spanish translations, and others in French and Latin, all published during Botero's lifetime. The book circulated around the imperial courts of Madrid, Munich, Graz, and Rome. Botero himself retired to his local court of Savoy, where he spent sixteen years tutoring the children of Duke Charles Emmanuel, while *Reason of State* found followers across the Old and New Worlds.[66]

Empires

Botero influenced Spanish Jesuits, English Puritans, French nationalists, and American colonists. The appeal of reason of state to such a diverse lot is evidence of its elasticity. It could mean and sanction almost anything, giving rulers the moral authority to do what they deemed necessary while forswearing Machiavellian motives and dirty tricks. To Jesuit casuists like Pedro de Ribadeneira and Juan de Mariana, reason of state entailed a greater Spanish empire whose prince could practice guile and secrecy for the common good. To Puritan divines like John Saltmarsh, it called forth a community of saints whose leaders were allowed to deceive and otherwise break rules if good could come of it. To French monarchists like Cardinal Richelieu, it implied a sacred state whose king had the absolute, divine right to crush any resistance for the general welfare as he saw it.[67]

Richelieu, prime minister of France under Louis XIII, did more to advance his ideas than any of them. He summed up the implications of reason of state in a mirror for princes addressed to his king "for use after my death for policy-making and the management of your realm." It is titled *The Political Testament or Maxims of State of Cardinal Richelieu*. It urges the king to embrace Richelieu's own view of the general welfare and reason of state—namely, "to ruin the Huguenot [Protestant] Party, to abase the pride of the nobles [who defied the crown], to bring all your subjects back to their duty, and to restore your reputation among foreign nations to the station it ought to occupy." Toward these ends, Richelieu's *Testament* is filled with tips for tyrants.[68]

The prince must have a vision, a goal in mind, and pursue it doggedly, not "proceed in the aimless way customary with most men," Richelieu says. A prince should never let himself be deflected from his goal by "distracting interests, pity and compassion, favoritism and importunities of all sorts." He should be decisive in dealing with great nobles of the realm—else "knowing the hesitancy of their prince to play the part of master, they in turn get bored with playing the part of subject." He should not permit anyone to question his will. "Obedience is the most important part of the subjection so necessary to the well-being of states," Richelieu asserts; "whatever else one may do in governing states, one must be inflexible in punishing those who fail to obey."[69]

Richelieu argues that "it is absolutely necessary for a prince to be severe in order to avoid misdeeds which might be attempted in the hope of obtaining clemency." Severity "makes a good impression on the people." Clemency, on the other hand, "is more dangerous than cruelty even, since leniency gives rise to the ultimately necessary exercise of a degree of cruelty which could have been avoided by the employment of an efficacious punishment at an earlier time." The prince needs to anticipate threats and stop disorders before they occur; "with enemies of the state, as with diseases, it is better to advance to the attack than to wait and drive them out after they have invaded." This means that ordinary processes of justice—say, "authenticated proof" of guilt—may be suspended in cases which affect the state. "In such instances what appears to be circumstantial conjecture must at times be held sufficiently convincing, since plots and conspiracies aimed at the public welfare are ordinarily conducted with such cunning and secrecy that there is never any persuasive evidence of them until they strike, at which time they are beyond prevention." Richelieu suggests that crimes against the state can be prevented with "such innocuous measures as the banishment or imprisonment of suspected persons." A peevish populace may raise issues of fairness; but "at the very worst, the abuses which can be committed will injure only private individuals, which really has little bearing on the matter and should not be taken too seriously, since their interests are hardly comparable to those of the state."[70]

Like Machiavelli and Botero, Richelieu counsels the prince to inspire fear but not hate: "Of all the forces capable of producing results in public affairs, fear, if based on both esteem and reverence, is the most effective, since it can drive everyone to do his duty." Richelieu says, "both foreigners and subjects take the same view of redoubtable power and both refrain from offending a prince whom they recognize as being able to hurt them if he so wishes." The prince's ability to control people though fear and awe is enhanced by denying them education and economic security.[71]

Richelieu claims that "a knowledge of letters . . . should not be indiscriminately taught to everyone. A body which had eyes all over it would be monstrous, and in like fashion so would a state if all its subjects were learned; one would find little obedience and an excess of pride and presumption." Learning would divert the lower ranks of people from their proper jobs, he goes on: "It would ruin agriculture, the true nourishment of the people, and in time would dry up the source of the soldiery, whose ranks flow more from the crudities of ignorance than from the refinements of knowledge. It would, indeed, fill France with quibblers more suited to the ruination of good families and the upsetting of public order than to doing any good for the country. If learning were profaned by extending it to all kinds of people one would see far more men capable of raising doubts than of resolving them, and many would be better able to oppose the truth than to defend it." (Learning is a privilege best reserved for churchmen, Richelieu feels, "since so many of its truths bear a natural relationship to the sacred mysteries which divine wisdom has entrusted to the care of the ecclesiastical order.")[72]

Even better for managing the masses, a lack of education keeps people needy. "All students of politics agree that when the common people are too well off it is impossible to keep them peaceable," Richelieu says. "If not preoccupied with the search for the necessities of existence, [subjects] find it difficult to remain within the limits imposed by both common sense and the law." So, for example, "it would not be sound to relieve them of all taxation and similar charges, since in such a case they would lose the mark of their subjection and consequently the awareness of their situation. Thus being free from paying tribute, they would consider themselves exempted from obedience. One should compare them with mules, which being accustomed to work, suffer more when long idle than when kept busy."[73]

Richelieu has related tips for maintaining secrecy and silencing women. Secrecy is "so necessary to the success of affairs as to dwarf all other attributes," he says. Rulers and their administrators should make plans in secret and take people by surprise: Opponents can't conspire to block government policies they don't see coming. To Richelieu, "it follows that women, by nature indolent and unable to keep secrets, are little suited to government, particularly if one also considers that they are subject to their emotions and consequently little susceptible to reason and justice, attributes which should exclude them from all public office." The ultimate judge of reason and justice—the Lord's anointed head of state—was of course the king.[74]

In the name of King Louis, Richelieu applied the teachings of his *Political Testament*, pursuing his objectives for the state, subjecting the Huguenots, nobles, and French people to the will of his prince. He acted ruthlessly on the belief that higher ends sanctified the means to attain them, that for reason of state "one may employ any means against one's enemies" (which could be nearly anyone).[75] Despite the cardinal's far-reaching power, however, he was after all only a courtier—always "suspended between hope and fear," in the words of one contemporary critic.[76] Richelieu himself never mastered the trick of arousing fear but not hate; the public and, in the end, even the king despised him. When he died in 1642 he left a personal estate of 20,000,000 livres—one of the richest in the history of France—and a country teetering on the edge of bankruptcy. The French monarchy and others like it eventually came crashing down, although not before their agents introduced reason of state to a New World.[77]

Mirrors for princes taught that reason of state called for overseas empires and entrepreneurial leaders to build them: In theory, foreign trade and colonies enhanced the reputation of the prince and the survival of his kingdom. In practice, they also enhanced the profits of stockholders, such as Cardinal Richelieu. Richelieu took the lead in colonizing New France. In 1625, in his first year as prime minister, he authorized Samuel de Champlain to "bring into subjection, submission and obedience, all the peoples of the said country."[78] The next year, Richelieu added to his own titles the job of "grandmaster, chief, and general superintendent of the Navigation and Commerce of France," overseeing transatlantic trade.[79] The following year, he created a joint stock company, known as the Company of the Hundred Associates, to expand New France, govern the colony, and control the fur trade. Richelieu, who ran the company with a board of twelve directors, conveyed the usual vision of a colony dedicated to God, country, and the common good of its members. He also ensured that, as historian David Hackett Fischer observes, "on the list of the hundred stockholders dated January 14, 1628, Richelieu appeared as number 1."[80]

Richelieu was one among many competitors for the Atlantic trade. Other European leaders were establishing their own colonies in the Americas, stressing the Christianizing mission of these ventures in accord with Botero's *Reason of State*. A Christian reason of state, Botero preached, gave glory to God plus greatness to the nation and prosperity to its people; princes who made Christianity their goal in colonizing the earth received wealthy empires to rule in return. "Colonies with their mother out of which they issued make, as it were, but one body," Botero wrote, "by which means the country grows to be more populous and rich."[81]

Botero's ideas were appropriated by British publicists at the forefront of colonization, notes Atlantic historian Andrew Fitzmaurice. Walter Raleigh, who held the patent from Queen Elizabeth I to colonize America and sent the first English settlers to Roanoke Island, and Robert Johnson, an officer of the Virginia and Bermuda companies, incorporated Botero's prosperity theology into their own promotional tracts. Raleigh and Johnson were careful to stress both the Christian goals of their enterprise and the wealth that would be returned to support-ers (as in modern social-purpose-washing). Whether colonial promot-ers sincerely believed in the godliness of their goals or not is beside the point. Either way, the potential for abuse is clear. Contrary to Botero's teaching that better goals make better policy, it is not the specific goal that's problematic in states (or corporations); it's the unchecked pursuit of any official goal that fuels coercive practices.[82]

Botero's followers sometimes glimpsed the terrible costs of coloniza-tion to Native Americans. Robert Johnson condemned the terror spread by the Spanish conquistadors, for example. He pledged, in colonizing Virginia, to enlarge British dominions "not by stormes of raging cruelties (as West India was converted) with rapiers point and musket shot, mur-dering so many millions of naked Indians, as their stories doe relate, but by faire and loving meanes, suiting to our English natures, like [God's] soft and gentle voice." But no aversion to cruelty, no promise of fairness, no twinge of conscience trumped reason of state. Holy ends justified Machiavellian means—in New Spain, New France, New England, all along the Atlantic—just as they had in in the kingdoms of old Europe.[83]

NINE
Puritan Mirrors

The Indians are infamous, especially for three scandalous qualities: They are lazy drones and love idleness exceedingly! They are also most impudent liars and will invent reports and stories at a strange and monstrous rate; and they are out of measure indulgent unto their children—there is no family government among them. But O how much do our people Indianize in every one of those abominable things! We must repent of these our miscarriages or else our God will take up that resolution concerning us: "I will even forsake them, saith the Lord" [Jer. 23.33]. . . . Let there be a public spirit in us all for the good of the whole—the rarity and mortality whereof among us, New England bewails among the greatest of its calamities.

Cotton Mather, *The Way to Prosperity*

The Puritans were English Protestants on an errand for God—or so their leaders told them. They came to New England, said John Winthrop, the first governor of the Massachusetts Bay Colony, to build a holy "city upon a hill," a model Christian community where "the rich and mighty should not eat up the poor, nor the poor and despised rise up against their superiors and shake off their yoke," but where everyone "might be all knit more nearly together in the bond of brotherly affection . . . for the glory of his creator and the common good of the creature, man." If they stayed true to this vision, Winthrop promised the colonists, God would bless their enterprise and reward them with prosperity. If they turned away from God and one another to seek selfish ends, the Lord would withdraw His blessing and they would perish in shame.[1]

The Puritans who colonized New England brought with them a set of beliefs that had been percolating through old England for three-quarters of a century. Not all Puritans held the same beliefs, but they shared a cause—a zeal for moral purity—that was recognizable and often irritating to their neighbors. In 1623 a Cambridge University don named Joseph Mead identified three kinds of Puritans: those who wished to purify their own lives, those who wished to purify the Anglican Church, and those who wished to purify the English nation. Many Puritans, like John Winthrop, yearned for all three.[2]

Puritans looked within themselves and saw sinfulness. They suffered guilt over the smallest pleasures of life. Winthrop, the lord of an English country manor, for example, worried that he dined too richly, relaxed too frequently, loved his wife too passionately, and otherwise sorely disappointed his God. Puritans believed they were children of Adam and so bore the stain of original sin. They were told from the pulpit that "every natural man and woman is born full of all sin, as full as a toad is of poison, as full as ever his skin can hold; mind, will, eyes, mouth, every limb of his body, and every piece of his soul is full of sin."[3] Fear and shame, government and religion, may restrain man's sinfulness, but inside "he hath no more good in him (whatever he thinks) than a dead carrion hath."[4] You may appear to all the world like a decent Christian, said Puritan minister Thomas Shepard, but no matter how white your sepulchre is painted you are full of rottenness, of sin, in your heart: "Guilty thou art therefore of heart whoredom, heart sodomy, heart blasphemy, heart drunkenness, heart buggery, heart oppression, heart idolatry; . . . These sins of thine heart are all ready armed to fight against God at the watchword or alarm of any temptation."[5]

Puritans looked outside themselves at the Church of England and saw corruption. They deplored the vestiges of Catholicism left over from the reformation of Henry VIII—the fancy liturgical vestments, daily celebrations of supposed saints, popish rites of baptism, confirmation, and communion. They questioned the scriptural basis for the ecclesiastical bureaucracy—all the bishops, archbishops, and petty office holders who lived off church revenues. They found fault with the clergy hired on the cheap to serve in parishes—the ordained "Shoemakers, Barbers, Tailers, even waterbearers, shepheards, and horse keepers." Puritans kept a list of unfit ministers, warning Parliament of "dumme doggs" such as "Mr Levit, parson of Leden Roding, a notorious swearer, a dicer, a carder, a hawker and hunter, a verie careles person, he had a childe by a maid"; "James Allen, vicar of Shopland, some time a serving man, unable to preach, for he cannot render an accompt of his faith, neither in Latine nor English, yet made a minster"; "Mr Phippe, vicar of Barling, Sometime a sadler by occupation, convicted of whoredome, who kept a whore long time in his house, a man far unable to preach." The list goes on.[6]

Puritans looked across England and saw a country awash in drunks, fornicators, cheats, vagrants, and backsliders. Go by the alehouses, they cried, "on the Sabboth dayes, there is as well solde all kinde of looseness as victuals. Goe to Greenes, there is myrth that would wound a Christian mans heart with heauinesse. Go to Fayres, there is a shew and trafficke, as well of all lewdnesse, as of wares."[7] The popular Puritan preacher Henry "Silver-Tongued" Smith tallied just a few of the sins of Elizabethan England:

Item—for lending to usury.
Item—for racking of rents.
Item—for deceiving thy brethren.
Item—for falsehood in wares.
Item—for starching thy ruffs.
Item—for curling thy hair.
Item—for painting thy face.
Item—for selling of benefices.
Item—for starving of souls.
Item—for playing at cards.
Item—for sleeping in the church.
Item—for profaning the Sabbath Day.[8]

Smith pictured all the places reserved in hell for greedy lawyers, covetous judges, gouging landlords, slothful bishops, lusty youths, wanton dames, thieves and robbers who filled the kingdom. "Woe, woe, woe," he lamented, "that ever we were born."[9]

To the Puritan mind, the cause of societal disorder—the root of all evil—was individuals' selfishness. The solution was a shared goal, "the common good," and a leader to uphold it. William Perkins, a Cambridge theologian and Puritan founding father, made the case with the old analogy of human and social bodies. "In mans body," he wrote, "there be sundry parts and members, and every one hath his severall use and office, which it performeth not for it selfe, but for the good of the whole bodie." The office of the eye is to see, the ear to hear, the foot to walk, and so on, all for the body's sake. Similarly, Perkins said, social groups—families, churches, nations, and the like—are bodies, and the members in each of them have an office, a calling, that they must fulfill not for their own advancement but for the common good. As in natural bodies, members of a social body are able to cooperate because there is a hierarchy of authority among them, Perkins preached. "God hath appointed, that in every society one person should bee above or under another; not making all equall, as though the bodie should bee all head and nothing else." So, for example, the calling of a magistrate is to govern his subjects, the calling of a minister is to teach his people, the calling of a master is to manage his servants—and the calling of subjects, people, and servants is to do as they're told.[10]

Because members' duties in a social body and their rank in the hierarchy are ultimately given by God, it is against God's will, it is sinful and worthy of damnation, to neglect one's calling or overstep its boundaries. Perkins's organic metaphor left no room for slackers; his vision of a purer England would not permit rouges and vagabonds to wander the country begging and stealing, monks and friars to sit around expecting farmers to feed them, dreamers and idlers to waste their days gambling and drinking. Perkins had no use for social climbers who imagined that others' callings were preferable to their own; from these "come treacheries, treasons, and seditions, when men, not content with their own estate and honors, seeke higher places." Perkins's ideal "church and commonwealth is when every person keepes himselfe to his owne calling."[11]

Now, it is the special calling of princes and governors to bring this ideal world into being. Puritans complained that England wouldn't be sinking in corruption if rulers would do their jobs and stop winking at sin. Puritan preachers denounced "timorous and flexible" rulers, "lukewarme neuter-passive magistrates," "scarecrow constables, and mealemouthed under officers," urging them to get tough and purge the land of vice.[12] In Puritan teachings, kings and their deputies were installed by God not just to enforce His laws but to make their own laws and punishments for the commonweal. "God hath given these gods upon earth, a power," Perkins claimed, "to make these lawes, and annexe these punishments" so that "they may in many cases (if the common good so require) inflict even death itselfe." Of course a ruler should show some mercy—say, by sparing the life of a child who steals a bit of meat to relieve his hunger. But, as usual, the ruler should choose a punishment of sufficient severity "to reforme the party from this sinne" and "to terrifie others."[13]

Puritans like Perkins tried to distance themselves from Machiavelli and from Catholic casuists who excused official cruelty for reason of state. But some scholars see little difference between them. Machiavelli, Botero, and Perkins all shared a belief that "the true goodness of actions depends principally upon the goal toward which they are directed," notes historian George Mosse. English Puritans merely substituted, for reason of state, the goal "reason of faith." They offered a rationale for almost anything that pious princes and other "gods upon earth" judged necessary for the common good. And they transplanted these ideas to New England, along with the ancient clichés of mirrors for princes.[14]

The Good Ruler

Most Puritans preferred to reform their church and their country from within. Some "separatists" chose instead to leave the Anglican Church, hoping to purify at least themselves and their neighbors. But John Winthrop and a church remnant took the extreme step of leaving England, to plant a purer colony of that "sinfull lande" in the New World.[15]

Winthrop led a fleet of eleven ships and some seven hundred colonists across the Atlantic, arriving in New England on June 12, 1630. Their colony was governed as a commercial corporation, the Massachusetts Bay Company, run by a governor, a deputy governor, and a board of directors or assistants. Elected by stockholders or "freemen," the officers and directors of the Massachusetts Bay Company were expected to meet regularly in order to make rules "for the good and welfare of the said Company, and for the government and ordering of the said lands and Plantation, and the people inhabiting and to inhabit the same."[16] It was customary for such company meetings to take place in London, where groups like the Virginia and East India companies were headquartered. But before the colonists left for Massachusetts Bay, company leaders decided that future meetings would be held in New England—out of sight of the king's ministers and bishops—and Winthrop was elected governor of the colony. Once in America, Winthrop's word was law, and he was reelected year after year by the founding freemen of Massachusetts.[17]

As eligible voters expanded from the first company shareholders to include church members and eventually most male residents of the colony, the annual election day was the closest thing there was to a holiday for New England Puritans (who shunned popish feast days like Christmas and Easter). Each spring, villagers would gather to install their governor and assistants in a celebration of community. This was an exercise in building unity, if not exactly democracy. From the outset, the role of citizens was chiefly to ratify a self-selected slate of candidates. And election day—taken up with pomp and ceremony—looked more like the old-time acclamation of a tribal prince than a modern democratic process. Historians vouch for the atmospheric depiction of election day in Nathaniel Hawthorne's novel *The Scarlet Letter*, where the story's protagonist, Hester Prynne, tells her young daughter to "look about thee, and see how cheery is everybody's face to-day. The children have come from their schools, and the grown people from their workshops and their fields, on purpose to be happy. For, to-day, a new man is beginning to rule over them; and so—as has been the custom of mankind ever since a nation was first gathered—they make merry and rejoice; as if a good and golden year were at length to pass over the poor old world!"[18] The centerpiece of each election day was a sermon by a distinguished preacher who would instruct the rulers on their social responsibilities and the populace on their communal goal. These yearly election sermons carried on the timeworn tradition of mirrors for princes.[19]

Elections sermons were preached in Massachusetts from 1634 into the late nineteenth century. Many got preserved in one form or another. They were copied down by listeners and shared with neighbors. They were printed in pamphlets and distributed to churches. They were expanded by their authors and published as books of advice on governance. Today you can read them online and compare the language from one generation to the next. Pre-Revolutionary sermons reflect more clearly the rhetoric of mirrors for princes. The most memorable of these, according to A. W. Plumstead, a specialist in early American literature, sound like "New World versions" of *The Prince*.[20]

The oldest surviving example is an election sermon preached in 1638 by Thomas Shepard, then pastor of the First Church in Newtown (Cambridge) and a close friend of John Winthrop. Winthrop's journal alludes to Shepard's reputation as a fearsome orator: After hearing one of his sermons, a chronic sinner was so "wounded in conscience" he "drowned himself in a little pit where was not above two feet water."[21] An open sin which had disturbed the peace of the colony was a rise of willfulness among the members, and Shepard saw fit to remind those going their individual ways that they were called to build a *united* city upon a hill. His election sermon laments the perversity of human beings. Shepard likens the sins of men to a "raging Sea, which would overwhelm all if they have not bankes."[22] The sea banks symbolize moral laws and magistrates that channel the "fickle minds of a heady multitude" toward a common good.[23] Foolhardy people want to break free of restraints, to enjoy more liberty, to govern themselves, but sinners, Shepard teaches, cannot be trusted to choose their own laws or rulers.

The topic of Shepard's sermon—"Then sayd all the trees to the Bramble raine over us"—refers to a story in the Old Testament book of Judges. A prophet by the name of Jotham told the Israelites this parable about selecting rulers: One day the trees went in search of a king to rule over them. They first asked the wise olive tree to be their king, but the olive would not leave his job of providing oil to light all the houses. They next asked the bountiful fig tree to be their king, but the fig would not leave his job of bearing fruit to feed everyone. They then asked the sacred vine to be their king, but the vine would not leave his job of producing wine to nourish their spirit. Finally they asked the bramble—a low and thorny scrub—to be their king, and the bramble accepted, demanding that all trees stoop to serve him or suffer his wrath. The trees, Shepard says, resemble men in a commonwealth. They grow difficult to govern, so they drive away wise leaders (like the olive tree), rich leaders (like the fig tree), and holy leaders (like the grape vine). If they don't mend their ways and cheerfully submit to their betters, they will get thorny leaders (like the bramble).[24]

As in prior mirrors for princes, election sermons address both leaders and followers. Shepard tells the people of New England to beware of shopping for governors. He argues, when all men have a hand in choosing their ruler, they are apt to flit from good to bad: "The multitude are exceedingly apt to be led by colours like birds by glasses & larkes by lures"; they are seduced by ambitious politicians who stir up discontent and divide the people into factions; they are deceived by religious "innovators" who preach freedom of conscience and feign concern for the public good. No doubt Shepard had in mind recent events in Massachusetts where a brash upstart, Sir Henry Vane, had replaced Winthrop as governor and allowed an outspoken woman, Anne Hutchinson, to challenge the teaching authority of Bay Colony ministers. (Shepard had denounced Hutchinson as a heretic; Winthrop saw that she was expelled from the colony and Vane from the governor's chair). Through God's providence, Winthrop became governor again; now, Shepard suggests, citizens should be thankful for a ruler with the virtues of an olive tree and grape vine, instead of the snares of a bramble.[25]

For rulers, the lesson of the sermon is that governors, like kings of old, should be wise, selfless, pious, and so on. They should strive for eminence to encourage their people's submission. But their authority comes from God, not from man; their duty is to uphold God's law, not pander to popular opinion. In Shepard's view, rulers must not shrink from severity in policing and punishing sin. If men and women will not freely follow the laws of God and his earthly deputies, they must be compelled by whips and chains, as with the backsliders of ancient Israel. Should there be any confusion about what God expects, rulers can consult prophets like Jotham and ministers like Thomas Shepard.[26]

Backsliding was a recurrent theme of New England election sermons. It found expression in the jeremiad, recognized by scholars as the Puritans' distinctive contribution to American literature. The term comes from the biblical book of Jeremiah, another prophet, who lamented the loss of faith and virtue among God's chosen people. Laments of this type feature prominently in the election sermons of John Higginson (1663), William Stoughton (1668), Samuel Danforth (1670), Urian Oakes (1673), Samuel Willard (1682), William Adams (1685), Cotton Mather (1696), Nicholas Noyes (1698), and others.[27]

In *The Cause of God and His People in New-England*, Salem pastor John Higginson scolds the colonists for losing sight of their common goal, their divine mission in America. He faults them for seeking worldly gain and forsaking religious purity. He reminds them that "New England is originally a plantation of Religion, not a plantation of Trade. Let merchants and such as are increasing Cent per Cent remember this." Let everyone remember that "when the Lord stirred up the spirits of so many of his people to come over into this wilderness, it was not for worldly wealth, or a better livelyhood here." Rather, it was to escape profane rituals of religion. But now a lax generation foolishly tolerates all manner of religion, Higginson complains. "A toleration of all religions," he warns, becomes "a toleration of any false religion." And this is "a heinous back-sliding which the Lords jealousy will not bear."[28]

In *New England's True Interest; Not to Lie*, Dorchester preacher William Stoughton compares the colonists to the chosen people of Israel who embraced pagan idols and turned their backs on God after being delivered from bondage. He tells New Englanders that God expected better things from them:

> not Worldliness, and an insatiable desire after perishing things; not Whoredomes and Fornications; not Revellings and Drunkenness; not Oaths & false Swearings; not Exactions and Oppressions; not Slanderings and Backbitings; not Rudeness and Incivility, . . . not Contentions and Disorders; not an Itching after new things and wayes; not a rigid Pharisaical Spirit; not a contempt of Superiours, not Unthankfulness and disrespect to Instruments of choice Service; not a growing weary of Government, and a drawing loose in the Yoke of God.

Stoughton charges that New Englanders have lost all resemblance to their Christian forebears: They have sunk so low, they're "Sermon proof and Ordinance-proof"; they've come to loathe the word of God and "despise holy things." Stoughton, however, would one day hold them to account; a quarter-century after giving this election sermon, he became God's instrument of choice—the chief justice in the Salem witch trials. (Stoughton's court put twenty persons to death for witchcraft in 1692.)[29]

The appearance of witches at Salem, among other afflictions, was God's punishment for New England's moral decline, according to leading Puritan ministers. A vocal representative of these ministers was Cotton Mather, pastor at Boston's North Church, who delivered no less than three election sermons (1690, 1696, and 1700). In *Things for a Distressed People to Think Upon*, Mather begins his jeremiad with the nostalgic story of New England's golden age when the Puritans embarked on their errand into the wilderness. The first planters, he says, were "Generous, Notable, Brave Spirited men": As in a biblical epic, "New-England once abounded with Heroes worthy to have their Lives written, as Copies for future Ages." But, Mather mourns, "*These are ancient things!*" The first officers of the plantation were imbued with a public spirit: Their "fervent Inclination to Do Good, joined with an Incomparable Ability to do it, once ran through New England." But, alas, "*These are Ancient Things!*" The first citizens of the colony were paragons of virtue: A New England man was "one whose word is as good as his Bond." But, again, "*These are Ancient Things!*"[30]

Now, two generations later, Mather says, the great men, all the heroes, are gone. "We grow Little every way; Little in our Civil Matters, Little in our Military Matters, Little in our Ecclesiastical Matters; we dwindle away to Nothing" in all deeds but sin. In the most renowned families of New England, the grandchildren of God's chosen people have become "Children of the Devil." Almost every house in New England is a scene of horrid sins, bloody crimes, scarlet abominations, Mather claims. "There is not one of all the Ten Commandments, in the Law, which our God has given us, but people are notoriously violating of it, from one end of the Land unto the other." This land, he says, was initially defiled by the Natives; instead of Christianizing them, New Englanders have become just like them, adopting "the Indian Vices of Lying, and Idleness, and Sorcery, and a notorious want of all Family Discipline." Other vices are all too evident. Every day, one can see drinking and swearing in public, hating and vexing of neighbors, unchastity and injustice throughout society, insolence and discontent from top to bottom. God's displeasure is evident as well. His wrath has poured down on New England in a long train of disasters—crop failures and famines, epidemics of disease and death, fires and devastation of cities, shipwrecks and pirates at sea, wars and attacks by savage Natives, loss of the colony's charter and right to self-government, now the dreadful prospect of Irish and Catholic settlers in New England, and the evil magic and demonic possessions darkening the country. As in medieval mirrors for princes, Mather portrays such calamities as the voice of God, calling people to repent and refocus their lives on the common good.[31]

The cause of New England's distress is clear to Cotton Mather; it is "the Selfishness which depraves the most in all Societies." His solution is for individuals to unite as one body, recognize they share a purpose beyond themselves, and cleanse the land of vice. If people cannot agree on all that is necessary, at least they can agree on first steps toward reform: They can, for example, shut down the drinking houses, revive the practice of prayer, strengthen the authority of families, and restore respect for public officials. As God's watchmen, clergymen play a lead role in reforming society. They can bring the word of God to the most remote communities and, while visiting their flocks, monitor the morals of persons in every quarter. They can then report, with voices raised like trumpets, anything they find offensive to the Lord. (Not even Machiavelli goes so far in urging the use of spies and informants—although this is a common tip for tyrants in mirrors for princes, from Aristotle's *Politics* to Botero's *Reason of State*).[32]

As in ages past, the inquisitors envisioned by Cotton Mather depend on help from civil authorities to reform the populace. Sinful New Englanders have shown they won't return to God on their own. They need pious rulers—governors, constables, grand-jurymen, officials at every level—to enforce God's law. Impudent citizens gossip about whether this leader or that one is true to the interest of the country, Mather observes. He explains, in reply, who is *really* true to the interest of the country: "Those men, that will do all they can, for the Reformation of the Country, from Ignorance, from Idleness, from Dishonesty, from Uncleanness, from all Profaneness, and Paganism, and from Drunkenness, and all the Execrable Incentives thereunto; THAT, That is the man! Those men are *True to the Interest of the Country*."[33]

Cotton Mather likens the good ruler to a guardian angel who guides people to God and away from evil. He allows that these rulers are few and hard to find. To cultivate good leaders, Mather recommends moral education of "Learned and Pious Young men, from a well-governed Colledge" (such as his alma mater Harvard—even though, he gripes, graduates tend to flee public service for more lucrative jobs as fast as they can). To improve ordinary leaders, Mather supports voluntary codes of ethics. Counselors, justices, constables, clerks, all the officers of New England must take an oath to discharge their duties faithfully, with justice and impartiality. They should be taught what their oaths mean, given copies and reminders so that they "Read and Think, what they are Sworn to Do." Finally, Mather concludes, New Englanders should look to heaven and *pray* that "God will send us a Governour, who will cast a Favourable, and a Fatherly Aspect, upon all that is valuable to us; a Governour, who shall have the brave Motto of the Emperour Hadrian Engraved upon his Heart, *Not for my self, but for my People*."[34]

These old refrains from mirrors for princes were echoed by other election day preachers. Cotton Mather's father, Increase Mather, the senior minister at Boston's North Church and president of Harvard College, gave the election sermons in 1677, 1693, 1699, and 1702.[35] (Increase, his son recalled, was so "heart serious" that "his very Countenance carried the Force of a Sermon with it."[36]) In *The Great Blessing of Primitive Counsellours*, the elder Mather testifies to the selfishness of New Englanders. The "great sin" of his generation, he says, "is their forgetting the Errand on which their Fathers came into this Wilderness which was not to seek great things for themselves, but to seek the Kingdom of God and His Righteousness."[37] He affirms the need for civil rulers to redirect people toward the goal of God's kingdom. And he thanks God for the ruling king of England, William III, who had just issued a new charter for Massachusetts and assumed more control over the colony. Indeed, Mather praises King William and Queen Mary with fulsome rhetoric that would make a medieval courtier blush: "God has Blessed Our Nation with a King in the Preservation of whom the Fate of Europe and of the Church of God is more concerned then it has been in the life of any one Person for these Thousand Years. A King that Fights the Battels of the Lord." Moreover, "God has blessed the Nation with a Queen . . . the like unto whom . . . never sat on the English Throne. . . . A Queen that is a pattern of Vertue to the Nation." Mather prays that "as long as Their present Majesties shall hold the English Scepter in their Hands, we in New England may hope to see Good days."[38]

Increase Mather's hope for New England is conditional, however. Because a sinful nation "does provoke God to take away Good Rulers, and to send Bad ones," he says, and because even good rulers are not always well served by their deputies, godly *counselors* are essential to manage the commonwealth. "The wisest Ruler in the World needs the assistance of Counsellers," Mather states. Moses, David, and Solomon all needed counselors to advise them; so did the kings of Egypt and Persia and other great civilizations. Counselors share the burden of governance, which "will be too heavy for one alone." They see more of life than any one ruler can. They bring more knowledge to bear on public policies. They discern who best to appoint as judges and governors over the people. Politically, Mather declares, people are better off under a bad prince with good counselors than under a good prince with bad counselors.[39]

Mather elaborates on the traits of good counselors. They should show wisdom, justice, courage—the classical virtues. As scripture teaches, they must also exhibit piety and fear of God. They should be men of vision. Their goals should be "the Advancement of Gods Interest" and the common "Interest of the People." God calls only a select few to this job; not many men in this world "are fit to give Counsel, especially in the difficult affairs of State," Mather says. He cites some biblical exemplars, including the prophets Jeremiah, Nathan, and Isaiah; and he submits that, happily, New England is home to just such servants of God. Isaiah-like figures have been ministering in her churches and counseling her rulers from the beginning. On election days in particular, prophetic ministers counsel the entire country. Citizens should honor them and thank the Lord, for good counselors "are a singular mercy and Blessing of God to a People."[40]

Increase Mather was, of course, speaking of himself as a good counselor. His sermon was a defense of his own role in colonial politics. A defense was in order because Mather had personally negotiated a controversial new charter for the colony—which, he granted, "makes the Civil Government of New England more Monarchial and less Democratical than in former Times."[41] Among other revisions, the new charter replaced the previously elected governor of Massachusetts with a royal appointee. The surrender of self-rule was unpopular enough, but Mather had also persuaded the Crown that the best candidate for governor was Sir William Phips, a roughneck who earned his title by hunting Spanish treasure for the king. Royal Governor Phips went on to convene the Salem witchcraft court, sow dissension in Boston, make enemies of neighboring colonies, and face arrest back in London on charges of bribery, piracy, and misconduct in office. Despite Phips's failures, Increase Mather never questioned his own fitness as a wise counselor and a singular blessing to New England. But Mather's reckless counsel caused citizens to question what their ministers were preaching—and to resent paying them for it.[42]

As their influence waned, preachers fell back on a timeless ploy to engage wary New Englanders and shore up their own teaching authority. In the style of classic mirrors for princes, they told tales of heroic leadership, trusting that everyone loves a good story. In 1725, for instance, Azariah Mather, from the Connecticut branch of the family, gave the election sermon in Hartford. Titled, *Good Rulers, A Choice Blessing*, it paints the usual picture of authority: Civil rulers are God's vicegerents, "Cloathed with his Image, Adorned with Majesty and Power by him." Their goal is "the Publick Good," their duty to discern the true interest of the commonwealth and "not suffer any Private Views to come in Competition therewith." Only learned men steeped in the virtues (prudence, justice, temperance, and courage) are qualified to exercise sound judgment in the art of governance, Azariah Mather insists: "'Tis especially dangerous when Un-skilful men sit [as] Judges in heavy and weighty Cases," for they can be outmatched by cunning lawyers who know how to twist the law for the self-interest of their clients.[43]

Azariah Mather brings this picture to life with stories of exemplary rulers from scripture, Roman literature, and English folklore. He talks about the biblical kings David and Solomon and the English monarch Edward VI, all of whom took time from the business of state to hear the pleas of their subjects. He repeats the old fable of the emperor Trajan, who stopped on his way to battle, got down from his horse, and patiently listened to the grievances of a poor woman. He tells of Queen Elizabeth, who on a visit to Suffolk marveled at the teamwork between clergy and civil officials, declaring she now understood why England was better governed than any other country. He waxes about legendary rulers of New England, such as Connecticut's late governor Gurdon Saltonstall (like Mather, an ordained minister and staunch defender of officialdom): "A Man TRULY Great," a perfect prince, Saltonstall "shin'd with distinguishing Excellencies in every Station." Just imagine him, Mather says, "walking in his House and when under the greatest Trials, in Patience and self-Command, Uncommon." See him "at the head of his Troops, and you'll see Mars shining in his Lustre and Glory." Look at him, "on his little Throne surrounded with his Councillors, he was their Oracle; and his word gave Law." Reflect on his countenance, "which Charm'd and Commanded the Admiration of Beholders. His frowns were more than a match for the daring and impudent."[44]

Mather's sermon instructs the rulers of New England to imitate these great leaders and set examples for their own subjects to follow. The examples of great men are like pocket mirrors for princes; they "are the Country Peoples Looking-glasses, by which they Dress themselves" and model their behavior. Good rulers encourage good citizens; bad rulers encourage the unruly. If New England magistrates and ministers happen to visit taverns, for instance, other men will go "tipple, and spend a great part of their Time there." Mather exhorts the leaders of Connecticut to aim for higher things, to wage war on vice, to fight the "Levelling Spirit" of "Giddy and Head-strong" persons, and to win reform through their virtue and charisma. They should act like rulers of old, like King Cyrus—of whom Xenophon said not even a blindfolded man could miss his goodness.[45]

Reverend Mather closes with a personal appeal for better treatment of clergymen. He admits "how invidious a Theam 'tis to many, and how Neglected and Censured Discourses of this Nature have been before"; nevertheless, he goes on about the "low and mean State" of the New England ministry. He bemoans the loss of public respect for ministers. He complains there are "few if any that can live upon their Salaries." He faults taxpayers who begrudge their assessment of but two-pence on the pound to support the ministry. He blames backsliders who prefer "a cheap Minister," an uneducated one, or none at all. Mather's laments, reminiscent of the first Egyptian mirrors for princes, suggest how far New England had diverged from John Winthrop's vision of a Puritan commonwealth. Mather's exasperation reveals an awareness that his exemplars of heroic leadership had become, in New England just as in ancient Egypt, mainly stories for schoolchildren.[46]

For over a century, New England election sermons had repeated the same old talking points. One historian who has studied these sermons, T. H. Breen, finds that "much of the rhetoric dealing with the character of the good ruler in Massachusetts and Connecticut appeared the same in 1730 as it had in 1630." In fact, the rhetoric remained much as it was in the Middle Ages, when mirrors for princes urged kings to fight a crusade or jihad for some heavenly goal and urged citizens to honor their rulers as God's vicegerents on earth. Increasingly, this rhetoric proved irrelevant to rulers and citizens alike. While Puritan preachers chastised them with jeremiads, Breen says, "civil leaders paid less and less attention to the complaints of the churchmen." As sermons trumpeted New England's Puritan mission, colonists went their own ways in manners, business, religion, and government. And, despite prophecies that God would punish their willfulness, Americans prospered in their independence. A hundred years after settlement, for instance, Boston was a hub of Atlantic commerce, a teeming cosmopolitan city, a crucible of democracy unimaginable to its Puritan founders and prophets.[47]

Democracy

Like past mirrors for princes, New England election sermons looked back to a golden age that never really was, and they mythologized leaders whose visions were never to be. Stories of visionary leaders and once-perfect communities can be entertaining, even inspiring, but they are poor guides to governing. If viewed simply as aspirational social ideals, they have little to offer rank-and-file participants struggling to get by in nonideal communities (suggesting, for example, that dissatisfied individuals just pray for a better leader). And, if taken too seriously, they can worsen participants' struggles (suggesting that leaders rein in or get rid of dissatisfied individuals). These real-world hazards of mirrors for princes become clearer when you compare the idealized story of New England, as taught in Puritan election sermons, with the empirical accounts of the Bay Colony taught by professional historians.

Most scholars agree that John Winthrop started with a godly vision for the colony. "We are a company professing ourselves fellow members of Christ," Winthrop told the colonists enroute to New England; our goal "is to improve our lives to do more service to the Lord . . . that ourselves and posterity may be the better preserved from the common corruptions of this evil world." In this endeavor, our care for the common good "must oversway all private respects." So "we must delight in each other, make others' conditions our own, rejoice together, mourn together, labor and suffer together: always . . . as members of the same body."[48]

While Winthrop and company sailed to Massachusetts Bay as one body, they were not exactly of one mind. In recruiting the first colonists, Winthrop wanted people who shared his vision, but he needed people for specific jobs—a "sawyer, cooper, surgeon, or whatever," notes historian Edmund Morgan.[49] It's a classic problem in managing purpose-driven organizations: Should Winthrop hire the best *Puritan*, who embraced the official goals of the company, or the best *carpenter*, who could build sturdy houses to withstand New England winters? As a businessman, Winthrop did his best to assemble the skills needed to survive in the wilderness. But he had to compromise the purity of his team. Contrary to the myth of a close-knit community on a mission for God, Winthrop's fleet held a heterogeneous crowd of colonists with a mix of motives for emigration. They came from different counties in England, according to the premier historian of colonial America, Bernard Bailyn; they came from Yorkshire in the north, Hampshire in the south, Suffolk in the east, Cheshire in the west—with different economies, folkways, and farming traditions. They came from different stations in life—masters and servants, craftsmen and laborers, elders and children—with different assets, educations, and expectations. They came from different religious backgrounds—hotly Puritan among the leadership, cooler among the common sort. They came not only to serve God but to escape economic depression, onerous taxation, swelling population, rising cost of living, and scarcity of land.[50]

As soon as they set foot in New England, the colonists began to pull in separate directions. Their original landing site at Salem "pleased us not," wrote Deputy Governor Thomas Dudley, but company leaders could not agree on an alternative place to settle. Dudley opted for a location on the Charles River (to be named Newtown). Sir Richard Saltonstall led a splinter group upriver to found Watertown. William Pynchon led another to Roxbury. Governor Winthrop took a group south along the bay to a spot they called Boston. Within a few months of landing, the colony was not united in one city but scattered over seven settlements, and Winthrop was fretting that Satan's forces were undermining his communal vision for New England, such that "I thinke heere are some persons who never shewed so much wickednesse in England as they have doone heer."[51]

Off in a wild and strange country, with diverse and dispersed members, the leaders struggled to maintain their objectives for the colony and their own authority. The governor, deputy governor, and assistants of the Massachusetts Bay Company—known collectively as *magistrates*—proceeded to act like any company directors, running the plantation as they saw fit. They distributed land, created courts, commissioned public works, regulated wages and prices, compelled religious worship (midweek and twice on Sundays), and made up other rules for the common good as they defined it. If people didn't like the rules, they were reminded that the magistrates were duly elected to govern the colony, and they could always be replaced at the next annual election. The men and women of the colony did not just go along like passive stakeholders, however. By nature, colonists were plucky people; these were pioneers with the self-determination to sail an ocean, clear a wilderness, farm rocky land. Much as they enjoyed the yearly election day holiday, they did not trust a ritual corporate election to protect them from oppressive leaders. The truth is, few even bothered to vote. Instead, they began to organize themselves and demand a voice in the actual governance of the colony: They formed autonomous "congregational" churches, hired their own ministers to interpret the common good, and took responsibility for community services. They dispersed further into the wilderness, founded independent towns, and sent representatives to meet with the colony's magistrates on their behalf. These representatives, called deputies, signaled the advent of democracy in New England.[52]

The founding fathers of the Bay Colony assured potential investors in England that Massachusetts would never become a "mere democracy" but would be governed by eminent men of wisdom, courage, justice, temperance, the traditional virtues. After all, one mused, "if the people be governors, who shall be governed?" Nevertheless, in 1632 the magistrates agreed to meet with activists from Watertown to discuss grievances over—predictably—taxation without representation. Afterward they authorized each town in the colony to choose two or three deputies to represent its residents at the magistrates' general meetings. By 1634 the deputies had gained full membership in the colony's governing body, the General Court. They could vote alongside the governor and assistants on a wide range of issues, and, given their greater numbers, they threatened to outvote the magistrates. To retain their authority, the magistrates insisted on a negative veto over any decision (law, order, or sentence) of the General Court. The deputies objected but settled for a veto of their own. Obviously, this was *not* the kind of governance envisioned in mirrors for princes, Puritan election sermons, or by John Winthrop. The deputies had no special qualities of leadership, they had no calling from God to govern. They were just "civil men," the very people the jeremiads accused of bad behavior and condemned to hell. Yet here they were, trying to rule the commonwealth.[53]

As any student of books on rulership could tell, the deputies upset the natural order—the organic organization of society and the hierarchy of authority described, for example, by John of Salisbury in the twelfth century. Governor Winthrop, the assistants, and ministers of the Bay Colony reached back for the old arguments to keep the deputies in their place. Winthrop reiterated that the magistrates and people of New England shared a common identity as members of one body politic. He held that, like a human body, the body politic needs a head—a central authority—to control the actions of its members who would otherwise act on impulse. The magistrates of New England were that central authority, Winthrop declared. Their goals were the goals of the whole colony: the common good and the will of God. The goals of the deputies, on the other hand, represented the narrow good of their towns and the self-interest of their residents. In speaking for their constituents, Winthrop argued, the deputies were mere counselors in the body politic, not the equals of the magistrates as decision-makers. To give equal standing to the deputies would create a monster, a democracy, which the ancients recognized as "the meanest and worst of all formes of Government." There is nothing in the Bible to justify democracy, Winthrop said; "there was no such government in Israell."[54] Rather, God sent wise and just kings to rule over His people. So too in New England, He endowed the magistrates with unique gifts and sent them to govern as "Gods upon earth."[55] Because "we have our authority from God," Winthrop concluded, not from the voters of New England, the people and their deputies should "quietly and cheerfully submit unto that authority which is set over you, in all the administrations of it, for your good"—just as the church submits to the authority of Christ and the good wife to the authority of her husband.[56]

The deputies, and many a good wife, were unmoved by this medieval rhetoric. What exactly were these God-given gifts, they asked, that set the magistrates above other people? What can they do that no one else could? The magistrates referred such questions to a council of ministers, who replied that the magistrates were privileged to exercise authority in three areas: legislative, judicial, and executive. On further reflection, they allowed that maybe the magistrates were not the only ones capable of exercising legislative and executive functions; the deputies could do these as well. But they still insisted the magistrates alone had the competence to judge cases. This was the ultimate attribute of authority, as Breen points out: "Since the Lord granted magistrates unique skills for discerning Christian equity, the deputies could not make judgments without encroaching upon the duties of the ruler's calling."[57]

With the public behind them, the deputies encroached all the same. Conflicts with the magistrates came to a head in the famous case of Goody Sherman's pig. In 1636 Goodwife Sherman lost her sow around Boston harbor. Subsequently, Capt. Robert Keayne found a stray sow and put it with his hogs for slaughter. Sherman accused Keayne of killing her pig; she sued him, lost, and appealed her case to the magistrates and deputies, then sitting together as the General Court of Massachusetts. The deputies and the court as a whole sided with Sherman. But a majority of the magistrates voted in favor of Keayne, and because of their negative veto over General Court decisions, he was exonerated. The case dragged on for years and garnered widespread publicity. The public sympathized with the deputies and Goody Sherman, a working woman of modest means. People distrusted Robert Keayne, who was a rich merchant known for sharp dealings. Keayne was also known to have family connections to the magistrates—his son was married to the daughter of former governor Thomas Dudley—and the court's verdict fueled distrust of the magistrates as well. Their claims to have superior virtues of leadership and to care for the common good looked like pretexts to take care of one of their own. The appearance of bias struck a direct blow at their alleged calling to judge Christian equity.[58]

Governor Winthrop lamented that the case led "many to speak irreverently of the court, especially of the magistrates, and the report went that their negative voice had hindered the course of justice."[59] After the case was decided, Winthrop proposed that the magistrates and deputies issue a declaration of unity from the General Court, stating that "howsoever the members of the court dissented in judgment, yet they were the same in affection, and had a charitable opinion of each other."[60] Winthrop's proposal was curtly rejected. In frustration, he lashed out against "a position maintained in the Countrye" that the public was better served by factions than by a court united in brotherly love: "If this past for good doctrine," he said, "then let us no longer professe the Gospell of Jesus Christ, but take up the rules of Matchiavell and the Jesuits, for Christ saythe Love is the band of perfection, and a kingdome or house divided cannot stand but the others teache (or rather the Devill teacheth them) divide et imperia."[61] This reproach fell on deaf ears. To check the authority of one another, the magistrates and deputies each held fast to their negative veto powers. The two groups soon stopped sitting together, and they divided into separate, coequal houses of government—the kind of bicameral legislature you see across America today.

What this signified, of course, was not repudiation of the Christian gospel but of mirrors for princes, which had glorified central authority, downplayed the potential for abuse of power, and endorsed only weak restraints on rulers (moral education, voluntary codes of ethics, social responsibilities, and so on). Thanks to Goody Sherman, Americans came to view division of power as an essential check on their leaders.

Enemies

While the magistrates and deputies fought over power, pigs, and other profane things, John Winthrop's holy vision for New England was further undermined by Puritan ministers in their midst. Here again, historians stress the fact that these were not timid souls. The clergy who emigrated to the Bay Colony had found fault with the church, the state, and their neighbors in England. They suffered the enmity of people high and low in return. And they left, rather than compromise their ideals. With no Anglican archbishop in Massachusetts to demand conformity, and without a mature body of Puritan doctrine to direct them, ministers were often at odds with each other and with the colony's civil leaders.[62]

A particular source of conflict was Roger Williams, who came to Boston in 1631 preaching that Puritans in Winthrop's city on a hill were not nearly pure enough. A Cambridge-educated theologian, Williams refused an invitation to minister in the Boston church because its members would not separate formally from the polluted Church of England. Williams objected to worship with unholy people and to regulation of religion by secular authorities, including officers of the Bay Colony. He criticized, for instance, Massachusetts laws requiring both saints and sinners to attend official Sabbath services. He went on to challenge the colony's title to land inhabited by Native Americans. He ridiculed colonial charters by which English rulers assumed they could "take and give away the Lands and Countries of other men."[63] Governor Winthrop maintained that people gained ownership of public land by enclosing it, building houses, and raising livestock. Because the Native people did none of these things, they had no civil rights to the land they occupied, Winthrop felt, so "if we leave them sufficient for their use, we may lawfully take the rest, there being more than enough for them and us."[64] Williams deemed this nonsense, responding that colonists could not just take land from the Native inhabitants but must buy it from them; anything else was "a sin of unjust usurpation upon others' possessions."[65] For such "new and dangerous opinions," Williams was tried for heresy and sedition, convicted, and sentenced to banishment from the colony.[66] He took refuge with the Wampanoag people and purchased land from them for a new plantation. With a small group of followers, he eventually settled among the related Narragansetts, in present Rhode Island. He called the settlement Providence and set it on a fresh footing. It promised freedom to anyone "distressed of conscience."[67] It sheltered believers in any religion or none. It separated governance of church and state. As it grew, it stood as a noxious irritant to the magistrates and ministers of Massachusetts, such as Cotton Mather, who disparaged Providence as "the cesspool of New England"[68]—a pit filled with "everything in the world but Roman Catholics and real Christians."[69]

What divided Puritans like Roger Williams and Cotton Mather was not their devotion to God or the common good. It was how they practiced devotion to God and defined the common good. Williams supposed that "forced worship stinks in God's nostrils."[70] He concluded that an ideal commonwealth sought no godly goals but only the peace and safety of its citizens. And he defined the common good in terms of civility among those citizens. Roger Williams reached unorthodox conclusions by following, to their logical limit, orthodox Puritan beliefs. Like all Puritans, he believed that human beings were sinful, that they required governance to check their selfish impulses, and that rulers needed broad powers to manage them. He thought people were so sinful, in fact, that they corrupted anything they took part in—churches and governments as well as alehouses. There had been no pure church since Christians' alliance with Constantine in the fourth century, Williams claimed, certainly no pure government, and there was no use mixing them together. God did not delegate authority to civil rulers any more than he commissioned ship captains, who perform a similar function, Williams argued. A captain's job is to take his passengers safely to their destination. It is beyond the scope of his contract to dictate final ends to them or to command "the consciences of the passengers—whether Jews, Turks, Persians, Pagans, Papists, [or] Protestants—whom he transports from port to port upon a civil account of payment."[71] In a similar sort of contract, Williams suggested, citizens empower governors, for the common good of the ship of state, to weather "storms and tempests, want of provisions, sickness and diseases, treacherous and professed enemies, fires, leaks, and mutinies."[72] To alleviate such common woes, to maintain civility, governors can regulate behavior but not belief.[73]

Williams dismissed the exemplars of heroic leadership featured in mirrors for princes. The history of bloody Roman emperors and even more bloody princes of the Church showed, he said, the danger of messianic leaders. By using the sword of civil power to further a holy vision, such as the goal of a Christian empire, zealous leaders created fear, suffering, and veritable nations of hypocrites. Williams cited examples from the Spanish Inquisition and the European wars of religion, wherein "the Emperours, Kings, and Magistrates of the World," at the direction of Rome, unleashed their forces upon "the Waldenses, Wicklevists, Hussites, Hugonites, Lutherans, Calvinists, Protestants, Puritans, Sectaries, etc. to imprison, to whip, to banish, to hang, to head, to burne, to blow up such vile Hereticks, Apostates, Seducers, Blasphemers etc."[74] While "the voice of so many rivers of blood cry to heaven for vengeance," Williams reminded Englishmen that Protestant rulers behaved just as badly when they took power and persecuted Catholics. Who could possibly think this kind of leadership advanced the common good?[75]

Apparently, Cotton Mather thought so. Unlike Roger Williams, Mather attributed a religious purpose to New England. Civility to heretics, apostates, and blasphemers was not his idea of the common good. He made that clear in his election sermon of 1690, *The Serviceable Man.* "New England above all the Countries of the world," he declared, "is a Plantation for the Christian and Protestant Religion"; the colony was founded by "Pious and Worthy men" in order to practice "the Religion of the Lord Jesus here, without such Obstructions as in Europe"—"without that Episcopacy, that [Anglican] Common-Prayer, and those unwarrantable [Popish] Ceremonies, which the Land of our Fathers Sepulchres, has been defiled with." For Mather, the common good required universal commitment to "the Great Ends which this Plantation was first erected upon." And it demanded great leaders such as John Winthrop, whom God tasked to rule as "the terror of the wicked, and the delight of the sober, the envy of the many, but the hope of those who had any hopeful design in hand for the common good of the nation, and the interests of religion."[76]

As Mather wrote in his epic jeremiad, *Magnalia Christi Americana,* Governor Winthrop and fellow leaders of the Puritan exodus not only delivered God's people from bondage in Europe, but they protected God's church from enemies in America that beset her like "hungry lions, wolves, boars and bears, and all manner of cruel and hurtful beasts."[77] These enemies included Roger Williams, who represented "the first rebel against the divine church-order established in the wilderness."[78] They included the deputies in the notorious stray-sow (*Sherman v. Keayne*) case, who managed "by over-driving to have run the whole government into something too democratical." They included the witches who brought not just Salem but the whole commonwealth under "assault from hell."[79] They included Quakers, Baptists, Catholics, the usual enemies of the common good. And they included, above all, the Native people—whose "savage inclinations," Mather said, "ill suit, either with honor, or with the design of Christianity."[80]

Cotton Mather's depiction of the Native Americans harkens back to Gerald of Wales's denigration of the Irish in the twelfth century. "These doleful creatures are the veriest ruines of mankind which are to be found any where upon the face of the earth," Mather asserted. The Natives are "infinitely barbarous" and "abominably slothful." They inhabit a country rich in iron and copper, but "our shiftless Indians were never owners of so much as a knife till we come among them." They live in woods "full of the best ship-timber under heaven," yet they make only crude canoes, in which they paddle about like dogs and get nowhere. "Their chief employment, when they'll condescend to any, is that of hunting." They have no arts and almost no culture, "except just so far as to maintain their brutish conversation, which is little more than is to be found among the very beavers upon our streams." (Strangely, according to Mather, they seem adept at astronomy, tracking the motions of the stars and observing the same constellations as the Europeans.) What passes for religion among them amounts to this: "They believe that there are many gods, who made and own the several nations of the world; of which a certain great God in the south-west regions of heaven bears the greatest figure." Moreover, "they believe that when any good or ill happens to them, there is the favour or the anger of a god expressed in it; and hence, as in a time of calamity, they keep a dance, or a day of extravagant ridiculous devotions to their god; so in a time of prosperity they likewise have a feast, wherein they also make presents one unto another." The obvious similarities to English rituals escaped Cotton Mather.[81]

Like Gerald of Wales before him, Mather encouraged a crusade against the infidels. In 1689 he preached a sermon to a company of militiamen mobilized for a "just war" against the Native Americans. "You are Fighting," he told the troops, "that the Churches of God may not be Extinguisht, and the Wigwams of Heathen swarming in their room: You are Fighting that the Children of God may not be made Meals or Slaves to the veriest Tygers upon Earth." As soon as you see the "Tawny Pagans," he instructed the militia, "Turn not back till they are consumed: Wound them that they shall not be able to Arise; Tho' they Cry; Let there be none to Save them; But Beat them small as the Dust before the Wind, and Cast them out, as the Dirt in the Streets."[82]

The following year Mather backed a wider war against Canada, which he vilified as the Papist "seminary of our troubles from the Indians."[83] Indigenous tribes and their French Catholic allies had been skirmishing with New Englanders for control of lands along the Northern frontier; Mather felt an assault on Canada would reduce both these enemies and extend the Protestant empire in America. To lead this crusade, Mather recommended a friend of the family: the old treasure-hunter, Sir William Phips. The opportunistic Phips took a hastily organized force and sailed off for Nova Scotia, where he sacked the Acadian village of Port Royal and looted its Catholic church. Despite murmurs that he was more pirate than Puritan, Phips then procured a commission from the Massachusetts General Court to lead a seaborne strike on Quebec. The expedition was poorly planned and badly executed, resulting in a humiliating defeat. Phips's soldiers and sailors died by the hundreds— not from enemy fire but from disease, lack of supplies, and failures of navigation. Lukewarm from the start, popular support for the war cooled as Phips's sick and starving men straggled home, bringing smallpox with them to local communities and overwhelming the colony's treasury with demands for back pay. Unfazed, Cotton Mather defended the holy goal of the war and praised Phips's dedication to the common good. He immortalized Sir William as "Phippius Maximus," New England's knight who Christianized "the old heathen virtue of Pietas in Patriam"—love of country—"and so notably exemplified it" that he lives on as a model of leadership for the ages.[84]

The crusade preached by Cotton Mather and led by William Phips grew into a series of French and Indian Wars that plagued Americans for the next three-quarters of a century. English monarchs stoked these wars in an effort to unite their colonies against a common, French Catholic enemy. New England ministers gave their blessing: Military sermons upheld Cotton Mather's imperial notion of the common good against Roger Williams's civil alternative. Thanksgiving sermons voiced gratitude to the Crown for protecting New England from chaos. Even as England imposed insufferable royal governors on the colonies, election sermons urged Americans to obey their rulers as God's deputies on earth. In 1701, for example, Joseph Belcher, pastor of the church at Dedham, preached that people should count their rulers "a great and necessary blessing to them," for "even bad government is acknowledged better than none at all. Who is there but will grant that tyranny (except it grow to a great extremity indeed) is better than anarchy?"[85]

As the years and the wars wore on, however, more and more Americans looked beyond the rhetoric—past the fiction that self-proclaimed agents of God had privileged knowledge of the common good, reason of state, ends of empire, or other goals for society. After all, if learned divines like Cotton Mather and Roger Williams could not agree on the common good, then it must be a matter of opinion. And ordinary Americans were coming to the conclusion that their opinions were as good as those of their rulers or their ministers.

Equals

Ministers finally bowed to democratic sentiments and abandoned the language of mirrors for princes in the 1760s, after the British Parliament passed a notorious law called the Stamp Act. Preachers went on giving election sermons, but they were never the same.

The Stamp Act, taxing colonists without their consent for the upkeep of British troops in America, met bitter opposition from merchants, mechanics, and ministers alike. Printers especially resented the act, which taxed (among other items) newspapers, pamphlets, and almanacs—the major media outlets of the day—and so threatened freedom of the press, not to mention publishers' profits. Up and down the Atlantic Seaboard, local papers raised alarms, inflamed passions, and incited resistance. The law was tantamount to slavery, "as fatal to almost all that is dear to us, as the Ides of March were, to the life of Caesar," cried the *New-Hampshire Gazette*.[86] The "Stämpfel-Acte" was "the most unconstitutional law imaginable," claimed *Der Wöchentliche Philadelphische Staatsbote*, a German-language paper taxed at twice the rate of English publications.[87] Stamp tax collectors were "mean mercenary Hirelings or Parricides among ourselves, who for a little filthy lucre would at any time betr[a]y every Right, Liberty, and Privilege of their fellow subjects," said the *Boston Gazette*—which made sure to print their names.[88] Defy these "vile minions of tyranny" and "never ... pay one farthing of this tax," exhorted the *Constitutional Courant*, punctuated with the famous cartoon of a segmented snake (representing the separate colonies) and the caption, "JOIN or DIE."[89]

When mass protests and demonstrations forced repeal of the act in 1766, ministers joined their countrymen in celebration. Across New England, sermons of thanksgiving portrayed rebellious Americans not as the self-ish sinners charged in the jeremiads but as heroic patriots. Suddenly, observes professor of religious history Harry Stout, the grandsons of ministers from Cotton Mather's generation "reversed the teachings of their predecessors and taught that tyranny was a greater threat than anarchy." Like their neighbors, preachers at long last tired of the old homilies about visionary leadership. Some of those homilies may have been inspiring. Parts of their stories about godly kings, emperors, and governors may have even been true. Still, they were irrelevant to most Americans because they addressed a question of interest to a privileged few.[90]

By definition, mirrors for princes and, by association, Puritan election sermons asked how to enable a great leader. This seemingly neutral question reflects the concern of rulers and powerholders to enhance their authority over other people. Of more concern to most people, however, is the question of how to inhibit a bad leader. No one in New England had experienced the perfect rulers imagined by election day preachers. Some, certainly, had prospered under patriarchal rulers like John Winthrop. Many had not and had resisted (such as Goody Sherman) or left (such as Anne Hutchinson). Yet, everyone saw the harm wrought by some petty despot like Sir William Phips—or, worse, some bully with real power like British prime minister George Grenville, the architect of the Stamp Act. And just about everybody wished to avoid such leadership. Now, how to avoid a bad leader is a very different question from how to enable a great one. The two questions are not simply obverse sides of the same coin; they have opposing implications for public policy.

To enable great leaders, for example, mirrors for princes told everyone else to follow. In human societies, just as in natural bodies, God gives some members the "power to command, while others are required to obey," William Hubbard said in his election sermon of 1676. "It is not then the result of time or chance, that some are mounted on horse-back, while others are left to travell on foot"; but "the Almighty hath appointed her that sits behind the mill, as well as him that ruleth on the throne." Indeed, "the greatest part of mankind are but as tools and Instruments for others to work by." It offends God to turn creation upside down, to resist nature's hierarchy of authority, or "to think that because we were all once equal at our birth, and shall be again at our death, therefore we should be so in the whole course of our lives."[91]

To inhibit bad leaders, on the other hand, one would tell everyone just the opposite: God did not appoint rulers and workers; no one is subservient by nature, but persons are equal in rights all their lives. On the heels of the Stamp Act crisis, Edward Barnard from the church in Haverhill gave the election sermon in 1766 and warned the royal governor of Massachusetts that "unlimited submission,—submission in all cases, cannot be a duty" of New Englanders. When peoples' liberties are threatened, he said, it is their duty under God's law to resist. In another sermon Barnard compared Americans' resistance to the Stamp Act with their ancestors' struggle for Magna Carta.[92]

Cambridge pastor Samuel Cooke went further in his election sermon of 1770 after British soldiers fired on protestors in Boston, killing five civilians. Cooke declared that, while the institution of government was ordained by God, the particular kind of government is for its citizens to decide. Governments are unlike organic bodies of higher and lower members—they are more like social contracts between consenting parties. Men are "by nature equal" and cannot "yield unlimited subjection" to any earthly prince. From a state of nature, people form governments "not to ennoble a few and enslave the multitude" but so that individuals "may be protected in their persons and secured in the enjoyment of all their rights." Among those rights Cooke included liberty to lead a quiet and peaceful life, freedom of speech and assembly, freedom of conscience and worship, rights to submit grievances and seek redress, title to fairly acquired property, and immunities from oppression. Cooke proposed extending property rights to Native Americans and immunities to Africans oppressed by trade in "the merchandise of slaves and the souls of men."[93]

Civic leadership, according to Cooke, is a public trust to secure these rights. It is based on popular consent rather than personal callings from God, superior birth, or unique virtues. Of course civil authorities should act with justice, prudence, mercy, and such—all citizens should—but no one should display "arrogant pretenses to infallibility in matters of state or religion." In Cooke's view, the duty of authorities is not to proclaim some common goal for the state or define the common good for everyone. Authorities are responsible to the people who empower them to defend their goals for the nation and their visions of the common good. Even kings are accountable to the public; they "greatly tarnish their dignity when they attempt to treat their subjects otherwise than as their fellowmen."[94]

Pastor Cooke was Harvard educated (though not by birthright, like Cotton Mather—Cooke worked in the college commissary to make ends meet). He had heard the arguments against democracy advanced in mirrors for princes. It is possible, he acknowledged in his election sermon, that under a popular administration people "may degenerate into licentiousness, which in its extreme is subversive of all government, yet the history of past ages and of our nation shows that the greatest dangers have arisen from lawless power." History also shows that traditional cures for abuses of power are ineffective—for instance, education for kingship, oaths of office, counselors on ethics, and pleas for benevolence. These folk remedies for tyranny, promulgated in mirrors for princes, underestimate the problem of bad leaders. The best way to keep authorities accountable to the people, Cooke concluded, is to divide power among different branches of government. "The whole power cannot with safety be entrusted with a single person, nor with many acting jointly in the same public capacity," he preached: Peoples' rights are more secure when "various branches of power . . . are a mutual check to each other." (Cooke realized that divided power may slow the operations of government; even so, he pointed out, it enhances deliberations and lends weight to policy decisions.)[95]

Within a few years Thomas Jefferson and James Madison would say similar things in announcing America's independence, then nationhood, to her former rulers. Before the American Revolution turned the world upside down, however, the nostalgic song of mirrors for princes beckoned one final time.

A Patriot King

On the eve of the Revolution, when even their preachers had eschewed monarchist rhetoric and took a more populist tone, some patriotic Americans still had kind words for their king. Benjamin Franklin, a colonial agent in London who had worked to repeal the Stamp Act, wrote in 1768 that Britain had "the best Constitution and the best King any Nation was ever blest with."[96] Americans by then had come to hate British tax collectors, British soldiers, British governors, and the British

Parliament, but some held out hope that a British constitutional monarch might yet protect their rights. Loyalists took heart from a mirror for princes titled *The Idea of a Patriot King*, penned by a British lord with grudges of his own against Parliament. This book has been called "the last major example in the English speaking world" of the mirror-for-princes genre.[97]

In 1738 Henry St. John, Viscount Bolingbroke, was facing circumstances much like those that vexed Machiavelli in 1513. Once a senior civil servant in Britain, Bolingbroke had been banished from government after the Crown and House of Commons turned against him. He was burdened by debt and filled with regret over his forced retirement. I am "surrounded with difficultys, exposed to mortifications, and unable to take any share of the service, but that which I have taken hitherto," he wrote to his friend Sir William Wyndham. "My part is over," he sighed, "and he who remains on the stage after his part is over, deserves to be hissed off." Like Machiavelli before him, Bolingbroke sought refuge in the countryside and found comfort in rural pastimes—roaming the woods, hunting boar, breeding dogs, grousing about taxes and public officials. Yet, like Machiavelli, he yearned to play one more role in the national theater of politics and he needed a patron to back him. So, to ingratiate himself with Britain's royal family, to showcase his experience and patriotism, he wrote a mirror for princes.[98]

Bolingbroke's mirror, *The Idea of a Patriot King*, continues the tradition of *The Prince*, *The Education of Cyrus*, and so many others. It starts with the age-old clichés about people behaving badly. Once upon a time the Britons were a virtuous race, headed by great landed families, but now "the greatest part of the present generation; not of the vulgar alone, but of those who stand foremost, and are raised highest in our nation" all pursue "the same course of self-interest, profligacy, and corruption," Bolingbroke says. He blames the moral breakdown of Britain on the selfishness of her subjects. And he links the growth of selfishness to the rise of big financial institutions—the central Bank of England, the London stock-market, corporations like the South Sea and East India Companies. Such corrupting institutions, he complains, fuel state spending and public debt, mass moneylending and security speculation, lust for riches and luxury goods, all kinds of excesses. The exemplar of corruption, for Bolingbroke, is Sir Robert Walpole, who as prime minister empowered Britain's moneymen and lured her citizens away "from the love of liberty, from zeal for the honour and prosperity of their country, and from a desire of honest fame, to an absolute unconcernedness for all these, to an abject submission, and a rapacious eagerness after wealth."[99]

Bolingbroke prescribes the customary remedy for the avarice of a corrupt age: a common goal and an extraordinary leader to unite people behind it. Forsaking self-interest, everyone's common goal should be "the interest of the state," as articulated by a patriot king. A patriot king is a transformational leader whose virtue is an example for the nation and whose vision draws subjects to follow. "A Patriot King is the most powerful of all reformers," Bolingbroke says; "for he is himself a sort of standing miracle, so rarely seen and so little understood, that the sure effects of his appearance will be admiration and love in every honest breast, confusion and terror to every guilty conscience, but submission and resignation in all." Such a king will not abet "the divisions of his people" stemming from greed, faction or party; but he will "be himself the centre of their union . . . in order to govern, or more properly to subdue all parties." In Bolingbroke's view, "the true image of a free people, governed by a Patriot King, is that of a patriarchal family, where the head and all the members are united by one common interest, and animated by one common spirit: and where, if any are perverse enough to have another, they [are] soon borne down by the superiority of those who have the same."[100]

Bolingbroke wrote *The Idea of a Patriot King* for Frederick, the Prince of Wales and eldest son of King George II. He tried to instruct Frederick using all the flourishes of ancient mirrors for princes: He discussed classical virtues to practice, faults to avoid, legendary monarchs to emulate, and case studies to inspire the self-confidence required for leadership. He told the prince that if he acted like a patriot king, "a new people will seem to arise" almost as if "they are changed into different beings." Bolingbroke prophesied that "as soon as a Patriot King is raised to the throne," corruption will cease. Then "concord will appear, brooding peace and prosperity on the happy land; joy sitting in every face, content in every heart; a people unoppressed, undisturbed, unalarmed; busy to improve their private property and the public stock; fleets covering the ocean, bringing home wealth by the returns of industry, carrying assistance or terror abroad by the direction of wisdom, and asserting triumphantly the right and the honour of Great Britain, as far as waters roll and as winds can waft them."[101]

When *The Idea of a Patriot King* was published in the mid-eighteenth century, politicians such as Horace Walpole (Sir Robert's son) ridiculed "the absurdity and impracticality of this kind of system."[102] In 1781 a popular pamphlet expressed the feeling of cynical Londoners that a patriot king was "romantic nonsense. A monster, a chimaera in politics, what never did and never will exist."[103] As the century came to an end, Edmund Burke sneered, "Who now reads Bolingbroke, who ever read him through?"[104] Modern scholars have been just as critical; political historian Isaac Kramnick, by no means the most judgmental reader, has called the *Patriot King* "a hopeless anachronism" and a "ludicrous example" of befuddled rhetoric.[105]

Still, many eighteenth-century opinion leaders did read Bolingbroke. (American patriot John Adams claimed to have "read him through more than five times."[106]) And many ordinary people who never read him knew what he said. Like Machiavelli's "Prince," Bolingbroke's "Patriot King" became a familiar figure of English culture, sharing playbills with "John Bull." Prince Frederick died before he could take the throne, but his son George—the future King George III—was taught what it meant to be a patriot king. British subjects on both sides of the Atlantic expected Prince George to live up to it. Bolingbroke was well known in the colonies. He was, Kramnick points out, "the century's most famous critic of parliamentary corruption."[107] As Americans' grievances with Parliament increased, so did their wish for a savior, and Bolingbroke offered one: The idea of a patriot king was aired in essays and newspapers, churches and alehouses throughout the colonies. Accordingly, Americans had high hopes for King George III from the beginning of his reign in 1760. Remarkably, many maintained their hopes—blaming government ministers and excusing the king for their woes—until the Revolutionary War was upon them. In 1775, after the battles of Lexington and Concord, George Washington himself referred to the Redcoat enemy as "the Ministerial Troops (for we do not, nor can we yet prevail upon ourselves to call them the King's Troops)."[108] Another Revolutionary leader, William Henry Drayton, said that in 1775 South Carolinians still believed King George III "would heal our Wounds, and thereby prevent the Separation" of the colonies from the British empire.[109]

The world changed in 1776. War brought home to Americans "that George III was no patriot king," observes historian William D. Liddle; "George III swiftly degenerated from potential savior to principal villain in the eyes of American patriots." The Declaration of Independence fixed blame squarely on the king for a long list of abuses. It charged that he invaded the people's rights, dissolved representative assemblies, obstructed the administration of justice, sent swarms of soldiers to harass citizens and plunder their property. It declared that "a Prince whose character is thus marked by every act which may define a Tyrant, is unfit to be the ruler of a free people." Americans imbued with the spirit of '76 did not just turn on George III but against the sentimental illusion of a patriot king. Their civic rhetoric dismissed Bolingbroke and cheered Thomas Paine.[110]

The whole idea of a king is "absurd and useless," Paine wrote in *Common Sense*: "There is something exceedingly ridiculous in the composition of monarchy; it first excludes a man from the means of information, yet empowers him to act in cases where the highest judgment is required. The state of a king shuts him from the world, yet the business of a king requires him to know it thoroughly." Out of touch, addicted to luxury, and desperate for adulation, "a thirst for absolute power is the natural disease of monarch[s]." So instead of hoping for a better king, Paine advised Americans to "let the crown . . . be demolished, and scattered among the people whose right it is."[111] *Common Sense* was an immediate sensation. Shortly after it appeared in January of 1776, George Washington accurately predicted that its "sound doctrine and unanswerable reasoning" would convince his countrymen to admit "the Propriety of a Seperation" and repel (what he now called) "the Kings Troops."[112]

Americans were never of one mind, of course. A few patriot leaders held on to royalist ideas long after 1776. John Adams, who signed the Declaration of Independence, later disclosed that it used "expressions which I would not have inserted, if I had drawn it up, particularly that which called the King tyrant." Among the framers at the Constitutional Convention of 1787, James Wilson argued for a strong chief executive to check legislative tyranny, claiming that the Revolution was not against a king but against the "corrupt multitude" of Parliament. Alexander Hamilton favored an even more powerful chief-executive-for-life, modeled after the king of Great Britain who could stand above factions and who "can have no distinct interests from the public welfare." But the convention rejected these views. The chief executive of the United States would not be a patriot king with the prerogative to determine the common good, public welfare, or joint goals for the nation. As Paine urged, the framers of the Constitution demolished the powers of an old-fashioned monarch and scattered them across different branches of government.[113]

The age of monarchy, of patriot kings, was ending, and with it the books that told princes how to rule the world. Burke's oft-quoted words suggest an epitaph not just for Bolingbroke but for the entire genre of mirrors for princes: *Who now reads them? Who ever read them through?*

TEN

Madison versus Mirrors for Princes

By the article establishing the Executive Department, it is made the duty of the President "to recommend to your consideration, such measures as he shall judge necessary and expedient." The circumstances under which I now meet you, will acquit me from entering into that subject, farther than to refer to the Great Constitutional Charter under which you are assembled . . . It will be more consistent with those circumstances, and far more congenial with the feelings which actuate me, to substitute, in place of a recommendation of particular measures, the tribute that is due to the talents, the rectitude, and the patriotism which adorn the characters selected to devise and adopt them.

George Washington

On Thursday, April 30, 1789, George Washington, the first president of the United States, addressed members of the first Congress, officers of the new nation, and distinguished guests. The president looked nervous. It was the day of his inauguration, and the pomp might have given King George III stage fright.

For the previous two weeks, as he journeyed from Mount Vernon to New York City for the inauguration, Washington had been toasted at banquets, hailed with fireworks, saluted by cannon, heralded by bands, showered with flowers, crowned with laurel, and cheered by crowds all along the route. Today was the big finale. At dawn, guns boomed from the Battery. At nine, bells pealed from the churches. At noon, Washington paraded through Manhattan in a state coach behind a grand marshal, aides-de-camp, a cavalry troop and regiment of artillery, companies of grenadiers and infantry, a corps of Scottish bagpipers, committees of US senators and representatives, and six masters of ceremony on horseback.

The parade ended at the old New York City Hall, remodeled to house the new federal Congress. Washington walked through the door, past an honor guard, and up the stairs to the Senate chamber, where he faced an audience of the rich and the famous. Land baron Charles Carroll and state chancellor Robert R. Livingston were among the rich, Vice President John Adams and Foreign Secretary John Jay among the famous. Members of Congress in attendance included Richard Henry Lee and Elbridge Gerry, who signed the Declaration of Independence; William Patterson and Oliver Ellsworth, who helped frame the Constitution; and George Read and Roger Sherman, who did both. There were Revolutionary War generals Henry Knox and Arthur St. Clair, ministers from Spain and France, Gov. George Clinton, and renowned orator Fisher Ames watching to see what the "father of his country" would say. Portraits of Christopher Columbus and George Washington himself stared down from the walls.[1]

Before addressing the assembled dignitaries, Washington was escorted across the room and onto a balcony overlooking Wall Street, where he swore to "faithfully execute the office of President of the United States and . . . defend the Constitution." Below the balcony, the neighborhood was jammed with spectators who had streamed into the city to glimpse the inauguration ceremony. "I was on the roof of the first house in Broad Street," said Eliza Morton, a young New Yorker, who was "so near to Washington that I could almost hear him speak. The windows and roofs of the houses were crowded; and in the streets the throng was so dense that it seemed as if one might literally walk on the heads of the people."[2] Looking up from the crowd was a six-year-old boy named Washington Irving, who would one day regale the nation with his stories of George Washington and New York. Already, Americans everywhere looked up to Washington. Like the Irvings, they named their babies after him. Like the Congress, they hung his picture in their public buildings, their homes, and their taverns. Last winter they gave him every one of their electoral votes. Now, as he stepped back into the Senate chamber, it was his turn to address Americans' hopes for the future.[3]

Washington had prepared carefully. He ordered a brown American-made suit to wear, a nod to local industry. He picked out silver buttons crested with spread eagles, the national logo. He gathered advice on what to say. His aide, David Humphreys, gave him the same advice that consultants give modern chief executives: Articulate a vision, talk about your leadership philosophy. He and Humphreys drafted a seventy-three-page speech detailing Washington's vision for the country. It called on Congress to take steps to promote the general welfare: "to improve the education and manners of a people; to accelerate the progress of arts and sciences; to patronize works of genius; to confer rewards for inventions of utility; and to cherish institutions favorable to humanity." The speech went on with proposals for the federal budget, national defense, international trade, domestic manufacturing, other common goals and patriotic virtues uniting the states.[4]

In the end, Washington had the prudence not to give that speech. Some weeks earlier he quietly sought a second opinion and enlisted a ghostwriter who knew better than he did what the first president should say. Today, at his inauguration, he held in his hands the new draft, only six paragraphs in length. Eyes down on the paper, at last he began to read. He said something about his deficiencies for the job. He prayed for guidance to nonsectarian entities, from an "Almighty Being," to an "invisible hand." When he came to recommending "such measures as he shall judge necessary," he deferred to the wisdom of Congress, offering a few words of tribute instead of directions. It was not his vision that mattered, after all, but the views of the American people and their elected representatives. If they wanted to amend the Constitution, for example, he invited Congress to lead the way; he expressed "entire confidence" in members' ability to protect the rights of individuals and still preserve the effectiveness of government. In less than twenty minutes it was all over.[5]

Pennsylvania senator William Maclay noticed "this great man was agitated and embarrassed more than ever he was by the levelled cannon or pointed musket. He trembled, and several times could scarce make out to read." But, if Washington flubbed a few lines, most of his audience enjoyed the performance. The Spanish minister was inspired by the president's words. Fisher Ames was moved by his humble delivery. Others no doubt thanked the invisible hand for his brevity. Congressman James Madison, who had pledged to amend the Constitution with a bill of rights, was especially pleased with the speech. He wrote it.[6]

It took almost two centuries for editors of Madison's papers to finally flesh out his role in the story. Madison never let on that he had written

Washington's inaugural address. He played along when the House of Representatives asked him to draft a reply to the president. The House, Madison wrote Washington, shared the president's concern for the American people and vowed to get to work on constitutional amendments. He kept the dialogue going when Washington privately asked him to answer the House. The president, Madison wrote back, would do his best to cooperate. Madison finished the conversation by writing Washington's response to the Senate as well. The president, Madison said, wished the Senate would cooperate too. Only George Washington knew this whole exchange between the first president and the first Congress was actually James Madison talking to himself. And Washington was too proud to tell anyone.[7]

Religions

Other Founding Fathers courted fame, but Madison was used to anonymity. He had already written much of *the* founding text, *The Federalist*, under a pen name, Publius. He "was simple, modest, bland and unostentatious, retiring from the throng and cautiously refraining from doing or saying anything to make himself conspicuous," said his presidential secretary Edward Coles. (Madison looked inconspicuous. He was short, around five feet six, and thin, barely one hundred pounds.) At work, he displayed the habits of a Jesuit: By night he studied, wrote, and kept a candle burning so he could grab his book or pen whenever he woke; by day he walked the back corridors of power, clothed all in black. A Scottish correspondent said James Madison "reminded him of a schoolmaster dressed up for a funeral."[8]

Born to an old Virginia family, Madison received a more progressive education than most Virginians of his class. He was introduced to literature of the Enlightenment by Scottish schoolmasters, completing his coursework with John Witherspoon, who headed the College of New Jersey at Princeton (now Princeton University). Under Witherspoon, the school had a stated liberal mission: "In the instruction of the Youth, care is to be taken to cherish the spirit of liberty, and free enquiry; and not only to permit, but even to encourage their right of private judgment, without presuming to dictate with an air of infallibility." At Princeton, Madison learned political theory from books, from liberal writers like John Locke, but he also saw firsthand something that proved fateful to his career and set him apart from his neighbors: By choosing to attend the College of New Jersey—instead of the local school for Virginia gentlemen, the College of William and Mary at Williamsburg—Madison experienced at an impressionable age the plurality of religious thought that only existed in the middle colonies of America.[9]

The northern and southern colonies drew settlers mainly from England. These colonists supported, by law, a majority religion—Puritanism in New England and Anglicanism in Virginia. The middle colonies of New Jersey, New York, Pennsylvania, and Delaware in contrast attracted settlers from all over Europe; there were Dutch, Germans, Swiss, Swedes, Finns, Norwegians, Flemings, Walloons, French, Welsh, and Irish. Those immigrants brought with them a variety of religions, which coexisted in relative peace because no single denomination could command a majority, dictate the "public good," and dominate the others. On his way to Princeton, Madison passed through nearby Philadelphia where at least eight different sects had built churches within a few blocks of one another, and still more, including a congregation of Spanish and Portuguese Jews, met in private homes. By the time he left Princeton, Madison held the unshakable belief that every person had a right to religious freedom, and every society could profit from religious diversity.[10]

He revealed the depth of that belief in letters to a former classmate, William Bradford, written after Madison returned home from college. "I want again to breathe your free air" in Philadelphia, he told Bradford.[11] For "that liberal catholic and equitable way of thinking as to the rights of Conscience, which is one of the Characteristics of a free people and so strongly marks the People of your province is but little known among the Zealous adherents to our Hierarchy."[12] Madison complained that the dominant Anglican clergy in Virginia suppressed any dissenters who they feared may "rob them of the good will of the people and may in time endanger their livings & security."[13] He expressed outrage at the treatment of separatist Baptist preachers in an adjacent county who were jailed just for professing their religion. Madison said he "squabbled and scolded" neighbors to no end over it, but "that diabolical Hell conceived Principle of persecution rages among some and to their eternal Infamy the Clergy can furnish their Quota of Imps for such business. This vexes me the most of any thing whatever." Madison asked Bradford to "pray for Liberty of Conscience."[14] Then he chose a vocation where he could do something about it.

His Princeton education, old Virginia connections, and income from the family plantation (more on that later) allowed Madison to devote his life to politics. He began his career just as royal government dissolved in the colonies and Americans scrambled to rebuild governments from the ground up. He was elected in 1774 at the age of twenty-three to the Committee of Safety for Orange County, Virginia, the local revolutionary council chaired by his father. Two years later he was elected to the Virginia Provincial Convention, the de facto legislature of the colony. There in Williamsburg Madison listened as seasoned leaders— Edmund Pendleton, George Mason, Patrick Henry, and others—called for a continental declaration of independence and drafted a new constitution for Virginia. Madison's moment to contribute came when the convention debated a Virginia Declaration of Rights. Mason proposed an article on religious freedom, stating that "all men should enjoy the fullest Toleration in the Exercise of Religion."[15] Madison thought toleration was not enough. He felt such language left freedom of religion a mere favor, dependent on the mercy of the majority and their state-sponsored church. And he'd seen how merciless they could be. So he moved to declare freedom of conscience a fundamental right, and he sought to secure that right by separating church and state. The state convention was not ready to disestablish the Anglican Church in Virginia, but it did approve Madison's amendment that, by right, "all men are equally entitled to the free exercise of religion, according to the dictates of conscience."[16]

In 1777 Madison was elected to the Virginia Council of State, an executive board that handled day-to-day duties of government. On his first day on the job, the council took up an urgent request to resupply the Continental Army, now poised, in General Washington's words, to "starve—dissolve—or disperse" at Valley Forge.[17] The council authorized the purchase of "all the pork Beef & Bacon that can be procured" for Washington's troops.[18] It also sent an expedition to New Orleans to get more supplies and meet with the Spanish governor about securing the Mississippi River. Madison dealt with issues like these for two years in the Virginia statehouse and for nearly four more in the Continental Congress, where he shouldered the task of persuading loosely confederated states to do their fair share for the war effort. Madison's ability to broker cooperation and reach compromise enabled the fragile union to keep troops in the field, outlast the British, and stave off bankruptcy. In the process he made lifelong friends and allies, none closer than Thomas Jefferson. In Jefferson's estimate, Madison's practical experience during the war years, along with his knowledge of political theory, "rendered him the first of every assembly afterwards of which he became a member."[19]

While James Madison had good friends like Jefferson, he had enemies too—none worse than Patrick Henry. After the Revolutionary War, Madison returned to the Virginia legislature to face off with Henry over freedom of (and from) religion. During the Revolution, Virginia had suspended collection of taxes for the Anglican Church. Without state support, clergy began to leave, parishes closed, and religious observance decreased. When the war was over and "the world turned upside down," county leaders raised alarms about moral decay in their communities and they petitioned the legislature to restore support for religion. As in ages past, "moral decay" was a sort of dog whistle, implying that workers were getting big ideas and acting above their station. Plantation owners lamented that "the poor are seduced from their Labor" by collapse of the established church. Qualified ministers, the gentry complained, had given way to itinerant rabble-rousers who preached to enslaved workers "disobedience & insolence to Masters & glorying in what they [the slaves] are taught to believe to be persecution for Conscience's sake."[20] Conservative groups lobbied the Virginia Assembly to rescue their churches, claiming that professional pastors enhanced the virtue of the whole commonwealth and should be everybody's responsibility: Petitioners from Isle of Wight County appealed to the common good, "a principle as old as society itself that whatever is to conduce equally to the advantage of all should be borne equally by all."[21]

Patrick Henry responded with a proposed bill to tax Virginians for the support of "teachers of the Christian religion."[22] Henry introduced his bill in the Virginia Assembly with his trademark fiery oratory. He delivered jeremiads about the cancer of sin and vice in the country. He told stories about the fall of nations after the decline of religion. He argued that his assessment plan was reasonable: It did not aim to reestablish any specific state church or privilege any particular denomination; it simply required people to pay "a moderate tax or contribution annually" for the maintenance of a Christian church of their choice.[23] The old guard lined up behind Henry.

Madison replied that the proposed tax violated the Virginia Declaration of Rights. The state could not authorize *any* religion, not even one as broad as Christianity. Besides, he asked, how would courts decide what sects qualify as "Christian"? History is full of wars over which group of believers, which books of scripture, which tests of faith are truly Christian. History also shows that state-imposed religion is no guarantee of public morals or safety; the "downfall of states mentioned by Mr. H[enry] happened when there was establishment." Such arguments failed to coax enough delegates to oppose Henry and derail his bill. So Madison worked around them. He nudged Henry from his leadership role in the assembly. (Gov. Benjamin Harrison's term was expiring, and Madison managed to get Henry elected to the weak governor's office.) Madison then took his case against the assessment bill directly to the voters. In 1785 he published—anonymously, as usual—a "Memorial and Remonstrance against Religious Assessments" in which he reminded Virginians that the establishment of religion for some hypothetical common good has all too often meant the oppression of minorities for whatever faith their rulers believed in.[24]

The assessment bill, Madison wrote, implies "that the Civil Magistrate is a competent judge of Religious Truth," an "arrogant pretension" falsified by fifteen centuries of bigotry and persecution by Christian princes and ecclesiastical courtiers. The bill assumes that authorities can legislate uniformity of thought by employing teachers of religion. But "torrents of blood have been spilt in the old world, by vain attempts of the secular arm, to extinguish Religious discord, by proscribing all differences in Religious opinion." No matter how pure the legislators' goals, it is a "perversion of the means of salvation" to "employ Religion as an engine of Civil policy." The future of America, Madison insisted, depends on its "offering an Asylum to the persecuted and oppressed of every Nation and Religion." Yet the assessment bill "is itself a signal of persecution. It degrades from the equal rank of Citizens all those whose opinions in Religion do not bend to those of the Legislative authority. Distant as it may be in its present form from the Inquisition, it differs from it only in degree." The bill is, therefore, a warning beacon to immigrants in search of liberty to avoid our shore and "to seek some other haven." Madison's Remonstrance moved Virginians to flood the assembly with counter petitions against the assessment bill. Fearing a backlash from voters, the delegates finally tabled the bill and left it to die.[25]

Far from just a tax protest, the fight over the assessment bill was a clash of two worldviews. As in Puritan New England, the gentry in

Virginia imagined society as an organic body of stratified members—natural workers at the bottom doing the labor, natural leaders at the top doing the planning, and everyone united as one for a common goal. This organic image of society, taught in mirrors for princes since antiquity, was reflected in the nostalgic assessment bill. Madison rejected the organic image in favor of the emergent view of society as a social contract (made popular by John Locke and disseminated in America by teachers like John Witherspoon). A social contract is a cooperative agreement between independent parties for the good—for the goals and rights—of individual persons. It has no natural hierarchy, no human faculties, no goals or good of its own. The measure of its success is not how well it achieves the alleged aims of some social body but how fairly it treats the participants. James Madison developed this view in his Remonstrance. Invoking the Virginia Declaration of Rights, he argued that "all men are by nature equally free and independent." They enter into civil society and subsequent associations for mutual benefit, but they do not give up the natural rights bestowed on them by "the Governour of the Universe" prior to any such agreement. Among these unalienable rights is freedom of conscience. In religion, "it is the duty of every man to render to the Creator such homage and such only as he believes to be acceptable to him." More generally, "the opinions of men, depending only on the evidence contemplated by their own minds[,] cannot follow the dictates of other men." It is a violation of natural rights and "a dangerous abuse of power" for authorities to try to force unity of opinion. Madison carried this view into the most important assembly of his career, the Constitutional Convention of 1787.[26]

States

Communitarian critics charge that liberals like James Madison, by discounting common goals, normalize selfishness. Classic liberals, however (especially Madison), recognized that people value goals and causes greater than themselves. Madison would say that of course people seek goals for their churches, for their workplaces, for their communities, and for their country as well as for themselves. The trouble is, people usually don't agree on these goals; participants have different goals for complex institutions—religious purity or inclusiveness, good wages or profits, public projects or austerity. Still, despite varied and often opposing goals, people can cooperate. With enough effort, individuals may agree on customs and work rules that further their different goals for an institution they all care about. And with more effort they may agree on a constitution and laws that further their diverse goals even when they care about different institutions.

What Madison, Jefferson, and their allies cared about was the stability of the nation emerging from the American Revolution; their goals for the nation included sound credit, a continental foreign policy, and the respect of other countries. What Patrick Henry and his allies cared more about was the rights of *their* country—by which they meant the state of Virginia. They seemed willing to tax Virginians for goals like keeping the faith of their fathers, but they were less willing to support national causes—say, paying Revolutionary War debts. Frustrating the goals of almost all Americans after the war, there was no firm agreement to cooperate between the states, just loose Articles of Confederation. And there was no proper government to tie people together as a nation, just a feeble Confederation Congress.

Across America, therefore, postwar differences over public policies grew into pitched conflicts. New York merchants wanted a treaty of commerce with Spain, and they would grant in return Spanish control of the Mississippi River. Kentucky farmers cared more about navigation on the Mississippi, and they were prepared to fight for free access to the river. Up and down the Atlantic Seaboard, states ran competing economies; they issued their own currency, with wildly fluctuating exchange rates, and they imposed their own tariffs (or not) to lure shipping to their home ports. Great Britain played states off against one another and took away much of their Atlantic trade by closing British colonies to American ships. One London magazine reported gleefully, "By the latest letters from the American States, the restraint laid upon their trade with the British West India islands has thrown them into the utmost perplexity; and by way of retaliation they are passing laws inimical to their own interest; and what is still worse, inconsistent with each other.... Hence the dissentions that universally prevail throughout what may be called the thirteen Dis-United States."[27]

Lack of a national trade policy cost states jobs, fueling unrest. Massachusetts, for example, went from building about 125 ships per year before the war to 15 or 20 in 1786, ruining not only shipyards but their whole supply chain of "blacksmiths, rope-makers, riggers, block-makers, sailmakers" and related businesses, notes historian Frederick Marks.[28] As its economy weakened, Massachusetts shifted the tax burden from seaport towns to backcountry farms. Farmers rebelled. "I have been greatly abused," said one farmer, according to a newspaper report on a county protest meeting; "[I] have been obliged to do more than my part in the war; been loaded with class rates, town rates, province rates, Continental rates and all rates . . . been pulled and hauled by sheriffs, constables, and collectors, and had my cattle sold for less than they were worth," complained the farmer.[29] He told his neighbors, "The great men are going to get all we have, and I think it is time for us to rise and put a stop to it, and have no more courts, nor sheriffs, nor collectors, nor lawyers."[30] Massachusetts farmers and their supporters *did* rise up and try to stop tax collections. In late 1786 and early 1787, protesters by the hundreds closed the courts in five counties, and an army of well over a thousand led by Daniel Shays raided the main armory at Springfield for weapons to shut down the government. Massachusetts militia routed Shays's forces, but the rebellion stirred backcountry resistance elsewhere and sent shockwaves throughout the states.[31]

No appeal to common goals—the traditional nostrum of mirrors for princes—could resolve the postwar disputes that were pushing Americans apart. No transforming leader—not even the famed George Washington—could articulate a shared vision for the country. From the comfort of his Mount Vernon home, the retired general followed the news about "the disorders which have arisen in these states," but he did not envision anything he could do. "Good God!" Washington despaired, "There are combustibles in every State, which a spark may set fire to," and no one can "say when—where—or how it will end." James Madison, however, had an idea. What Americans needed, he decided, was not a common purpose, not a unifying leader, but a better social contract.[32]

Madison first tried for an agreement to limit "commercial warfare among the states."[33] He promoted a meeting of state representatives to cede powers over trade to the Confederation Congress. Held at Annapolis in September of 1786, this meeting was poorly attended and inconclusive, but Madison, Alexander Hamilton, and the other attendees called on Congress to hold a follow-up convention "to render the constitution of the federal government adequate to the exigencies of the Union."[34] The Congress went along and invited states to send delegates to Philadelphia the next May, 1787, to discuss revisions to the Articles of

Confederation. Every state but fiercely independent Rhode Island sent delegates to the Philadelphia convention. No one knew exactly what the convention was supposed to accomplish; but the Virginia delegation had a plan—a proposal for a brand new constitution—and the chief architect of the Virginia Plan was James Madison.[35]

Madison came to Philadelphia better prepared than any delegate to the convention. During the prior year, he read every book on government he could find. He had asked Thomas Jefferson, off in France, to purchase the latest works from booksellers in Paris; Jefferson sent him two full trunks. Much like Machiavelli in 1513, Madison retreated to his wooded farm in the spring of 1786 to study what great thinkers had said about the leadership and design of states. Unlike Machiavelli, he did not undertake another mirror for princes; he did not conjure a hero on horseback to save his country from ruin. Rather, from his books of theory, Madison compiled an analysis: "Of Ancient and Modern Confederacies." From his own experience, he applied this analysis to a case study titled "Vices of the Political System of the United States." And, combining his political theories and his practical experience, he drew up a blueprint of government.[36]

The fatal flaw of all confederacies, Madison determined, was their lack of a central authority to enforce mutually beneficial laws. Americans had cast off an oppressive central authority in their war with King George III, but now they had no agent capable of protecting their hard-won liberties. Under the Articles of Confederation, Madison observed, America was not a union of fellow states but a "league of sovereign powers."[37] This confederation allowed states to usurp federal responsibilities, for example, by conducting their own foreign policies. It allowed states to disregard one another's interests, for example, by placing punitive taxes on interstate commerce. What's worse, the American confederation allowed member states to violate the rights of their own citizens, for example, by denying freedom of conscience. Over time, Madison reflected, such vices of confederations cause them to fragment and precipitate greater evils—including nostalgia for monarchy, which he already detected in "some leading minds."[38]

The siren song of monarchy that lured sages like Xenophon, Seneca, John of Salisbury, Aquinas, Erasmus, and even contemporaries like John Adams was lost on James Madison. *His* mind was set, in 1787 and thereafter, on solving an age-old problem of governance—how to design a central authority sufficiently competent "to controul one part of the Society from invading the rights of another, and at the same time sufficiently controuled itself." A prince, he thought, might be able to control others but not himself. A small republican state might control itself but fail to protect all its citizens. However, Madison reasoned, a constitutional government over a large enough territory could do both.[39]

He explained his reasoning in letters to George Washington and Thomas Jefferson, written just before and after the Philadelphia convention. Society, Madison wrote, is composed of different interest groups— what, in management jargon today, might be called "stakeholders." The task of government and national leaders is not to unite *all* stakeholders for a common purpose; that would be futile. It is not to rally *some group* of stakeholders for a common purpose; that might impassion some but jeopardize the rights of other stakeholders who stand in their way. Rather, the job of civil leadership is to impartially balance the rights of every stakeholder group, to serve as a "disinterested & dispassionate umpire in disputes between different passions & interests in the State."[40]

Now the practical question is what sort of government may be plausibly impartial in balancing the rights of different stakeholders. The classical answer is a monarchy ruled by a perfect prince. "In absolute monarchies," Madison told Jefferson, "the Prince may be tolerably neutral toward different classes of his subjects, but may sacrifice the happiness of all to his personal ambition." The problem is, a prince and his courtiers are themselves stakeholders, and when it comes to their own stakes, they are apt to be biased judges, not impartial umpires. Certainly, a prince could be schooled in virtue, and moral education might improve the whole system, as mirrors for princes preach. But history shows that partisan princes are nevertheless the rule. The American people deserve better than being taught to pray for the best and suffer the worst.[41]

The traditional alternative to monarchy is the plain democracy of a small republic. This, too, is problematic, Madison wrote Jefferson. A small republic removes the prince as a source of oppression, "but it is not sufficiently neutral toward the parts composing it": The dominant stakeholders are still able to invade the rights of others. Americans can look to their own history for evidence. Massachusetts, for instance, was founded by the Bay Company as a shareholder democracy, but it denied religious freedom to nonconforming colonists. More recently, democratic assemblies in other states have threatened the religious rights of minorities (as in Virginia, with its assessment bill). Madison drew on his earlier experience in Philadelphia, his collegiate exposure to the "free air" of religious pluralism, and he concluded that religious rights would be more secure in a larger representative democracy—containing so many sects, with such dispersed members, that none could impose their faith on their neighbors. Madison's key insight now was to extend this conclusion to nonreligious rights as well. "The same security seems requisite for the civil as for the religious rights of individuals," he said: Everyone's rights are safest in a large republic composed of multiple interest groups, represented by multiple officials, none of whom have unchecked power to impose their goals on the rest.[42]

Madison described to Washington in April of 1787 what the government of an impartial republic might look like, and his ideas shaped the Virginia Plan that became the agenda for the Philadelphia convention the following month. The centerpiece of the plan was a national legislature where the citizens of America were supreme, replacing the Confederation Congress where the separate states were supreme. The new Congress would have powers to manage national defense, conduct foreign policy, regulate continental trade, and otherwise do what the states could not. To check injustice in the states and to strengthen the central authority that Madison found wanting in the confederation, Congress would have the power to veto state laws. To check abuse of its authority, Congress would be divided into two houses, with members apportioned on state population or taxes. The powers of the central government would be further divided between a federal judiciary and a national executive of some kind.[43]

Madison's plan did not hinge on the availability of a chief executive of George Washington's caliber; it was designed to guard against a brute like George III or a zealot like Cotton Mather. But Washington's popularity could help to sell the plan, so Madison coaxed the general out of retirement to join the Virginia delegation at the convention. (Patrick Henry declined an invitation to attend, saying he "smelled a rat.") The Virginia delegation tapped Gov. Edmond Randolph, a gifted orator, to introduce their plan in Philadelphia. The convention debated its provisions, lobbed counterproposals, and hammered out details through the summer of 1787.[44]

Delegates fought especially over state representation in the national legislature. The Virginians' bid for representation proportional to population would obviously give their state—the most populous in the country—the most influence in the federal Congress; less populous states, which enjoyed equality of representation in the current Confederation Congress, protested their diminished role. Siding with Madison, James Wilson of Pennsylvania (the second most populous state) took the view that a government where the people, not the states, were supreme must represent the people, not the states, equally: "Can we forget for whom we are forming a Government?" Wilson challenged the delegates. "Is it for *men*, or for the imaginary beings called *States*?"[45] John Dickinson of Delaware (the least populous state) took a different view, warning that the small states "would sooner submit to a foreign power, than submit to be deprived of an equality of suffrage, in both branches of the legislature, and thereby be thrown under the dominion of the large states." Positioning himself among "friends to a good national government" as well as friends of states' rights, Dickinson sought a middle way, to reinforce the division of power between state and national sovereignties in a federal system of government.[46] His view convinced the small states to hold out for a "Great Compromise," which provided for proportional representation in one house of Congress and state equality in the other.

While proportional representation divided large and small states, another divide split the northern and southern states. Any plan to base representation on state population forced the convention to consider who exactly to include in that population. The framers would allow states to count most permanent residents: free men, women and children, indentured servants, even taxpaying Native Americans. Enslaved people were the problem. States such as South Carolina, where enslaved persons comprised half the population, wanted to count them all—not to grant them actual representation but to increase their state's representatives in Congress. (With slaves included, notes legal historian Michael Klarman, the combined population of the five southern states and their representation in the House would have equaled that of the eight northern states in 1787.[47]) States such as Massachusetts objected to counting any enslaved persons. Non-free blacks were treated as property, said Elbridge Gerry, "used to the southward as horses and cattle are to the northward; and why should their representation be increased to the southward on account of the number of slaves, than horses or oxen to the north?" Wilson offered another compromise, proposing to apportion representatives "in proportion to the whole number of white and other free Citizens and inhabitants of every age, sex and condition including those bound to servitude for a term of years and three-fifths of all other persons not comprehended in the foregoing description." And thus were *slaves*, those unnamed "other persons," dealt with in the Constitution by men who were too ashamed to use the word.[48]

The framers went on to define the powers of Congress, the responsibilities of the executive branch, the jurisdiction of the federal courts. Assuming that any authority could and would be abused, the framers adopted all sorts of checks and balances: election of officials for fixed terms, legislative approval of executive and judicial appointments, restrictions on officeholders' compensation and emoluments, separation of House and Senate powers, judicial review of legislative acts, executive vetoes of congressional bills, and veto overrides by Congress, among others.

Much debate concerned the creation of a national executive, a vague detail (down the list of ideas at number 7) in Madison's Virginia Plan. The Articles of Confederation did not even provide for an executive, and the delegates had no obvious model to copy. Almost nobody but Alexander Hamilton leaned toward a philosopher-king.[49] Americans were sick of kings and wary of philosophers who thought their goals for the country were morally superior to everyone else's. Still, delegates conceded that an executive branch headed by a single chief executive could be a useful check on abuses of legislative power, so they made up the office of the president, adding more checks on *its* power. Madison was particularly intent on an impeachment provision "for defending the Community against the incapacity, negligence or perfidy of the chief Magistrate." Madison argued that a fixed term of office was not enough security. The president "might lose his capacity after his appointment. He might pervert his administration into a scheme of peculation or oppression. He might betray his trust to foreign powers." The potential of the president to do harm was much greater than that of individual legislators, Madison pointed out. It was unlikely that all or most members of Congress would succumb to incapacity or bribery, and "if one or a few members should only be seduced, the soundness of the remaining members, would maintain the integrity and fidelity of the body." However, "in the case of the Executive Magistracy which was to be administered by a single man, loss of capacity or corruption was more within the compass of probable events, and either of them might be fatal to the

Republic."[50] Finally, as the convention came to a close, an impeachment provision was adopted.

After four months, the framers wound up with a constitution that most of them found fault with but nearly all of them could support. James Madison had supplied the framework for debate and won agreement on a federal government of divided powers, but he clearly did not get all that he hoped for. He was disappointed, he told Jefferson, that the convention failed to give Congress a veto over state laws. The delegates substituted a clause making the Constitution and federal legislation the supreme law of the land, with state laws subject to Supreme Court review. (Madison objected that "it is more convenient to prevent the passage of a law, than to declare it void after it is passed," especially "where the law aggrieves individuals, who may be unable to support an appeal against a State to the supreme Judiciary."[51]) Madison was displeased, too, that the convention did not sustain proportional representation in both houses of Congress but only in the House of Representatives. Less fateful but personally grating was action on a last-minute proposal of Madison's authorizing Congress "to establish an University, in which no preferences or distinctions should be allowed on account of religion"; tired of tinkering with language, the delegates voted it down and went home.[52]

Despite these disappointments, Madison signed off on the Constitution and began the fight for ratification. Nine states had to approve the Constitution for it to take effect. This promised to be trickier than the "miracle," as Madison called it, of negotiating the document in Philadelphia. However spirited their debates, the Constitutional Convention was a relatively small meeting between men of similar wealth and standing with some continental views. (A total of fifty-five delegates attended but never all together; daily attendance averaged about thirty, and the regulars numbered only around twenty, reports Max Farrand, a longtime student of the convention.[53]) Ratification of the Constitution was a different business—a state-by-state campaign to win over skeptical Americans. Americans were skeptical not necessarily because they were small-minded or uninformed but because they asked themselves a logical question: Was this Constitution the best way to divide power and govern? Many suspected—as many suspect today—that it was not. The framers, politicians after all, tried to steer public attention away from this question. They focused instead on whether their plan was preferable to the status quo: Was the Constitution better than the Articles of Confederation? The framers bet most Americans would concede that it was.

Factions

Once the Philadelphia convention adjourned, the Constitution was published in the *Pennsylvania Packet* and sent to other newspapers around the country. At that point the document, in Madison's words, "was nothing more than the draft of a plan, nothing but a dead letter, until life and validity had been breathed into it by the voice of the people, speaking through the several State Conventions." Madison had seen to it that the Constitution would be subject to ratification not by state legislatures, all of which stood to lose power, but by special state conventions of popularly elected delegates. Pennsylvania was the first state to schedule an election and a convention. Supporters of the Constitution—who called themselves Federalists—insisted that the state convention simply vote *yes* or *no* on ratification, precluding amendments by their opponents— whom they stigmatized as Antifederalists.[54]

Opponents reacted with angry words. Typical Antifederalist broadsides appeared in the Philadelphia newspapers under the pen name "Centinel" (likely Samuel Bryan, the son of a state judge). Centinel charged that the Constitution was framed by "the wealthy and ambitious" to "lord it over" their fellow Americans. He argued that the planned federal government was so far removed from the people that "it would be in practice a *permanent* ARISTOCRACY," and it was so complicated that "the people will be perplexed and divided in their sentiments about the source of abuses or misconduct." Despotism was inevitable in any plan to "bind so great a country under one government," Centinel maintained. In the larger states, people already complained that governments were unresponsive to their concerns. Americans wanted smaller units of government—closer to home, with better access to information, able to act faster—not a bigger government that fuses the United States into one huge empire. "It is the opinion of the greatest writers," according to Centinel, "that a very extensive country cannot be governed on democratical principles, on any other plan, than a confederation of a number of small republics." Maybe the US Confederation *was* weak, but states like Pennsylvania with simple structures of government were competent to secure the rights of their people, he said. The Federalists' contention that Americans must accept the Constitution—one lacking the most basic declaration of rights—or face ruin was the argument of tyrants. Centinel concluded with a call for a second "general Convention" to consider amendments and frame a more democratic plan of government.[55]

Federalists resisted calls for amendments or, God forbid, a second convention because they feared that renegotiating the compromises reached in Philadelphia would prolong debate and doom the Constitution. Backed by business leaders and urban workers, Pennsylvania Federalists held firm on an up-or-down vote and ratified the Constitution on December 12, 1787. By month's end, the states of Delaware, New Jersey, and Georgia had also ratified. But trouble was brewing in the key states of New York and Virginia as local politicians stoked opposition. So Federalists stepped up their campaign, publishing scores of pro-Constitution essays in friendly newspapers. The most famous series, *The Federalist*, was written for the New York press by Alexander Hamilton, John Jay, and James Madison under the pseudonym Publius.[56]

Madison's essays respond to critics of an extended republic and federal government. In *Federalist* No. 14, he claims that Antifederalists like Centinel are stuck in the past: They gaze backward to the civic ideals enshrined in ancient literature, and they take on faith that democracy must be confined to "a small number of people, living within a small compass of territory." They tell Americans—who together "accomplished a revolution which has no parallel in the annals of human society"—that they cannot aspire to be fellow citizens of a proud nation, cannot even "live together as members of the same family." Don't listen to these melancholy voices, Madison pleads. Don't fall for stale rhetoric "rending us in pieces, in order to preserve our liberties and promote our happiness." Don't look back to the clichés of august writers but forward to the promise of America: "Is it not the glory of the people of America, that whilst they have paid a decent regard to the opinions of former times and other nations, they have not suffered a blind veneration for antiquity, for custom, or for names, to overrule the suggestions of their own good sense?"[57]

In *Federalist* No. 10, Madison builds a stronger case for an extended republic, using his own good sense to dispel the clichés of mirrors for princes. The tiredest of these clichés, now peddled by Antifederalists, says that people need a common goal in order to live in peace or cooperate effectively. Antifederalists assumed their states *had* common goals (or at least *could* have them given the right leadership). New York's Antifederalist governor, George Clinton, viewed the states "as moral persons, having a will of their own."[58] In this view, states were close-knit, virtuous communities whose citizens shared interests, values, and a public good. Antifederalists further assumed that a large, continental republic could *not* have common goals and therefore "can never form a perfect union, establish justice, insure domestic tranquility, promote the general welfare, and secure the blessings of liberty," as pledged in the Constitution. Citizens of the United States, Antifederalists said, would have such a "dissimilitude of interest, morals, and politics" that a national government would be "like a house divided against itself"; such a government, where "the public good is sacrificed to a thousand views," could only end in dictatorship.[59] Madison attacks the hypocrisy of this position. Antifederalists, he suggests, were vocal denouncers of tyranny at the national level but tacit enablers of tyranny in their states. In fact, states were not the cozy, single-minded bodies of Antifederalist myth. Real states, in Madison's experience, were arenas of clashing interests dominated by majority factions (say, a church or industry) that presumed to speak for the whole. What Antifederalists got right is that people in a large republic will normally not share common goals. What Antifederalists got wrong is thinking that people in small states *do* share common goals. And what Antifederalists got very wrong is supposing that common goals are necessary in any social body to cure the mischiefs of faction.

"There are two methods of curing the mischiefs of faction," Madison argues. "The one, by removing its causes; the other, by controlling its effects." The first is the method taught since antiquity in mirrors for princes: Ancient sages saw their countrymen behaving badly, their states ridden with factions; they diagnosed the problem as a lack of civic purpose, and they called for a visionary leader to provide unity—to somehow transform people's selfish goals and refocus them on the public good. But attempting to remove the causes of faction by instilling in citizens the same passions and interests, Madison contends, is illiberal in principle and unworkable in practice.[60]

For Madison, the problem of faction arises not because people are too selfish but because they have different ideas and opinions. "A zeal for different opinions concerning religion, concerning government, and many other points," a devotion to different leaders or different cultural figures, all such attachments have divided mankind into factions, Madison writes. No doubt, "the most common and durable source of factions, has been the various and unequal distribution of property. Those who hold, and those who are without property, have ever formed distinct interests in society. Those who are creditors, and those who are debtors, . . . a landed interest, a manufacturing interest, a mercantile interest, a monied interest, with many lesser interests, grow up of necessity in civilized nations, and divide them into different classes, actuated by different sentiments and views."[61] These different interests and opinions can clash and flare into harmful animosities if not managed in some way. The safest way, Madison asserts, is through constitutional structures to control the *effects* of faction, not transformational leadership to remove the *causes* of faction.

"It is in vain to say, that enlightened statesmen will be able to adjust these clashing interests, and render them all subservient to the public good," Madison submits. For one thing, "enlightened statesmen will not always be at the helm." For another, "the public good" is itself open to conflicting interpretations.[62] On person's "public good" for the nation (for example, a state-supported religion) is often another's cost (for example, unjust taxation). So long as people are free to think for themselves, they will continue to have different goals for their lives, for their communities, for their country. And leaders who try to deny that freedom are worse than the disease of faction they purport to cure. Madison takes issue with academic statesmen and philosophers who admonish individuals, in management-speak, to get on the same page—who trivialize differences that cause faction and dissention: "However erroneous or ridiculous these grounds of dissention and faction, may appear to the enlightened Statesman, or the benevolent philosopher, the bulk of mankind who are neither Statesmen nor Philosophers, will continue to view them in a different light."[63] The vast majority of Americans feel they are entitled by right to different opinions, interests, and visions—just as they are entitled to different religions. And, consequently, even the most transforming leader will not transform everyone's goals but will at most command a majority of followers, whose shared passion can put at risk the rights of individuals who stand in their way.

Madison endorses a constitution for controlling the effects of faction that is the very opposite of what mirrors for princes teach for removing the causes of faction. Instead of trying to consolidate factions behind a common goal, Madison wants to disperse factions through a larger republic so "that no common interest or passion will be likely to unite a majority of the whole number in an unjust pursuit."[64] Using a constitution, a social contract, to deter rather than to promote group goal-seeking defies centuries of wisdom on leadership. But seriously, Madison asks, what else is there to restrain majority factions from violating minorities' rights? He questions the theoretical restraints invoked in mirrors for princes—for example:

- Voluntary ethical codes, such as an honest concern for the common good. In the ideal world of political theory, Madison writes, this is considered a sufficient social control. "Experience however shews that it has little effect on individuals, and perhaps still less on a collection of individuals, and least of all on a majority with the public authority in their hands. If the former are ready to forget that honesty is the best policy; the last do more."
- Respect for reputation or character. "This motive," Madison says, "is not found sufficient to restrain individuals from injustice, and loses its efficacy in proportion to the number which is to divide the praise or the blame. Besides as it has reference to public opinion, which is that of the majority, the standard is fixed by those whose conduct is to be measured by it."
- Religion. "The inefficacy of this restraint on individuals is well known," Madison goes on. "The conduct of every popular assembly, acting on oath, the strongest of religious ties, shews that individuals join without remorse in acts against which their consciences would revolt, if proposed to them separately in their closets." (No doubt recalling his youthful outrage at religious bigotry in Virginia and his fight against Christian establishment in the state assembly, Madison observed that religious passion at its hottest is not necessarily a force for good: "Even in its coolest state, it has been much oftener a motive to oppression than a restraint from it.")[65]

Madison had no quarrel with Christianity or religion per se. Again, he uses religion simply as an exemplar, an illustrative case of a broader principle: "In a free government, the security for civil rights must be the same as for religious rights. It consists in the one case in the multiplicity of interests, and in the other, in the multiplicity of sects." Madison worried about the power of organized groups, whatever their goals, to abridge individual rights. Of course, Madison knew that churches could inspire goodwill, encouraging members to "love your neighbor as yourself." Of course, he knew what Adam Smith wrote about the societal benefits of goal-seeking groups in general—they can leverage effort, manufacture cheaper pins, and all that. What he also knew and took more seriously than almost anyone was the potential cost of purposeful groups to vulnerable individuals. Students of management have pointed out that goal-seeking in organizations has a dark side: Unchecked, it can create a dominant culture where anything goes to post a number, reach a quota, or make a buck. James Madison in 1787 sought to protect Americans from the dark side of mass interest groups: He thought, "If a majority be united by a common interest, the rights of the minority will be insecure." But "in the federal republic of the United States," under the Constitution, "the society itself will be broken into so many parts, interests and classes of citizens, that the rights of individuals or of the minority, will be in little danger from interested combinations of the majority."[66]

Madison's analysis continues in *Federalist* No. 51: If a large republic of divided interests is Americans' best protection against overbearing groups, a federal government of divided powers is their best protection against overbearing leaders. Madison stipulates that the primary control on government leaders is their dependence on the people who give them power. "But," he writes, "experience has taught mankind the necessity of auxiliary precautions." The precautions prescribed in mirrors for princes, such as training in moral leadership, are sometimes helpful yet generally inadequate. To address "the defect of better motives" among leaders, the Constitution provides for a government of opposite and rival interests— the "aim is to divide and arrange the several offices in such a manner as that each may be a check on the other."[67]

"In the federal system of America," Madison explains, "the power surrendered by the people, is first divided between two distinct governments," state and national. Avoiding the extreme nationalism of his co-Federalist, Alexander Hamilton, Madison insists that the states, for all their flaws, would act as counterweights to the central government. Each government would have different jurisdictions and furnish different channels for public opinion so that "the different governments will control each other, at the same time that each will be controuled by itself." Self-control of these governments results from dividing their own power between independent branches and separate departments. It is the independence of these branches and departments—not paper declarations, not wishful codes of ethics—that provides security for individual rights, according to Madison. Independence consists in "giving to those who administer each department, the necessary constitutional means, and personal motives, to resist encroachments of the others." Through numerous checks and balances, "ambition must be made to counter ambition. The interest of the man [the officeholder] must be connected with the constitutional rights of the place." In government as in the marketplace, one can hope for benevolent leaders but one is better off in a system where "the private interest of every individual, may be a centinel over the public rights."[68]

Debates

Early in 1788 Federalists won an easy vote for ratification of the Constitution in Connecticut and scored a narrow win in Massachusetts. Elsewhere in New England, New Hampshire was split, postponing its vote; feisty Rhode Island refused to even hold a ratifying convention. In the South, Maryland and South Carolina voted for ratification, bringing the total number of ratifying states to eight—one short of the requirement to approve the Constitution. All eyes now turned to Virginia, the largest (both in size and population) of the states.

Virginians were of two minds. The same delegation that proposed the Virginia Plan in Philadelphia left there at odds over the Constitution. Gov. Edmond Randolph and elder-statesman George Mason refused to sign the document, the latter going public with his objections that "there is no declaration of rights," that the federal government would turn into "a monarchy, or a corrupt oppressive aristocracy."[69] On the other side, George Washington and James Madison swallowed their reservations and backed the Constitution. After the Philadelphia convention, Madison traveled to New York to serve out his term in the Confederation Congress and stave off trouble from Antifederalists there. Washington once more retired to Mount Vernon, where he could monitor local opinions. As Madison was writing his scholarly *Federalist* No. 51, an apprehensive George Washington wrote to him relaying the "anxious sollicitude" of Virginians that he should come home and stand for election to the state ratifying convention.[70] George Mason was out cam-paigning on his objections to the Constitution. Worse yet, the state's populist leader and Madison's old adversary, Patrick Henry, was rousing his rural rabble against the elitist motives of the framers and the parade of horribles sure to come from big government. Washington's secretary, Tobias Lear, expressed the feelings of many that Madison was "the only man in this State who can effectually combat the influence of Mason & Henery."[71]

Madison dutifully finished his last *Federalist* essay, put down his pen as Publius, and returned to Virginia. Elected to represent Orange County at the state convention, the soft-spoken, diminutive James Madison squared off against the greatest orator of his generation—Patrick Henry. (Thomas Jefferson said Henry was the laziest reader he ever saw but the finest orator: He "spoke as Homer wrote."[72]) In June of 1788 Virginians flocked to Richmond to watch Patrick Henry take on James Madison and the Federalists at the state ratifying convention. Hundreds of specta-tors filled the box seats and galleries at the town's theater for performing arts, while 170 delegates shared the stage. Luckily, one of the spectators was an attorney named David Robertson who took shorthand notes and published a full stenographic account of the debates—or as full as pos-sible, since Madison spoke with "a feebleness of voice" and Robertson up in the gallery often could not hear what he was saying.[73]

Everyone heard Patrick Henry when he took the floor and challenged the very first words of the Constitution. Glaring at Madison, ringleader of the framers, Henry demanded to know "what right had they to say, *We, the People?*" Surely, "the people gave them no power to use their name." What about, "*We, the States*"? Professing his "anxious solicitude for the public welfare" of Virginia, Henry proclaimed himself as the voice "of the people of this Commonwealth, as a sentinel over their rights, liberty, and happiness." The people are *not* happy, Henry declared, over the fatal proposal to change from a confederated to a consolidated government, "a proposal that goes to the utter annihilation of the most solemn engagement of the States." I share the people's alarm, Henry said: "I conceive the republic to be in extreme danger" from "this perilous innovation." If you adopt this new government, Henry warned his fellow delegates, "instead of securing your rights, you may lose them forever; . . . the Republic may be lost forever; . . . liberty will be lost, and tyranny must and will arise."[74] As Henry thundered that they'd be enslaved by the

Constitution, one listener "involuntarily felt his wrists to assure himself that the fetters were not already pressing his flesh."[75]

Madison replied calmly, "I shall not attempt to make impressions by any ardent professions of zeal for the public welfare." That's empty rhetoric, just like Mr. Henry's "general assertions of dangers" lurking in the Constitution, just like his charge that the framers of the Constitution ignored the states and presumed to speak for people. "Sir, no state is bound by it," Madison reminded Henry, "without its own consent"—as expressed by its own people at these very ratifying conventions. Never in history were "We, the people" given so much voice; nowhere have so many "free inhabitants ... been seen deliberating on a form of Government, and selecting such of their citizens as possessed their confidence, to determine upon, and give effect to it." So let's skip the histrionics and put passions aside, Madison suggested. Let's not dispute one another's "honor, candor, and rectitude of motives." But let's "examine the Constitution on its own merits solely."[76]

Mercifully, Madison had rules of the convention on his side. George Mason, to buy time to feel out the delegates, had proposed at the outset that they discuss the Constitution "clause by clause, through all its parts"; the Federalist camp gladly agreed. Such a plodding, systematic process played to the advantage of a knowledgeable policy wonk like James Madison, not a soaring orator like Patrick Henry. Day after day, for three weeks, Henry went on telling Virginians to be afraid of this Constitution, while Madison and his allies—John Marshall, George Nicholas, and by now Edmund Randolph—patiently explained its features.[77]

Henry complained that the Constitution would create an all-powerful national government that "cannot reign over so extensive a country as this is, without absolute despotism." He said that states' rights would disappear because "this Constitution can counteract and suspend any of our laws." He claimed that Virginia's sovereignty would be surrendered to elites up North, that her future could be determined "by a despicable minority at the extremity of the United States." He alleged that supporters of the Constitution wanted a big, splendid government, with a large "standing army—a great powerful navy—a long and rapacious train of officers and dependents," at the service of senators and representatives and other grandees, all headed by "a great and mighty President, with very extensive powers; the powers of a King." He predicted that Virginians would pay dearly for it: "The whole of our property may be taken by this American Government, by laying what taxes they please, giving themselves what salaries they please," and squandering whatever they please of the public's money. Federal tax collectors sent from Philadelphia or New York, he raged, would be even more voracious than "our State Sheriffs, those unfeeling bloodsuckers." Henry insisted that at the very least "a Bill of Rights [is] indispensably necessary." Without major amendments, Henry concluded, the Constitution would never bring harmony between the states and federal government: "If you attempt to force it down men's throats, and call it Union, dreadful consequences must follow."[78]

Madison responded that Henry was as confused on his facts as he was in his opinions on the Constitution. If Henry read more, "upon a review of history he would have found, that the loss of liberty very often resulted from factions and divisions;—from local considerations," from "the majority trampling on the rights of the minority" rather than from big governments. As for standing armies and federal taxation to support them, Madison expressed his own misgivings. But he cautioned Virginians that their shores and borders remained vulnerable to attack, their fortunes subject to threats and extortions from foreign empires. Madison disputed that members of Congress would be giving themselves whatever salaries they please; the voters wouldn't stand for it. He dismissed the notion that the president would degenerate into a tyrant; the legislature and judiciary would frustrate a would-be king. He disagreed that the national government would be all powerful; its powers were defined and limited by the Constitution. "It has never been denied by the friends of the paper on the table, that it has defects," Madison concluded. But it is better for all Americans than "the present inadequate, unsafe, and pernicious confederation." And it can be amended if required—after it takes effect.[79]

Madison pushed back on demands for amendments, including a bill of rights, prior to ratification. A bill of rights is not needed, he said; the Constitution protects rights not with parchment promises but with concrete checks and balances. Besides, a hasty enumeration of rights can put freedom at risk; it implies that individuals have no more rights against their government—just as an enumeration of powers implies that governments have no more powers over individuals. Patrick Henry scoffed, "The middle and lower ranks of people have not those illuminated ideas, which the well-born are so happily possessed of." Ordinary Virginians just want liberty; they take comfort in the plain guarantee of rights under their state Declaration. But under the proposed Constitution, according to Henry, "there will be no checks, no real balances, in this Government: What can avail your specious imaginary balances, your rope-dancing, chain-rattling, ridiculous ideal checks and contrivances?"[80]

Madison knew that the Virginia Declaration of Rights was no guarantee of liberty, that Patrick Henry was the same demagogue who ignored it in 1784 when he tried to ram his religious assessment bill through the Virginia legislature. In principle, Madison confided to Thomas Jefferson, he did lean toward a federal bill of rights, provided it was properly framed. But now was not the time, not with Patrick Henry working to derail the Constitution by offering some forty amendments. As the convention prepared for its final vote, Madison asked the delegates to reflect: What if every state insisted on such a list of amendments, all addressing different local concerns? The states would never agree on a constitution, and its enemies know it. To placate Antifederalists, Madison invited the convention to propose subsequent amendments, to be recommended *after* ratification for consideration in the new Congress. Then Madison urged the weary delegates to choose hope over fear and approve the Constitution unconditionally. And so they did, on June 25, 1788, ratifying the Constitution by a vote of 89–79 and recommending that the First Federal Congress consider "whatsoever amendments may be deemed necessary."[81]

Before Madison could echo that recommendation in Washington's inaugural address, he faced one more round with Patrick Henry. While Henry lost the vote on ratification, he held his grip on the Virginia legislature, which would now choose the state's two US senators and draw up districts for electing representatives to the lower house. Madison was eager to join the first Congress to help implement the Constitution. But Henry denied Madison a Senate seat, and he configured congressional districts to force Madison into a tough race against James Monroe, an Antifederalist from a neighboring county. Opponents yet friends, Madison and Monroe campaigned together, traveling to small community gatherings and debating the Constitution all over again. Madison described one such debate, held on a cold winter day at a rural Lutheran church:

> Service was performed and then they had music with two fiddles. They are remarkably fond of music. When it was all over we addressed these people

and kept them standing in the snow listening to the discussion of constitutional subjects. They stood it out very patiently—seemed to consider it
a sort of fight of which they were required to be spectators. I then had to
ride in the night twelve miles to quarters; and got my nose frostbitten, of
which I bear the mark now.[82]

Madison campaigned on a pledge to support a bill of rights in the
First Federal Congress. And he swayed enough voters to give him a
comfortable win over Monroe. On his way to New York to take up
his congressional seat, he stopped by Mount Vernon at the request of
George Washington. It was there that the presumptive first president
enlisted Madison to write his inauguration speech. A few months later
Washington took the oath of office and repeated Madison's message to
the nation: It was not the president's goals or vision for America that
mattered but the diverse goals and visions of the American people.[83]

Regrets

James Madison is often called "the father of the Constitution." After all,
he led the movement that convened the framers in Philadelphia. He prepared the Virginia Plan that was the agenda for the Federal Convention.
He fought the battle for ratification, writing the most famous essays in
US history and winning the dramatic face-off with Patrick Henry. But
Madison was not the author of the Constitution; it was the product of
many compromises in Philadelphia. He did not agree with all of it; he
defended it because he thought it was fairer for Americans than the
Articles of Confederation. And he did not venerate it in the fashion of
modern "originalists." He had regrets.

Madison viewed the Constitution as an incomplete social contract,
and he tried after ratification to make it fairer yet. Sometimes he succeeded, as in the party battles of the 1790s, when Madison and Jefferson
formed the Democratic-Republicans to check the monarchical drift of
the new Federalist Party (under the Washington and Adams administrations) and turn public opinion against the Alien and Sedition Acts.
Often he failed, for instance, in challenging Federalist economic policies,
devised by Treasury Secretary Hamilton, to please businessmen who
believed "those who owned the country ought to run it." But Madison's
regrets and failures are as instructive as his achievements.[84]

Madison regretted that the Constitution did not go far enough in righting injustice within the states. By omitting a federal veto on state laws, he wrote Jefferson after the Philadelphia convention, the framers allowed local encroachments on individual rights that were "so frequent and so flagrant as to alarm the most stedfast friends of Republicanism."[85] Madison glossed over the issue during the fight for ratification. In *Federalist* No. 10, he reassured Americans that the Constitution would protect them from factional wildfires in the nation at large; still, he acknowledged that "the influence of factious leaders may kindle a flame within their particular states": "A religious sect," for example, "may degenerate into a political faction in a part of the confederacy; but the variety of sects dispersed over the entire face of it, must secure the national councils against any danger from that source."[86] Madison took another stab at the problem while moving the Bill of Rights through the first Congress. (Many of the bill's former champions, after taking office, lost interest; it became law through Madison's dogged leadership.)

Madison assumed the difficult task of distilling into a consensus bill over one hundred different amendments regarding rights and liberties recommended by the state ratifying conventions. He explained to Congress his earlier misgiving about a bill of rights, that an enumeration of specific rights "would disparage those rights which were not placed in that enumeration," making them insecure.[87] But now he proposed to mitigate the danger of a narrow bill of rights by adding, in the words of the final Ninth Amendment: "The enumeration in the Constitution, of certain rights, shall not be construed to deny or disparage others retained by the people."[88] (Madison's fears were well founded. Unenumerated rights were not taken seriously by the Supreme Court until 1965, when Justice Arthur Goldberg invoked the Ninth Amendment to defend an unenumerated right of privacy in *Griswold v. Connecticut*; the Roberts Court has once more disparaged unenumerated rights.) Madison's chief concern then, in 1789, just as before, was not to list all the rights that deserved protection—there were too many—but to identify and constrain the various entities that threatened individual liberties.[89]

The Constitution focused on threats from executive and legislative departments of the federal government. But Madison told the first Congress that an even greater threat to liberty was present in "the body of the people, operating by the majority against the minority" in the states. Some states, he noted, had no bills of rights protecting minorities;

other states had defective or improper ones. Madison proposed, among a list of important amendments in a federal bill of rights, that "no state shall violate the equal rights of conscience, or the freedom of the press, or the trial by jury in criminal cases." He called this "the most valuable amendment in the whole list; if there was any reason to restrain the government of the United States from infringing upon these essential rights, it was equally necessary that they should be secured against the state governments." Madison's amendment was included in the bill of rights passed by the House of Representatives, whose members were elected by the people, but stripped from the bill by the Senate, whose members were then chosen by state legislatures. (It was not until after the Civil War that the Constitution was finally amended to protect basic rights against state encroachment.)[90]

Years later, Madison also expressed regret that individual rights were not better protected from state-chartered *corporations*—from towns to banks to churches. He saw the same problems in municipalities that he addressed in his *Federalist* essays on societal factions: At the neighborhood level, factions form around "different sorts of property, sometimes on divisions by streets or little streams; frequently on political and religious differences." Just as in society at large, these divisions are often exploited by local bosses to control followers and enrich themselves. In neighborhoods where people are in proximity, Madison reflected, passions are more contagious, "animosities are the more violent," and majorities can oppress minorities in ways limited only by "the ingenuity and interest of those who possess the power." Local law enforcement ought to protect minorities, but it often partakes in the oppression: "Is there a single regulation of police which will not differently affect the component parts of the society, and afford an opportunity to the majority to sacrifice to their prejudices or their conveniency the conveniency or the interests of the minor party?" wondered Madison (again, perhaps remembering his post-college dismay at seeing Baptist preachers jailed for professing an unsanctioned religion). He concluded that municipal officials should in turn face regulation by some neutral authority "to preserve a just, a uniform, and an impartial exercise of their subordinate powers."[91]

Madison thought individual rights deserved more protection as well from commercial corporations. The most important such corporations in the early republic were banks, which supplied the necessary capital for other ventures. There were only three state banks in 1791 when Alexander

Hamilton prompted Congress to create the First Bank of the United States. There were almost 250 by 1816 when Madison authorized the Second Bank of the United States (nearly 600 were spread across the states by 1836). Banks' ability to create and lend money as if by magic awed Americans. Fears that banks could just as suddenly destroy money troubled those who knew the magic consisted of printing bank notes in quantities far exceeding the capital invested in these institutions. James Madison worried about something else. "The greatest, certainly the most offensive abuses of Banks," he observed, "proceed from the opportunity and interests of the Directors."[92] They help themselves to low-interest loans. They speculate with other people's money and trade on inside information from borrowers. They use favorable financing to monopolize other businesses, like shipping, and they impose extortionate credit terms on their customers. Some bank directors willingly served without salary, Madison reported, because they pocketed personal fortunes from their position.[93]

Madison kept some hope that banks and their directors could reform themselves with traditional controls, such as education in social responsibilities and solemn oaths of office (as suggested in mirrors for princes). But he recognized that voluntary restraints are less reliable than regulatory remedies in shielding people from financial abuses; he did not mistake self-regulation for the real thing. Madison recommended that bank directors be prohibited, for example, "from holding Bank Stock & from borrowing directly or indirectly from the Institution." These regulations might protect creditors and benefit banks in the long run, he argued: "If it be objected that by holding an interest in the Institution they [directors] will be more solicitous to increase its profits, the answer is that that at present they may promote their particular interest, in ways impairing those profits."[94]

Madison called for checks on "the power of all corporations," for "the growing wealth acquired by them never fails to be a source of abuses." Even religious corporations abuse their power, he said, by amassing property and by claiming special privileges for church leaders and their estates. At the very least, they should pay taxes like anyone else, Madison felt. And they should not be allowed to encroach on the civil rights of anyone else, for instance, by naming military chaplains—who assume "political authority in matters of religion" and bar the door of worship against minority creeds. ("Look thro' the armies & navies of the world,"

Madison tells you, "and say whether in the appointment of their ministers of religion, the spiritual interest of the flocks or the temporal interest of the Shepherds, be most in view.")[95]

James Madison's specific proposals for regulating churches, banks, and towns may sound quaint to experts today. What remains forward-thinking is Madison's approach to governance in general, to the leadership of societies, states, or corporations (be they municipal, commercial, or ecclesiastical). The cornerstone of his approach is his emphasis on justice as the first duty of leaders. For Madison, justice is not merely one among many virtues of a perfect leader, as mirrors for princes purport. It is not simply an open-door policy that serves some strategic goal. Understood by Madison as impartiality or fairness, "Justice is the end of government. It is the end of civil society." It is the ultimate measure of any social contract.[96]

Madison's case against mirrors for princes all came down to this. Typical mirrors for princes teach rulers to pay attention to subjects for the sake of their realm. In *The Prince*, Machiavelli tells rulers to heed public opinion and try to satisfy the city's guilds, neighborhood associations, and other stakeholder groups based on their power to affect a reason of state. "Whether they are businessmen, farmers, or are engaged in any other activity," Machiavelli writes, the ruler "should ensure that those who improve [property] and invest are rewarded, as should be anyone whose actions will benefit his city or his government." A ruler should not overlook but need not pay the same attention to stakeholders who have little to offer but their forbearance. The prince can merely, from time to time, "amuse the populace with festivals and public spectacles." Rulers may not actually care or know how to *be* just to different interest groups, but they should *seem* just. Even toward enemies, Machiavelli says, "victors still need to appear just"—to build allies, silence skeptics, and enhance the reputation of their regime.[97]

Madison rejected this utilitarian notion of justice. It's not fair, he submitted, to respect persons simply for what they can do for the state or its ruler. Individual persons deserve respect for their own sakes. Madison did not lay out a theory of justice with the rigor of a philosopher like John Rawls, but he reached similar, Rawlsian conclusions. In Madison's view of government as a social contract, all participants have equal worth; they have basic rights regardless of social position or power, as spelled out, for instance, in the US Bill of Rights. Beyond such basic liberties, with respect to public policies affecting wealth and income, Madison leaned toward the least advantaged rather than the most favored groups in society.[98]

A case in point precipitated Madison's break with the Federalist policies of George Washington and Alexander Hamilton in the 1790s. Among the many problems facing the First Federal Congress, one of the thorniest was what to do about debts from the Revolutionary War. The nation owed about $12 million to foreign banks and governments. The states owed another $25 million to various creditors. The bulk of the debt, over $40 million, consisted of securities issued to citizens of the United States—bonds purchased by patriotic Americans, certificates used to pay Continental soldiers, IOUs for war supplies and services. At the request of a house committee chaired by James Madison, Treasury Secretary Alexander Hamilton prepared a report for Congress on ways and means of paying the debt. Hamilton's "Report on Public Credit" called for the United States to refinance (with gilt-edged bonds) the entire debt— foreign, domestic, and state—at full face value. Hamilton argued from expediency that nations, like individuals, who honor their debts gain the trust of lenders and reduce their cost of borrowing. Fully funding the public debt, he informed Congress, would secure the nation's "great and invaluable ends": It would boost the reputation of America, increase trade, promote agriculture and manufacturing, improve national security, and establish public order. It would cement the union of states, Hamilton figured, and unite wealthy investors—financiers, entrepreneurs, merchants, and other businessmen—behind an energetic national government. Madison, however, challenged Hamilton's funding plan. Whatever good it might do for the American government, he maintained, it would not do justice to the American people.[99]

Madison stipulated that, yes, the United States must honor valid debts of the old confederation. Paying foreign lenders was not only just; it was clear to everyone that America would find it hard to ever borrow again if the government defaulted. Refinancing the state debts was more controversial since northern states generally owed more than southern; but disparities could be ironed out through political bargaining. (Thomas Jefferson, it seems, brokered a deal between Madison and Hamilton to allow assumption of state debts in return for relocation of the nation's capital from New York to a southern site on the Potomac.) Redeeming at face value all the debt paper issued to Americans was the sticking point. This domestic debt, Madison warned Hamilton, "is well known to be viewed in different lights by different classes of people." Madison focused on two classes: There were the people who originally owned wartime securities—the people who fought the British, supplied the army, or bought the war bonds. Most of these people would get nothing under Hamilton's plan because they had sold their certificates and IOUs for what they could, often for a fraction of their face value. Then there were the people who now held the securities—mainly speculators, some with close ties to the government, who bought the paper for pennies on the dollar. These people stood to reap fortunes from Hamilton's scheme.[100]

During congressional debates over Hamilton's report, Madison underscored the unfairness of the domestic funding plan. He reminded Congress that many soldiers of the Revolution and the farmers who fed them were not fairly compensated in the first place. Instead of the money they were promised, they were paid with a piece of paper worth "no more than one-eighth or one-seventh of that value." They accepted this devalued paper only because "the government offered that or nothing. The relation of the individual to the government, and circumstances of the offer, rendered the acceptance a forced, not a free one. The same level of constraint would viciate a transaction between man and man, before any court of equity on the face of the earth," Madison stated. There is obviously no consent, no justice, "where the property of the planter or farmer has been taken at the point of the bayonet, and a certificate presented" in lieu of payment. Why, Madison asked rhetorically, did the farmers or soldiers sell off their depreciated certificates? "In some instances from necessity; in others, from a well-founded distrust of the public" to raise taxes and pay the debt; but "whether from one or the other, they had been injured: they had suffered loss" at the hands of the government. The new Treasury plan adds insult to injury, Madison said, by enriching security traders at the expense of the original debt holders, many of whom "were poor and uninformed."[101] Their exploitation has in fact worsened since Hamilton's report to Congress, Madison observed. Speculators have bid up prices for public securities, and their "emissaries are still exploring the interior & distant parts of the Union in order to take advantage of the ignorance of holders."[102] Madison concluded that "at present the transfers extend to a vast proportion of the whole debt, and the loss to the original holders has been immense. The injustice which has taken place has been enormous and flagrant, and makes redress a great national object."[103]

Madison proposed a compromise plan to restore some semblance of justice. He urged Congress to fund the whole domestic debt but adjust the payouts to different classes of creditors. Under Madison's plan, the original owners—the Revolutionary War veterans, widows, and farmers—who *still held* their securities would receive the full face value. The new owners—the wealthy speculators—who *purchased* their securities would receive "the highest price which has prevailed in the market." No investor would lose money, and most would make a healthy profit. The original owners who were issued inflated paper and *had to sell* their securities for a pittance would receive the remainder. "This will not do perfect justice; but it will do more real justice" than the Treasury plan, Madison said.[104]

Hamilton's supporters raised all sorts of objections to Madison's plan: It was too complicated, and it cost too much. It invited fraud and perjuries. It robbed one group to pay another and smacked of class warfare. "If there were robbery," Madison replied, "it had been committed on the original creditors." Now was the time for a grateful nation to compensate those who bore the brunt of war and left empty handed, he declared. This was not a simple management case to be decided on principles of bookkeeping, Madison told Congress. "It was a great and an extraordinary case. It ought to be decided on the great and fundamental principles of justice." The first Congress decided otherwise. Madison's proposal went down to defeat in the House of Representatives; Hamilton's plan became law, and the seeds were sown for the party battles of the 1790s. Although Madison lost this initial skirmish with the emerging Federalist Party, he showed Americans what moral leadership, freed from the long shadow of mirrors for princes, looks like. It prioritizes justice, as fairness to the least advantaged, over collective goals, as defined by the most advantaged. For fair-minded managers in large institutions, he also showed what a fraught choice that could be.[105]

Enslaved Stakeholders

By his own standard of justice, Madison's biggest failure in life was his accommodation to the institution of slavery. From early on, he realized that his theories of politics were at odds with the practice of slavery. In 1785 Madison sent a copy of his "Memorial and Remonstrance" for religious freedom to Edmund Randolph, and in an accompanying letter he expressed his wish "to depend as little as possible on the labour of slaves."[106] Yet he did nothing to free himself from that dependence. Ironically, on September 17, 1787, the very day that Madison signed the Constitution pledging to establish justice and secure the blessings of liberty in America, his father signed a will leaving the family farm—and the slaves to work it—to his son James. James Madison depended on the labor of those enslaved workers for the rest of his life.[107]

As master of the plantation, called Montpelier, Madison displayed what was considered at the time enlightened management. Visitors to Montpelier said that Madison's slaves were treated kindly and fed well. One guest reported, "Each family raise their own pigs and poultry, eat meat twice a day, and have meal, vegetables, milk, and fruit without restriction."[108] Another remarked that Madison rewarded his slaves with beer and whiskey for strenuous work, especially at harvest time. And Madison was known to respect the customary "rights" of enslaved persons in Virginia—for instance, to Sundays off plus a few holidays every year. Madison's own correspondence indicates that he gave some African Americans considerable responsibility and autonomy. Like most plantations, Montpelier was divided into several farms or "quarters," and one of these was managed by an enslaved worker named Sawney, to whom the oft-absent Madison delegated quite general objectives—for example: "To stem & get down as soon as may be convenient his crop of tobacco"; "To plant about 200 apple Trees [chosen by Sawney from any local nursery] either before Christmas or very early in the spring, in the little field on the top of the Mountain."[109] Madison trusted Sawney to market the farm's produce in Fredericksburg; and Mrs. Madison's niece, Mary Cutts, recalled that Sawney ran a small entrepreneurial sideline of his own: "He had his house and ground, where he raised his favorite vegetables, cabbages and sweet potatoes, as well as chickens and eggs, to be sold to Miss 'Dolley.'"[110] (Sawney wound up caring for Madison's aged mother Nelly, working into his eighties.[111])

Of course, this was not enlightened management. This was not benevolent leadership. This was exploitation, bondage pure and simple. Madison knew it, and he said so, calling slavery "the most oppressive dominion ever exercised by man over man."[112] Throughout his public career, notes historian Drew McCoy, Madison never wavered in condemning slavery as a violation of justice and human rights. In retirement, Madison agonized over how America might shed the stain of slavery. He proposed that the national government sell western lands from the Louisiana Purchase and buy slaves' freedom. He suggested that freed slaves be resettled in Liberia to escape the prejudice of white Americans. But these were impractical ideas. It would take a civil war to free America's enslaved population. And people of color, including those in bondage to the Madisons, did not want to leave America for a foreign land, even if their liberators paid their way.[113]

As a politician of his day, Madison could do little to eradicate slavery in the antebellum South or the nation at large. As a business owner, however, there was something Madison could have done in his own back yard. He could have freed his enslaved workers upon his death or his wife's, as George Washington had done. He could have freed Sawney and the others sooner, as his friend and presidential secretary Edward Coles had done. Coles—who moved his former slaves to Illinois, bought them farms, then became an abolitionist governor of that state—wrote to Madison in 1832, urging him at least to "make provision in your Will for the emancipation of your Slaves." Coles alluded to Madison's apprehensions, his concerns about casting adrift enslaved workers of advanced years, his anxiety over separating the families of slaves who intermarried with the slaves of his neighbors. "There will of course always be these kinds of difficulties," Coles wrote, "but they are temporary, and nothing compared to the example of your countenancing, and as far as you can of perpetuating the bondage of so many unfortunate human beings." Coles warned Madison that "it would be a blot and stigma on your otherwise spotless escutcheon, not to restore to your slaves that liberty and those rights which you have been through life so zealous & able a champion."[114]

For whatever reason, Madison did not heed Coles's plea "to put a proper finish to your life and character"; he did not emancipate his enslaved workers in his will.[115] Some of Madison's biographers speculate that, after years of bad crops and financial woes, he could not afford to free his slaves and still provide a secure future for his beloved wife, Dolley. But Madison's own will suggests otherwise. As documented by Holly Shulman, an editor of Dolley's letters, James Madison staked his wife's future not on his plantation but on the sale of his personal papers. He estimated that publishing his notes from the Constitutional Convention and other writings would bring her $100,000. In his will Madison bequeathed the value of Montpelier and its slaves to a bunch of collateral relatives and a few of his favorite institutions. He left $9,000 ($290.32 apiece) to thirty-one nieces and nephews, some who were estranged from the family, others whose whereabouts were unknown. He left an additional $6,500 for the education of great-nieces and -nephews. He left $2,000 to the American Colonization Society, $1,500 to the University of Virginia, $1,000 to the College of New Jersey at Princeton, and $1,000 to Madison College of Pennsylvania—uncommonly large philanthropic gifts for wills of the day. All these were certainly generous gestures, but they were not required by justice. The money might have instead gone to free some of Madison's enslaved workers. (The average market price of a slave in Virginia at the time was not far from the $290.32 Madison gave each of his nieces and nephews; according to one estate appraiser, the cost to maintain elderly slaves like Sawney, whose auction value was nil, was about $60 for life.) Edward Coles—not only a confidant of James but a first cousin to Dolley—concluded that a man with Madison's mind and heart should have found a way to do justice to both his wife and his slaves.[116]

In the end, Coles was right; Madison's failure to free his enslaved workforce would forever tarnish his reputation. That does not mean Madison is no longer worth reading. James French, chair of the Montpelier Descendants Committee representing the descendants of the plantation's enslaved workers, said recently, "I'm a huge fan of the intellectual achievement of James Madison. I think he was a genius. I read about him all the time," but "he compromised on the evil of slavery," and that needs to be acknowledged.[117] The lesson is to learn from Madison's management mistakes as well as his political insights. As a political theorist, James Madison recognized that "justice is the end of government."[118] As a manager, he lost sight of the truth that justice, not some master's purpose, is the end of any organization.

Finally, once more bear in mind that this is a book about mirrors for princes, not the full story of any big thinker like Aristotle or James Madison. It is Madison's capacity to steer readers past the clichés of the genre that's still profound.

ELEVEN
Toward Mirrors for Managers

Community, the joyful sound,
What pleasure to our ears;
A healing balm for every wound,
A rescue for our fears.

Owenite hymn

Ex-presidents of the early United States spent much of their time and money entertaining visitors. Besides the regular guests, strangers from far and near would show up with a letter of introduction at Thomas Jefferson's home, Monticello, or James Madison's home, Montpelier: Foreign statesmen, writers, and celebrities on tour all came to see these living monuments to America's founding. Sore from the bad roads and tired of the filthy inns along the way, some callers would stay for days, chatting with their hosts, enjoying the fine food and wine. The Madisons never knew from one day to the next how many beds to make up or places to set for dinner. So it was not unusual when a traveler from Great Britain rode up to Montpelier and spent a few nights in the spring of 1825. This visitor did have an unusual tale to tell, however. His name was Robert Owen.[1]

Owen needed no introduction. A world-famous industrialist, he was touring America promoting his management system as a cure for the ills of society. He had just come from the city of Washington, where he met with President James Monroe and President-elect John Quincy Adams and where he addressed members of Congress and the city's elite in the Hall of Representatives—not once but twice. In his speeches Owen told how he turned a grim cotton mill into a joyful community at New

Lanark, Scotland. He said he'd transformed "a population that had been indolent, dirty, imbecile, and demoralized" into men and women "who had become actively industrious, cleanly, temperate, and very generally moral." He'd reformed their children too, he said; freed from millwork until age ten, they were "trained and educated, from two years of age and upwards, without individual reward or punishment." Astonished visitors to New Lanark (some twenty thousand over the prior decade) "had never seen children who were their equals, in disposition, habits, manners, intelligence, and kind feelings, or who appeared to enjoy an equal degree of active happiness."[2]

Owen explained that he achieved these amazing results through a series of management experiments wherein he changed working conditions for the better, in turn changing workers' character for the better so they reached higher levels of productivity and created more wealth to further improve their circumstances. "Having discovered that individuals were always formed by the circumstances, whatever they might be, which were allowed to exist around them," Owen said, "my practice was to *govern* the circumstances; and thus by means imperceptible and unknown to the individuals, I formed them, to the extent I could control the circumstances, into what I wish them to become." What Owen wished individuals to become was "a race of very superior beings," united in affection for each other, working as one for their mutual benefit. What Owen urged Americans to embrace was a new system of organization that he derived from his experiments in Scotland. "In the new system, union and co-operation will supersede individual interest," he vowed; "the powers of one man will obtain for him the advantages of many, and all will become as rich as they will desire."[3]

Owen proposed to teach leaders in the United States and the world at large how to use his system to dispel the "ignorance, poverty, and disunion, pervad[ing] the earth" and to create "a new people, having but one common interest," the good of their community.[4] Owen called on members of Congress and other men of influence to put aside superstition and prejudice, to reject divisive parties and sectarian differences, and to learn from his experience. "We all know," he said, "the increased power acquired by a small army, united, and acting as one body, over the same number of men acting singly and alone—and if such advantages can be gained by union to destroy, why should it not be applied to our benefit for civil purposes?"[5] Owen would show the way, not as a political leader but as a private businessman. He announced that he had purchased property in America, the existing town of Harmony and surrounding land in Indiana, where he intended to found a new community based on his principles of management—"which principles, in due season, and in the allotted time, will lead to that state of virtue, intelligence, enjoyment, and happiness, in practice, which has been foretold by the sages of past times, would, as some distant period, become the lot of the human race!"[6] Owen invited the "industrious and well-disposed of all nations" to join his backwoods utopia, renamed New Harmony, and demonstrate the promise of his system to humanity.[7]

A "New" View

It was on his way to develop this community that Robert Owen stopped to visit James Madison. The former president was known to be a gracious host; after dinner (normally lasting from four to six o'clock) he liked to talk with guests well into the night. No one recorded what Owen and Madison said to one another during their evenings together, but you can be sure Owen presented his plan for a new social system. He wrote a book on it (*A New View of Society*), and he repeated his plan wherever he went, to whoever would listen.

The famous British essayist William Hazlitt said a few years earlier that "Mr. Owen is a man remarkable for one idea"—to model the world after his Lanark cotton mill, with Owen himself as chief executive. "He comes into a room with [his plan] in his hand, with the air of a school-master and a quack-doctor mixed, asks very kindly how you do, and on hearing you are still in an indifferent state of health owing to bad diges-tion, instantly turns round and observes that 'All that will be remedied in his plan.'"[8]

After meeting with Owen, Madison shared Hazlitt's skepticism, com-menting that Owen's "panacea" for the diseases of society was just one more of the "great palliatives" prescribed by impractical theorists.[9] Both Madison and Hazlitt had heard schemes like Owen's before. As Hazlitt noted, Owen touted everything he thought of as *new*—his reform of *New* Lanark, his essays on "A *New* View of Society," later his vision for *New* Harmony, and his "Book of the *New* Moral World." But, Hazlitt pointed out, even if it all proves true, "it is not new." Owen's big idea is as old as the medieval borough of Lanark, as old as the *Utopia* of Thomas

More, as old as the philosopher-kings imagined by ancient Greeks; in fact, "it is as old as society itself."[10] What Owen had done was simply to translate the old formula of mirrors for princes into jargon for a new type of leader, the modern manager.

As in past mirrors for princes, Owen's writings and speeches framed a problem: Owen saw people behaving badly. "The poor and working classes of Great Britain and Ireland," he claimed, are prone to "extreme vice and misery; thus rendering them the worst and most dangerous subjects in the empire."[11] Owen saw it among his own workers when he took over management of the New Lanark mill from his father-in-law, David Dale—"Theft and the receipt of stolen goods was their trade, idleness and drunkenness their habit, falsehood and deception their garb, dissentions, civil and religious their daily practice; they united only in a zealous systematic opposition to their employers."[12] Owen diagnosed a cause for bad behavior: Individuals learn from their social circumstances to be selfish. From infancy, he argued, children are taught that they have interests separate and different from those of their neighbors, disposing them to compete rather than cooperate with others; their continued belief as adults in this "individual selfish system" is the root of poverty, crime, social unrest in general, and ill will toward employers in particular.[13] But Owen had a remedy: Children should be educated from birth, and workers reeducated as best they can, to believe they all share a goal, a common interest. Their goal should be to maximize "happiness for the greatest number of human beings" through "the creation of wealth."[14] Mobilizing people behind such a goal is the mission of a transformational leader, like Robert Owen.

Owen, no doubt, described for Madison how he transformed the workforce at New Lanark. As he spelled out in *A New View of Society*, Owen patiently instructed workers on the advantages of honesty over theft, sobriety over drunkenness, harmony over dissention. He tightened security for property, removed alehouses from the village, and opened a company store charging moderate prices. He provided decent housing for workers and introduced insurance for the aged, sick, and disabled. He financed free schools for workers' children, who were taught basic skills—"reading, writing, and arithmetic"—from ages five through nine (ages when children were routinely employed at other factories). He sponsored adult education, dances, and other community-building activities. Gradually Owen gained the trust of workers, he wrote, and they "became industrious, temperate, healthy, faithful to their employers, and kind to each other."[15]

In the end, he concluded, workers came to share Owen's vision, seeing themselves as one system of action with one common interest. "When men work together for a common interest, each performs his part more advantageously for himself and for society," Owen theorized. Workers who toil just for pay will do just what's required to earn it, he figured, but those who work for a common goal will be more effective and "may be easily regulated and superintended." Once workers see "the inseparable connection which exists between individual and general [well-being], between private and public good," Owen insisted, they will care more about producing wealth than how much they each get in return for their labor. In most firms, employees and owners quarrel perpetually over the division of profit because they make too little of it; mismanagement of personnel and inefficiencies in production restrict output, causing the parties to fight over any surplus. But if workplaces were so organized for unity of action that persons could "procure the necessaries and comforts of life in abundance, they might be trained to dispute as little about the division of them as they now do about the commonly attainable products of nature—such as water." In Owen's plan, cooperation that enriches the company trickles down to satisfy each individual member.[16]

William Hazlitt and James Madison found this wishful thinking or, worse, propaganda. In his review of *A New View of Society*, Hazlitt took aim at its central premise: Owen's "teaching that the good of the whole is the good of the individual"—the oldest cliché of mirrors for princes— is "an opinion by which fools and honest men have sometimes been deceived, but which has never yet taken in the knaves and knowing ones." Princes of old and statesmen of Owen's day entertained this teaching not because they were all fools or honest men but because it respected their authority. Politicians continue to give Owen a forum, Hazlitt remarked, because "his schemes . . . are remote, visionary, inapplicable. Neither the great world nor the world in general care anything about New Lanark, nor trouble themselves whether the workmen there go to bed drunk or sober, or whether the wenches are got with child before or after the mar- riage ceremony." Owen's rhetoric was a diversion from the real world of power and thus no threat to men behind the curtain.[17]

Seasoned executives like Madison were not fooled by Robert Owen. Madison warned a young friend of his, Nicholas Trist, who was caught up in the hype of New Harmony, not to put much faith in "Mr. Owen's scheme with all the successes he assumes for it." Owen's ability to transform human beings by "force of education & habit" is limited, Madison said. Of course social *circumstance* can shape behavior; of course *custom* can become second nature to people, but "Mr. Owen makes it nature herself," Madison protested. Owen thinks he can teach everyone what to value. He supposes that he can motivate workers without the ordinary inducements, that he can make everyone care more about meeting management's goals for an enterprise than they care how rank, reward, and effort are distributed among themselves. Owen dreams he can ensure the prosperity of the world through closer management of souls in small industrial communities—rather than, for example, through "freedom of commerce among all nations." Madison could contemplate nothing of the sort; a veteran of the fight to secure individual rights, especially liberty of opinion, he detected in Owen's vision for New Harmony the germ of tyranny.[18]

Robert Owen espoused a particular view that had long troubled Madison. In his first recorded speech to followers at New Harmony, Owen articulated his errand into the wilderness: "I am come to this country," he declared, "to introduce an entire new state of society; to change it from the ignorant, selfish system, to an enlightened, social system, which shall gradually unite all interests into one, and remove all cause for contest between individuals."[19] This was precisely the view that Madison had cautioned against in his famous *Federalist* essay No. 10 on the problem of faction. Madison argued it was impractical to remove the causes of faction by uniting all interest into one; interests were too deeply rooted in different human faculties, different personal experiences, "different degrees and kinds of property"—sorting individuals into creditors and debtors, farmers and merchants, manufacturers and mechanics, holding "different opinions concerning religion, concerning government, and many other points." Uniting all interests into one was not just impractical but also cause for oppression, Madison said; it prompted "leaders ambitiously contending for pre-eminence and power" to demonize people with differing opinions, inflame followers with animosity toward nonconforming neighbors, and mobilize "the superior force of an interested and over-bearing majority" to suppress minority interests. Better to manage the *effects* of faction by seeking agreement on rules, Madison thought, than to attack its *causes* by seeking consensus on goals.[20]

The history of the Owenite community at New Harmony supports Madison's analysis.

New Harmony

As Madison anticipated, New Harmony failed to live up to its billing by Robert Owen. Close to a thousand people flocked to the town in response to Owen's open invitation. What they found was a place without functioning institutions to house and feed them all. They were told, writes historian Arthur Bestor, that "members were to work for the common good and were to be 'fully supplied with the necessaries and comforts of life,' but whether their labor was to be balanced against their consumption, and how, was unexplained." Owen's grand vision overlooked such mundane details. As Owen continued to travel around the country on his publicity tour, he left his twenty-three-year-old son, William, to sort things out in New Harmony. William confessed in his diary that "the enjoyment of a reformer, I should say, is much more in contemplation, than in reality. . . . I doubt whether those who have been comfortable and contented in their old mode of life, will find an increase of enjoyment when they come here."[21]

The former town of Harmony was a going concern before Robert Owen bought it, lock, stock, and barrel, in January of 1825. Built by a sect called the Rappites (led by George Rapp), it contained factories, shops, homes, and public buildings, plus three thousand acres of farmland under cultivation. The Rappites produced what they needed, they sold their surplus grain and pork, they made wine and woolen goods for market, and they took away chests full of money when they left. But *New* Harmony, under Robert Owen's leadership, could never produce enough to support its population. Long after Owenites replaced the Rappites, mills sat idle for lack of skilled workers and supervisors. Fields lay fallow for want of able farmers. The best-staffed operation was the school, which "boarded, clothed and educated [hundreds of children] at public expense" according to the *New-Harmony Gazette*, further straining community resources.[22] Owen kept the town going with subsidies from his own pocket until the spring of 1827, when he effectively abandoned the whole project.[23]

Communitarians have blamed the failure of New Harmony on its people, who've been portrayed as too diverse, too selfish, too indolent.

Owen's son Robert Dale Owen disparaged the New Harmonites as "a heterogeneous collection of radicals, enthusiastic devotees to principle, honest latitudinarians and lazy theorists, with a sprinkling of unprincipled sharpers thrown in."[24] However, in what is still the most detailed history of New Harmony, Bestor shows that the community's collapse was the fault of Robert Owen, and the problem was his brand of leadership. Owen's plan to transform individuals and unite them for a common goal was simply unrealistic and, when tested, it proved oppressive.[25]

From the outset, Owen's communitarian goals for New Harmony undermined its economy and quality of life. If anything, the community was not diverse enough. It attracted plenty of high-minded members who were sympathetic to Owen's mission (as each understood it). Yet the town offered little, Bestor notes, to "the superior workman, whose incentives were not professional but strictly economic, and whose abilities could command far more in the open market" than in a closed society like New Harmony.[26] By the time Robert Owen addressed the skills shortage and advertised for various trades—almost a year into the venture—there was no place left in New Harmony to house new workers. William Owen's frustration in trying to manage the situation comes through in a letter he wrote toward the end of 1825, warning his father that building houses for more workers "is at present out of the question. We have no lime, no rocks (ready blasted), no brick, no timber, no boards, no shingles, nothing requisite for buildings," and no way to buy such things. "We must ourselves produce the whole of them, before we can build, we must dig and burn the lime, dig and blast the rocks, mould and burn the bricks, fell and hew the timber, fell and saw the boards and split the shingles, and to do all these things, we have no hands to spare, or the branches of business in the Society must stop, and they cannot stop, or the whole Society would stop too." (Without lumber, William added, it was not even feasible to partition existing buildings for extra bedrooms, and there was no bedding for people or spare stoves to heat them anyway. People here remain in good spirits, he reported, although all "the sugar is gone" and "the store will be quite empty in six weeks.")[27]

Robert Owen was out of touch with on-site conditions because he spent less than eight weeks in New Harmony during all of 1825. After signing the purchase papers on January 3, he left immediately for his promotional tour, capped by the speeches in Washington and calls on the US presidents. He returned to New Harmony in mid-April and gave more speeches on his new social system: He told the residents that their community was a work in progress—"a halfway house on this new journey from poverty to wealth."²⁸ They needed time, he said, to break "their individual, selfish habits," change their self-interested attitudes, and pull together toward a common goal. He assured everyone that his plan would resolve their problems, and he urged them all to work harder. Owen left New Harmony again in early June to continue proselytizing and was gone until the next January. Despite his absence (or perhaps because of it), New Harmonites gradually adjusted to their conditions. In fact, Owen's distance from New Harmony served to immunize him from the defects of his plan and the deprivations of his followers. To many, he remained the mythic leader of mirrors for princes, Machiavelli's hero on horseback, who inspired hope that he would eventually appear, relieve their woes, and lead them to their fill of milk and honey.²⁹

Hope turned to disappointment in 1826. What Owen brought back to New Harmony when he returned in January was not milk or honey, sugar or shingles, but a new program of education. His theories had resonated with a group of distinguished educators and scientists in Philadelphia, so Owen partnered with a fellow philanthropist, school reformer William Maclure, to hire the lot of them for a model academy in New Harmony. That winter Maclure and Owen ferried some forty academics, artists, and musicians downriver from Pennsylvania on a keelboat dubbed the "Boatload of Knowledge." It held the makings of the best public school in the west. But it also sowed seeds of division in the little community of New Harmony. Upon arrival, the academics were heralded as very important people; they were afforded special privileges, housing, and compensation. This ran counter to Owen's stated emphasis on common goals over individual incentives to gain cooperation, and it undercut his pledge that New Harmony would be a "community of equality."³⁰

Fresh off his triumphal return with the Boatload of Knowledge, Owen assembled a committee of loyal townsmen (including his two sons) to draft a governing charter for New Harmony: On February 5, 1826, they issued a "Constitution of the New Harmony Community of Equality." The charter copied lofty sounding phrases from the American Declaration of Independence and the US Constitution, proclaiming "Equality of Rights," and it prefigured later communitarian manifestos, adding "Equality of Duties."³¹ However, this "constitution" contained none of the checks and balances that James Madison considered necessary to hold leaders to their promises. The New Harmony Constitution was ahead of its time in promising equal rights to women, for instance, but many women found those rights not worth the paper they were printed on. One such woman was a teacher named Virginia Dupalais who came from Philadelphia on the Boatload of Knowledge. Her treatment was recorded in the travelogue of a German aristocrat, Duke Bernhard of Saxe-Weimar-Eisenach. During his visit to New Harmony in April of 1826, the duke noticed this delicate young woman's distress at being called away from an evening's entertainment: "While she was singing and playing very well on the piano forte, she was told that the milking of the cows was her duty, and that they were waiting unmilked. Almost in tears, she betook herself to this servile employment, deprecating the new social system, and its so much prized equality."[32]

Virginia Dupalais's experience was not at all unusual. Women as a group had more duties than rights and certainly more duties than men who ruled the town as if their interests were the interests of the whole. While some women found equal opportunities to work in New Harmony, they were expected to shoulder traditional female responsibilities as well. One of the most accomplished teachers in New Harmony was Marie Duclos Fretageot. Madame Fretageot had a reputation as a brilliant educator, running avant-garde schools in Paris and Philadelphia. She had introduced Owen to Maclure, becoming a driving force behind the Boatload of Knowledge. Yet she wound up doing as much cooking in New Harmony as teaching. A letter to William Maclure outlines her daily schedule—eight hours of classes, plus another eight-hour shift of housework. "I get up regularly at four o'clock," she writes. "Twelve young men . . . board and sleep here" in the house; she gives them lessons until six-thirty, then prepares breakfast. From nine to eleven, she teaches "the class of the children under twelve; at two o'clock the same children till four; at six all the children above twelve, including the boarders, till eight. The other hours I am occupied cooking for the whole family. I may say that I have but very little the occasion of wearing out the chairs of the house."[33]

Male teachers reported casual school days and frequent vacations, in contrast to Marie's grind. But women without her professional status had it even worse in New Harmony, observes Carol Kolmerten, who has studied many such intentional communities.[34] At least elites like Marie had access to creature comforts—delicacies, dresses, and finery from Owen's store—and they gained some voice in the community. Many middle- and lower-class women worked two jobs, doing both social service and domestic chores; they spent their Sundays washing and ironing while the men relaxed; they did it all with little reward and less say over their treatment. Their despair is memorialized in a letter from Mrs. Sarah Pears, who grieved to her uncle: "Only in the grave can I see any prospect of rest."[35]

Some outspoken women complained about their conditions; others rebelled by feigning illness and withholding work (or missing assignments after actually getting sick). Owen and his male colleagues dismissed them as malcontents and trivialized New Harmony's "woman problem." The problem, Owen claimed, was that females spend too much "time in talking, which should be devoted exclusively to work." Women's gripes about doing more than their fair share of labor were jealous "trifles," he felt, which could be easily cured by reeducating them to see the big picture. He proposed adding to everyone's schedule three evening classes per week to instill "the same general and particular ideas and feelings" in tune with "the New Social System." Robert Owen's reaction suggests he learned nothing from James Madison. Owen continued to believe that by setting a single vision for New Harmony he could remove the cause of friction between different groups. He resisted sharing power and bargaining over work rules to control the effects of friction between interest groups.[36]

Meanwhile, as Madison foresaw, economic inequalities, social differences, and group interests were dividing New Harmony into factions—male and female, rich and poor, professional and unskilled, agricultural and industrial, religious and secular. In 1826 these factions broke into open conflict. Besides the "woman problem," rustic New Harmonites—male *and* female—resented the educators, intellectuals, and wealthy "aristocrats"; conversely, the better classes sneered at the "rough uncouth creatures" who aspired to be their equals.[37] Owen's disdain for religion caused a group of "native back-woodsmen, strongly tinctured with methodism" to split off and found a new community, named Macluria (after William Maclure).[38] Owen's ignorance of agriculture, along with the ethnic prejudices of a group of English farmers, drove the farmers to separate and form another community called Feiba Peveli (code words for its geographic coordinates). But the fatal division in New Harmony arose between its top leaders, who, as often happens, did not themselves have the same interests.[39]

When Robert Owen teamed up with William Maclure to launch the Boatload of Knowledge, they had agreed that Owen would oversee the government and industries of New Harmony, and Maclure would manage the schools, library, and any scientific research. As New Harmony's troubles deepened—prompting Owen to suspend its constitution and try one restructuring after another—he blamed the schools and the teachers for neglecting their mission. Owen and Maclure, it turns out, had very different goals for New Harmony's schools. Owen's goals for the schools were to teach "good habits" and inspire individuals to put the community's good (as Owen defined it) above their own.[40] He believed that cradle-to-grave education should standardize the formal lessons and informal experiences that formed people's character in order to channel them into "honest and useful employments."[41] Maclure, on the other hand, believed that "knowledge is power in political societies" and that education should be liberating, not indoctrinating.[42] His goals for New Harmony's schools were to teach understanding of the world (through sciences like geology) and develop skills for mastering one's world (through arts like drawing).[43]

Conflict between these different goals came to a head in August 1826, when Owen stood up at a community meeting and threatened to do something about the schools and teachers "if they fail . . . or fall short in their conceptions or practice of the education which the new system requires."[44] Maclure reacted with anger, expressing to Madame Fretageot his intention to defend the schools "to the utmost extent." Owen knows nothing of education or management, and the schools "must be independent of his metaphysics," Maclure said. "However willing I might be to spend my money on my own education visions, I'm positively determined to waste none of it on the visions of others" who would train people like parrots.[45]

Owen addressed the next community meeting to rally support for his educational agenda. As soon as small children learn a language, he stated, they are "competent to understand, when the subject shall be properly explained to them, the necessity for, and the advantages of, an annual production being made by every society somewhat exceeding its wants,—and to discover, that it will be more beneficial to them to acquire the knowledge and practice of producing their proportion of it in the best and easiest manner." As they get older, Owen went on, children should be taught what they need to know in order to contribute to the community, especially "knowledge of gardening, of agriculture, and of surveying" ("with this exception, that the females instead of mechanics, agriculture, and surveying, will be taught to perform the domestic operations requisite for a Community"). Continuing instruction should be provided for adults to ensure that everyone is on the same page. Owen charged that professional educators overthink the process—they make it all too complicated and time consuming. He said the schools need to cooperate better in instructing "all, young and old, the learned and the untaught," how to implement his new social system. Therefore, he urged the New Harmonites, "Let us now, at once, adopt measures, that shall well educate and enlighten the whole Community,—so as that we may become as one body, having one mind, with one determination to overcome all the evils of the individual system."[46]

Maclure was dismayed when he read Owen's speech in the *New-Harmony Gazette*. "O's sermon on education," he told Madame Fretageot, "is the greatest mixture of contradictions I ever read. But he's incorrigible, and we must get out of the alliance as well as we can." Maclure feared that if Owen had his way, New Harmony's children would wind up like "all the children of New Lanark, none [of whom] got above the merit of twisting a thread of cotton." The adults would fare no better: Owen's scheme to convert the entire population of New Harmony to his system through thrice-weekly reeducation meetings will please only his courtiers, just like "the wreck he has surrounded himself with." Sadly, in Maclure's judgment, Owen is impervious to facts: He thinks "every blunder he commits is a master stroke of policy that could not possibly have happened better"; "he rants in big vague and undefined words"; he traffics in "imperial and sweeping principle[s], which might suit a Bonapart." The Chief, as Maclure dubs him, suppresses any opinions that differ from his and he imagines "that nothing but monarchy or despotizm can make men happy." (Everyone might be happier, Maclure suggested, if Owen would shut up for a year.)[47]

The next spring Maclure did sever his alliance with Robert Owen. In May of 1827 he purchased New Harmony's educational property from Owen—who cut his losses, gave a self-pitying farewell address faulting misfits for spoiling his plan, then left the town to its fate. William Maclure and Marie Fretageot kept the schools running while the community collapsed around them. Maclure offered an education to children who had nowhere else to go. He maintained a research program and established a scientific press. Poor health forced Maclure from Indiana to a warmer climate in 1828. Madame Fretageot stayed to manage the town's schools, supervise the press, run her own farm, and no doubt cook yet more meals, until she retired in 1831.[48]

Opinions

Three hundred miles due south of Chicago, on the left bank of the Wabash River, some of the original New Harmony buildings are still there—monuments, in Arthur Bestor's view, as much to Marie Fretageot as to Robert Owen. You can read, in the files of the New Harmony Working Men's Institute (founded by William Maclure) and other archives online, letters from men and women who survived the Owenite regime. You'll find few words of tribute to Robert Owen. Speaking for many of those around in 1827, Lydia Eveleth mourned the community's downfall but not the disgrace of "its once highly celebrated founder, who has now become the abhorrence of this people, as much as ever he was their idol."[49]

Sociological studies of the Owenite community at New Harmony note it was short-lived, as if that defines its failure. But longevity is not the only or best measure of organizational success; some short-lived organized groups have been good for people, and some long-lasting ones have caused harm. The real failure of New Harmony under Robert Owen was not its collapse but, rather, its unfairness to individuals, especially women who had to toil month after month, as one wrote, "without any leisure, sewing, cooking, teaching, and nursing the sick."[50] Their mournful letters to friends and family show that, as difficult as it was for a powerful man like William Maclure to witness Owen's leadership from close up, it was harder—unjust by almost any measure—for vulnerable women to suffer it from below. In another letter to her uncle, Sarah Pears reveals deeper dismay over Owen's governance than that felt by her husband or even William Maclure: You've heard from Mr. Pears, she says, "that our government is an aristocracy. He ought to have called it a despotism. Our feelings are perpetually irritated by some or other of their acts and Resolutions; and if we should unfortunately be so bold as to express our sentiments upon them, we are told that we are liable to expulsion. It makes my blood boil within me to think that the citizens of a free and independent nation should be collected here to be made slaves of."[51]

So long as they kept quiet and working, Robert Owen wouldn't have cared how Sarah Pears felt about his acts and resolutions; he wouldn't have cared that Lydia Eveleth was tired of listening patiently to "old Bob" drone on about "his much loved System."[52] He didn't care that much about *individuals*. As an ardent utilitarian, Owen expressed concern for the happiness of mankind in the abstract and the community in the aggregate, but he did not take seriously the distinctiveness of persons (in John Rawls's terminology).[53] He did not take seriously individuals' opinions, and he did not take seriously their rights—in contrast to James Madison. Madison declared that persons have intrinsic value and unalienable rights *against* their communities; Owen assigned people instrumental value and overriding duties *to* their communities. Madison held that "the opinions of men, depending only on the evidence contemplated by their own minds cannot follow the dictates of other men"; Owen treated men, women, even adolescent children as "living machines" for the express use of their employers.[54]

In *A New View of Society*, Owen laid out for fellow employers his philosophy in running the New Lanark Mills: Like many of you, he wrote, "I am a manufacturer for pecuniary profit." At New Lanark, "from the commencement of my management I viewed the population, with the mechanism and every other part of the establishment, as a system composed of many parts, and which it was my duty and interest so to combine, as that every hand, as well as every spring, lever, and wheel, should effectually co-operate to produce the greatest pecuniary gain to the proprietors." Owen perceived that workers are as valuable as the machinery (no more, no less). And, just like machines, they require proper upkeep. Most managers know not to neglect expensive machines, Owen pointed out: Manufacturers "expend large sums of money to procure the best devised mechanism of wood, brass, or iron; to retain it in perfect repair; to provide the best substance for the prevention of unnecessary friction, and to save it from falling into premature decay." By taking care of their inanimate machinery, owners obtain returns of 5, 10, maybe 15 percent on their investment; but, Owen argued, managers can make even more money by taking care of their "living machines." A worker, too, needs maintenance; it's important "to keep it neat and clean; to treat it with kindness, that its mental movements might not experience too much irritating friction; . . . to supply it regularly with a sufficient quantity of wholesome food and other necessities of life, that the body might be preserved in good working condition, and prevented from being out of repair, or falling prematurely to decay." Owen said he "expended much time and capital upon improvements of the living machinery" at New Lanark, "producing a return exceeding fifty per cent" on invested capital. He assured employers they could double that if they tried: Well-maintained living machines could be easily trained and directed to return profits of 100 percent.[55]

Owen proclaimed in "An Address to the Working Classes" that his system was fair to "the rich and the poor, the governors and the governed, [who] have really but one interest":[56] Everyone gains by maintaining workers as instruments for the production of wealth. Contemporary critics like William Hazlitt knew better (Hazlitt compared Owen's system to a "lucky lottery" scam where everybody's promised a winning ticket).[57] Founders of the American republic like James Madison knew better. The women of New Harmony knew better. And Owen's son Robert Dale knew better. Robert Dale Owen—who managed the New Lanark mills in his father's absence, followed him to New Harmony, then went on to a distinguished political career in Indiana—strongly disagreed with his father's management philosophy:

> It appears to me the greatest mistake to suppose it rational to make men mere producing machines and to treat them as such, and to estimate their happiness by the quantity of their productions. We must be careful, too, not to forget that happiness is the object of our pursuit; and that we succeed, not in proportion to the extent of our surplus productions, but in proportion to the measure of happiness which the members of the society enjoy.[58]

While New Harmonites such as Sarah Pears had to "put happiness entirely out of the question," Robert Owen carried on blissfully touring America, Britain, Mexico, France, Ireland, wherever he could lecture an audience on his "New System" of leadership.[59] Owen's doggedness in his beliefs, command of the public stage, and penchant for publicity ensured that it was *his* self-promotion, not Mrs. Pears's or her neighbors' testimony against him, that captured the imagination of future generations.[60]

To this day, Owen is hailed as the "Father of Scientific Management," a forerunner of the "Human Relations" school of management, and a "pioneer of human resource development." He's been acclaimed, by experts on modern management, "the Thomas Edison of social invention," a "genius as a leader of change" on par with Henry Ford and other visionaries: "A hundred years ahead of the pack, Owen perceived instinctively that effective leadership is a matter of communicating a vision," states management professor James O'Toole. Owen's problem, O'Toole submits, is that he did not know how to overcome resistance to change, although "in hindsight, he was clearly right, and the reforms he proposed were in the self-interest of the people who opposed them."[61] Such rhetoric is Robert Owen's legacy to modern management theory—assertions that leadership is a matter of communicating a vision, that leaders' goals are one and the same as the interests of workers, that opposing goals are rooted in selfishness and retained in ignorance. Readers with longer hindsight than O'Toole will recognize these as ancient clichés of mirrors for princes, revived for today's management textbooks and corporate public relations.[62]

Scientific Management

Following Robert Owen, one theorist after another propagated a "new" system of management that hewed to the classical formula of mirrors for princes. With the dawn of the twentieth century, along came Frederick Winslow Taylor—a second "Father of Scientific Management"—with ideas much like those preached by his predecessor.

Taylor saw people behaving badly. An industrial engineer, he pictured workers shirking their duties and deceiving their employers with slowdown tactics; he called it "soldiering": "The natural laziness of men is serious," Taylor wrote in "Shop Management," "but by far the greatest evil from which both workmen and employers are suffering is the *systematic soldiering* which is almost universal." So virulent is soldiering, he complained, "that hardly a competent workman can be found in a large establishment . . . who does not devote a considerable part of his time to studying just how slowly he can work and still convince his employer that he is going at a good pace." As usual, Taylor attributed soldiering behavior to the selfishness of workers, specifically their attitude that employers' interests are different from and antagonistic to their own. And as ever, his remedy was a common goal; he conceived a system of scientific management to unite labor and management, to instill "the feeling that they are all working for the same end."[63]

Frederick Taylor is most famous—infamous, to workers—for introducing time study and for standardizing tasks to maximize industrial efficiency. But Taylor insisted that scientific management is not what most people think, or fear. In the early 1900s his system raised apprehension among American workers, who felt it was shifting all job decisions to managers and reducing workers to low-cost machines. (Everyone heard tales of some minion like the rate-busting "Schmidt," whom Taylor programmed what to lift, where to walk, when to sit, how to talk.[64]) And in 1911 Taylorism sparked a labor strike at the federal arsenal in Watertown, Massachusetts. "This method is un-American in principle" and unfair in practice, the workers protested.[65] To investigate labor unrest over scientific management, a special committee of the US House of Representatives held hearings at which Taylor was called to explain his system. He testified that, contrary to popular belief, "Scientific management is not any efficiency device. . . . It is not holding a stop watch on a man and writing things down about him; it is not time study; it is not motion study." While these are useful tools in nearly any system of management, they are not at the core of scientific management, Taylor said: "In its essence, scientific management involves a complete mental revolution on the part of the workingman" and the employer.[66]

Taylor argued that labor troubles occur in organizations because workers and employers worry too much about how the costs and benefits from their cooperation are distributed. Unproductive disputes go on over the proper allocation of earnings to owners and wages to workers, for example, leading to soldiering, strikes, and demonization of the counterparties. But "the great revolution that takes place in the mental attitude of the two parties under scientific management is that both sides take their eyes off of the division of the surplus as the all-important matter, and together turn their attention toward increasing the size of this surplus until this surplus becomes so large that it is unnecessary to quarrel over how it shall be divided."[67] You'll recall, this is the same argument made by Robert Owen. Taylor and Owen both assumed that more production renders it possible to make life better for everyone, which may be true. They both assumed further that unfettered leaders and markets could be trusted to distribute the fruits of cooperation fairly and actually make life better for everyone, which James Madison and many workers knew to be false. Nevertheless, scientific management caught on because it addressed an age-old question of rulers and managers: *How can I get people to do what I want?*

Frederick Taylor defined the art of management "as knowing exactly what you want men to do, and then seeing that they do it in the best and cheapest way."[68] Taylor's advice for managers has a Machiavellian tinge, observes his biographer Robert Kanigel—at times resembling the tips for tyrants found in *The Prince*: When imposing a new system of rules, for instance, managers will meet resistance to change; workers "look upon all change as antagonistic to their best interests," Taylor warned. "The first changes, therefore, should be such as to allay the suspicions of the men and convince them by actual contact that the reforms are after all rather harmless and are only such as will ultimately be of benefit to all concerned. Such improvements then as directly affect the workmen least should be started first." Although managers should begin cautiously, "the new system should be started at as many points as possible, and constantly pushed as hard as possible."[69]

Workers pushed back, of course. What workers sought was not to veto all change but to negotiate rules with their employers, collectively and increasingly through labor unions, which leveled bargaining power and kept management from always having its own way. Taylor saw little use for unions. He understood why workers might seek protection from arbitrary management. But he maintained that *scientific* management, properly applied, "will confer far greater blessings upon the working people than can be brought through any form of collective bargaining."[70] Science can show the one best way to achieve common goals, Taylor claimed; it "prevents arbitrary and tyrannical action on the part of the foremen and superintendents quite as much as it prevents 'soldiering' or loafing or inefficiency on the part of the workmen."[71] In his system, Taylor concluded, a "union is absolutely unnecessary and only a hindrance."[72]

Critics of Taylor's *Principles of Scientific Management* found in there fishy calculations of a proper day's work and fudge factors for variables like fatigue, suggesting that his system was about as scientific as the magic ring prescribed in the medieval *Secret of Secrets* (which promised princes similar mastery over people). In the tradition of mirrors for princes, Frederick Taylor reinvented management theory with doctrines that were old in the twelfth century. A contemporary of Taylor's, labor activist Abraham Jacob Portenar, made the point, notes Robert

Kanigel, that "the Taylor system was nothing but feudalism in modern dress." Portenar explained in a letter to Taylor: "The baron allotted to each man his task—so do you. The baron took a large part of the task upon himself as leader—so do you. The baron allotted to each his share of the usufruct in spoils or produce—so do you. The baron was the sole judge of whether a man was right or wrong—so are you." Real cooperation, Portenar chided Taylor, can never come from a system that gives workers no voice and makes managers the sole judge of what is fair.[73] Portenar was prophetic: Labor activism intensified, and union representation doubled in the decade after *The Principles of Scientific Management* appeared (growing from 10% of the nonfarm workforce in 1910 to near 20% in 1920).[74]

After Taylor's death in 1915, managers looked for a better way to achieve their goals. Taylor had lit their path forward. His lasting legacy, just as he wished, was not management by stopwatch; it was a mental revolution—toward management by objectives.

TWELVE

Classic Mirrors for Managers

There has never been a more efficient, a more honest, a more capable and conscientious group of rulers than the professional management of the great American corporations today.

Peter Drucker

Following World War I, employers and management experts responded to the challenge of organized labor by modifying Frederick Taylor's system—smoothing its sharp edges while retaining its core philosophy. No organization was more concerned to soften its image than the American Telephone and Telegraph Company. One of the earliest adopters of Taylorism and one of the biggest employers in America, AT&T was a particular target of union organizers. The International Brotherhood of Electrical Workers had unionized telephone operators in Boston, and the company was determined to stay union free elsewhere. With a virtual monopoly over phone service, AT&T was also a focus of government regulators, who posed an existential threat. By 1913 every major country except the United States had nationalized its telephone system, and AT&T was taken over by the federal government during the war. Returned to private hands in 1919, the company's management vowed to keep it that way.[1]

AT&T tried to neutralize regulators, discredit unions, and win the hearts and minds of Americans with a display of corporate social responsibility, commonly called welfare capitalism. Bell System companies adopted an array of employee welfare policies to build loyalty. The Western Electric manufacturing subsidiary offered workers a pension, a stock purchase plan, and social programs through its Hawthorne Club at the huge Hawthorne Works outside Chicago. Open to all employees, club benefits included a cooperative store, a comprehensive library, athletic facilities, golf and bowling leagues, and an evening school teaching everything from electricity to "health, appearance, and personality." "To promote a get-together spirit," the Hawthorne Club sponsored noon-hour entertainment for workers; the Western Electric employee booklet advertised "outdoor dances with fine orchestra music," celebrations on holidays like Armistice Day, "theatrical programs by professional talent; and talks by outstanding men and women from the government, stage, screen and sports."[2]

Elton Mayo

At the same time that Western Electric was crafting paternalistic personnel policies in the style of Robert Owen, the company was conducting efficiency studies in the mode of Frederick Taylor. In 1924, as part of a campaign by General Electric and the lighting industry to sell more bulbs, the Hawthorne Works collaborated in experiments to assess the effect of illumination on productivity. Results were ambiguous; there seemed to be no direct relation between factory lighting and worker output (to GE's dismay). When the illumination tests ended in 1927, Hawthorne Works' technical superintendent, George Pennock, steered research into other factors that might bear on efficiency.[3]

So began the famous Hawthorne studies. Pennock and his staff set out to gauge fatigue, Taylor's notorious fudge factor, and find means to reduce it: Would rest periods or a shorter workday raise productivity? The investigators ran tests on a group of six women, seated together in a special room, assembling telephone relays (electromagnetic switches built by hand from three dozen small parts). Experiments with different rest breaks and working hours did increase output over time, but results were still hard to decipher—especially since management decided two of the women "talked too much" and replaced them during the tests. To make sense of the data, Pennock sought expert advice; he consulted social science professors from MIT and Harvard University. It was Elton Mayo from the Harvard Business School who would interpret the results in light of his own theories and, with his students, teach managers around the world what the Hawthorne studies showed.[4]

Mayo's path to Harvard was circuitous. Born and raised in South Australia, he tried medical school but dropped out; he earned a bachelor's degree in philosophy from the University of Adelaide, then found a faculty position at the new University of Queensland where he taught ethics, metaphysics, psychology, and economics. Early on he developed an interest in the psychoanalytic theories of Freud and Jung. He went on to treat anxious patients and shell-shocked soldiers from the Great War. And he gave a series of public lectures applying psychological diagnoses to perceived ills of industrial society.[5] In 1919 Mayo published his views in a mirror for managers and politicians. Titled *Democracy and Freedom*, the book portrays people in democratic countries behaving badly, caught up in class hatred, civic warfare, workplace strikes, and sabotage. As in olden mirrors, societal disintegration is attributed to members' selfishness. In Mayo's telling, modern democracies—Australia, England, and the United States—are corrupted by "excessive individualism," party politics, and a partisan press. These legacies of nineteenth-century liberal theorists (like James Madison) stoke neurotic fears of imagined enemies and preclude "the possibility of any real social unity." *Democracy and Freedom* prescribes a timeless remedy for both international and domestic disorder: a common goal. According to Mayo, cooperation for "a common social purpose"—not legalistic leagues of nations nor unions of workers— "is the ideal for democracy," the only alternative to war and strife.[6]

Democracy and Freedom did not specify exactly what the common purpose of countries or companies should be. But, like Owen and Taylor before him, Mayo suggested the goal of productivity growth. He lamented, for instance, state regulations and union rules that restrict industrial output: In one case, "The proprietor of a bacon factory in Brisbane asked his night-watchman to turn off a brine-tap at two o'clock in the morning; the union secretary informed him the next day that this act constituted the watchman a skilled worker . . . and necessitated a changed rate of wages." Such a practice "hampers commercial growth," Mayo complained; as a system of management, "its primary assumption is that the interests of masters and men cannot be made identical, that the intervention of an intermediary is necessary." Mayo brooked no interference with management's role in growing output. He accused union leaders of demagoguery and "a partisan hostility to all employers." He rebuked advocates of workplace democracy for introducing "all the ills of partisan politics into industrial management" and placing "the final power in the hands of the least skilled workers," who cannot be expected to solve problems they are "unable even to understand." He deplored the overreach of government regulators: Regulators revere competition and oppose monopolies, but this is shortsighted, Mayo wrote, given "the industrial anarchy of the last century." He argued that "industry has drifted into a condition of muddled competition between a multiplicity of [cut-throat] producers" in an "evil tradition of a competitive struggle for survival." What's needed is bold leadership to provide a "social vision and the inspiration of high purpose—these are the motives which have made our civilization" great, not the antisocial fear of competitors. In Mayo's view, even "a monopoly . . . could hardly fail to realize, if intelligently handled, that social service was its chief duty."[7]

Mayo, of course, meant "intelligently handled" by company management, not government officials. "The proper function of the democratic 'governor,'" he said, "is to record the achievements of society in the form of law, to criticize existing social relationships and to forbid any contravention of established morality. The more serious ills which democracy suffers are due to attempts on the part of political leaders, to control and direct social and industrial undertakings."[8] Mayo concluded: "The only person who is capable of controlling an industry, or sharing in its control, is the person who understands the methods and conditions of works, the nature of the market and who knows something also of the economic structure of the modern world"—the company manager.[9] This sort of rhetoric eventually got the attention of corporate leaders in America.

In 1922 Mayo gathered up letters of introduction and left Australia to seek a bigger stage for his ideas. He sailed to the United States, he gave a few lectures, he did a little consulting. Struggling to meet expenses, he knocked on doors until he found a patron by the name of Beardsley Ruml, who was just appointed director of the Laura Spelman Rockefeller Memorial Foundation. The LSRM, as it's known, was established by John D. Rockefeller, cofounder of the Standard Oil Company, to support his late wife's favorite causes. His son, John D. Rockefeller Jr., hired Ruml to refocus the foundation on funding social research that could be useful to business but was too controversial for the major Rockefeller philanthropies. Ruml had $20 million to spend on social science research. Mayo needed work. And the values of both men aligned with the interests of businessmen like the Rockefellers to run their companies without hindrance from government or conflict with trade unions. Ruml and Mayo, in the fashion of past royal advisers, presumed to teach them how.[10]

With Rockefeller's backing, Ruml funded a temporary appointment for Mayo as a research associate at the University of Pennsylvania's Wharton business school. Mayo's research called for the interviewing of workers at Philadelphia factories to uncover attitudes limiting productivity. He saw "an extraordinary resemblance between a 'shell-shock' hospital and a factory where the morale or will to cooperate is low."[11] Both kinds of organizations, Mayo inferred, are full of sick people who need treatment to function effectively. Just like shell-shocked solders, for example, workers are subject to irrational fears: He recollected that "one of the greatest industrial upheavals of recent years, the Sydney railway strike of August, 1917, was mainly caused by the workers' unreasoned terror of a mere word—'Taylorism.'"[12] Labor unrest, strikes, slowdowns, turnover, and other workplace ills are not really about wages or hours, Mayo surmised; they stem from "passionate misunderstandings."[13] Mayo had small success in curing labor misunderstandings himself; most of the companies he tried to study in Philadelphia rejected his approach. Still, he proposed that industrial counselors could be trained to listen to workers, reduce their fears, and thus gain their collaboration for organizational goals. This new psychological approach would be more productive, he predicted, than "the old method of 'collective bargaining,'" which kept managers and workers divided and "led nowhere but to further dispute and difficulty."[14]

While hunting hospitable research sites around Philadelphia, Mayo published several articles explaining his theories. And he submitted hopeful progress reports to the LSRM, encouraging Beardsley Ruml to find him a regular university position. Ruml turned to Wallace Donham, a trustee of the LSRM and dean of the Harvard Business School (founded with a Rockefeller grant in 1908). Harvard was willing to offer Mayo a position as associate professor of industrial research—so long as the LSRM paid his salary. Ruml agreed, and Mayo joined Harvard's business faculty in September 1926. The following year he addressed members of the Special Conference Committee (a secretive organization of antiunion corporate executives spearheaded by Rockefeller Jr.) at the Harvard Club in New York, where he met T. K. Stevenson, personnel director of Western Electric. In March of 1928 Mayo was invited to consult with local Western Electric management on their studies at the Hawthorne plant.[15]

Mayo visited the Hawthorne Works, conferred with study administrator George Pennock, and read company reports on the experiment with the telephone relay assemblers then underway. Western Electric researchers observed the six women in the test room and collected production data for five years, from 1927 to 1932, as they systematically changed working conditions: The experimenters introduced rest periods, increased their duration and frequency, served the workers lunch and snacks, shortened the workday, and lengthened the weekend. Group production rose 34 percent in the first two years and 46 percent over the five years of the experiment. But why?[16]

Mayo offered a preliminary answer in his 1933 book, *The Human Problems of an Industrial Civilization*: "Better output is in some way related to the distinctly pleasanter, freer, and happier working conditions" in the relay assembly test room. Besides the satisfying breaks and snacks and work shifts, normal plant supervision was replaced by "an interested and sympathetic chief observer" in the test room. "He took a personal interest in each girl and her achievement; he showed pride in the record of the group." The observer listened to the women—about their problems at home, comments on the study, any concerns over phased changes. In time the women came to trust the observer, they felt "a sense of participation" in decisions affecting them, and they became a "social unit" with a common purpose.[17]

It wasn't the working conditions themselves that motivated the relay assemblers, Mayo stressed. "What the company actually did for the group was to reconstruct entirely its whole industrial situation," transforming the women's attitudes and creating a "new orientation" aligned with organizational goals. Effective managers, he said, need to understand this total situation, including covert group norms and individual feelings that limit productivity. Managers, for example, must not only diffuse irrational fears of Taylorism that exist within some departments (as detected in a different, uncooperative Hawthorne test group composed of men wiring switchboards at their own pace); they must also help individuals overcome rebellious attitudes that stem from hard luck at home or other misfortunes. Resistance to authority, Mayo believed, is a sign of mental illness; it has treatable psychological causes. Once again Mayo proposed that just listening to workers' feelings can have a cathartic effect, improving morale and efficiency. He endorsed a plan to interview all employees in the Hawthorne plant to hear what's on their minds. Listening, he cautioned, does mean taking seriously employees' demands for, say, increased wages or union representation; such things only address workers' symptoms but don't cure their sickness.[18]

Reprising the argument from his earlier mirror for managers, Mayo alleged that worker sickness is widespread because of the social disintegration of industrial societies. From close-knit communities with common beliefs and customs, where "each individual knows his place and the value of his work to the communal purpose," people have migrated to tumultuous cities like Chicago where individuals seek the freedom to pursue their own goals regardless of any larger social purpose to one's work. Such disintegration of industrial nations—with ensuing crime, suicide, and mental instability—implies, Mayo wrote, that "the world over we are greatly in need of an administrative *élite* who can assess and handle the concrete difficulties of human collaboration." Now more than ever, Mayo said in late 1932, recovery from global economic depression requires business leaders capable of "analyzing an individual or group attitude," restoring confidence (as President Herbert Hoover preached), and directing people "to work together for a common end."[19]

This is the same kind of rhetoric—tailored for titans of industry such as John D. Rockefeller Jr. and his fellow members of the Special Conference Committee—that Machiavelli composed for Renaissance princes. Mayo acknowledged as much. He asserted, "Machiavelli's sage observations upon Florentine history and the education of princes make an admirable contribution to the study of industrial organization."[20] Mayo credited Machiavelli with seeing there must be skilled executives in authority over people not for petty politics but for efficient operations. Like Mayo himself, Machiavelli understood that class rivalries, feuds, and factions can destroy a nation; he grasped the need for extraordinary leadership to refocus the passions of men on service to the country. Elton Mayo preferred the perfect prince of Machiavelli to the messy democracy of James Madison. Mayo sought comfort in the old organic analogy "between the human body and a social group," where every member performs a natural function and shares a goal set by the body's head.[21] He scorned the "enlightened" Madisonian notion of associations as social contracts between parties with natural rights to different views: Where there is contention between groups, where there are partisan factions, where there is difference of opinion, Mayo supposed, "There is always something wrong."[22]

Mayo transformed "Machiavelli's Prince into the modern-day manager," concludes business professor Ellen O'Connor: "This transformation gave management the moral legitimation it needed to accompany its material success. Now, the manager would become the guardian of social order and Western civilization itself, for it would save humanity from its naturally dire state." Workers, Mayo hoped, would in time stop trading "tales of capitalistic conspiracy" and recognize the futility of selfish practices like collective bargaining. The views Mayo first espoused in Australia after the Great War—for example, that so-called industrial democracy "is based not on reason, but on delusions of conspiracy and lunacy"—were the views he brought to the Hawthorne studies and taught at the Harvard Business School until he retired after the next world war.[23]

Human Relations

What Mayo taught was called "human relations." It was billed as a new approach to management theory and business education. But it was not new. Just like Machiavelli, when he taught a new approach to political theory four centuries earlier, Elton Mayo and his industrial research team at Harvard said nothing original; they simply publicized for everybody to hear what the powers that be had been saying among themselves for some time.[24]

Business leaders did not need Mayo to tell them that the Great War would fuel worker unrest and embolden the labor movement. "Having thrown everything into the balance in the war for democracy in government," editors of the trade journal *Iron Age* warned steelmakers in March of 1918, "it would be strange if the people of the United States came out of the war without any concessions to the growing demand for more democracy in industry."[25] Nor did industry leaders need Mayo to tell them how to respond. Steel magnate Charles M. Schwab advocated a combination of paternalism involving job security, health protection, stock ownership and old-age benefits to address workers' material wants—along with an innovative tool for listening to workers, an employee representation plan, to give them "a voice in the regulation of conditions under which they work."[26] Schwab's representation plan at

Bethlehem Steel, he stated, "provides for election by shops or depart-ments of representatives to meet and deal with the management for the discussion, regulation, and adjustment of matters having to do with all the conditions which may arise out of employment"—in other words, a company union.[27]

Employee representation plans signified "the most celebrated labor experiment" prior to the Hawthorne studies, observes labor historian David Brody. One of the biggest boosters was John D. Rockefeller Jr., who introduced such a plan after a deadly strike at his Colorado Fuel and Iron Company. Representation plans were couched in idealistic language, such as Rockefeller's declaration that "employees in every industrial unit [have] a fundamental right, namely, the right to representation in the determination of those matters which affect their own interests," includ-ing the right to "adequate machinery for the uncovering and adjustment of grievances."[28] As James Madison wrote in 1788, however, paper rights are worthless to individuals without power to enforce them; and employ-ers knew it.[29] The practical effect, if not always the intended purpose, of representation plans was to maintain management's full authority over the employment relationship and to deter workers from joining trade unions with real machinery for handling grievances. One Bell telephone operator recalled that the only complaints that company union represen-tatives raised with management were trivial things like "the toilet tissue in the bathrooms was too rough, or there wasn't enough sugar, or the food was cold in the cafeteria."[30]

By the early 1920s, AT&T had introduced "friendly organizations"—as Bell president Henry B. Thayer called company unions and repre-sentation plans—to replace trade unions "practically everywhere except in New England." "It is our hope," Thayer told a major shareholder, that "before very long, the employees of the Bell System throughout the country will have no affiliation with any outside labor organizations and will cooperate thoroughly for the good of the business."[31] AT&T's vice president for employment relations, E. K. Hall, outlined the compa-ny's management philosophy in a 1928 speech to the National Industrial Conference Board. Prefiguring Elton Mayo's human relations approach, he explained that Bell's policy was to relieve employees of worry. "All human beings have worries at some time," Hall said. "We must find ways and means to help our workers get those worries out of their minds so they can come on the job 'rarin' to go.'" Besides providing an array of employee benefits, he went on, management must communicate with workers to find out what they are thinking about their jobs or about the business, to resolve performance issues and remove obstacles to cooperation. Most companies then communicated in one of three ways, Hall reported: "Certain establishments, for some time to come and perhaps always, must deal with their employees through representatives of groups which include employees in other organizations," that is, outside unions. "Others will deal with their own people through some form of employee representation," the company unions installed in most Bell subsidiaries. Still others "will deal with their employees through more or less direct contact." Hall preferred employee representation, but he allowed that listening to workers individually might be a satisfactory alternative.[32]

Mayo and his team provided AT&T with precisely such an alternative in their interpretation of the Hawthorne studies. Elton Mayo dealt in grand theory; he found research reports tedious, so he left it to his Harvard protégé Fritz Roethlisberger to write up the details of the Hawthorne studies. Roethlisberger and Western Electric's study coordinator, William Dickson, published the definitive account, *Management and the Worker*, in 1939. It has since become a classic mirror for managers. The book's central premise is that "the function of management" is to make sure "the purposes of the enterprise are realized." The authors' assumption is that an organization's ultimate purpose is specified by top management. It follows that managers must somehow get workers to see that official purposes are *their* purposes.[33]

To win cooperation and unify interests, *Management and the Worker* advised showing more attention to employees, as proposed in Mayo's plan to interview all employees at the Hawthorne plant. Roethlisberger and Dickson recommended that management enlist sympathetic personnel specialists to counsel workers one on one, interviewing employees to address performance deficiencies. A good counselor "comes to be regarded by everyone in the situation for what he is, as a person to whom anyone can talk freely, and if he has done his job well he will be regarded in the same light as the patient regards his doctor," wrote Roethlisberger and Dickson. Faced with a low-performing employee, the counselor would encourage her to talk about work, home, whatever is worrying her, so that she "might by that very process come to a new understanding of what her real difficulty is. . . . The counselor's sole object is to lead the employee to a clear understanding of her problem such that she herself comes to realize what action to take and then assumes responsibility for taking it."[34]

In recommending personnel counseling, Mayo's research team offered managers an alternative for dealing with workers that was even better than company unions (and, better yet, still legal after employee representation plans were banned by the Wagner Act). Mayo's assistant Richard S. Meriam compared counseling with employee representation plans in a 1931 *Personnel Journal* article: Both kinds of plans have the same aims, to foster cooperation and unity of interests, Meriam indicated. But employee representation may degenerate into partisan politics and actually create divisions, for "the grievances of a number of employees may be adopted by the employees as a body." From a few individual grievances, "a small group of employees may feel that the chance of getting a full hearing and a favorable decision depends on persuading others that they have the same complaints. The up-shot may be that employees become an organized group opposed to management." In contrast, Meriam pointed out, employee counseling or interviewing is easier for management to control. It isolates workers one-on-one with "a trained specialist in the service of higher executives." The worker is not influenced in the interview by the grievances of fellow employees; in fact, "he is not asked for grievances" at all. "He is not required to propose remedies or to listen to counter arguments or counter proposals." There is nothing political about the process. Indeed, "Absence of political machinery is the chief advantage of the interview plan."[35]

Without such "political machinery," employers were free to manage as they saw fit. They would no longer be forced to give night watchmen extra pay for extra duties—the requirement that appalled Elton Mayo in Australia. Without "our overlogicized machinery for handling employee grievances," workers would no longer try "to tell their bosses to go to hell"—a specter that haunted Fritz Roethlisberger in America.[36] To workers, on the other hand, the absence of reliable grievance machinery meant that their rights were unprotected from abusive employers. Some workers had good reason to tell their bosses to go to hell—for instance, women who regularly faced sexual harassment at factories in the 1930s. Asked why she joined the union, one female employee at Midland Steel replied, "When you belong to a union the foreman can't screw you. Last month my foreman asked me to go out with him. I told him, 'to hell with you, Charlie. I know what you want.' He got mad, but he did not try to spite me. He knew damn well the union would be on his neck if he did."[37]

Mayo and Roethlisberger assumed that workers joined unions from greed, sloth, wrath, or some such sickness. Like past advisers to princes, they further assumed that leaders, given proper instruction, could be trusted to wield power responsibly. But workers knew from bitter experience not to count on responsible bosses; they pleaded instead for relief from the tyrants who ruled some workplaces.

New Deal

Working Americans' experiences are documented in heartrending letters to the new administration after the presidential election of 1932. People from across the country wrote to Franklin and Eleanor Roosevelt, Secretary of Labor Frances Perkins, and others about the indignities they suffered at work. They told of carrying soiled and "diseased rags all day," inhaling "the grime and dirt of a nation," leaving work "too tired to even wash ourselves," lifting materials "so hot they burnt blisters on our hands," working for stingy wages "in cellars heated with gas stoves without fume flues throwing the fumes into the room," handling acids that "eat our fingers . . . almost to the bone," putting in twelve-hour shifts, seven nights a week (this from the wife of a night watchman in a salmon cannery: "In addition to the hourly rounds he has janitor work in five offices rooms and during working seasons he has to keep up steam in the boiler also attend the freight boat as they come and go. And keep pressure in the retorts. . . . for which he gets $75 a month and a shack to live in"). And those were the fortunate workers who still had jobs during the Great Depression. Workers who questioned their pay or conditions were fired or told, "Well if you don't like it you can quit." Many of the letters asking the Roosevelts and Secretary Perkins for help begged them not to tell the writers' employer that they complained for fear they'd be sacked. Together these letters delivered a poignant message: This is what work is like for Americans without political machinery to redress grievances—not always, but often enough that the government ought to do something about it.[38]

In 1935 the government did. Over industry objections, the National Labor Relations Act was passed by Congress, signed by the president, and upheld by the Supreme Court two years later. Sponsored by New York senator Robert F. Wagner, the act guaranteed the right of workers to join an independent union to negotiate with employers. It created the National Labor Relations Board to enforce the law. It also outlawed the company-dominated unions and employee representation plans used to avoid unionization at companies like AT&T. "No organization can be free to represent the workers when it is the mere creature of the employer," Senator Wagner argued; so long as employee representatives are subservient to top management, employees' rights are secondary considerations, granted "by the grace of the employer's whims."[39] In signing the Wagner Act, President Roosevelt said it assures "employees the right of collective bargaining [and] it fosters the development of the employment contract on a sound and equitable basis. . . . By preventing practices which tend to destroy the independence of labor, it seeks, for every worker within its scope, that freedom of choice and action which is justly his."[40]

In Roosevelt's view, the employment relationship is more like the social contract that James Madison had in mind than the social organism imagined by Elton Mayo—it is an agreement on rules of behavior to further the separate interests of management and labor, not a single-minded entity wherein employee and employer goals are one and the same. As Roosevelt recognized, the appropriate standard for evaluating a social contract is justice to the contracting parties, not efficiency in achieving the goals of one party. And justice in the employment relationship is better served by the checks and balances of an independent union than a sham system of governance in which employers dictate the terms.

Elton Mayo joined industry in attacking Roosevelt's efforts to rein in corporate power and level the playing field for labor relations. Speaking to Boston businessmen a few months after passage of the Wagner Act, Mayo compared the administration's New Deal to the fascist regimes of Europe. Roosevelt answered such rhetoric with a memorable speech accepting his party's renomination for the presidency in 1936. Likening Americans' struggle for industrial democracy to their Revolutionary War for political democracy (a "rendezvous with destiny"), FDR placed his views squarely in the tradition of Madison and the founders.[41]

"In 1776 we sought freedom from the tyranny of a political autocracy—from the eighteenth century royalists who held special privileges from the crown," he said. These political royalists governed without concern for the governed, denied rights of free speech and assembly, and put the lives of ordinary people "in pawn to the mercenaries of dynastic power." The American Revolution was fought to win freedom from such political tyranny. "That victory gave the business of governing into the hands of the average man, who won the right with his neighbors to make and order his own destiny through his own Government."[42]

Since then, Roosevelt said, Americans' innovative genius has reshaped people's lives with electricity and railroads, telegraph and radio, mass production and distribution—all contributing to modern civilization but posing a new challenge to freedom. "For out of this modern civilization economic royalists carved new dynasties. New Kingdoms were built upon concentration of control over material things. Through new uses of corporations, banks and securities, new machinery of industry and agriculture, of labor and capital—all undreamed of by the fathers—the whole structure of modern life was impressed into this royal service." Mincing no words, FDR called out the "privileged princes of these new economic dynasties": Imposing their will on government and working Americans, uniting with employer associations and antiunion lawyers, the princes of industry have dictated, for instance, "the hours men and women worked, the wages they received, the conditions of their labor." As a result, Roosevelt continued, "the average man once more confronts the problem that faced the Minute Man." The testimony of hardworking Americans has shown that "for too many of us life was no longer free; liberty no longer real"; "the political equality we once had won was meaningless in the face of economic inequality."

With their hopes for the future and their very lives at stake after the collapse of 1929, Roosevelt noted, Americans turned in desperation to their government for help. But "the new economic royalty" tried to shield their privilege behind the flag and the Constitution: Their publicists "have conceded that political freedom was the business of the government, but they have maintained that economic slavery was nobody's business. They granted that the government could protect the citizen in his right to vote, but they denied that the government could do anything to protect the citizen in his right to work and his right to live." Now, with false analogies to fascism, "these economic royalists complain that we seek to overthrow the institutions of America. What they really complain of is that we seek to take away their power."

American institutions like freedom of enterprise deserve our allegiance, Roosevelt concluded. But "today we stand committed to the proposition that freedom is no half-and-half affair. If the average citizen is guaranteed equal opportunity in the polling place, he must have equal opportunity in the market place." FDR declared: "This generation of Americans has a rendezvous with destiny." Elsewhere in the world, people who once lived and fought for freedom "seem to have grown too weary to carry on the fight." They have accepted economic submission "for the illusion of a living. They have yielded their democracy." But here in America, he vowed, we stand for freedom of voice in the workplace: "It is not alone a war against want and destitution and economic demoralization. It is more than that; it is a war for the survival of democracy."

Big business battled on against the New Deal, but the Roosevelt administration gave ordinary Americans a say in their conditions of work with the Wagner Act. Despite the material benefits of welfare capitalism and the friendly management of human relations in firms like Western Electric, workers increasingly elected independent unions to represent them when given a free choice. After a steep decline in union membership during the 1920s (coincident with the rise of employee representation plans), unionization in America rebounded from about 13 percent of the nonfarm workforce in 1935 to 35 percent within a decade. In 1937 Hawthorne plant workers formed a local union, the Western Electric Independent Labor Association, although they remained relatively passive compared to other Bell employees such as telephone operators—a testament, management believed, to the effectiveness of its personnel counseling in containing grievances. Nevertheless, the Hawthorne union gradually asserted itself and finally affiliated with a national union, the International Brotherhood of Electrical Workers, in 1954.[43]

Elton Mayo could never make sense of it, why workers of sound mind would choose a labor union to represent them rather than collaborate with management, or why it was any business of government. While Franklin Roosevelt enacted his New Deal for American workers, Mayo backed the chief executives who opposed it. As he prepared to retire from the Harvard Business School, Mayo summarized his views in yet another mirror for managers—*The Social Problems of an Industrial Civilization*, published in 1945. The book restates his objection to government regulation of industry and continues his attack on the progressive theories of "many of our liberals and our lawyers [who] have come to enunciating doctrines that are only with difficulty distinguished from the pronouncements of a Hitler or a Mussolini" (quite a provocative statement in 1945, outside of executive suites). Mayo longed for the self-regulated communities of single-minded members, forever mythologized in mirrors for princes. He pictured society as a complex of cooperative organizations, such as industrial companies, headed by leaders with "a capacity for vision and wise guidance"—private-sector philosopher-kings. He wanted to educate managers of those organizations in the social skills needed to ensure "that the avowed purpose for which the whole exists may be conveniently and continuously fulfilled."[44] Business leaders and business educators applauded. An article in *Fortune* after the book's release praised Mayo's erudition and experience: "Scientist and practical clinician, Mayo speaks with a rare authority that has commanded attention in factories as well as Universities. . . . Mayo's view gives promise of exerting through the field of business administration a significant influence on the future relations of US management and labor."[45]

Father of Modern Management

As the business press spread the legend of Elton Mayo and the gospel of human relations, social scientists in the late 1940s questioned Mayo's ideology. His sharpest critics included sociologists Wilbert Moore and Daniel Bell, who raised some of the same complaints made by critics of Robert Owen. Mayo, Moore said, "is insensitive to problems of ends or values":[46] He thinks that managers can learn the skill of cooperation—"which will settle all issues from those in industry to those in international affairs"[47]—without addressing different "aims of the cooperative endeavor, the distribution of the product, or the distinct interests of the cooperators."[48] Moore called Mayo a captive of "nostalgia for the good old days," when princes and prelates supposed *their* goals should be the goals of all; Mayo, he observed, tries "to make the factory the functional equivalent of the primitive kinship system or the medieval church."[49] Bell charged Mayo and his fellow industrial researchers of abandoning the impartial search for truth and espousing unconscionable bias: "They uncritically adopt industry's own conception of workers as *means* to be manipulated or adjusted to impersonal ends," forsaking "the belief in man as an end in himself." Consequently, "the social science of the factory researchers is not a science of man, but a cow-sociology" (teaching that contented cows give more milk).[50]

Such ethical critiques of the human relations movement are now accepted even by analysts schooled in its founding traditions. A former managing editor of *Fortune* and the *Harvard Business Review*, Walter Kiechel III, writes that the "Harvard Circle" centered around Elton Mayo and Dean Donham displayed "an elitism, a class-arrogance, almost incomprehensible by today's standards." They "ardently believed that an educated managerial cadre—a new 'managing class'—was the answer to the nation's problems: to the Depression, to inept government, to social upheaval." They "looked down on the typical worker as a lesser being, one to be manipulated in the service of higher purposes." And their aim in the Hawthorne studies "was always to discover how psychology could be used to raise productivity, resist unionization, and increase workers' cooperation with management." Ethics aside, however, the fatal critique of human relations was that it didn't accomplish the first of those goals for management: Scientifically flawed, it did not reliably raise productivity. Subsequent empirical research showed that happy workers were not necessarily good workers.[51]

In the 1950s and '60s a new generation of business theorists tried to fix Mayo's system, retaining his principle of managerial supremacy but revising his formula for motivating subordinates. Leading thinkers posited that high productivity causes pleasant human relations, not the reverse, and the key to productivity is employee participation, not employee satisfaction. This came to be called a *human resources* view, in contrast to Mayo's *human relations* approach, and it dominated management thought in the latter half of the twentieth century. Early adopters of this view wrote mirrors for managers promoting some variant of the human resources idea. For example, Douglas McGregor taught Theory Y; Frederick Herzberg urged job enrichment. But *the* exemplar, widely acclaimed as the "Father of Modern Management," was Peter Drucker, who prescribed management by objectives.[52]

Drucker's mirror for managers, *The Practice of Management*, outlined his philosophy: "Any business enterprise must build a true team and weld individual efforts into a common effort. Each member of the enterprise contributes something different, but they all must contribute toward a common goal," Drucker stated. Teamwork does not occur automatically. In many organizations, supervisors face opposition and conflict; workers waste effort, either goldbricking for personal reasons or gold-plating their work for professional aesthetics. It is the function of management to turn everyone's attention away from personal or professional goals and toward the organization's goals, ensuring "that each job [is] directed towards the objectives of the whole business."[53]

Drucker proposed management by objectives as a holistic method to focus vision and effort on common goals: Top management should set goals for the organization as a whole. Managers further down the hierarchy should participate in setting their own objectives to meet management's goals and in deciding how to achieve those objectives. Workers below them should be given as much discretion as feasible to align their efforts with company goals. From top to bottom, increased participation is meant to enhance the meaning of one's job by seeing the "big picture" from a general management point of view. Drucker made the point with the old story of three medieval stone masons who were asked what they were doing. "The first replied: 'I am making a living.' The second kept on hammering while he said: 'I am doing the best job of stonecutting in the entire country.' The third one looked up with a visionary gleam in his eyes and said: 'I am building a cathedral.'" The aim of management by objectives is to give everyone in an organization that third "cathedral" viewpoint where the interests of leaders and workers are identical.[54]

Drucker advised managers that it's not enough to give subordinates "'a sense of participation' (to use a pet phrase of the 'human relations' jargon)."[55] Employees must find opportunities for self-control and take responsibility for the results of their particular jobs. "The corporation simply cannot afford to deprive itself of the intelligence, imagination and initiative of ninety percent of the people who work for it, that is, the workers."[56] To help nonsupervisory workers acquire a "managerial vision" and identify with company objectives, Drucker recommended giving them greater control over activities pertaining to "the social life" of the organization: activities "entirely incidental—even irrelevant—to economic performance," for example, the company cafeteria "or, in places where women work, the day nurseries."[57] As in the human relations approach, however, Drucker insisted that "in managing the business employees as such cannot participate. They have no responsibility—and therefore no authority"—for setting company goals and policy.[58] "Management must remain the governing organ of the enterprise."[59]

Drucker does not say precisely what the goals of a company should be. But, as with management gurus since Robert Owen, he suggests a general

goal of productivity in meeting societal needs and wants. Like his predecessors, he bemoans the obstacles to such a goal posed by recalcitrant
individuals and intrusive government agencies. He gripes, for instance,
that in the last decade of the twentieth century, "the number of sexual-
harassment claims filed with the Equal Employment Opportunity
Commission more than doubled, from 6,883 a year to 15,889. And for
every case filed, up to ten or more were being settled in-house—each
requiring many hours of investigation and hearings, and substantial legal
fees as well." Expressing the same annoyance voiced by Robert Owen
over New Harmony's "woman problem," Drucker exclaims, "No wonder
that employers . . . complain bitterly that they have no time to work on
product and service, on customers and markets, on quality and distribution—they have no time to work, that is, on *results*. They work instead on
problems, that is, on employee regulations."[60]

In his futuristic mirror, *Managing in the Next Society*, Drucker tells
employers they can avoid these problems by hiring consultants to manage employee relations, by outsourcing the jobs of nearly everyone else,
and by using temporary workers who are exempt from labor regulations
and their associated costs. In plants and hospitals and universities, managers almost anywhere can give contract or temporary workers the same
responsibilities as legally recognized "employees" but without the same
expensive entitlements (overtime pay, unemployment insurance, old-age
and disability benefits, etc.).[61] Not simply the father of modern management, Drucker properly deserves the title father of the gig economy. It is
a dubious honor. "Today the so-called gig companies present themselves
as the innovative future of tomorrow, a future where companies don't
pay Social Security or Medicare," California state senator María Elena
Durazo recently remarked, but "let's be clear; there is nothing innovative
about underpaying someone for their labor."[62]

In Drucker's writings, there is nothing innovative about many of his
ideas, but there are lots of tired clichés one sees in mirrors for princes. The
tiredest cliché is that, with no common goal, social groups descend into
chaos and anarchy. Drucker claims, "Every enterprise requires commitment to common goals and shared values. Without such commitment
there is no enterprise; there is only a mob."[63] Turning a mob into a productive organization by setting "simple, clear, and unifying objectives" is
the singular job of management; the success of any enterprise depends
on leaders who instill "common vision, common understanding, and

unity of direction and effort."[64] Drucker views organizations as the sort of organic, living bodies depicted in mirrors for princes: They "decide, act and behave," but only as their managers—their governing organs—direct. Like the perfect prince of yore, "the manager is the dynamic, life-giving element in every business," Drucker asserts.[65] Other members are functional organs, valuable resources for attaining organizational goals, but not valuable in themselves and ultimately disposable. "In the Next Society's corporation," Drucker predicts, "top management will, in fact, be the company. Everything else can be outsourced."[66]

In actual societies, this strategy has troubling consequences. While outsourced employees can be just as dedicated to their jobs as perma-nent staff, the outsourcing firms that supply them may be committed to shortsighted goals. For example, most US hospitals outsource their emergency departments to for-profit physician management firms. Their doctors are qualified, and sick patients might not care who employs them—until the bill arrives. Emergency-room patients treated at hos-pitals in their insurers' network have been shocked to receive huge bills from out-of-network specialists. Contracting with such specialists ap-pears to be a deliberate tactic to boost profits by the private-equity-backed firms (EmCare and TeamHealth) that dominate emergency-department outsourcing, according to a Yale University study. The Yale researchers point out that unexpected bills of hundreds or thousands of dollars can be financially devastating to many Americans. Surprise bills cause reputational harm to hospitals, which are seen to collude in a "kind of ambushing of patients"—taking their insurance but handing them to doctors who don't. And the attendant bad press has led to repeated calls for legislation to regulate the practice, finally resulting in a bipartisan federal ban on surprise billing in 2022.[67]

Contrary to Drucker's managerial view, the more organizations en-gage in outsourcing, the less they look *empirically* like organic bodies of functional members with common goals, and the more they look like contractual arrangements between participant groups with rational goals of their own. The more organizations look like contracts, the less reason-able it seems *ethically* to judge them based on one party's goals, and the more appropriate it seems to rate them on fairness to all participants, especially the most vulnerable. The more organizations are held to stan-dards of fairness, of course, the less apparent it is that one stakeholder—that is, management—should be entrusted to decide the terms of the contract. Nevertheless, Drucker has maintained from the outset that "it is undoubtedly management's duty to manage; and management's proper function must be preserved. Its authority must be strengthened; for management in this country today has been weakened" by bloated government, divisive unions, and uninformed public opinion.[68]

In his 1950 mirror for managers, *The New Society*, Drucker preached that free enterprises "are the firmest basis on which a free society could be built." The free-enterprise system has inspired business leaders to found great industries like the electrical industry, the chemical industry, the automobile industry, and the aluminum industry, which Drucker argued would never have been started in a planned economy. Yet, he warned, modern welfare states are teaching citizens to depend on a flow of benefits they can have for nothing from a central government. Drucker urged that every citizen must instead "learn that the satisfaction of his hopes depends on increasing output, increasing productivity and increasing efficiency, that, in other words, it depends on *his efforts*." Every worker should learn as well that the main contributors to productivity (and therefore the most entitled to profit from it) are the managers of an enterprise. Drucker lamented that unions discourage workers from cooperating with managers or from seeing the connection between their own welfare and productive efficiency. Unions focus on how profits are divided, not produced, and how power is balanced, not leveraged—to the extent that "management and union may be likened to that serpent of the fables who on one body had two heads that, fighting each other with poisoned fangs, killed themselves." There can be only one head, Drucker insisted. Ambitious union leaders pretend otherwise, calling regular ritual strikes ("very much akin to the carefully arranged 'spontaneous' demonstrations of a totalitarian regime") designed to establish *their* authority, to display their members' power and cohesion, or to intimidate rival unions. Ultimately, workers must learn, "the enterprise can operate without the union but cannot operate without the management."[69]

Drucker concluded that business should take the lead in educating workers how the American economy makes prosperity possible for everyone—how, for example, "it is to the interests of the workers to have maximum efficiency and maximum profitability" and why "management must have full authority over all matters affecting the company's economic performance."[70]

In practice, top managers can tie almost anything to their company's economic performance (the way princes could tie whatever they fancied to some "state goal"); and Drucker would place few checks on their discretion. The authoritarian potential of his approach has not escaped professors of management. Critics of management by objectives, for instance, have described it as a one-sided bargain, not real participation, since bosses have the final say on objectives, and subordinates are forced to accept duties without rights and responsibilities without control. Others have charged that management by objectives leads managers to focus on short-term, easily measured results (like speed of production or service), to the neglect of outcomes important to weaker stakeholders (like product safety or service quality).[71] However, Drucker put his trust in management—not unions or government or public watchdogs—to self-regulate excesses, to balance different interests in the firm, and to focus everyone's vison on a common goal for the good of society. Sure, there are some poor managers, Drucker allowed in his book, *Management: Tasks, Responsibilities, Practices*. But in free economies no other authorities are so competent to define and achieve socially responsible objectives, he declared: "If the managers of our major institutions, and especially of business, do not take responsibility for the common good, no one else can, or will."[72]

During World War II, Peter Drucker shared the same fear that gripped Elton Mayo in World War I—that "society has been slowly disintegrating into anarchic masses in all industrialized countries." Like Mayo, Drucker found salvation in purposeful work; he imagined that the modern corporation could become "an autonomous organic social entity," a new authentic community much like the church of old, that gives meaning to life through the vision of its leaders. Updating the prayer of mirrors for princes for an industrial age, Drucker gave thanks that "there has never been a more efficient, a more honest, a more capable and conscientious group of rulers than the professional management of the great American corporations today."[73]

As always, the rulers said *amen*.

Voice of Industry

Even now business chroniclers call Peter Drucker a "truly revolutionary thinker" whose ever-fresh ideas contradict conventional wisdom. Yet "the professional management of the great American corporations" to whom Drucker wrote decades ago had heard such ideas many times before. Just as Machiavelli mirrored rulers' own views, Drucker said essentially what leading industrialists had been saying themselves. Their words are preserved for you to read (and compare to Drucker's) in the annals of the National Association of Manufacturers.[74]

Established in 1895 for "the promotion of the industrial interests of the United States," the National Association of Manufacturers (NAM) set out from the beginning to educate the public on the virtues of private enterprise. Association officials decried the hostility shown toward employers by labor organizations, newspapers, and other popular media of the Progressive Era. "The greatest menace that our country has today," the NAM magazine *American Industries* warned in 1913, "is a so-called 'free press,' bidding for popularity with the thoughtless mob." NAM's mission was to combat bad business press with pro-industry speeches, educational literature, and "public news" releases (issued without attribution to the association, in acknowledgment that its voice "is naturally discounted" as propaganda). As trade unions gained strength during World War I, NAM preached to "the workingmen of this country that their employers are their best friends" and "that the worst enemy of the workingmen is the 'outsider' who is always promising impossible advances in wages and impracticable shortening of working hours, and otherwise misleading them." NAM's stated aim in 1918 was to teach the wage earner "that his interests and those of his employer are identical."[75]

In the 1920s NAM's efforts were reinforced by the publicity efforts of large corporations like AT&T, which used folksy slogans and images to advertise their concern for improving the lives of all Americans. "Ma Bell's" early publicity manager, William P. Banning, said his job was "to make the people understand and love the company," to make it "an admired intimate member of the family." This familial face of business lost all credibility in the 1930s. Between 1929 and 1933, over fifteen million Americans lost their jobs, millions more saw their hours and pay cut, five thousand banks and nine million savings accounts vanished, farm income fell by half, and one in three farmers lost their land. Business leaders such as NAM's president, John Edgerton, felt that jobless workers and homeless farmers had only themselves to blame "if they gamble away their savings in the stock market or elsewhere." Most Americans thought otherwise—that the businessmen who took credit for America's great standard of living before 1929 were the ones to blame for the Great Depression. People heard it on the radio in FDR's speeches faulting the "economic royalists." They read it in the newspapers that covered congressional hearings into banking corruption. They saw it in magazines that ran photographs of down-and-out citizens in bread lines shuffling past locked businesses or signs advertising some faded real estate dream. Those who had jobs learned it at work from union organizers energized by the Wagner Act: corporations could not be trusted, left unchecked and unregulated, to ensure Americans' prosperity.[76]

After Roosevelt's "rendezvous with destiny" broadside and his landslide reelection victory in 1936, NAM spearheaded a counterattack to win hearts and minds for free enterprise. Enlisting specialists in the new art of public relations, NAM's leadership launched a campaign for the "American Way," described by media historian Stuart Ewen as a Holy War "to challenge the fundamental social assumptions of the New Deal and to project a picture of American business as a system that—through its normal routines—responds to and meets the concerns and aspirations of ordinary Americans." The idea of the American Way campaign was to persuade what NAM called "the folks along Main Street" that they were partners in "the United States, Inc.," that their interests were corporate America's interests, and that the goal of business was their common good.[77] NAM communicated its message via newspaper and magazine ads, editorials and feature stories, radio programs and film productions, outdoor billboards and direct mail advertisements, speakers at civic events and community groups, instructional materials for schools and workplaces, comic strips and cartoons—every media imaginable. NAM's yearly spending on such informational programs increased from $36,500 in 1934 to $1 million by the end of the decade (plus millions more in free airtime and advertising donated by affiliated companies), and it kept growing. "The central theme of NAM public relations material," notes business professor Richard Tedlow, "was that industry's managers were the true leaders of the nation. The public interest, and especially the workingman's interest, was safe in their hands." NAM ads portrayed workers and managers in perfect harmony, united in "the spirit of good will among all groups." A common tagline read, "Prosperity dwells where harmony reigns." The subtext was: No need here for intrusive government or unions.[78]

To help spread its message, NAM formed alliances with local opinion makers including news editors, civic leaders, school teachers, and church ministers. Historian Kevin Kruse credits NAM with forging the link between business and Christian conservatives when the association tapped the Reverend James W. Fifield Jr. to address its members at their 1940 convention. Pastor of the elite First Congregational Church in Los Angeles (and nicknamed the "Apostle to Millionaires"), Fifield delivered a jeremiad deploring the New Deal as an "encroachment upon our American freedoms" and, moreover, an affront to God. Reverend Fifield enlisted like-minded ministers in a crusade for prosperity against the "pagan statism" of bureaucrats in Washington and against the Social Gospel preached in mainline churches. Even more direct and systematic was NAM's outreach, through schoolteachers, to America's children.[79]

In November of 1939 NAM's chair, Charles Hook, addressed Missouri public school teachers at their state convention, urging them to explain and defend free enterprise in their classrooms. "Private enterprise should be presented fairly for what it is," he said, "namely, an essential element in the preservation of representative democracy and in the creation of better living for our people." Too many educators hold outdated views of industry, envisioning ruthless capitalists bent on maximizing their profits, Hook lamented; but that's not what businessmen do. Hook described his own job as president of the American Rolling Mill Company: "I am a manager whose function it is to operate a business in such a way that the three chief elements in the business all receive proper consideration. These three elements are the investors, labor (or the workers) and the consumer." Hook claimed it was his responsibility (not the government's) to manage these stakeholders, "to see that the interests of all three are satisfactorily balanced." It was NAM's role, he said, to deepen "management's awareness of its social responsibilities" and to enlighten the public on issues of mutual interest, such as keeping America safely away from the conflict in Europe. Some of our own educators, Hook added, espouse "alien philosophies" (socialism, communism, and other totalitarianisms) now resurgent abroad. Just as they vex Europeans, these long-discredited political and economic theories divide Americans; they perpetuate the "class consciousness, sectional jealousies, and loss of confidence" brought on by the Depression. Hook called on "patriotic educators" to help "all groups in this country work together" as one. He urged them to teach that the American Way is to "*produce* more" so "our people *have* more."

And he pledged NAM's assistance "to inculcate that philosophy in the hearts and minds of the oncoming generation." For that purpose, NAM would provide, free of charge, a series of "You and Industry" booklets prepared by the association specifically for use in schools.[80]

From 1936 to 1942, NAM published twenty different "You and Industry" titles for students, plus a study guide for teachers. Written at a middle-school level, the booklets were used mostly in high school social studies classes. NAM reported that over one million copies were distributed annually, reaching two-thirds of all high school students in America in the early 1940s.[81] The series covered all the topics of NAM's public relations campaign. Booklet number 1, *The American Way*, taught students that the American free-enterprise system is the best social system in the world, responsible for the highest standard of living and the happiest citizens with "the highest per capita ownership of wealth on earth."[82] Successive booklets told students the following story: American prosperity is the fruit of the initiative and ingenuity of far-sighted businessmen—exemplified by Robert Fulton, John Deere, Charles Goodyear, Alexander Graham Bell, George Westinghouse, Thomas Edison, and others. Suddenly, in the 1930s, America's success came under attack. The dynamic companies launched by business pioneers, along with the free-enterprise system itself, fell victim to the Great Depression. Investors lost money, employees lost jobs, consumers lost confidence; and when prosperity declined, people behaved badly. Workers saw themselves in competition with one another and with employers, causing class warfare and industrial strife. Government officials tried to bring back prosperity with an exuberant burst of social legislation, such as the Wagner Act, the Social Security Act, the Fair Labor Standards (Wage and Hour) Act, and so on. But these New Deal laws burden business with regulation that "puts brakes on individual initiative and ingenuity—on the freedom that private enterprise needs to do its work well."[83]

The series booklet *Employer-Employee Cooperation* cast the Wagner Act as especially onerous, saying the act "has granted labor rights without assigning commensurate responsibility," thereby trampling employers' rights and stoking even more conflict. Students learned, "This law has been a major factor in the growth of irresponsible labor leadership and in the large number of strikes obstructing vital defense production." Students learned further that labor strikes, while selfishly endangering the nation's security, are frequently not over wages or working conditions but about forcing workers to join a union: "Bloody clashes have occurred between rival unions for jurisdiction over certain workers, or over particular types of work"; and in big cities like Chicago "various types of racketeering have resulted from the monopolistic power wielded by closed-shop unions." Yet, students were reassured, with their cooperation business can reclaim its leadership, restore prosperity at home, and turn the tide of war overseas (now that America was engaged).[84]

NAM's "You and Industry" booklets prescribed a remedy for America's ills that propagated, to a new generation, the ageless clichés of mirrors for princes. The remedy is a common goal, as formulated by visionary leaders: "Despite the industrial strife, which is more prevalent than anyone interested in the preservation of our social order desires, employers and employees have important common interests," students read; "both benefit most when industry best performs its primary social function—the efficient production of goods."[85] Echoing Robert Owen, Frederick Taylor, Elton Mayo, and other sages, NAM taught that *everyone* benefits when industry pursues its basic social purpose of producing more goods for more people. To attain this goal, government and unions should get out of the way and let leaders of industry manage. "Only industry, ever and more productive, can produce enough goods to go around. It is not possible to create the things we need by legislation. Food must be grown; clothing made; houses built; equipment manufactured. There must be more, and more, and more, until there is abundance for all. Standards of living cannot be raised by dividing up what already exists. The only way by which standards of living can be raised and broadened is by more production."[86]

NAM's lesson to the nation's youth was that company executives deserve the right to manage as they see fit; they are the country's best hope to pursue goals that Americans have in common. "You and Industry" warned students that leftist labor leaders were demanding a bigger voice in company management, just as their fellow travelers in government were overreaching into business affairs. But "one of the cardinal principles in the management of any organization is that executive authority and responsibility must be centralized in one individual"; a chief executive "must reconcile the interests of capital, labor, and consumer," ensuring that each constituent group benefits sufficiently to continue cooperating.[87] A related principle of the American way of life is that free people cooperate most responsibly through "self-discipline and self-regulation," students were informed.[88] Self-regulation may not have stopped slave masters from irresponsible conduct in times gone by, but today's system of "free private enterprise makes it certain that management must meet *all* of its social responsibilities if managers are to hold their jobs."[89] NAM's booklet on *The Profession of Management* concluded confidently: "The industrial and business managers today, most of whom have come up through the ranks, have generally had good training in both the principles and practice of modern management. They know its requirement of efficiency, in order that the interests of labor, capital, and market may be well served. And they are conscious of their broad social responsibility—for the preservation of a free society and for making freedom work ever better for the common welfare."[90]

Lest these homilies be lost on children, NAM's study guide for teachers suggested test questions, subjects for class discussion, essay topics, and group activities to reinforce key points. Students might be asked, for example, to "tell in your own words the different wants of capital, labor, and consumers that management must recognize, also their common interest." Or students might "make a chart or a poster showing how producing more goods for more customers benefits all parties concerned: investors, workers, management, consumers." Or teachers could lead a class discussion on "provisions of the Wagner Act which industrial management finds unfair to employers and contrary to public interest."[91] To keep teachers on message, NAM supplied them with teaching aids, including cinema-quality motion pictures to entertain and inspire their students; NAM's 1940 short film *Your Town*, for example, portrays wise old Grandad telling his grandson Jerry how the town's factory owner made everybody's life better and explaining why labor agitators are wrong, un-American, to stir up trouble. (You can watch it now at https://archive.org/details/YourTown1940—go ahead, it's only eleven minutes—and you can imagine its effect on children of "the greatest generation.")[92]

Professors of education, media studies, and business history have all criticized NAM's campaign of indoctrination and the pro-management bias of the "You and Industry" materials. Members of Congress raised objections early on. In 1936 Wisconsin senator Robert M. La Follette Jr. launched a congressional investigation into corporate violations of workers' rights to unionize. His Committee on Education and Labor began by looking into industry's use of spies and private police, but in 1939 the

spotlight turned to NAM's campaign of "public education." The committee found that, under the guise of education, "the National Association of
Manufacturers has flooded the country with biased propaganda directed
against organizations of American workingmen and against social legislation adopted by Congress." The committee reviewed, among other
public relations communications, NAM's "You and Industry" booklets.
Their stated purpose is to increase understanding of the American economic system by providing "the facts about industry," the committee
noted, yet the booklets are more about shaping opinions than providing facts. Students are told in booklet number 1, *The American Way*, for
instance, that "it is essential, in a free system, that there should be no
bureaucratic control of the citizens," yet the United States has authorized
so many federal (i.e., New Deal) agencies "that it has become increasingly
difficult to know what the Government chooses to do," imperiling the
liberty and prosperity of all Americans. When "facts" *are* given, the committee observed, they are not supported by any references. Some information appears to be simply made up. Other data are presented in misleading charts or pictures—in graphs of per capita wealth, for example,
which mask gross inequalities. (At any neighborhood bar Bill Gates
walks into, the joke goes now, everyone is per capita a billionaire.) NAM's
own officers "recognized their program as propaganda," the La Follette
Committee reported: "In writing of the association's 'education program'
for school children, James P. Selvage, director of the public relations
department, did not speak of truth, or facts, or education, but referred
to the theory that 'pictures have become accepted more and more as the
most impressive medium for leaving a lasting impression on children . . .
during their formative years.'" Selvage indicated that industrialists who
supported such a program "considered 'its propaganda value good.'"[93]

The NAM—the self-styled "Voice of Industry"—spoke mostly for
powerful corporations like DuPont, General Motors, US Steel, Mon-
santo, Borg-Warner, Swift, Standard Oil, and, high on the list of contributors, Western Electric. Association spokesmen used language typical of
mirrors for princes. To mute calls for fairness or oversight, they spread
stories of shiftless youths, uppity laborers, subversive rabble-rousers,
and wasteful politicians; they said strong leadership was required to
restore harmony, and they taught citizens to rely on leaders of industry
to transform people, to unite them for a common goal. The La Follette
Committee summarized NAM's scheme: "Unnerved by the impact of

the depression, apprehensive of the growing strength of labor, enraged at critics of the failures of business and rejecting almost in toto the devices of the new administration in Washington to find solutions to the problems it inherited in 1933, the leaders of the association resorted to 'education.'"[94] Industrialists' overriding goal was better and faster production. It was a goal that even children could learn, as one professor of economic education later testified to Congress: "First-graders can realize that the faster and better men can produce goods and services, the more wishes and dreams can be fulfilled."[95]

This was the same sort of "education" advocated by Robert Owen in New Harmony; the same sort of education proposed by Peter Drucker in his mirrors for managers; indeed, the same sort of education taught by the earliest mirrors for princes in ancient Egypt.

Full Circle

Egyptologists have translated many mirrors not from the actual books (fragile papyrus scrolls, long lost) but from heaps of fragments scrawled by schoolchildren on ostraca, potsherds or limestone flakes, and wooden writing tablets. The lessons children copied in pharaohs' schools closely resemble what children in America learned from the National Association of Manufacturers:

> The country is in chaos, "topsy-turvy."
> The servants are demanding. The nobles are in fear. The officials are corrupt.
> And "Every man's heart is concerned with himself."
> You—everyman but aspiring leaders in particular—must do better.
> Don't be so selfish. "Know your place, be it lowly or exalted."
> Don't be a layabout, expecting handouts from the king's storehouse.
> Don't listen to the hotheads who create factions among the young.
> Instead, "emulate the great ones of old."
> Denounce troublemakers and harness the heat of the multitude.
> Pull together like a single team for a worthy goal.
> "Do *maat* for the king, for *maat* is what the king loves."
> Your boss will tell you what *maat* (truth, harmony, social responsibility) means.

Everybody has a boss.

Obey him, don't talk back. Work hard. And be content with what he
   gives you.

That is the way to prosperity.[96]

As in modern mirrors for managers, these first mirrors for princes
reflected how top bosses wished to be seen: Egyptian "kings presented
themselves as the key element in maintaining the prevailing social and
economic order," writes Egyptologist Juan Carlos Moreno García: To
ensure order and prosperity, to balance different subjects' duties and des-
erts, kings' "sovereignty could simply not be shared"; there was no room
for politics as "a deliberative process about long-term *goals*" between
"actors enjoying executive agency." As in executive suites today, "hierarchy and subordination were thus essential in an ideal pyramidal
order . . . in which there was only a place for one actor at the summit":
Pharaoh. For four thousand years, mirrors for princes have said virtually
the same thing—not because it's true, not because it's been good for
society, but because it's what pleased the prince.[97]

There remains good reason to read mirrors for princes. But it's not
what some theorists suppose. The ancients who wrote mirrors for princes,
claimed Peter Drucker, "knew all that has ever been known about leadership." According to Drucker, "The first systematic book on leadership:
the *Kyropaidaia* of Xenophon" (*The Education of Cyrus*) "is still the best
book on the subject."[98] Xenophon's book, you'll recall, is a fictionalized
biography of the Persian King Cyrus the Great; it "is composed of dialogues that were never spoken, battles that never took place, and people
summoned and dismissed from the written page without any shadow of
historical reality," notes classicist Philip Stadter.[99] The book describes
Xenophon's own theory of the ideal leader—a benevolent autocrat who
commands willing obedience by setting lofty objectives and inspiring
others to believe their interests are identical. It's an entertaining story
and has attracted all kinds of readers. "Xenophon's best-known and
most devoted reader," remarks political scientist Christopher Nadon,
was Machiavelli.[100]

What authors from Machiavelli to Peter Drucker learned from
Xenophon was not the actual art of leadership, however. Xenophon
taught his admirers how to *talk* about leadership to impress an audience,

as classics professor Melina Tamiolaki suggests: Xenophon showed how to argue that a strong king might effectively rule a great empire, what to say, for example, "in front of a Greek audience who had no tradition of monarchy and had, on the contrary, constantly experienced the failure of empires."[101] Since antiquity, mirrors for princes told kings how to impress audiences skeptical of their right to rule. (It was Xenophon who influenced King James of Scotland and England to write his 1599 mirror, *The Royal Gift*, and remind his son that the Divine Majesty hath "made you a little GOD to sit on his Throne, and rule ouer other men."[102]) The reason to still read this clichéd genre of literature, then, is not to discover secrets of leadership but to help you recognize propaganda when you see it.

THIRTEEN

Beyond Mirrors for Leaders

A Social Contract for Organizations

This book has addressed *readers* of management literature, revisiting teachings that once passed for wisdom in mirrors for princes, to help readers spot the clichés. This concluding chapter addresses *writers* on management, particularly teachers of leadership and business ethics, to suggest how one might avoid those clichés in explaining organizations.

Now and again business leaders will launch a campaign, sponsored by some trade group, asking the public to trust them and promising to act in the interests of everyone, for the common good. Most recently it was the Business Roundtable, an association of more than two hundred chief executives from America's largest corporations. The association had long espoused the view that corporations' primary goal was to maximize profits for shareholders. But in 2019 member CEOs proudly released a new "Statement on the Purpose of a Corporation" pledging "to lead their companies for the benefit of all stakeholders—customers, employees, suppliers, communities and shareholders." This "modernized" goal of balancing multiple stakeholder interests, said Roundtable chair and JPMorgan Chase chief executive Jamie Dimon, reflects "the business community's unwavering commitment to continue to push for an economy that serves all Americans."[1]

Professors of management and business ethics hailed the announcement as "a sea change" for the Business Roundtable and "an important moment in our understanding of how management is studied and practiced."[2] But the business media has not been so sanguine. Editorial writers have derided the Roundtable statement as just another public relations exercise. Chicago Booth School financial economist Luigi Zingales wrote:

The same business leaders who signed this statement have knowingly sold fraudulent mortgages to investors and defective products to customers, aggressively marketed addictive drugs, dumped toxic products in their communities and used every possible trick to elude (if not evade) taxes. If the top executives were serious about improving the way their companies are run, what about a commitment to reduce their lobbying and making it more transparent? Or a commitment to reduce the amount of taxes they elude by transferring intellectual property rights in fiscal paradises. At best, the new statement seems an attempt to present a kinder and gentler image to cover the reputational blow that daily scandals are imposing on corporate America: a marketing ploy with no real bite.[3]

Political economist Robert Reich singled out, for shameless hypocrisy, Business Roundtable director Dennis Muilenburg, since fired as chief executive of Boeing for discounting the risks to stakeholders posed by the company's ill-starred 737 Max jet (which killed 346 of them).[4]

Veteran business columnist David Lazarus spoke for many critics, calling the Business Roundtable's statement a "populist flavor of corporate propaganda" reminiscent of the business community's crusade against the New Deal.[5] Issued in a press release with great fanfare, the Roundtable's statement harkens back to the National Association of Manufacturers' American Way campaign, eighty years earlier. It affirms that "the free-market system is the best means of generating good jobs, a strong and sustainable economy, innovation, a healthy environment and economic opportunity for all." It declares that all these benefits are provided by independent businesses that sell consumer products, make industrial equipment, supply defense weaponry, grow food, deliver health care, generate energy, and offer communication and financial services to Americans everywhere. The Roundtable states that "each of our individual companies serves its own corporate purpose"; and it upholds management's right to act for "*all* of our stakeholders"—to judge what each requires—in pursuit of the corporate purpose.[6] Skeptics' concern, just as with NAM's publicity campaign, is that Roundtable executives do not acknowledge that stakeholders have any rights of their own that trump management's goals for the corporation.

Most critics agree that corporations should benefit all stakeholders; the question is whether chief executives can be trusted to make the hard calls required. What happens when the interests of different stakeholders conflict, as they often do? Should a company executive be the final judge, for example, of whether profits for stockholders (and other beneficiaries) outweigh the safety of a few hundred airplane passengers? PR statements ceding such authority to management are understandably viewed with suspicion by stakeholder and stockholder advocates alike. Shareholder activist Nell Minow notes that, as in its past rhetoric, the Business Roundtable statement serves to entrench management: "The CEOs who signed this statement know that accountability to everyone is accountability to no one. It's like a shell game where the pea of obligation is always under the shell you didn't pick."[7] Former labor secretary Reich likewise views the Roundtable declaration of "corporate social responsibility" as a classic con. He argues, "The only way to make corporations socially responsible is through laws requiring them to be—for example, giving workers a bigger voice in corporate decision-making . . . and preventing dangerous products (including faulty airplanes) from ever seeing the light of day."[8]

Business ethics and management scholars have acknowledged that the Roundtable statement appears one-sided in stressing value *creation* for stakeholders while overlooking value *destruction* or harms to stakeholders. Still, many remain supportive of the new statement because it seems to exorcise the ghost of stockholder value, which the Roundtable previously emphasized (following Milton Friedman's provocative dictum that the prime responsibility of business is to maximize profits). Far from representing a sea change in corporate social responsibility, however, there's actually nothing new in the 2019 Business Roundtable statement. It's virtually identical to the Roundtable "Statement on Corporate Responsibility" issued in October of 1981 (before the Roundtable opted to espouse shareholder primacy in 1997). The 1981 statement differs from the most recent version mainly in terminology, holding corporations responsible to multiple "constituencies"—instead of "stakeholders"—and calling on managers to weigh the interests of customers, employees, suppliers, shareholders, communities, and society at large. Both statements assign top management the right to balance stakeholder interests in light of the corporate purpose that management decides for itself. And therein lies the problem; many stakeholders would deny that management has any such moral right.[9]

The issue came up centuries ago in a confrontation between Machiavellian and anti-Machiavellian mirrors for princes. The amoral Machiavelli and his clerical opponent Giovanni Botero both supposed that states were organic entities with goals of their own, articulated by their rulers. But Botero faulted Machiavelli for prioritizing the wrong goal: *The Prince*, he maintained, taught rulers to focus on the survival of a secular regime, a bad reason of state, whereas Botero told rulers to focus on building a Christian empire, a good reason of state. The type of goal makes all the difference in eliciting ethical behavior, Botero presumed. It was all nonsense, in the opinion of James Madison: Rulers on a mission for God were not the best at reconciling rival interests. The holiest of goals, Madison pointed out, have inspired participants in religious wars, inquisitions, and state-sponsored churches to "join without remorse in acts against which their consciences would revolt, if proposed to them separately in their closets."[10] It's not the particular social purpose, then, but the unbridled pursuit of any so-called common goal—be it a heavenly cause or worldly profits—that's morally problematic. This poses a fundamental challenge for organization and management theory.

Goals

Specialized theories of organization and management proliferated in the second half of the twentieth century. One famous article painted the picture of a bewildering "management theory jungle," where isolated tribes spoke about organizational behavior in different languages.[11] Amid all the babble, however, the study of organizations retained a singular focus, observed political scientist Petro Georgiou: It's "been dominated since its inception by the conceptualization of organizations as goal attainment devices."[12] Whatever theoretical scheme organizational researchers conceived, whatever new jargon management gurus minted, they all agreed that organizations are systems to achieve some goal.

The trouble, Georgiou said, is that this goal model of organizations is descriptively flawed. Empirically, organizational goals are contested concepts. In corporations, government departments, universities, and most large organizations, people generally don't agree on goals. What some participants consider goals (e.g., wages or profits), others may see as costs. Because goals of the organization as a whole are contentious, they get expressed as vague aspirations that may have little bearing on individuals' behavior. The reality is that individuals participate in organizations for different personal reasons, they take satisfaction in different system outcomes, and organizations must address these different interests to remain going concerns. The dominant "goal paradigm" of organizations cannot explain this reality, Georgiou noted. "Organizational analysts have been unable to cope with the reality of organizations because their vision is monopolized by an image of the organization as a whole; an entity not merely greater than the sum of its parts, but so superior that it is effectively divorced from the influence of the parts. . . . The organization is endowed with a personality while the individuals constituting it are depersonalized, role players in the service of the organization's goals." Georgiou urged researchers to abandon this outdated goal model in favor of a more true-to-life image of organizations. Organizations, he argued, are best viewed not as purposeful bodies but as "marketplaces whose structures and processes are the outcomes of the complex accommodations made by actors exchanging a variety of incentives and pursuing a diversity of goals."[13]

Similar arguments have been advanced over the years, but the goal model of organizations remains central to management theory despite its empirical failings. The reason is that theoretical social models are not just descriptive tools, depicting how people actually behave. They are also prescriptive tools, idealizing how people *should* behave. The old organic model of social systems as goal-seeking bodies, for example, implies that societies, states, and other associations should have goals, even (or especially) if they don't. A long time ago Aristotle imagined that states seek goals, like the common good, that transcend the goals and goods of individuals. Yet his study of 158 Greek states did not reveal a single one that actually sought such a goal; "all the constitutions which now exist are faulty," he reported. The foremost political scientist of the ancient world, Aristotle recorded much the same behaviors that Petro Georgiou saw in modern organizations. He found people allied in different factions, contesting the common good, putting their interests before their duties to the state, buying cheap and selling dear to further their own purposes. However, Aristotle did not conclude that his social model, the "goal paradigm," was wrong. He assumed that his research subjects were wrong, that people were behaving selfishly. He insisted that a state does not exist "for the sake of exchange"—"nor does a state exist for the sake of alliance and security from injustice" or merely "for the prevention of mutual crime." Rather, "a state exists for the sake of a good life" that everyone can share, or at least everyone that matters (i.e., free, male citizens). What Aristotle meant, of course, was that states *should* have one goal, everyone *should* share a common good, not that they actually do.[14]

In the same way, when professors of business ethics tell you that "corporations are first of all communities, social groups with shared purposes," they're largely echoing Aristotle's claim that communities *should* have shared purposes.[15] Anyone can see that big corporations and other modern organizations do not *in fact* have shared goals (unless one defines their "members" so narrowly as to include only a core executive team). That's why Frederick Taylor and Elton Mayo and Peter Drucker and others proposed new systems of management—to convince self-interested workers they *should* share a purpose. The whole point of scientific management, human relations, management by objectives, all such schemes, is to remake workplaces that don't exhibit common goals into organizations that do. And it's the main point of modern leadership theory. Leadership researchers, recognizing that the goal paradigm fails to accurately describe corporations, do not fault the goal model but claim it is the organization—and specifically employees—that ought to change: "It is thus imperative that leaders influence employees not only to acquire a sense of purpose—but a sense of purpose that is construed by different organizational members in the same way," write management professors Andrew Carton, Chad Murphy, and Jonathan Clark.[16]

Leaders

Early on, theorists distinguished leaders from managers based on the formers' ability to build belief in organizational goals. Pioneering leadership authority James MacGregor Burns explained that management involves the administration of necessary tasks, the prompt disposition of everyday problems in organizations. "Leadership," he said, "is something else": It reshapes human behavior and institutions "toward desired ends," toward "broader, more substantive goals." Managers are necessary in all organizations, he supposed, but visionary leaders make some organizations great.[17]

Burns shifted terminology in his popular book *Leadership*. Here Burns referred to conventional management as "transactional leadership." It seeks cooperation through the exchange of incentives between individuals to reach independent objectives: "Thus Dutchmen (colonists in America) give beads to Indians in exchange for real estate, and French legislators trade votes in the Assembly on unrelated pieces of legislation. This is *transactional* leadership. The object in these cases is not a joint effort for persons with common aims acting for the collective interests of followers but a bargain to aid the individual interests of persons or groups going their separate ways." Such leadership treats organizations as marketplaces, just as Georgiou and other realists picture them. But Burns viewed exchange-based transactional leadership as "superficial and trivial." Leaders should do better, he felt; followers should aim higher: "Leaders can [and should] also shape and alter and elevate the motives and values and goals of followers through the vital *teaching* role of leadership. This is *transforming* leadership. The premise of this leadership is that whatever the separate interests persons might hold, they are presently or potentially united in the pursuit of 'higher' goals." Transforming leadership is not only motivating and uplifting, Burns said, but ultimately "*moral* in that it raises the level of human conduct and ethical aspiration of both leader and led."[18]

Since Burns published his *Leadership* mirror in 1978, writing on transforming or transformational leadership has grown into a cottage industry. Setting the agenda for recent theory and research, organizational psychologist Bernard Bass developed Burns's theme that "leadership is nothing if not linked to collective purpose."[19] Bass dismissed attempts by theorists to model everyday behavior in organizations—especially theories normalizing "leadership as an exchange process, a transactional relationship in which followers' needs can be met if their performance measures up to their contracts with their leader." Bass set out instead to model extraordinary behavior. Citing cases of storied leaders like CBS founder William S. Paley, Bass advanced a theory of leadership as a transformational process that engaged followers' unmet needs to achieve their potential and to lead fulfilling lives. He identified three main components of transformational leadership: The first and most important component, "charisma," is displayed by leaders "to whom followers form deep emotional attachments and who in turn inspire their followers to transcend their own interests for superordinate goals." The second component, "individualized consideration," is shown by leaders who mentor and enhance the confidence of subordinates. The final component, "intellectual stimulation," occurs as leaders arouse awareness of shared problems and foster visions of new possibilities.[20]

Bass associated these three aspects of transformational leadership with exceptional levels of effort and high degrees of organizational effectiveness. While he stopped short of insisting that transformational bosses are always more moral than transactional ones, he followed Burns in portraying the former as true *leaders* who raise attitudes and behavior to a "higher plane" of maturity, the latter as mere *managers* mired in "compromise, intrigue, and control." According to Bass, transactional managers act like "everyone has a price; it is just a matter of establishing it," whereas transformational leaders motivate individuals to put aside selfish aims for the sake of some greater, common good.[21]

Leadership specialists Daan van Knippenberg and Sim Sitkin have documented the dominance of the "charismatic-transformational" perspective in leadership research over the past twenty-five years. They review study after study in which attributions of charismatic-transformational leadership seem to predict attributions of leaders' effectiveness (with a laundry list of at least fifty-eight moderating variables, such as team diversity). Yet, the authors point out, this research is not all that it appears. The big problem is that studies confound charismatic-transformational leadership with its supposed effects. Does it surprise you, for example, that a questionnaire study finds most employees who say their boss "Instills pride in me for being associated with him/her" would also say their boss "Increases my willingness to try harder"? Is it clear to you why the first question is a valid measure of leadership (the independent variable) and the second a valid measure of effectiveness (the dependent variable)—rather than aspects of an overall perception of one's supervisor? Not all studies share this fatal ambiguity, of course. But van Knippenberg and Sitkin demonstrate that leadership research is beset by conceptual and methodological problems. They argue that charismatic-transformational leadership is a fuzzy concept with no empirical mechanism for how it works its magic. And they conclude that "the state-of-the-science suggests that leadership research and practice are better off abandoning the construct of charismatic-transformational leadership."[22]

As van Knippenberg and Sitkin infer, belief in charismatic-transformational leadership is ultimately a matter of faith, not facts—

what leaders *should* do, not what they *really* do. In the style of mirrors for princes, leadership theory and research has long had a homiletic tone. "Transformational leadership should be encouraged," proclaimed Bernard Bass. At the individual level, Bass expounded, factors associated with transformational leadership "should be incorporated into managerial assessment, selection, placement, and guidance programs." At the organizational level, institutional constraints on managerial behavior should be reduced to allow transformational leaders more freedom of action: "Organizational policy needs to support an understanding and appreciation of the maverick who is willing to take unpopular positions, who knows when to reject the conventional wisdom, and who takes reasonable risks."[23]

With such leadership, what could possibly go wrong? Why would anyone *not* appreciate leaders who act like mavericks, who disregard public opinion and conventional norms, who take risks they deem reasonable in exerting authority over others? Despite the obvious potential for abuse of power, proponents of transformational leadership seldom ask about its hazards. Instead, they cast aspersions on alternatives like transactional leadership—which Bass calls "a prescription for mediocrity."[24] The modern father of transforming leadership, James MacGregor Burns, offered this depiction of transactional leaders in government organizations:

> [They] grope along, operating "by feel and by feedback." They concentrate on method, technique, and mechanisms rather than on broader ends and purposes. They protect, sometimes at heavy cost to overall goals, the maintenance and survival of their organization because they are exposed daily to the claims of persons immediately sheltered by that organization. They extrude red tape even as they struggle with it. They transact more than they administer, compromise more than they command, institutionalize more than they initiate. They fragment and morselize policy issues in order better to cope with them, seeking to limit their alternatives, to delegate thorny problems "down the line," to accept vague and inconsistent goals, to adapt and survive. Thus they exemplify the "satisficing" model, as economists call it, far more than the "maximizing" one.[25]

This, Burns suggests, is what leadership looks like if we view organizations as marketplaces for the exchange of incentives between actors with a diversity of goals. It's a gross caricature, however, a rhetorical flourish that puts transformational leadership in a better light and diverts attention from *its* dark side. Burns's disdain for government "satisficers" is telling. It reflects his quarrel with the framers of the American Constitution, and James Madison in particular, who saw very clearly the dark side of transformational leadership and took steps to temper it.

Framers

Many of the governmental practices that dismay Burns and his followers are the legacy of the framers. Burns took issue with this legacy in an early book lamenting "the deadlock of democracy"—an allusion to "the system of checks and balances and interlocked gears of government that requires the consensus of many groups and leaders before the nation can act." Burns wrote that this system exacts a "heavy price of delay and devitalization" and that it was "designed for deadlock and inaction" from the start—by Madison and those delegates to the Constitutional Convention who shared his fear of strong leadership.[26]

But the framers were not naive about leadership. They were experienced in practical affairs; most were lawyers, businessmen, or politicians who shouldered responsibilities themselves. They were educated as well, familiar with leadership theories and historical exemplars from mirrors for princes. Even those who never read such books knew what they said. Bolingbroke's *Idea of a Patriot King*, which called for a transforming leader two centuries before Burns did, was a commonplace of political rhetoric among English speakers—as famous in the colonies as Machiavelli's *Prince*. What's more, the framers had a shining example of patriotic, transformational leadership right in front of them.[27]

The unanimous choice to preside over the Constitutional Convention was George Washington—father of the country, symbol of virtue, and a larger-than-life monument even in 1787. Washington's fame stemmed from his ability to transform a fractious band of rebels into a victorious army in the American War of Independence. This was no small feat: Rank-and-file Americans were not eager to risk their lives and fortunes fighting for the sacred honor of Congress. Volunteers from some states wanted nothing to do with militia from others. Farmers and merchants were reluctant to take Continental currency and provide food or supplies to Washington's forces. His staff included quarrelsome, treasonous, and just useless officers. (While short of good officers, for instance, Washington had a surplus of unemployed European officers sent by friends abroad; historian Samuel Eliot Morison remarked, "since Americans disliked serving under foreigners, there was nothing for most of [the Europeans] to do except serve on Washington's staff, and tell him in French, German, or Polish as the case might be, that his army was lousy."[28])

Washington's army lost most of the battles, yet somehow won the war. In describing Washington's behavior as commander-in-chief, his biographer James Flexner portrays a transformational leader in every sense of the term. From the outset, Washington displayed heroic acts. Upon accepting command of the Continental Army, he informed Congress that he would take no salary, a selfless and inspiring gesture in an age when it was customary for military officers to enrich themselves at public expense. Throughout the war, shortages of money and equipment drove Washington to devise unconventional means of motivating his troops. British and other professional soldiers of the day were paid to carry out orders without concern for what the fight was all about—European kings and generals did not want their armies thinking about which way to point their weapons. Lacking the funds to employ such compliant professionals, Washington united and motivated a bunch of rugged individualists by refocusing their attention on higher ends: "Washington labored to inspire his soldiery with confidence in the value and nobility of the cause," wrote Flexner. This military innovation—encouragement of combat by appeals to nationalism—transformed not only the Continental Army but the very nature of modern warfare.[29]

If ever there was a model of charismatic-transformational leadership, that leader was George Washington. And if ever there was a time for such leadership, the year was 1787. Under the weak Articles of Confederation, the newly independent states had turned from fighting the British with muskets to fighting one another with tariffs, currencies, and other weapons of commercial warfare. These civil conflicts were textbook cases of bad behavior for which mirrors for princes promised a cure; sages from Isocrates to Bolingbroke had prescribed visionary leadership to unite people behind a common goal. (The exemplar of leadership, Bolingbroke told the Prince of Wales, was Queen Elizabeth I, who "united the great body of the people in her and their common interest" and "inflamed them with one national spirit.") But books of advice for rulers and tales of legendary leaders, written for the most part to please some prince or patron, were not serious blueprints for governing, the framers realized.

George Washington knew his own leadership of a small army in time of war was a special case, not a responsible prototype for running a nation. With one or two exceptions, delegates to the Constitutional Convention felt it would be irresponsible to entrust the well-being of their fellow citizens and their descendants to a "standing miracle, so rarely seen," as Bolingbroke characterized the true, transforming leader.[30]

Their knowledge of history, their practical experience, and their good sense taught the framers that trying to cure social ills with common goals and uncommon leaders could be worse—much worse, for some persons—than the disease. James Madison explained that personal circumstances give rise to different goals and opinions, which are valid to individuals holding them "however erroneous or ridiculous these . . . may appear to the enlightened Statesman, or the benevolent philosopher."[31] Conflict ensues not because individuals have different goals but when groups with similar goals, "factions," become so passionate in pursuing their interests that they invade the rights of others, imposing costs on people without their consent. In the ideal world of patriot kings, conflicts between factions are happily resolved by firm leadership. But this solution compounds the problem in the real world, Madison argued: Strong-willed "leaders ambitiously contending for pre-eminence and power . . . have in turn divided mankind into parties, inflamed them with mutual animosity, and rendered them much more disposed to vex and oppress each other, than to co-operate for their common good."[32] It would be fairer for all over the long haul, Madison concluded, not to seek consensus on goals, as prescribed in mirrors for princes, but on terms of collaboration, as in a social contract of government.

By 1787 the social contract idea of John Locke was as familiar to Americans as the patriot king of Lord Bolingbroke. Thomas Jefferson had endorsed the former and debunked the latter in his draft of the Declaration of Independence: People are created free and equal in rights, he wrote; to protect their rights, governments are instituted by the consent of the governed. Official goals and princes to articulate them are not required, only agreement to rules and laws. James Madison concurred that "the idea of a compact among those who are parties to a Gov[ernmen]t is a fundamental principle of free Gov[ernmen]ts."[33] He viewed the framing of the Constitution and its ratification by the people as a social contract uniting the states in one system of government, which freed people from both princes and the anarchy such leaders were supposed to prevent.[34]

That's not to say the US Constitution deserves the veneration it's now granted by nostalgic originalists. The framers turned a blind eye to women and enslaved persons; they left all sorts of minorities at the mercy of state extremists. Even as revised by amendments, expanded by legislation, and reinterpreted by landmark court decisions, the Constitution seems like an unfulfilled promise to many Americans. But in that promise is the germ of an idea—the idea of a social contract—that has given voice to millions of citizens and could expand voice for workers as well. What the social contract idea did in offering an alternative to the ideology of mirrors for princes, it could do as an alternative to the ideology of mirrors for managers.

The Social Contract

A Milwaukee newspaper reported in 1862 that Abraham Lincoln was speaking to a group of abolitionists when one asked him why he didn't declare people held in slavery to be free then and there. Lincoln replied: If I told you that a lamb's tail was a leg, how many legs would a lamb have? Five, someone answered. No, said Lincoln: *Four*—Calling a tail a leg doesn't make it one. As he proclaimed the following year, freedom is a worthy ideal, but emancipation is not a fact simply by announcing it. President Lincoln knew he had to win a war for it.[35]

The social contract represents another worthy ideal, but calling a constitutional government (or a corporation) a social contract doesn't make it one either. The social contract is a general social model, a historic rival to the organic model of social systems featured in mirrors for princes. Both models are descriptive as well as prescriptive tools. The organic model suggests that societies, states, and other associations are analogous to living bodies: They consist of functional members working together for a common goal—and if some associations don't look like goal-directed bodies, then they *should* (perhaps with the aid of a transformational leader to articulate a shared vision). In contrast, the social contract model suggests that societies, states, and organizations are analogous to contracts. They consist of consensual agreements between autonomous persons with diverse goals—and if some associations don't look like freely made contracts, then they *should* (perhaps with the aid of a constitution or a labor union to protect individual rights).

The dual descriptive and prescriptive faces of the organic goal model are clear enough in mirrors for princes, textbooks on management, and studies of leadership as outlined earlier. The dual aspects of the social contract model are best illustrated in the works of classical liberal philosophers like John Locke. Political philosopher Jeremy Waldron points out that Locke's *Second Treatise* tells two different stories about how organized societies come about. One is a descriptive story: Locke reflected that social organization arose first in families where members accepted basic rules for cooperation under the authority of some father figure. Subsequent generations gave express or tacit consent to more elaborate customs and practices, and families grew into tribes led by a patriarch or chief who demonstrated the ability to settle disputes and protect members from aggression by enemies. Successful tribes in time developed into communities with gainful economies and working political institutions under the leadership of kings and such. Locke described societal evolution as an ongoing contract-like process where people commit in gradual, almost "insensible" steps to more or less agreeable rules and rulers for mutual benefit.[36]

Locke's descriptive story is empirically plausible. But it is morally iffy. Although naturally developing communities as Locke describes them look more like serial contracts than organic goal-seeking bodies, they may not look like very *good* contracts. The many tacit agreements they involve may not be altogether voluntary, and their terms may not all be fair to weaker parties. Locke was well aware that some regimes survived through force and fraud. So to assess the fairness of actual institutions, he told another story about how organized societies might come about.

Locke's second story is a prescriptive one: Imagine, he said, that before individuals joined in civil societies, they lived free and equal in a state of nature. This state of nature is not necessarily a war of all against all; people of good will can discern moral laws to guide them, and they may trade with one another for reciprocal benefits, as in barter between European emigrants and Native Americans. But since some persons may not act with good will, and since even those who do may be biased toward their own cause in parsing moral laws, people may derive additional benefit by agreeing to positive laws and impartial judges to enforce them. This is what Locke understood by a social contract—the establishment of binding rules by mutual consent to secure individuals' rights and liberties.

Locke went on to imagine the sort of governance that parties to a social contract might agree on. He left the door open to a range of institutional possibilities, but he left no doubt about what the parties would reject. They would never accept, Locke insisted, an absolute prince ("however intitled, *Czar*, or *Grand Signior*, or how you please"), which people of his day "counted the only Government in the World." By an absolute prince, Locke meant one who stands above the laws that bind other persons, one who has both executive and legislative powers and "there is no Judge to be found, no Appeal lies open to any [independent authority] ... from whose decision relief and redress may be expected of any Injury or Inconveniency, that may be suffered from the Prince or by his Order." While such a prince offers subjects some protection from violence between themselves, they risk punishment by death if they so much as question the prince's violence toward any of them. Locke could not imagine that free and equal persons, quitting the state of nature to escape faction and aggression, would ever agree "that all of them but one, should be under the restraint of Laws, but that he [the prince] should still retain all the Liberty of the State of Nature, increased with Power, and made licentious by Impunity. This is to think that Men are so foolish that they take care to avoid what Mischiefs may be done to them by *Pole-Cats* or *Foxes*, but are content, nay think it Safety, to be devoured by *Lions*." Locke supposed that social contractors would prefer a government of mutually agreeable checks and balances to thwart abuse of power.[37]

Locke's social contract is a theoretical ideal, as imaginary as Aristotle's community for the common good (but arguably more fair). It is useful nonetheless for evaluating social institutions. "The point of the social contract story," notes Jeremy Waldron, "is to provide a moral template to be placed over historical events and over our present predicament, for the purpose of ascertaining what is right and wrong for us and our political rulers to do."[38] To eighteenth-century British pundits, Locke's descriptive story did not seem too bad a fit with the unwritten English constitution—that happy blend of monarchical, aristocratic, and democratic conventions that had evolved over centuries. To the American colonists who had no say under that constitution, however, Locke's prescriptive template was revolutionary. It led the Continental Congress to denounce "the present King of Great Britain" as an absolute prince—indeed, an absolute *tyrant*—to whom free and equal persons owed no submission. It emboldened the colonists to declare their right to abolish his rule and institute a new government for their own safety and happiness.[39]

Organizations

Just as the social contract ideal showed political theorists centuries ago a way to escape the clichés of mirrors for princes, it shows business theorists today a way past the clichés of mirrors for managers and the "goal paradigm" of organizations. For organizations can be viewed as social contracts much as portrayed in John Locke's descriptive story. This does not imply that corporations and other organizations are modeled after political institutions but that they can be social contracts in their own right, evolving alongside social contracts of government. A business, for instance, may develop from agreements among a small group of stakeholders—investors, entrepreneurs, maybe a few hires or family members and clients. Initially, staff and, no doubt, legal counsel work out basic rules for cooperation under the authority of some leader or other. Over time, stakeholders give express or tacit consent to more complex customs and practices, and start-ups mature into firms led by chief executives who demonstrate the ability to grow the enterprise and fend off competitors. Successful firms may acquire others whose stakeholders commit in matter-of-fact steps to more or less agreeable rules for mutual benefit. As in Locke's descriptive story, the process is empirically credible. It is consistent with modern theories of business anthropology. It is consistent with economic theories of the firm as a nexus of contracts. And it is consistent with Petro Georgiou's view of organizations as systems of exchange.

Again, however, although organizations historically may look more like serial contracts than organic goal-seeking bodies, they may not be very good contracts. The many tacit agreements they involve may not be altogether voluntary, and their terms may not be fair to weaker parties. Classic examples include employment in company towns once used to keep coal miners, railroad laborers, loggers, and other remote workers in debt and on the job. Still common but troublesome cases involve "contracts of adhesion"—standardized leases, credit agreements, insurance policies, travel tickets (contracts of carriage), and other form contracts that are skillfully drafted by and for the benefit of the issuing organization, then offered to stakeholders on a take-it-or-leave-it basis. Adhesion contracts are found with increasing frequency in all sorts of "terms of service" that consumers are required to accept and that amount to "mass-market boilerplate right deletions," in the words of legal scholar Margaret Jane Radin.[40] These boilerplate contracts enable organizations to shift the risks and costs of nonroutine events to the adhering party, who may not understand the implications or be in a position to object. And they lead to abuses such as surprise billing by hospitals, recently outlawed by the US Congress.[41]

So, like Locke, social contract theorists also need a prescriptive story about organizations—a moral template for distinguishing right from wrong behavior, better from worse leadership: Imagine that free and equal parties with general knowledge of the corporate world (but, to preclude bias, not their individual place in that world) were to design an ideal social contract for multistakeholder organizations. What would they consider and what would they agree to, or reject? One of the first things the parties might grant is that what they are joining in *is* a contract—not some organic entity analogous to a living body with a will and goals of its own. Contracting parties would know that contracts are not just personal but social enterprises; they have objective outcomes that occur because of how people act together. So, too, organizations built from contracts have collective consequences that are the "more than the sum" of individual behaviors—profits, jobs, goods, and services as well as losses, waste products, industrial diseases, air and water pollution. But contracts and organizations do not themselves intend any of these consequences. Only natural persons can prefer one organizational outcome over another, and different stakeholders generally prefer different outcomes; they seek different goals *for* organizations—investors, profits; workers, wages; customers, goods or services, and so on. Top managers sometimes designate certain outcomes as official organizational goals, but these remain simply management's goals *for* the organization, not goals *of* the organization as such.

Recognizing the diversity of persons' goals for most organizations, now, free and equal parties are unlikely to agree on a social contract that gives one set of stakeholders final authority over all the others. No doubt the parties would allow some stakeholders to manage operations, to coordinate the contributions of others, but not on their own terms. Free and equal contractors would likely insist on some process independent of management to adjudicate conflicts between their individual rights and goals for the organization. Such processes could involve independent boards, labor unions, elected officials, safety regulators, civil courts, tenure systems—different possibilities for different stakeholders. More theoretical development is needed to assess whether specific processes are appropriate in particular cases. But for any proposed process, social contractors might reasonably feel that more independence is better, fairer, than less. Recall, for example, management's choice of employee relations channels in the Hawthorne studies, where Western Electric preferred employee counseling over company unions, a company union over independent labor organizations, to further corporate goals. Free and equal social contractors are apt to reverse this priority, ranking independent representation over company unions over paternalistic human relations.

Organizational social contractors need not suppose that top managers are generally tyrants. The parties need not think they're at risk of being devoured by lions, as feared in John Locke's version of the theory. They need not assume managers are corrupt but, as in economic theories of the firm, that *"even fairly dutiful managers* will be prone to pursuing strategies that turn out to be in their individual interest more than they are in the interest of the firm or of society."[42] One can imagine free and equal social contractors reaching the same conclusion as critics of the Business Roundtable "Statement on the Purpose of a Corporation": Top managers cannot be trusted to prioritize goals for an organization and balance stakeholder interests as they deem best. As suggested by Nell Minow, Robert Reich, and other stakeholder advocates, fairness requires actual checks on managerial authority beyond public relations pledges (or invisible forces that chief executives have a hand in shaping).

There's a lot more that organizational social contractors might consider. (Interested readers can turn to the afterword.) But it is plausible that *free and equal parties to a social contract of organizations would choose to protect their individual rights and goals for the organization with some process independent of their managing stakeholders.* (Whether individuals ever invoke that process is of course up to them.) Even if one could imagine nothing else that organizational contractors might agree to, such a principle has implications with bite in the real world. It implies, for example, that arrangements where managers define "the organization's purpose" for themselves are suspect. That would include not only the traditional governance envisioned by the Business Roundtable but also arrangements like "benefit corporations."

Instead of protecting workers or shareholders with checks on managers, benefit corporations extend "legal protections for managers and directors to manage for the common good" as they define it.[43] Critics have pointed out that, akin to patriot kings, "Benefit Corporations' managers are largely free unilaterally to proclaim some thing or activity to be beneficial" despite adverse outcomes for some stakeholders.[44] Ethics professor Daryl Koehn worries that "directors are free to decide which interests deserve priority" and they are free to put their own interests first—perhaps to "claim a First Amendment-based exception to otherwise applicable anti-discrimination laws or insurance mandates."[45] Defenders of benefit corporations reply that laws and regulations stifle innovation, that "the more effective pathway to promoting good is not through devising mechanisms of governmental enforcement, but liberating corporations' desires to do good." Advocates assert confidently that "benefit corporations are effectively self-regulating, adjusting their aims and function with input from the market and its constituents."[46] However, recurring crises in financial markets have shown the dangers of self-regulation—for instance, in the unregulated trading of complex derivative products by Enron and credit default swaps by Lehman Brothers. Business ethicists would do well to remember the warning of veteran bank economist Willem Buiter after the financial crisis of 2008: "Self-regulation is to regulation as self-importance is to importance."[47]

Suggestions

While regulation by publicly accountable authorities is unnecessary in the ideal world of mirrors for princes, it is inherent in a social contract to secure individuals' rights. Social contract theory does not prescribe a particular type of regulation, but it helps to expose practices that are ripe for regulation. A social contract theory of organizations suggests that researchers should do more to analyze management practices that weaken independent processes protecting stakeholders' rights and goals. Researchers could focus more attention, for instance, on typical tactics to deny workers the free choice to join a union. Management theorists and business law scholars could heighten awareness of how companies skirt labor laws by misclassifying employees as independent contractors, or how they void all sorts of laws through forced-arbitration provisions and class-action bans. A social contract theory suggests further that organizational researchers should look behind self-serving public relations like the Business Roundtable "Statement on the Purpose of a Corporation"—to question the behavior of member firms, say Wells Fargo, who engage in dubious practices. (Again, interested readers can consult the afterword for details.)

More broadly, a social contract theory suggests that management teachers should stop telling top executives that their goals are the be-all and end-all of organizations. Like princes of yore, CEOs of the Roundtable don't need to be told. They already believe in their visions and their right to rule. Since time immemorial, all manner of princes and leaders have used the rhetoric of grand "common purposes" to justify their authority and gild their own goals for some group of stakeholders. They have resisted checks on their authority and goals—by courts and parliaments and regulators and unions and other independent parties that get between themselves and their subjects or workers. But in writing about organizations, it may not be practical—or fair—to continue the rhetoric of mirrors for princes, to idealize leadership that transforms individuals' goals into a vision shared by everyone.

After all, most of us who teach in universities don't think *we* need transforming by visionary leaders. Many readers might judge from their own experience that the academic freedom and goal diversity allowed to tenured professors makes for better institutions than the conformity asked of contingent educators beholden to their bosses. In a classic study of academic leadership, professor of higher education Robert Birnbaum found that "transformational leadership, through which extraordinary people change organizational goals and values, is an anomaly in higher education." Because operational goals for a university are shaped by a variety of participants, "rather than by an omnipotent leader, attempts at transformational leadership are more likely to lead to disruption and conflict than to desirable outcomes."[48] (Good university presidents know what James Madison knew—It's safer to manage the *effects* of conflicting goals than try to eliminate the diversity that *causes* goal conflict.)

Given a free choice, academic professionals seek employment in universities with some process independent of management to adjudicate

conflicts between their individual rights and goals for the organization—tenure systems, labor unions, grievance procedures, accreditation
requirements, committees representing every interest imaginable. If this
is the sort of social contract we choose for ourselves, if we claim academic
freedom as our right, why should we prescribe so much less freedom
for others?

AFTERWORD

This afterword addresses some of the thornier issues raised by a social contract model of organizations. It offers an agenda of sorts for further research.

Scholars have shown new interest in the social contract idea in the wake of John Rawls's theory of justice as fairness. Rawls famously renewed John Locke's attempt to prescribe a moral social contract template. He imagined what principles free and equal parties in a state of nature might choose for evaluating the basic structure of society. After careful deliberation, such hypothetical parties, Rawls concluded, would agree to two principles: (1) Each person has an equal right to the most extensive liberty compatible with a like liberty for all, and (2) Social and economic inequalities should provide the greatest benefit to the least advantaged persons. Philosophers have questioned Rawls's argument for these specific principles. But even his critics acknowledge that Rawls has achieved much success in his stated aim of challenging the general doctrine of utilitarianism.[1]

Utilitarianism is the moral view that a society should maximize the aggregate or average good of its members. This view makes sense if one imagines society as an organic entity, as portrayed in mirrors for princes—or in the fable of "the belly and the members." For society as a whole, more good is better than less, whether some members get more than others, whether some have more voice than others, whether a few members have any voice or liberty at all. The coherence of this organic view is sustained by conflating all persons into one, a single spokesperson for the entire body (like the prince or a chief executive).[2] But, according to Rawls, utilitarianism makes less sense if one imagines society as a social contract between a "plurality of distinct persons with separate systems of ends."[3] Free and equal parties would not agree to a social contract that does not take seriously this separateness of persons. Individual persons would expect a justification for some to get more than others (such as Rawls's second principle), and they might see no justification whatsoever for denying basic liberties to anyone (as in Rawls's first principle).[4]

Compared to his theory of justice, Rawls says utilitarianism "treats persons both as ends and means. It treats them as ends by assigning the same (positive) weight to the welfare of each; it treats them as means by allowing higher life prospects for some to counterbalance lower life prospects for others who are already less favorably situated." Rawls's theory and principles of justice, on the other hand, "rule out even the tendency to regard men as means to one another's welfare. In the design of the social system we must treat persons solely as ends and not in any way as means." Ethicists may discover better theories and principles of justice than Rawls's for evaluating social systems. (Credible alternatives focus on the fairness of social *relations*, not simply the distribution of social *goods*.) But Rawls leaves little reason to believe that better options will be utilitarian. Just as Locke's key contribution to practical politics was what his social contract theory ruled out—namely, an absolute prince— so too Rawls's key contribution to applied ethics may be what his theory of justice rules out—namely, a utilitarian, goal-based moral template.[5]

Fairness

Why, back in the real world, should one care about an imaginary social contract that hypothetical parties consent to? What obligates living persons to respect a theoretical agreement they never made? Some theorists have suggested that people give implicit consent to a system of rules, like a social contract, by participating in its benefits; however, this seems too legalistic for comfort (similar to stipulating that consumers agree to a company's policies just by clicking through its website). There's a better argument: The rationale for the social contract is not that one actually agreed to it in some technical sense but that free and equal parties would consent to it under conditions that are *fair*. It's the fairness, above and beyond any historical agreement, that gives an imagined social contract moral force. And the virtue of a social contract approach is that it makes the fairness of social relations and outcomes a priority.

The application of social contract theory to corporations and other organizations is a relatively new frontier. A number of business ethics professors have opened up promising paths of inquiry. Edward Freeman, for example, has imagined what kind of contract might be accepted as fair by corporate stakeholders "behind a Rawls-like veil of ignorance"—a state of nature where the parties know generally how the corporate world works but not the positions they occupy in that world. He proposed that such parties would agree to ground rules like clear routes of exit and "The Principle of Governance," which "says that the procedure for changing the rules of the game must be agreed upon by unanimous consent."[6] Nien-hê Hsieh has expanded on how hypothetical parties to an organizational social contract might deliberate behind a Rawlsian veil of ignorance. He's suggested that workers would not be content with a right of exit—like it or leave it—to safeguard their interests but would insist on "a basic right to protection from arbitrary interference at work" (freedom from mandates such as unsafe working conditions).[7] Others have explored the relevance of Rawls's general arguments, if not his exact principles, to organizations. Magali Fia and Lorenzo Sacconi have argued that organizational social contractors, recognizing "stakeholders as autonomous moral agents having separate lives to be lived," would not agree to a utilitarian management principle, such as maximizing total wealth or minimizing transaction costs.[8]

Perhaps the most robust approach is the Integrative Social Contracts Theory laid out by Thomas Donaldson and Thomas Dunfee in their book, *Ties That Bind*. The authors build on the two kinds of contracts associated with the social contract tradition: what they call "extant" or micro contracts, "reflecting an actual agreement within a community," and theoretical or macro contracts, "reflecting hypothetical agreement among rational members of a community." Donaldson and Dunfee imagine that rational contractors, with general knowledge of how economies and organizations work but not their own membership in any given community or institution, would want as much opportunity ("moral free space") as possible to enjoy the benefits of cooperation but would choose to protect themselves from flagrant violations of human rights. Hypothetical contractors, therefore, would agree to be bound by the explicit rules, implicit terms, and ethical norms of the extant contracts that constitute organizations so long as members retain rights of voice and exit, so long as a "substantial majority" of members support a given rule or norm, and so long as a rule or norm is compatible with universal moral principles or "hypernorms." Hypernorms, such as respect for persons, are distilled from wider community standards, different philosophical and religious traditions, international human rights declarations, global trade agreements, industry codes of conduct, and so on. Donaldson and Dunfee do not express a preference for any particular hypernorms, prompting critics to call for more specificity. But their theory has broad applicability, and it has attracted researchers' attention to the social contract approach.[9]

Critics like Richard Marens have detected a managerial bias in social contract theories of organization. Such a bias is possible in any theory that normalizes existing social relations; one needs to be careful about calling a one-sided agreement a "social contract" (a lamb's tail, a leg, in Lincoln's words). Carefully applied, however, the social contract model is potentially less biased than the prevailing goal paradigm of organizations: It challenges the orthodox belief that organizations must have common goals and that managers are privileged to set them. It prioritizes fairness among all stakeholders of an organization over maximization of goals *for* the organization of a few. And it is not impractically utopian; many of our settled moral judgments would support a principle such as proposed in chapter 13—"free and equal parties to a social contract of organizations would choose to protect their individual rights and goals for the organization with some process independent of their managing stakeholders."[10]

We generally accept, for example, that investors with money at stake would not freely give top management final authority over how their money is used; investors may not care to be involved in management decisions themselves, but they insist on some check on management's authority, such as a board of directors, to curb self-dealing. We accept that customers for goods or services would not freely give top management final authority over the quality of those goods and services; they insist on governmental regulation or some other independent authority to ensure that food and drugs are safe, airplanes are fit to fly, advertising is aboveboard, and more. We accept that suppliers, dealers, and franchisees would not freely give top management final authority over their own operations; they insist in many countries on fair trade regulation to prevent corporations from "abusing a superior bargaining position" in dictating store hours (to franchisees), product purchases (to retailers), staff support (from suppliers), and so forth. What needs more defense, perhaps, is the idea that employees are morally entitled to similar protection.[11]

The conventional corporate view is that, even if managers can't exercise authority over all stakeholders, they at least speak for employees and other "members" of an organization. Managers often claim to share an interest with employees, and management theorists have long assumed that managers and employees share common goals for organizations. As noted earlier, it's now widely recognized in leadership research that employees don't all have the same goals, but a basic premise of much research is that they *should*; therefore, transformational leaders are needed to instill a common purpose. It's unclear, however, *why* employees should have a common goal—and why managers have the moral authority (not just legal power) to define it.

There are a couple of traditional answers. One is a utilitarian justification taught by management sages like Robert Owen. Owen sought to reeducate workers from believing in "selfish individual" interests to belief in a common interest, a shared goal to maximize "happiness for the greatest number of human beings" through "the creation of wealth," which can trickle down to make everyone better off.[12] The flaw, of course, is that social goals like aggregate happiness, wealth, or production, which can in principle advantage everyone, may not in reality advantage everyone but instead permit gross inequities. (Robert Owen's indifference to the unfair workload borne by women is instructive.) John Rawls's argument that a utilitarian social contract does not respect the separate welfare of persons is as pertinent to organizations as to society in general—as is his conclusion that free and equal parties would not agree to such a contract.[13]

There's an even older justification for managers' authority to set common goals. For ages, mirrors for princes taught that people behaved badly on their own, that they faced conflict and chaos without a shared goal to guide them, and that they needed a leader to envision a unifying cause or common good. Mirrors for managers have carried on this tradition: They teach that workers behave badly on their own, that they perform poorly and suffer alienation without common goals, and that they need visionary leadership (or maybe management by objectives) to reach their full potential. All sorts of literature promotes this idea—ancient stories of princes like Cyrus the Great who melded disparate people into a mighty empire, business case studies of chief executives like Johnson

& Johnson's James Burke, who inspired employees with a lofty mission "Credo" to grow a socially responsible company, and research surveys of anonymous firms whose workers (on average) rate bosses they admire as transformational leaders. But there's another, darker side of goal-focused leadership. Historically it has unified only some people, mobilizing factions who pursued their goals at the expense of their neighbors, as James Madison warned.[14] More recently, management research has demonstrated that leaders bent on organizational goal attainment create conditions for a variety of unethical behaviors—from cheating on self-reports to full-blown financial frauds.[15] (Sociologist Guillermo Grenier provides a germane study of union busting at Johnson & Johnson under Burke's tenure.[16])

The final, fallback justification for managerial authority is to assume that employees really consent to management's goals, even if not explicitly. Business ethicists, following the classic economic theory of the firm, often suppose that "the members of a business organization, in assuming a particular position, take on new obligations to pursue the goals of the firm."[17] However, political philosopher Pierre-Yves Néron has suggested that such "obligations" are legal fictions reflecting the managerial ideology of the goal paradigm, not moral commitments voluntarily undertaken.[18]

The fact is, employment is normally an incomplete contract entered into for mutual advantage. All the terms, rules, and relationships cannot be specified in advance; managers and employees work out the details as they go.[19] Over time, the parties may behave opportunistically to tilt the terms toward their own or some other stakeholder's benefit. Mainstream business literature legitimizes efforts by managers to tilt rules toward their goals for an organization (calling it "transformational leadership") while disparaging efforts by employees to tilt rules toward their goals for the organization (calling this "resistance to change"). Nearly a century ago, management pioneer Chester Barnard described something like this in *The Functions of the Executive*. New hires join an organization to achieve personal goals without a clear idea of what's expected of them. They will accept some directives that align with their own goals and moral codes—Barnard's "zone of indifference"—but resist orders that do not. Wise managers know better than to press their advantage and give orders that will not be obeyed (although, Barnard says, "this principle cannot ordinarily be formally admitted"). The executive's job,

Barnard states, is "indoctrinating those at the lower levels with general purposes" to bring their zone of indifference more in line with management's goals and values. This "function of formulating grand purposes ... is one which needs sensitive systems of communication, experience in interpretation, imagination, and delegation of responsibility."[20]

Now, why is this one-way indoctrination proper? In fleshing out the incomplete contract of employment, why don't employees have the right to tilt management's zone of indifference toward their goals? Business books will tell you that management's goals are somehow better, more comprehensive or virtuous, than other stakeholders' goals, even if a few managers get too zealous in their pursuit. Like earlier mirrors for princes and later mirrors for managers, Barnard's *Function of the Executive* claims the "common purposes" formulated by executives "express the height of moral aspirations."[21] But philosopher Christopher McMahon observes that "managers are not moral experts"; their goals for an organization are often no more virtuous than anyone else's. Mirrors for managers insinuate that workers participate in organizations for selfish reasons; leaders must redirect them toward nonselfish, common goals. The reality is frequently the reverse: Many workers join organizations for nonselfish reasons but wind up working for managers focused on narrow, mercenary goals. Educators, for instance, may join universities to teach truth, research human well-being, or further the arts in society but then answer to administrators focused on building an endowment. Nurses may join medical staffs to care for the sick or save lives but work for bosses focused on cost containment. Scientists may join pharmaceutical firms to improve medicine and public health but report to managers focused on company stock price: McMahon cites the case of Pfizer, whose leaders decided to combine new and old cholesterol drugs in a single pill not to benefit patients but to extend patent protection for the old drug. (Negatively affected employees suffer a recognized psychological harm called "moral injury," first applied to soldiers forced by superiors to act contrary to deeply held values, and most recently applied to medical professionals.)[22]

Employees who disagree with management's goals or demands have one remedy open to them, according to the classical economic model of the firm: They can quit their jobs. The standard model depicts workers as willing agents of their bosses. Employment becomes a voluntary relationship where an employee "agrees to obey the directions of an entrepreneur" in return for compensation. This agency relationship justifies the authority of employers and is morally binding on workers so long as it remains voluntary. If either party becomes dissatisfied, they are free to terminate the relationship; employers can fire workers at will, and workers can exit the organization at any time. Bear in mind, however, the agency relationship is a legal fiction. It largely reflects management's understanding of the employment contract. A worker's understanding can be quite different, as Chester Barnard learned from long executive experience. Most workers have not in fact agreed to obey every (legal) direction their employers might give them—and therefore may feel no moral obligation to do so. If management's goals and demands become objectionable, workers may see no need to quit their jobs, given the potentially heavy costs of unemployment. Why, workers might ask, can't they instead join a union, work to rule, seek tenure rights, or otherwise do their jobs as though their goals for the organization had some legitimacy of their own? Legally, of course, at-will workers *do* risk being fired if they try to perform their jobs without submission to managers' wills; but the question is, *should* they?[23]

The problem is this: Prescriptively, standard goal-based theories of organization reduce the autonomy of individuals to free entry and exit. In between times, from the day a worker is hired to the day she leaves, she should be subject to her employer—to minimize transactions costs, maximize production, stave off anarchy, whatever. But, argues philosopher Elizabeth Anderson, "freedom of entry and exit from any employment relation is not sufficient to justify the outcome." To demonstrate, she asks you to imagine a marriage of coverture, which, like at-will employment, was once the default legal contract in the United States. Under coverture, husband and wife became one person, with a single interest, at law: "a woman, upon marrying her husband, lost all rights to own property and make contracts in her own name. Her husband had the right to confine her movements, confiscate any wages she might earn, beat her and rape her." The law derived from the old organic model, which portrayed social groups as natural bodies and prescribed unity through leadership of the head, king, husband, or other ruler. Nineteenth-century essayists defended coverture in the way that mirrors for princes once defended monarchy: "Whenever a married woman has a *separate and independent reputation*, a position, a power independent of her husband, she nurtures misery for herself and injury to the community. There can be, at home, but one head,—one chief. If both attempt to govern, anarchy ensues."[24] Coverture required the voluntary consent of both husband and wife to create a valid marriage contract, but divorce was hard to obtain, keeping many spouses in abusive relationships. Suppose, now, that states granted women legal rights of exit through at-will divorce. Would that be enough to justify such a one-sided contract of marriage? Elizabeth Anderson doesn't think so; free and equal social contractors probably wouldn't either. Likewise, Anderson submits, the right of exit cannot justify a one-sided contract of employment. Her point, obviously, is not to equate managers and wife-beaters but that "consent to an option within a set [such as coverture or employment-at-will] cannot justify the option set itself." Allowing "a lucky few to escape subjection" is not sufficient to vindicate a paternalistic or authoritarian regime.[25]

Nonetheless, Anderson says, one-sided contracts are all too prevalent in employment today. She contends that paternalism and authoritarianism are characteristic of the modern workplace, legal legacies of patriarchal rights to reign over the antebellum household. Anderson cites Apple's insistence that store employees wait on their own time for a security search of their bags and devices after each shift, Walmart's restriction of employee conversations to curb "time theft," and Tyson's norms prohibiting poultry workers' use of the toilet. Anderson concludes that these daily indignities, large and small, diminish the equal worth of workers through arbitrary, unaccountable governance "in which they have no voice other than what their employers care to give them (which is often none at all)." She calls for better government regulation of business, particularly in ensuring workers' rights to union representation.[26]

By this sort of reasoning (plus a bit more developed argument), free and equal social contractors may well choose to protect *all* stakeholders' rights and goals for an organization with some process independent of management. But finally, so what? What practical application might such an ideal social contract have to the study of real organizations?

Unions Today

A social contract principle subjecting corporate management to independent oversight calls into question attempts by managers to undermine the independence of stakeholder checks on their authority. And it suggests inquiry into tactics that managers would have a hard time defending in a court of ethics. Take a look at a few examples.

In 1935 President Franklin Roosevelt signed the National Labor Relations Act (NLRA) into law, he said, to put "the employment contract on a sound and equitable basis"—by assuring workers the free choice to bargain collectively with employers and by "preventing practices which tend to destroy the independence of labor." After the act, unionization in the United States increased to a high of about 35 percent of the nonfarm workforce in the 1950s. Since then it has declined to about 10 percent today. However, public support for unions has not changed all that much. A 2022 Gallup survey shows that 71 percent of Americans approve of unions—similar to opinions in the 1960s and not vastly different from the peak of 75 percent approval reported in 1953. A 2019 Massachusetts Institute of Technology study finds nearly 50 percent of nonunion workers would actually vote for a union, compared to only a third forty years ago. What appears to have changed the most since the NLRA is the willingness of employers to violate the spirit and the letter of the law to suppress unionization.[27]

Analysts at the Economic Policy Institute recount that unions maintained a decent if sometimes tense working relationship with US employers from the 1940s through the 1960s, similar to labor relations in Western Europe. But facing higher social welfare costs (from the American system of employer-based pensions and health insurance), US employers launched an aggressive campaign to cut expenses and specifically union members during the 1970s. "People began looking for ways to economize and found that . . . they had given [money] away in the contract," recalled Douglas Soutar, cofounder of the Business Roundtable—a successor organization to the antiunion Labor Law Reform Group.[28] So, advised by a new industry of union-avoidance attorneys and encouraged by business consultants in the mold of Elton Mayo, managers pressed their legal advantages to the limit, and then some, to disqualify workers from union membership and deter others from voting for union representation. In the decade from 1970 to 1980, charges brought against employers for unfair labor practices doubled. Over the years political pressure from employers has eroded the independence of the National Labor Relations Board (NLRB, the NLRA's enforcement agency), disposing unions to lose faith in the agency and underreport violations of

law. Still, charges of illegal coercion, threats, retaliation, and other violations are filed against employers in over 40 percent of all union elections (over 50 percent in elections with bargaining units larger than sixty
employees). Nearly 30 percent of elections result in charges of unlawful
discipline and firing of union supporters.[29]

One of those statistics is a man named Josh Coleman, who worked as
a customer service representative at the Wichita call center of T-Mobile.
The company recognized him as an exemplary worker, posting his image
on advertising billboards and awarding him a top prize for performance—a trip to Puerto Rico. That was before his bosses saw Coleman
urging his coworkers to join a union, the Communication Workers of
America (CWA). Soon after, management canceled his trip, terminated
his employment, and blamed his poor record for the firing. Such behavior would never be tolerated at T-Mobile's parent company in Germany
(Deutsche Telekom), declared leaders of the CWA, seconded by members of the German parliament. But firing union supporters is only the
most egregious way in which US employers deny workers' free choice to
bargain collectively.[30]

A study by Kate Bronfenbrenner, director of labor education and
research at Cornell University's School of Industrial and Labor Relations, surveyed a large sample of union respondents involved in NLRB-
supervised elections. She reports that, during the election campaigns,
almost 90 percent of employers required workers to attend antiunion
meetings; 63 percent subjected workers to one-on-one sessions with
a supervisor where they were questioned about their own and their
coworkers' support for the union; 57 percent of employers threatened to
close facilities if workers voted to unionize; 47 percent threatened to cut
wages and benefits; and 34 percent discharged workers for union activity, sending a clear signal that employers intend to make good on their
threats. Moreover, a comparison with prior studies reveals that extreme
antiunion tactics are more prevalent today than in the past; threats of
plant closings in union elections, for example, have doubled since the
1980s. Employers have increasingly deployed tough tactics because they
can, and they get their way. Bronfenbrenner finds that the more extreme
the antiunion measures used by an employer, the less likely the union is
to win an election. She concludes that workers'"aspirations for representation are being thwarted by a coercive and punitive climate for organizing that goes unrestrained due to a fundamentally flawed regulatory

regime that neither protects their rights nor provides any disincentives for employers to continue disregarding the law."[31]

The face of organized labor has changed with the times; from West Virginia coal miners, who once fought for safe workplaces, the movement has passed to their granddaughters, who now teach the children of Appalachia and fight for quality public schools. Yet, for most of America, labor laws have not kept pace in protecting workers from antiunion employers, who have normalized former Walmart chief executive Lee Scott's attitude: "We like driving the car and we're not going to give the steering wheel to anyone but us."[32] There are obvious legal reforms that might deter employers from using their economic power to inhibit workers' free choice to join a union as promised by the NLRA: Legislators could restore the credibility of the NLRB by authorizing monetary penalties for wrongful termination of workers seeking to unionize. They could enable workers to bypass the NLRB and bring actions in court to enforce their rights under the NLRA. They could expand the scope of the act by extending coverage to marginalized workers. They could prevent employers from interfering in union elections, say, by prohibiting companies from forcing workers to attend antiunion meetings. In fact, all of these proposals and more have been introduced by federal legislators— most recently in the Protecting the Right to Organize Act, which is stalled in Congress.[33]

Whether such reforms eventually become law or not, nonunionized workers face further obstacles from the one-sided contracts that managers routinely use to impose their goals on weaker stakeholders. Recall the potential for abuse of corporate power in contracts of adhesion— boilerplate service agreements, lease documents, employee handbooks, all kinds of "terms and conditions" that shift risks to adhering parties. Long ago, legal scholar Karl Llewellyn explained the problem: "Where bargaining power, and legal skill and experience as well are concentrated on one side ..., the drafting skill of counsel now turns out a form of contract which resolves all questions in advance in favor of one party to the bargain. It is a form of contract which, in the measure of the importance of the particular deal in the other party's life, amounts to the exercise of unofficial government of some by others, via private law." In 1931, Llewellyn observed, "Factory employment, employment in a company town or on a sugar beet farm, or farm-lease in some share-cropping districts—these press to the point where contract may mean rather fierce control." Twentieth-century government regulations freed many workers from the company towns ruled from shopfloor to barroom by industrialists like Robert Owen and Henry Ford. Yet, rather fierce control still goes on in the twenty-first century—through corporate misclassification of independent contractors, forced arbitration clauses, class action bans, stay-or-pay contracts, among other nonnegotiable arrangements.[34]

Private Government

"Sharecroppers on wheels" is how the National Employment Law Project describes the truck drivers who haul shipping containers full of TVs, tennis shoes, and whatnot from America's ports to local rail yards and warehouses. The vast majority are classified by their bosses as independent contractors, although they perform the same work as trucking company employees. These drivers report to work at scheduled times, submit to truck inspections and drug tests, line up and pick up loads as directed, drive and unload under monitoring, return to port, and do it again. They usually sign a contract, with no guaranteed income, stipulating they won't haul for any other firm. They are paid a floating rate set by the company—take it or leave it—for each cargo load. As independent contractors, they lack rights to benefits afforded employees under state and federal labor laws: minimum wage, overtime pay, paid breaks, medical leave, workers' compensation, retirement benefits, and the right to unionize.[35]

State governments have begun to rein in employers who misclassify workers and exploit their lack of opportunity to bargain for a fairer deal. (Many port truck drivers are immigrants who understand little English, much less the contract they have to sign). Yet artful contracting to skirt employment laws is a persistent problem, not only in port trucking but in construction, janitorial services, and other labor-intensive industries. And state regulation to control how workers are classified, such as the employee-friendly "ABC" test might not solve the problem.[36] Because no matter what rules state legislatures or local regulators devise to protect workers, they may be subverted at the stroke of a pen by skilled corporate lawyers. More and more corporations require both employees and independent contractors to sign arbitration agreements, giving employers rather than courts or regulators the power to adjudicate violations of workers' statutory rights. Claims of on-the-job injuries, employment discrimination, wage theft, nonpayment of overtime—all sorts of abuses that workers and their allies fought to control through a century of legislation and common law—are now subject to the kind of private government decried by Karl Llewellyn.[37]

Advocates of mandatory arbitration sometimes compare it to arbitration under a collective bargaining agreement, which has been accepted as fair by employers and unions alike. But in nonunion organizations the employer or their agent sets the rules, the employer vets the arbitrator, and the system gives management a clear advantage despite the veneer of impartiality. UCLA law professor Katherine Stone and Cornell School of Industrial and Labor Relations dean Alexander Colvin compared outcomes of mandatory arbitration cases with similar cases in federal and state courts. Employees won only 21 percent of arbitration cases but 36 percent of the federal court cases and 57 percent of state cases. The damages awarded compare even less favorably for employees, averaging $23,548 in mandatory arbitration cases versus $143,497 in federal cases and $328,008 in state courts.[38]

Worse yet, many employment contracts of adhesion combine mandatory arbitration with bans on class actions, forcing workers not just to arbitrate legal disputes but to do so *individually*. Colvin found that a majority of American workers are now subject to mandatory arbitration (up from 2 percent in the early 1990s), and a third of those must waive their rights to collectively challenge managers' abuse of power. Class action waivers deter complaints over practices like wage theft by forcing individual victims to shoulder the costs of attorneys, expert testimony, and other fees, which are prohibitive for the relatively small amounts recovered.[39] Without class actions, there is no check (even reputational) to petty cheating by corporations, resulting in sizable losses to large groups of stakeholders.[40] The National Employment Law Project estimates that nonunion employers use forced arbitration to cheat workers out of $12.6 billion every year in legally required minimum wage and overtime pay. Unsurprisingly, forced arbitration and class action waivers disproportionately affect the least powerful stakeholders; they are particularly prevalent, for example, among low paid retail and chain restaurant workers.[41] Law professor Myriam Gilles concludes, "Forced arbitration and class action bans serve only to immunize bad actors who regularly prey on these disadvantaged groups and leave them without remedy and vulnerable to future exploitation."[42] (Forced arbitration abusers are no respecters of pay grade, certainly. Gretchen Carlson, a well-known broadcast journalist who brought sexual harassment charges against Fox News chairman Roger Ailes, attested that "forced arbitration is a sexual harasser's best friend: It keeps proceedings secret, findings sealed, and victims silent."[43])

You may be fortunate to escape forced arbitration agreements at work, but you cannot avoid these contracts of adhesion in everyday life. If you shop online, if you use a credit card, if you stream movies, if you talk on a cell phone, if you rent a car, if you join a gym, almost any service you can imagine comes with a contract where someplace in all the legalese you will likely find a mandatory arbitration clause and a class action ban. But who bothers to read the terms of service that customers click through every day? You can't change the fine print; you can't outsmart the lawyers who drafted it; and you can't do business with a different bank or store or phone company to avoid it. You click or sign, use the service, and hope your risks are small. In fact, most risks are small, but by shifting the costs to consumers, they add up to big savings for corporations.[44]

One of the most notorious customer abuses of late involves Wells Fargo Bank. In a textbook case of what can go wrong with a goal-based model of organizations, the trouble stemmed from Wells Fargo managers' decision to impose their own short-term profit goals on employees. "In court papers," the *New York Times* reported, "prosecutors described a pressure-cooker environment at the bank, where low-level employees were squeezed tighter and tighter each year by sales goals that senior executives methodically raised, ignoring signs that they were unrealistic. The few employees and managers who did meet sales goals—by any means—were held up as examples for the rest of the work force to follow."[45] What the Wells Fargo workforce did to try to meet their goals was to open, from customers' data on file, millions of illicit accounts and credit cards, running up hefty fees and ruining victims' credit ratings when they didn't pay. Since the scandal broke, federal prosecutors and regulators have fined the company billions of dollars, penalized its executives millions, returned half a billion to investors, but recovered for customers not so much.[46] That's because Wells Fargo had required its customers to accept terms and conditions that mandated arbitration and banned class actions. In court after court, the bank successfully argued that arbitration was the only legitimate forum for hearing customers' complaints, killing costly lawsuits over the fraudulent accounts.[47] While arbitration is billed as a quick and easy alternative to litigation, it is a daunting process for ordinary consumers. Legal scholars Andrea Cann Chandrasekher and David Horton underscore that few win against big companies like Wells Fargo unless they hire an attorney, which is impractical without a large class of plaintiffs to represent. So forced arbitration and class action bans discourage consumers from contesting even outright fraud.[48] Victimized individuals see management's control over the process as a miscarriage of justice, shielding wrongdoers from exposure and responsibility. "It is ridiculous," said Jennifer Zeleny, one Wells Fargo customer who attempted to sue the bank. "This is an issue of identity theft—my identity was used so employees could meet sales goals. This is something that needs to be litigated in a public forum."[49]

In their dealings with corporate America, consumers are losing that opportunity to litigate. Over the past couple of decades, forced arbitration clauses have metastasized, writes David Horton. They now typically cover, as Sprint told phone customers, "ANY (we really mean ANY) disagreements." They govern not just the immediate parties to a consumer contract but "all persons whose claim is derived through or on behalf of the [signatory], including any parent, spouse, sibling, child, guardian, executor, legal representative, administrator, or heir." And they last for eternity; cable and satellite TV companies have insisted that your obligation to arbitrate "survives the termination of your service[s] with us" or "is indefinite."[50]

The explosion of forced arbitration and class action bans by corporations stems from a series of US Supreme Court decisions expanding the reach of the 1925 Federal Arbitration Act (FAA), which required federal courts to defer to arbitrators in limited circumstances. Echoing Court rulings of the pre–New Deal Lochner era, recent decisions have broadened those circumstances, permitting arbitration agreements to trump almost any federal or state labor and consumer regulations. So the most direct relief from forced arbitration entails congressional amendment of the FAA. Federal legislation has already been introduced—the Forced Arbitration Injustice Repeal Act (or FAIR Act) which states, "no predispute arbitration agreement or predispute joint-action waiver shall be valid or enforceable with respect to an employment dispute, consumer dispute, antitrust dispute, or civil rights dispute." (A stopgap bill has been passed to protect sexual misconduct victims from forced arbitration.)[51]

Corporate leaders and lobbyists have opposed any change in the FAA, viewing it as a bulwark of self-regulation for business. On the other side, cosponsor of the FAIR Act David Cicilline (D-RI) has summarized the case for such legislation: "Buried deep within the fine print of everyday contracts, forced arbitration deprives American consumers and workers of their day in court when they attempt to hold corporations accountable for breaking the law. This private system lacks the procedural safeguards of our justice system. It is not subject to oversight, has no judge or jury, and is not bound by laws passed by Congress or the States, but it has become a requirement of everyday life." According to Representative Cicilline, "This outrageous practice is nothing short of a corporate take-over of our Nation's system of laws, and the American people have had enough. The overwhelming majority of voters, including 83 percent of Democrats and 87 percent of Republicans, support ending forced arbitration. It is time to act."[52]

It is time for business researchers to respond as well, to study regulation not as an obstacle to be overcome by managers but as a power for fairness in organizations—an appropriate means to secure the independence of stakeholder checks on management—never mind the clichés of mirrors for princes.

NOTES

Introduction

1. Xenophon, *The Education of Cyrus*, trans. H. G. Dakyns (London: Dent, 1992), 270 [8.8.20].

2. James Tatum, *Xenophon's Imperial Fiction* (Princeton, NJ: Princeton University Press, 1989), xv; and Christopher Nadon, *Xenophon's Prince* (Berkeley: University of California Press, 2001), 3–4, 13–14.

3. Monographs on the genre are, hence, rather dated; see, for instance, Allan H. Gilbert, *Machiavelli's Prince and Its Forerunners* (Durham, NC: Duke University Press, 1938). Recent scholarship is summarized in mostly edited volumes wherein specialists each study a limited set of mirrors for princes over a limited period of history. See, for example, Regula Forster and Neguin Yavari, eds., *Global Medieval: Mirrors for Princes Reconsidered* (Boston/Cambridge, MA: Ilex Foundation and Harvard University Press, 2015); and Noëlle-Laetitia Perret and Stéphane Péquignot, eds., *A Critical Companion to the "Mirrors for Princes" Literature* (Leiden: Brill, 2023).

4. J. H. Hexter, *The Vision of Politics on the Eve of the Reformation* (New York: Basic Books, 1973), 215.

5. Jean-Philippe Genet, "Conclusion: Mirrors for Princes and the Development of Reflections on the State," in *A Critical Companion to the "Mirrors for Princes" Literature*, ed. Noëlle-Laetitia Perret and Stéphane Péquignot (Leiden: Brill, 2023), 533. Genet concludes one of the more recent (and sympathetic) surveys of mirrors for princes by questioning the value of these books: By the Late Middle Ages, "the damage caused by the modern state of war led the best minds to make this fatal observation"—that it was "impossible to educate or raise to the level of perfection" princes to meet the challenge. "So," Genet wonders, "what good are mirrors?" (538).

6. See, for example, Michael Arthur Leeden, *Machiavelli on Modern Leadership: Why Machiavelli's Iron Rules Are as Timely and Important as Five Centuries Ago* (New York: Truman Talley, 1999); and Thomas V. Morris, *If Aristotle Ran General Motors: The New Soul of Business* (New York: H. Holt, 1998).

7. Alasdair MacIntyre, *After Virtue*, 2nd ed. (Notre Dame, IN: University of Notre Dame Press, 1984), 172.

8. Derek L. Phillips, *Looking Backward* (Princeton, NJ: Princeton University Press, 1993), 194–95; Ted Robert Gurr, "Historical Trends in Violent Crime: A Critical Review of the Evidence," *Crime and Justice* 3 (1981): 306–7; and John of Salisbury, *Policraticus*, trans. Cary J. Nederman (Cambridge: Cambridge University Press, 1990), 93–96, 99, 104–7, 164–65.

Chapter 1: Egyptian Mirrors

Epigraph: *The Admonitions of Ipu-Wer* and *The Prophecy of Neferti, in Ancient Near Eastern Texts*, ed. James B. Prichard, 3rd ed. (Princeton, NJ: Princeton University Press, 1969), 441, 445.

1. *The Admonitions of Ipu-Wer* and *The Prophecy of Neferti*, 442–43, 445.

2. Miriam Lichtheim, "Didactic Literature," in *Ancient Egyptian Literature*, ed. Antonio Loprieno (Leiden: Brill, 1996), 243–62.

3. *Instruction for King Merikare*, in *Ancient Near Eastern Texts*, ed. James B. Pritchard, 3rd ed. (Princeton, NJ: Princeton University Press, 1969), 414–18; see also M. L. West, "Wisdom Literature," in *Hesiod: Works & Days*, ed. M. L. West (Oxford: Oxford University Press, 1978), 3–25.

4. Proverbs from *The Instruction of Papyrus Insinger*, in *Ancient Egyptian Literature: A Book of Readings*, ed. Miriam Lichtheim, vol. 3 (Berkeley: University of California Press, 1980), 189, 197. See also Lichtheim, "Didactic Literature," 243–62.

5. Emily Teeter, "*Ma'at*," in *Encyclopedia of the Archaeology of Ancient Egypt* (New York: Routledge, 1999), 458–60; and James Henry Breasted, *The Dawn of Conscience* (New York: Scribner's, 1934), 142. Definitions of maat are from Molefi Kete Asante, "The Egyptian Origin of Rhetoric and Oratory," in *Kemet and the African Worldview*, ed. Maulana Karenga and Jacob H. Carruthers, 182–88 (Los Angeles: University of Sankore Press, 1986); Norman Cohn, *Cosmos, Chaos and the World to Come* (New Haven, CT: Yale University Press, 1993), 9; Erik Hornung, *Idea into Image* (New York: Timken, 1992), 47, 136–41; William Kelly Simpson, "*Belles Lettres* and Propaganda," in *Ancient Egyptian Literature*, ed. Antonio Loprieno, 435–43 (Leiden: Brill, 1996); Emily Teeter, *The Presentation of Maat*, Studies in Ancient Oriental Civilization, no. 57 (Chicago: Oriental Institute of the University of Chicago, 1997), 1–2; and John A. Wilson, *The Culture of Ancient Egypt* (Chicago: University of Chicago Press, 1951), 48–50.

6. Miriam Lichtheim, *Maat in Egyptian Autobiographies and Related Studies* (Fribourg, Switzerland: University of Fribourg, 1992); and Wilson, *Culture of Ancient Egypt*, 48–50, 98–100.

7. Christopher A. Faraone and Emily Teeter, "Egyptian Maat and Hesiodic Metis," *Mnemosyne* 57, 4th ser., fasc. 2 (2004): 187.

8. Pascal Vernus, *Affairs and Scandals in Ancient Egypt*, trans. David Lorton (Ithaca, NY: Cornell University Press, 2003), 131.

9. Henri Frankfort, *Kingship and the Gods: A Study of Ancient Near Eastern Religion as the Integration of Society and Nature* (Chicago: University of Chicago Press, 1978), 56.

10. "The Instruction of Ptahhotep," in *Ancient Egyptian Literature: A Book of Readings*, ed. Miriam Lichtheim, vol. 1 (Berkeley: University of California Press, 1975), 65, 68–69, 70–71. The classic report on the Hawthorne studies, urging managers to listen to workers' worries, if not take them seriously, is F. J. Roethlisberger and William J. Dickson, *Management and the Worker* (Cambridge, MA: Harvard University Press, 1939).

11. Lichtheim, "Didactic Literature," 245.

12. Lichtheim, *Ancient Egyptian Literature: Readings*, 1:10; Frankfort, *Kingship and the Gods*, 8–9; and *The Instruction of King Amenemhet*, in *Ancient Near Eastern Texts*, ed. James B. Prichard, 3rd ed. (Princeton, NJ: Princeton University Press, 1969), 419.

13. *The Instruction of King Amenemhet*, 418–19.

14. See chapter 12 for modern examples. Historical background is provided by Gillian Adams, "Ancient and Medieval Children's Texts," in *International Companion Encyclopedia of Children's Literature*, 2nd ed., ed. Peter Hunt (London: Routledge, 2004), 1:227–30. Egyptian school practices are outlined by Ronald J. Williams, "Scribal Training in Ancient Egypt," *Journal of the American Oriental Society* 92 (April–June 1972): 216–18. The clichéd character of Egyptian instruction is noted in Lichtheim, *Ancient Egyptian Literature: Readings*, 1:10, 149–50. Relevant parallels between Egyptian teachings and *The Prince* by Machiavelli are suggested by Christian Langer, "The Political Realism of the Egyptian Elite: A Comparison between the *Teaching for Merikare* and Niccolò Machiavelli's *Il Principe*," *Journal of Egyptian History* 8 (August 2015): 49–79.

Chapter 2: Greek Mirrors

Epigraph: Isocrates, *Areopagiticus, in Isocrates*, vol. 2, trans. George Norlin (Cambridge, MA: Harvard University Press, 1956), 7.9, 7.18, 7.82.

1. Isocrates, 7.15, 7.31, 7.48, 7.49.

2. Isocrates, *To Nicocles,* in *Isocrates*, vol. 1, trans. George Norlin (Cambridge, MA: Harvard University Press, 1991), 2.9, 2.11, 2.18, 2.24, 2.38. Isocrates assumes "the teacher is the true lawgiver"; a wise teacher's guidance "makes a monarch legitimate: through instruction, a king becomes a worthy ruler." John R. Lenz, "Ideal Models and Anti-Models of Kingship in Ancient Greek Literature: Mirror of Princes from Homer to Marcus Aurelius," in *A Critical Companion to the "Mirrors for Princes" Literature*, ed. Noëlle-Laetitia Perret and Stéphane Péquignot (Leiden: Brill, 2023), 32.

3. Isocrates, *To Nicocles*, 1:3.2, 3.22, 3.48.

4. David Mirhady and Yun Lee Too, eds. and trans., *Isocrates I* (Austin: University of Texas Press, 2000), 157. Isocrates's fees from H. I. Marrou, *A History of Education in Antiquity*, trans. George Lamb (1956; repr. New York: Mentor, 1964),

80; and George Kennedy, *The Art of Persuasion in Greece* (Princeton, NJ: Princeton University Press, 1963), 203.

5. Frederick A. G. Beck, *Greek Education, 450–350 B.C.* (London: Methuen, 1964), 277.

6. Isocrates, *Evagoras*, in *Isocrates I*, ed. and trans. Mirhady and Too, 139–56; and Isocrates, *To Nicocles*, 2.31, 2.38.

7. John Ferguson, *Moral Values in the Ancient World* (London: Methuen, 1958), 122.

8. Isocrates, *Address to Philip* in *Isocrates*, vol. 1, trans. George Norlin (Cambridge, MA: Harvard University Press, 1991), 5.9; Isocrates, "Letter to Philip" (2) in *Isocrates*, vol. 3, trans. George Norlin (Cambridge, MA: Harvard University Press, 2014); and Kennedy, *Art of Persuasion*, 174, 191.

9. Colonial college entrance requirements from Robert Middlekauff, "A Persistent Tradition: The Classical Curriculum in Eighteenth-Century New England," *William and Mary Quarterly*, 3rd ser. 18 (1961): 54–67.

10. Aristotle, *The Politics* (Benjamin Jowett / Jonathan Barnes trans.), ed. Stephen Everson (Cambridge: Cambridge University Press, 1996): 1.1.

11. Robert C. Solomon, *Ethics and Excellence* (New York: Oxford University Press, 1992), 146, 131.

12. Aristotle, *The Politics*, trans. T. A. Sinclair (Harmondsworth, England: Penguin, 1962), 1.1, 3.6.

13. Aristotle, *The Politics* (Jowett/Barnes trans.), 2.1, 2.9, 5.3, 5.6.

14. Aristotle, 2.10, 2.11, 5.4.

15. Aristotle, 2.7, 2.12, 3.6, 4.11.

16. Although monarchy is only one of the ideals envisioned by Aristotle, it is significant; see W. R. Newell, "Superlative Virtue: The Problem of Monarchy in Aristotle's *Politics*," in *Essays on the Foundations of Aristotelian Political Science*, ed. Carnes Lord and David K. O'Connor, 191–211 (Berkeley: University of California Press, 1991).

17. Aristotle, *The Politics* (Jowett/Barnes trans.), 1.13, 3.17, 5.10. For Aristotle's attitude toward women and citizenship, see Jennifer Tolbert Roberts, *Athens on Trial* (Princeton, NJ: Princeton University Press, 1994), 88–91.

18. Aristotle, *The Politics* (Jowett/Barnes trans.), 5.11.

19. Aristotle, 5.11.

20. Aristotle, 5.11.

21. Aristotle, 5.11.

22. Frank Leslie Vatai, *Intellectuals in Politics in the Greek World* (London: Croon Helm, 1984), 113. See also Julia Annas, "Classical Greek Philosophy," in *The Oxford History of the Classical World*, ed. John Boardman, Jasper Griffin, and Oswyn Murray, 234–53 (Oxford: Oxford University Press, 1986), 245.

23. Jonathan Barnes, *Aristotle* (Oxford: Oxford University Press, 1982), 2–3, 82.

24. Thomas Renna, "Aristotle and the French Monarchy," *Viator* 9 (1978): 309; Jean Dunbabin, "Aristotle in the Schools," in *Trends in Medieval Political Thought*, ed. Beryl Smalley, 65–85 (Oxford: Basil Blackwell, 1965).

25. Anthony Black, *Political Thought in Europe, 1250–1450* (Cambridge: Cambridge University Press, 1992), 9–11.

Chapter 3: Roman Mirrors

Epigraph: Cicero, *In Defence of Lucius Flaccus*, in *The Orations of Marcus Tullius Cicero*, trans. C. D. Yonge, 7.15, accessed January 5, 2015, http://data.perseus.org /texts/urn:cts:latinLit:phi0474.phi017.perseus-eng1; and Cicero to Atticus, January 20, 60 BC, in *Letters of Cicero*, trans. and ed. L. P. Wilkinson (New York: Norton, 1968), 36–37.

1. Cicero, *Against Verres*, in *Cicero: Selected Works*, trans. Michael Grant (Harmondsworth, England: Penguin, 1971), 38, 41, 42.

2. Cicero, *Against Verres*, 37, 57. Background of the trial is given by Lily Ross Taylor, *Party Politics in the Age of Caesar* (Berkeley: University of California Press, 1949), 101.

3. Elizabeth Rawson, *Cicero: A Portrait* (London: Allen Lane, 1975), 53–54; and Michael Grant, introduction to *Cicero: Selected Political Speeches* (Harmondsworth, UK: Penguin, 1969), 10.

4. Cicero, *De Re Publica*, trans. Clinton Walker Keyes (Cambridge, MA: Harvard University Press, 1928), 1.8.

5. Cicero, 2.9, 2.12.

6. Cicero, 5.1; and Neal Wood, *Cicero's Social and Political Thought* (Berkeley: University of California Press, 1988), 179.

7. Cicero, *De Re Publica*, 2.42, 5.4, 6.13. For more on Cicero's ideal of leadership, see Jonathan Zarecki, *Cicero's Ideal Statesman in Theory and Practice* (London: Bloomsbury, 2014), 88.

8. Private contracting of state business in Rome is described in E. Badian, *Publicans and Sinners* (Ithaca, NY: Cornell University Press, 1983), 67.

9. Cicero, *On Duties*, ed. M. T. Griffin and E. M. Atkins (Cambridge: Cambridge University Press, 1991), 1.4, 1.15.

10. Cicero, 1.18, 1.19.

11. Cicero, 1.20, 1.26, 1.31, 2.77.

12. Cicero, 1.66, 1.67, 1.72.

13. Cicero, 1.101, 1.103, 1.141, 1.150.

14. Cicero, 2.20, 2.25, 2.53; see also Wood, *Cicero's Social and Political Thought*, 68, 110.

15. Rawson, *Cicero*, 299–303; and George A. Kennedy, "Cicero's Oratorical and Rhetorical Legacy," in *Brill's Companion to Cicero*, ed. James M. May (Leiden: Brill, 2002), 485, 487.

16. D. E. Luscombe and G. R. Evans, "The Twelfth-Century Renaissance," in *The Cambridge History of Medieval Political Thought*, ed. J. H. Burns (Cambridge: Cambridge University Press, 1988), 312. See also Kennedy, "Cicero's Oratorical and Rhetorical Legacy," 490.

17. Wood, *Cicero's Social and Political Thought*, 3–4; and Grant, introduction to *Cicero: Selected Works*, 29.

18. John Cooper and J. F. Procopé, general introduction to *Seneca, Moral and Political Essays* (Cambridge: Cambridge University Press, 1995), xii–xiv.

19. Seneca, *On Mercy*, in *Seneca: Moral Essays*, vol. 1, trans. John W. Basore (Cambridge, MA: Harvard University Press, 1958), 1.1. See also Emily Wilson, *The Greatest Empire: A Life of Seneca* (Oxford: Oxford University Press, 2014), 104–5; James Romm, *Dying Every Day: Seneca at the Court of Nero* (New York: Knopf, 2014), 65; and Mary Beard, "How Stoical Was Seneca?" *New York Review of Books* 61 (October 9, 2014): 31.

20. Seneca, *On Mercy*, 1.1, 1.4.

21. Seneca, 1.4, 1.11, 1.12, 1.23. The sack was reported to be favored by Nero's adoptive father, the emperor Claudius.

22. Seneca, 1.4, 1.12.

23. Miriam T. Griffin, *Seneca: A Philosopher in Politics* (Oxford: Oxford University Press, 1976), 64; Miriam T. Griffin, *Nero: The End of a Dynasty* (New Haven, CT: Yale University Press, 1984), 47, 95; and Tacitus, *Annals* (Cambridge, MA: Harvard University Press, Loeb Classical Library, 1937), 15.44, http://www.penelope.uchicago.edu/Thayer/E/Roman/Texts/Tacitus/Annals/15B*.html. Over the years writers have reinterpreted the historical record in an attempt to rehabilitate the reputation of tyrants like Nero; see, e.g., John F. Drinkwater, *Nero: Emperor and Court* (Cambridge: Cambridge University Press, 2019), 7–13. But as with Seneca's rhetoric, such revisions are controversial, and Nero remains an exemplar of the bad prince.

24. Stoics' evangelical side is described in Moses Hadas, introduction to *The Stoic Philosophy of Seneca* (New York: Norton, 1968), 19. Quintilian is quoted in Christina S. Kraus, "The Path between Truculence and Servility: Prose Literature from Augustus to Hadrian," in *Literature in the Roman World*, ed. Oliver Taplin (Oxford: Oxford University Press, 2000), 174. Philosophers' attitudes toward Seneca are discussed by Cooper and Procopé, general introduction, xxxi–xxxii. Historians' views are from Griffin, *Seneca*, 420–44; and *Dio's Roman History*, vol. 8, trans. Earnest Cary (London: Heinemann, 1925), 61.10.

25. Paul Veyne, *Seneca: The Life of a Stoic*, trans. David Sullivan (New York: Routledge, 2003), 11; Catherine Edwards, *The Politics of Immorality in Ancient Rome* (Cambridge: Cambridge University Press, 1993), 26–27; and Tacitus, *Annals*, 13.42.

26. Cooper and Procopé, introduction to *On Mercy*, 120.

27. On Roman informers, see Steven H. Rutledge, *Imperial Inquisitions* (London: Routledge, 2001), 65. On mercy as a mark of totalitarian regimes, see Slavoj Žižek, "Tolerance as an Ideological Category," *Critical Inquiry* 34 (2008): 675–76.

28. G. M. Ross, "Seneca's Philosophical Influence," in *Seneca*, ed. C.D.N. Costa (London: Routledge, 1974), 136.

29. Bryan P. Reardon, introduction to *Lucian: Selected Works* (Indianapolis: Bobbs-Merrill, 1965), xxxi.

30. Lionel Casson, preface to *Selected Satires of Lucian* (New York: Norton, 1968), vii–viii.

31. Lucian, *On Salaried Posts in Great Houses*, in *Lucian*, vol. 3, trans. A. M. Harmon (Cambridge, MA: Harvard University Press, 1960), 417, 425–27.

32. Lucian, 431–33.

33. Lucian, 437–43.

34. Lucian, 443–45.

35. Lucian, 447.

36. Lucian, 449–57.

37. Lucian, 457–61.

38. Lucian, 449, 469–75.

39. Lucian, 463–65, 475.

40. *Apology for the "Salaried Posts in Great Houses,"* in *Lucian*, vol. 6, trans. K. Kilburn (Cambridge, MA: Harvard University Press, 1959), 201, 205–9.

41. *Apology for the "Salaried Posts,"* 195. In *Peregrinus*, Lucian teased Christians as easy marks for any conman with a sob story because they imagine "they are all each other's brothers and sisters"; *Lucian: Satirical Sketches*, trans. Paul Turner (Bloomington: Indiana University Press, 1990), 11.

42. Christopher Robinson, *Lucian and His Influence in Europe* (Chapel Hill: University of North Carolina Press, 1979), 68–82; David Marsh, *Lucian and the Latins* (Ann Arbor: University of Michigan Press, 1998), 7–33; and Pauline M. Smith, *The Anti-Courtier Trend in Sixteenth Century French Literature* (Geneva: Librairie Droz, 1966), 18–21.

Chapter 4: Frankish Mirrors

Epigraph: From Nithard's *Histories*, in *Carolingian Chronicles*, trans. Bernard Walter Scholz and Barbara Rogers (Ann Arbor: University of Michigan Press, 1970), 174.

1. Nithard's *Histories*, 129–31.

2. Mayke de Jong, "From Scolastici to Scioli: Alcuin and the Formation of an Intellectual Elite," in *Alcuin of York: Scholar at the Carolingian Court*, ed. L.A.J.R. Houwen and A. A. MacDonald, Proceedings of the Third Germania Latina Conference (Groningen, Netherlands: Egbert Forsten, 1998), 47.

3. J. M. Wallace-Hadrill, "The *Via Regia* of the Carolingian Age," in *Trends in Medieval Political Thought*, ed. Beryl Smalley, 22–41 (Oxford: Basil Blackwell, 1965).

4. Eleanor Shipley Duckett, *Alcuin, Friend of Charlemagne: His World and His Work* (New York: Macmillan, 1951), 14–15, 19; and Donald A. Bullough, "Charlemagne's 'Men of God': Alcuin, Hildebald and Arn," in *Charlemagne: Empire and Society*, ed. Joanna Story, 136–50 (Manchester, UK: Manchester University Press, 2005).

5. *The Rhetoric of Alcuin and Charlemagne*, trans. Wilbur Samuel Howell (Princeton, NJ: Princeton University Press, 1941), 67.

6. *Rhetoric of Alcuin and Charlemagne*, 69.

7. *Rhetoric of Alcuin and Charlemagne*, 119–21, 127–29.

8. *Rhetoric of Alcuin and Charlemagne*, 125–27.

9. *Rhetoric of Alcuin and Charlemagne*, 131–33, 137, 145–53.

10. *Rhetoric of Alcuin and Charlemagne*, 151–53.

11. Alcuin to Charlemagne, ca. 796 (M.G.H. letter 121), in *Alcuin of York*, ed. Stephen Allott (York: Sessions, 1974), 12; and Duckett, *Alcuin*, 224.

12. Joseph Canning, *A History of Medieval Political Thought, 300–1450* (London: Routledge, 1996), 50; Alessandro Barbero, *Charlemagne, Father of a Continent*, trans. Allen Cameron (Berkeley: University of California Press, 2004), 86; Lawrence Nees, *A Tainted Mantle: Hercules and the Classical Tradition at the Carolingian Court* (Philadelphia: University of Pennsylvania Press, 1991), 115; and Bernard S. Bachrach, "Charlemagne and the Carolingian General Staff," *Journal of Military History* 66 (2002): 313–57.

13. Barbero, *Charlemagne*, 47.

14. Louis Halphen, *Charlemagne and the Carolingian Empire*, trans. Giselle de Nie (Amsterdam: North-Holland, 1977), 49.

15. Pierre Riché, *The Carolingians*, trans. Michael Idomir Allen (Philadelphia: University of Pennsylvania Press, 1993), 105.

16. Duckett, *Alcuin*, 131; and Barbero, *Charlemagne*, 244.

17. Duckett, *Alcuin*, 130.

18. Barbero, *Charlemagne*, 86; see also Bullough, "Charlemagne's 'Men of God,'" 140.

19. D. A. Bullough, "Alcuin's Cultural Influence: The Evidence of the Manuscripts," in *Alcuin of York: Scholar at the Carolingian Court*, ed. L.A.J.R. Houwen and A. A. MacDonald, Proceedings of the Third Germania Latina Conference (Groningen, Netherlands: Egbert Forsten, 1998), 25.

20. Bullough, 19.

21. Duckett, *Alcuin*, 305.

22. Halphen, *Charlemagne and the Carolingian Empire*, 159.

23. Karl Ubl, "Carolingian Mirrors for Princes: Texts, Contents, Impact," in *A Critical Companion to the "Mirrors for Princes" Literature*, ed. Noëlle-Laetitia Perret and Stéphane Péquignot (Leiden: Brill 2023), 82. See also Harry Randall Dosher, "The Concept of the Ideal Prince in French Political Thought, 800–1760" (PhD diss., University of North Carolina at Chapel Hill, 1969), 51; and Lester K. Born, "The Specula Principis of the Carolingian Renaissance," *Revue Belge de Philologie et D'Histoire* 12 (1933): 592–95.

24. Janet L. Nelson, "Women at the Court of Charlemagne: A Case of Monstrous Regiment?" in *The Frankish World, 750–900* (London: Hambledon, 1996), 240–41. See also Halphen, *Charlemagne and the Carolingian Empire*, 160.

25. J. M. Wallace-Hadrill, *The Barbarian West, A.D. 400–1000* (New York: Harper & Row, 1962), 121.

26. Thomas F. X. Noble, "Louis the Pious and His Piety Re-Reconsidered," *Revue Belge de Philologie et d'Histoire* 58 (1980): 297–316.

27. Riché, *Carolingians*, 147, 153–58.

28. Jonas of Orleans, *De institutione regia*, trans. R. W. Dyson (Smithtown, NY: Exposition Press, 1983), 5–6.

29. Jonas of Orleans, *De institutione regia*, 34, 36–38.

30. Jonas of Orleans, 41–43.

31. Jonas of Orleans, 15. A vernacular version of *The Twelve Abuses* is provided in *Two Ælfric Texts: The Twelve Abuses and the Vices and Virtues*, ed. and trans. Mary Clayton (Cambridge: Brewer, 2013), 109–37.

32. Jonas of Orleans, *De institutione regia*, 15–16.

33. Jonas of Orleans, 16, 18.

34. Jonas of Orleans, 31–32.

35. Jonas of Orleans, 10–13.

36. Riché, *Carolingians*, 41, 54.

37. Janet L. Nelson, "Making Ends Meet: Wealth and Poverty in the Carolingian Church," in *The Frankish World: 750–900* (London: Hambledon Press, 1996), 146.

38. Nelson, "Making Ends Meet," 146.

39. R. W. Dyson, introduction to *De institutione regia*, xiii.

40. Jonas of Orleans, *De institutione regia*, 20–22.

41. Halphen, *Charlemagne and the Carolingian Empire*, 186.

42. Timothy Reuter, "The End of Carolingian Military Expansion," in *Charlemagne's Heir: New Perspectives on the Reign of Louis the Pious*, ed. Peter Godman and Roger Collins (Oxford: Clarendon Press, 1990), 405.

43. Stuart Airlie, "Charlemagne and the Aristocracy, Captains and Kings," in *Charlemagne, Empire and Society*, ed. Joanna Story, 90–102 (Manchester, UK: Manchester University Press, 2005).

44. Wallace-Hadrill, *Barbarian West*, 133. See also Reuter, "End of Carolingian Military Expansion," 391–405.

45. The term "clerical party" comes from Riché, *Carolingians*, 169.

46. Florus of Lyon, "Lament on the Division of the Empire," in *Poetry of the Carolingian Renaissance*, ed. Peter Godman, 264–73 (London: Duckworth, 1985).

47. Canning, *History of Medieval Political Thought*, 3–4; Romans 13:1–2; and 1 Peter 2:13–17.

Chapter 5: Storybook Mirrors

Epigraph: *William of Tyre, A History of Deeds Done Beyond the Sea*, trans. Emily Atwater Babcock and A. C. Krey, 2 vols. (New York: Columbia University Press, 1943), 2:406.

1. William of Tyre, 1:75.

2. William of Tyre, 1:75.

3. William of Tyre, 1:75–76.

4. "The Speech of Urban: The Version of Robert of Rheims," in *The Chronicle of Fulcher of Chartres and Other Source Materials*, ed. Edward Peters, 2nd ed. (Philadelphia: University of Pennsylvania Press, 1998), 27–28.

5. Guibert de Nogent, *The Deeds of God through the Franks*, trans. Robert Levine (Woodbridge, Suffolk, UK: Boydell, 1997), 46–47.

6. Robert Bartlett, *Gerald of Wales: 1146–1223* (Oxford: Clarendon, 1982), 27.

7. Gerald of Wales, *The Autobiography of Giraldus Cambrensis*, trans. H. E. Butler (London: Jonathan Cape, 1937), 101.

8. Gerald of Wales, *The History and Topography of Ireland*, trans. John J. O'Meara (Atlantic Highlands, NJ: Humanities Press, 1982), 102, 106, 109–10, 124–25.

9. Gerald of Wales, *Autobiography of Giraldus Cambrensis*, 81.

10. Gerald of Wales, 81.

11. Bartlett, *Gerald of Wales*, 17.

12. Gerald of Wales [Giraldus Cambrensis], *Concerning the Instruction of Princes*, trans. Joseph Stevenson, in *The Church Historians of England*, vol. 5, part 1 (London: Seeleys, 1858), 134. For more translated excerpts, see Lester Kruger Born, "The Perfect Prince: A Study in Thirteenth and Fourteenth-Century Ideals," *Speculum* 3 (1928): 470–504; and István P. Bejczy, "Gerald of Wales on the Cardinal Virtues: A Reappraisal of *De Principis Instructione*," *Medium Aevum* 75 (2006): 191–201.

13. Charles T. Wood, "At the Tomb of King Arthur," Proceedings of the Illinois Medieval Association, *Essays in Medieval Studies* 8 (1991): 1–14.

14. Gerald of Wales, *Instruction of Princes*, 137–39.

15. Gerald of Wales, 140–42, 168–75. Some of the same material, but with a smoother translation, can be found in Gerald of Wales, *The Conquest of Ireland*, ed. and trans. A. B. Scott and F. X. Martin (Dublin: Royal Irish Academy, 1978), 125–33, 201–7. See also Bartlett, *Gerald of Wales*, 69–84.

16. Gerald of Wales, *Conquest of Ireland*, 205.

17. Gerald of Wales, 233.

18. Gerald of Wales, *Instruction of Princes*, 173.

19. Gerald of Wales, *Conquest of Ireland*, 233–47; and Gerald of Wales, *Instruction of Princes*, 172–73.

20. Christopher Tyerman, *England and the Crusades, 1095–1588* (Chicago: University of Chicago Press, 1988), 39, 50–51.

21. W. L. Warren, *Henry II* (Berkeley: University of California Press, 1973), 618; and Bartlett, *Gerald of Wales*, 84.

22. Bartlett, *Gerald of Wales*, 79.

23. David Rollo, *Glamorous Sorcery: Magic and Literacy in the High Middle Ages* (Minneapolis: University of Minnesota Press, 2000), 127.

24. Rollo, 127.

25. Rollo, 124.

26. Joseph R. Strayer, *The Albigensian Crusades* (New York: Dial, 1971), 101–2, 117–19, 123; and Mark Gregory Pegg, *A Most Holy War* (Oxford: Oxford University Press, 2008), 162–64, 172, 174–76.

27. John Lynch, *Cambrensis Eversus*, trans. Matthew Kelly (Dublin: Celtic Society, 1848), 103–7, 297, 301. "Gerald in effect laid the foundation for the historical fiction of Irish inferiority," concludes British literature professor David Rollo in "Gerald of Wales' 'Topographia Hibernica': Sex and the Irish Nation," *Romanic Review* 86 (1995): 169–90. Irish historian Nicholas Canny says this fiction allowed English forces to make war and commit atrocities "absolved from all normal ethical restraints" during the Elizabethan conquest of Ireland. Nicholas P. Canny, *The Elizabethan Conquest of Ireland* (New York: Barnes & Noble, 1976), 122. See also Hiram Morgan, "Giraldus Cambrensis and the Tudor Conquest of Ireland," in *Political Ideology in Ireland, 1541–1641*, ed. Hiram Morgan (Dublin: Four Courts, 1999), 22–44.

28. Social mobility in the twelfth century is described by R. Howard Bloch, *The Anonymous Marie de France* (Chicago: University of Chicago Press, 2003), 168–74. See also Frank Barlow, *Thomas Becket* (Berkeley: University of California Press, 1986), 26.

29. Christopher Brooke, "John of Salisbury and His World," in *The World of John of Salisbury*, ed. Michael Wilks, 1–20 (Oxford: Basil Blackwell, 1984); and Cary J. Nederman, introduction to John of Salisbury's *Policraticus*, ed. and trans. Cary J. Nederman (Cambridge: Cambridge University Press, 1990), xv–xxvi.

30. John of Salisbury, *Policraticus*, 133.

31. John of Salisbury, 135–36.

32. John of Salisbury, 132, 136.

33. Ruth Ilsley Hicks, "The Body Political and the Body Ecclesiastical," *Journal of Bible and Religion* 31 (1963): 29–35; and Karl R. Popper, *The Open Society and Its Enemies*, vol. 1 (Princeton, NJ: Princeton University Press, 1966), 294.

34. Cary J. Nederman, "Toleration, Skepticism, and the 'Clash of Ideas': Principles of Liberty in the Writings of John of Salisbury," in *Beyond the Persecuting Society*, ed. John Christian Laursen and Cary J. Nederman, 53–70 (Philadelphia: University of Pennsylvania Press, 1998); and Janet Martin, "John of Salisbury as a Classical Scholar," in *The World of John of Salisbury*, ed. Michael Wilks, 179–201 (Oxford: Basil Blackwell, 1984).

35. John of Salisbury, *Policraticus*, 66–67.

36. John of Salisbury, 93–96, 104–7.

37. John of Salisbury, 85–86.

38. John of Salisbury, 88, 164–65.

39. John of Salisbury, *Memoirs of the Papal Court*, trans. Marjorie Chibnall (London: Thomas Nelson, 1956), 54–55.

40. John of Salisbury, *Policraticus*, 99.

41. John of Salisbury, 142.

42. John of Salisbury, 28–37.

43. John of Salisbury, 35–38, 77–78, 140–41.

44. John of Salisbury, 51, 79–80.

45. John of Salisbury, 80–81.

46. John of Salisbury, 28.

47. Quentin Skinner, *Visions of Politics*, vol. 2 (Cambridge: Cambridge University Press, 2002), 12.

48. John of Salisbury, *Policraticus*, 32.

49. Robert S. Hoyt, *Europe in the Middle Ages*, 2nd ed. (New York: Harcourt, 1966), 278.

50. Barlow, *Thomas Becket*, 90. See also Cary J. Nederman, *John of Salisbury* (Tempe: Arizona Center for Medieval and Renaissance Studies, 2005), 20; and David Luscombe, "John of Salisbury in Recent Scholarship," in *The World of John of Salisbury*, ed. Michael Wilks, 21–37 (Oxford: Basil Blackwell, 1984).

51. John of Salisbury, *Policraticus*, 18–20, 36, 87.

52. Nederman, *John of Salisbury*, 20; and Amnon Linder, "John of Salisbury's *Policraticus* in Thirteenth-Century England: The Evidence of MS Cambridge Corpus Christi College 469," *Journal of the Warburg and Courtauld Institutes* 40 (1977): 276–82.

53. Barlow, *Thomas Becket*, 274.

54. Amnon Linder, "The Knowledge of John of Salisbury in the Late Middle Ages," *Studi Medievali*, 3rd ser., 18, pt. 2 (1977): 315–66; and Tilman Struve, "The Importance of the Organism in the Political Theory of John of Salisbury," in *The World of John of Salisbury*, ed. Michael Wilks, 303–17 (Oxford: Basil Blackwell, 1984).

55. Nederman, abstract to John of Salisbury's *Policraticus*.

56. Struve, "Importance of the Organism," 316.

57. George H. Sabine, *A History of Political Theory*, 3rd. ed. (New York: Holt, Rinehart and Winston, 1961), 246.

58. John of Salisbury, *Policraticus*, 6.

59. C. Stephen Jaeger, "Pessimism in the Twelfth-Century 'Renaissance,'" *Speculum* 78 (2003): 1153–54.

60. Joshua Byron Smith, *Walter Map and the Matter of Britain* (Philadelphia: University of Pennsylvania Press, 2017), 12–13; and Stephen Gordon, "Parody, Sarcasm, and Invective in the *Nugae* of Walter Map," *Journal of English and Germanic Philology* 116 (January 2017): 86.

61. Walter Map, *De nugis curialium: Courtiers' Trifles*, ed. and trans. M. R. James, rev. C.N.L. Brooke and R.A.B. Mynors (Oxford: Clarendon, 1983), 197, 207.

62. Map, 61–63, 495–97.

63. Map, 17.

64. Map, 501, 5, 503–5, 511–13, 3.

65. Map, 509–11.

66. Peter Brown, *Power and Persuasion in Late Antiquity* (Madison: University of Wisconsin Press, 1992), 50.

67. John Gillingham, "The Early Middle Ages," in *The Oxford Illustrated History of Britain*, ed. Kenneth O. Morgan (Oxford: Oxford University Press, 1984), 143; and John of Salisbury to John of Canterbury (letter 305) in *The Letters of John of Salisbury*, ed. and trans. W. J. Millor and C.N.L. Brooke, vol. 2, 724–39 (Oxford: Clarendon, 1979).

68. Map, *De nugis curialium*, 447, 449.

69. Map, 449.

70. Björn Weiler, "Royal Justice and Royal Virtue," in *Virtue and Ethics in the Twelfth Century*, ed. István P. Bejczy and Richard G. Newhauser, 317–39 (Leiden: Brill, 2005).

71. C.N.L. Brooke, introduction to *De nugis curialium*, xiii–l.

72. G. T. Shepherd, "The Emancipation of Story in the Twelfth Century," in *Medieval Narrative: A Symposium*, ed. Hans Bekker-Nielsen, Peter Foote, Andreas Haarder, and Preben Meulengracht Sørensen, 44–57 (Odense, Den.: Odense University Press, 1979); and Bloch, *Marie de France*, 19.

73. Bloch, *Marie de France*, 7; see also Karen K. Jambeck, "The *Fables* of Marie de France: A Mirror of Princes," in *In Quest of Marie de France*, ed. Chantal A. Maréchal, 59–106 (Lewiston, NY: Edwin Mellen, 1992).

74. Marie de France, *The Fables of Marie de France*, trans. Mary Lou Martin (Birmingham, AL: Summa, 1984), 33.

75. Marie de France, 57.

76. Marie de France, 63.

77. Mary Lou Martin, introduction to *Fables of Marie de France*, 1–30. The theft of Henry's clothes was alleged by Gerald of Wales.

78. Marie de France, *Fables*, 93, 51–53, 81.

79. Martin, introduction to *Fables of Marie de France*, 1–30; and *Pañcatantra*, trans. Patrick Olivelle (Oxford: Oxford University Press, 1997); see also a breezy translation by Arthur W. Ryder, *The Panchatantra* (Chicago: University of Chicago Press, 1956).

80. Bloch, *Marie de France*, 126–27; and Laurence M. Porter, *Women's Vision in Western Literature* (Westport, CT: Praeger, 2005), 35–57.

81. Marie de France, *Fables*, 231–33, 163–65.

82. Bloch, *Marie de France*, 159.

83. Marie de France, *Fables*, 213.

84. Bloch, *Marie de France*, 175.

85. Marie de France, *Fables*, 67–69.

86. Marie de France, 45–47; see also Porter, *Women's Vision*, 52.

87. Emanuel J. Mickel Jr., *Marie de France* (New York: Twayne, 1974), 34; and Edward Wheatley, *Mastering Aesop* (Gainesville: University Press of Florida, 2000), 28–29.

Chapter 6: Scholastic Mirrors

Epigraph: *Ghazali's Book of Counsel for Kings (Nasihat al-Muluk)*, trans. F.R.C. Bagley (London: Oxford University Press, 1964), 77.

1. Jean Dunbabin, *France in the Making, 843–1180*, 2nd ed. (Oxford: Oxford University Press, 2000), 44. The historical ambiguity of the word "prince" results in some controversy over the definition of "mirrors for princes." This book adopts the broad definition of prince as successful leader to allow for consideration of a wider range of mirrors.

2. Cicero, *The Republic*, trans. Clinton Walker Keyes (Cambridge, MA: Harvard University Press, 1928), 3.14; and St. Augustine, *The City of God*, trans. Marcus Dods (New York: Modern Library, 1993), 4.4.

3. "Magna Carta," in *The Middle Ages*, vol. 1: *Sources of Medieval History*, 3rd ed., ed. Brian Tierney, 278–82 (New York: Knopf, 1978), 280.

4. Maurice Keen, *The Pelican History of Medieval Europe* (Harmondsworth, Middlesex, UK: Penguin, 1969), 197; and Jean Dunbabin, "Government," in *The Cambridge History of Medieval Political Thought*, ed. J. H. Burns, 477–519 (Cambridge: Cambridge University Press, 1988).

5. John B. Morrall, *Political Thought in Medieval Times* (Toronto: University of Toronto Press, 1980), 59–60; and Dunbabin, "Government."

6. Erasmus, *The Education of a Christian Prince*, trans. Neil M. Cheshire and Michael J. Heath, ed. Lisa Jardine (Cambridge: Cambridge University Press, 1997), 1.

7. *Secretum Secretorum*, ed. Robert Steele, *Opera Hactenus Inedita Rogeri Baconi*, fasc. 5 (London: Oxford University Press, 1920), 176–78. See also Stephen J. Williams, *The Secret of Secrets* (Ann Arbor: University of Michigan Press, 2003), 7–9.

8. *Secretum Secretorum*, 224.

9. *Secretum Secretorum*, 185–86.

10. *Secretum Secretorum*, 186.

11. *Secretum Secretorum*, 187–88, 190.

12. *Secretum Secretorum*, 243, 237.

13. *Secretum Secretorum*, 239.

14. *Secretum Secretorum*, 236, 243, 245–46.

15. *Secretum Secretorum*, 221, 251, 255–56.

16. *Secretum Secretorum*, 257.

17. Williams, *Secret of Secrets*, 1–2, 183, 195, 254–55, 347.

18. Williams, 323, 335.

19. James A. Weisheipl, *Friar Thomas D'Aquino* (New York: Doubleday, 1974), 4, 10–15, 27; and Jean-Pierre Torrell, *Saint Thomas Aquinas*, rev. ed., trans. Robert Royal (Washington, DC: Catholic University of America Press, 2005) 1–12.

20. Anthony Kenny, *Aquinas* (New York: Hill and Wang, 1980), 2.

21. Kenny, 4–5; see also Christine Caldwell Ames, *Righteous Persecution: Inquisition, Dominicans, and Christianity in the Middle Ages* (Philadelphia: University of Pennsylvania Press, 2009), 6.

22. Jeremy Catto, "Ideas and Experience in the Political Thought of Aquinas," *Past and Present* 71 (May 1976): 3–21.

23. Thomas Aquinas, *On Kingship*, in *St. Thomas Aquinas: Political Writings*, ed. and trans. R. W. Dyson (Cambridge: Cambridge University Press, 2002), 5–7, 44.

24. Thomas Aquinas, *On Kingship*, in *St. Thomas Aquinas on Politics and Ethics*, ed. and trans. Paul E. Sigmund (New York: Norton, 1988), 15–18.

25. Aquinas, *On Kingship* (trans. Sigmund), 19–20.

26. Aquinas, *On Kingship* (trans. Dyson), 31–33.

27. Aquinas, 44.

28. Aquinas, 28.

29. Thomas Aquinas, *Summa Theologiae* in *St. Thomas Aquinas: Political Writings*, ed. and trans. R. W. Dyson (Cambridge: Cambridge University Press, 2002), 56.

30. Aquinas, *On Kingship* (trans. Dyson), 34.

31. Jean Porter, "The Common Good in Thomas Aquinas," in *In Search of the Common Good*, ed. Dennis P. McCann and Patrick D. Miller, 94–120 (New York: T&T Clark, 2005).

32. Thomas Aquinas, *On Princely Government*, trans. J. G. Dawson, in *Aquinas: Selected Political Writings*, ed. A. P. D'Entreves (Oxford: Basil Blackwell, 1978), 21.

33. Aquinas, *On Kingship* (trans. Dyson), 18, 20–21; see also Shadia B. Drury, *Aquinas and Modernity: The Lost Promise of Natural Law* (Plymouth, UK: Rowman & Littlefield, 2008), 48.

34. Aquinas, *On Kingship* (trans. Sigmund), 26–29.

35. Mark D. Jordan, *Rewritten Theology* (Malden, MA: Blackwell, 2006), 47.

36. Aquinas, *On Kingship* (trans. Sigmund), 26.

37. Aquinas, *On Kingship* (trans. Dyson), 25.

38. Aquinas, *On Princely Government* (trans. Dawson), 51.

39. Jordan, *Rewritten Theology*, 56.

40. Charles F. Briggs, *Giles of Rome's "De regimine principum"* (Cambridge: Cambridge University Press, 1999), 9; and John E. Rotelle, biographical introduction to *Commentary on the Song of Songs and Other Writings* by Giles of Rome (Villanova, PA: Augustinian Press, 1998), 11–45.

41. Giles of Rome, *On the Rule of Princes*, trans. Matthew Kempshall, in *The Cambridge Translations of Medieval Philosophical Texts*, vol. 2, ed. Arthur Stephen McGrade, John Kilcullen, and Matthew Kempshall (Cambridge: Cambridge University Press, 2001), 203, 210.

42. Giles of Rome, 205–6.

43. Giles of Rome, 205–6.

44. Giles of Rome, 205.

45. Giles of Rome, 205.

46. Briggs, *"De regimine principum,"* 1. On sermons and mirrors for princes as pop political philosophy, see Dunbabin, "Government," 478.

47. Elizabeth A. R. Brown, *Customary Aids and Royal Finance in Capetian France* (Cambridge, MA: Medieval Academy of America, 1992), 28. See also Lester Kruger Born, "The Perfect Prince: A Study in Thirteenth- and Fourteenth-Century Ideals," *Speculum* 3 (1928): 470–504.

48. M. S. Kempshall, *The Common Good in Late Medieval Political Thought* (Oxford: Clarendon, 1999), 133.

49. Allan H. Gilbert, *Machiavelli's Prince and Its Forerunners* (Durham, NC: Duke University Press, 1938), 61.

50. Paraphrased translation from Dunbabin, "Government," 484.

51. Quentin Skinner, *The Foundations of Modern Political Thought*, vol. 1: *The Renaissance* (Cambridge: Cambridge University Press, 1978), 62.

52. Giles of Rome, "On Civil Government," in *Medieval Political Theory—A Reader*, ed. Cary J. Nederman and Kate Langdon Forhan (London: Routledge, 1993), 150.

53. Giles of Rome, 151.

54. Giles of Rome, *On the Rule of Princes* (trans. Kempshall), 213.

55. Giles of Rome, *On the Rule of Princes*, in *Medieval Political Ideas*, ed. Ewart Lewis (New York: Cooper Square, 1974), 289.

56. Jean Dunbabin, "Aristotle in the Schools," in *Trends in Medieval Political Thought*, ed. Beryl Smalley, 65–85 (Oxford: Blackwell, 1965).

57. Giles of Rome, *De regimine principum*, ed. and trans. Samuel Paul Molenaer (1899; repr. New York: AMS Press, 1966), xxiii.

58. Dunbabin, "Aristotle in the Schools," 69, 73.

59. Giles of Rome, *De regimine principum*, xxiii.

60. Kate Langdon Forhan, *The Political Theory of Christine de Pizan* (Aldershot, Hampshire UK: Ashgate, 2002), 41.

61. Dunbabin, "Aristotle in the Schools," 77.

62. Elizabeth A. R. Brown, *The Monarchy of Capetian France and Royal Ceremonial* (Aldershot, Hampshire UK: Variorum, 1991), 283.

63. Joseph R. Strayer, *The Reign of Philip the Fair* (Princeton, NJ: Princeton University Press, 1980), 81, 238.

64. Brown, *Customary Aids*, 28–33.

65. Thomas Aquinas, "On the Government of Jews," in *St. Thomas Aquinas: Political Writings*, ed. and trans. R. W. Dyson (Cambridge: Cambridge University Press, 2002), 237.

66. Joseph R. Strayer, "The First Western Union," *Virginia Quarterly Review* 27 (1951): 196–205, reprinted in Joseph R. Strayer, *Medieval Statecraft and the Perspectives of History* (Princeton, NJ: Princeton University Press, 1971), 333–48.

67. Brian Tierney, *The Crisis of Church and State, 1050–1300* (Englewood Cliffs, NJ: Prentice-Hall, 1964), 176.

68. Tierney, 178, 179. See also Strayer, *Philip the Fair*, 291–99; and R. W. Dyson, *Normative Theories of Society and Government in Five Medieval Thinkers* (Lewiston, NY: Edwin Mellen, 2003), 141–85.

69. Giles of Rome, *On Ecclesiastical Power*, ed. and trans. R. W. Dyson (New York: Columbia University Press, 2004), 23.

70. Tierney, *Church and State*, 189.

71. Elizabeth A. R. Brown, "The Case of Philip the Fair," *Viator* 19 (1988): 219–46.

72. Elizabeth A. R. Brown, "Taxation and Morality in the Thirteenth and Fourteenth Centuries: Conscience and Political Power and the Kings of France," *French Historical Studies* 8 (1973): 1–28; Tomaž Mastnak, *Crusading Peace* (Berkeley: University of California Press, 2002), 239–41; Briggs, *"De regimine principum,"* 20; Thomas Renna, "Aristotle and the French Monarchy, 1260–1303," *Viator* 9 (1978): 309–24; and Nicholas Orme, *From Childhood to Chivalry* (London: Methuen, 1984), 90.

73. Charles Howard McIlwain, *The Growth of Political Thought in the West* (New York: Macmillan, 1932), 340.

74. William of Pagula, *Mirror of King Edward III*, ed. and trans. Cary J. Nederman in *Political Thought in Early Fourteenth-Century England* (Tempe: Arizona Center for Medieval and Renaissance Studies/Brepols, 2002), 74.

75. W. R. Jones, "Purveyance for War and the Community of the Realm in Late Medieval England," *Albion* 7 (1975): 300–316; and Cary J. Nederman, introduction to the *Mirror of King Edward III* by William of Pagula, 63–72.

76. William of Pagula, *Mirror of King Edward III*, 84.

77. William of Pagula, 88.

78. William of Pagula, 82, 86.

79. William of Pagula, 87.

80. William of Pagula, 109.

81. William of Pagula, 109–10.

82. William of Pagula, 110.

83. William of Pagula, 83–84, 95–96.

84. William of Pagula, 84, 94.

85. Cary J. Nederman, "Property and Protest: Political Theory and Subjective Rights in Fourteenth-Century England," *Review of Politics* 58 (1996): 58, 342.

86. Walter of Milemete, *On the Nobility, Wisdom, and Prudence of Kings*, ed. and trans. Cary J. Nederman in *Political Thought in Early Fourteenth-Century England* (Tempe: Arizona Center for Medieval and Renaissance Studies/Brepols, 2002), 29–30, 31, 57.

87. William of Pagula, *Mirror of King Edward III*, 116.

88. Nederman, introduction to the *Mirror of King Edward III* by William of Pagula, 63–72; and William of Pagula, *Mirror of King Edward III*, 116–17.

89. William of Pagula, *Mirror of King Edward III*, 74.

90. Nederman, "Property and Protest," 343; see also Nederman, introduction to the *Mirror of King Edward III* by William of Pagula, 63–72.

91. Jones, "Purveyance for War," 310.

92. J. R. Maddicott, "The Birth and Setting of the Ballads of Robin Hood," *English Historical Review* 93 (1978): 276–99.

93. David Matthews, *Writing to the King: Nation, Kingship, and Literature in England, 1250–1350* (Cambridge: Cambridge University Press, 2010), 112. Clerical support for Edward's wars as a divine mission is described in W. M. Ormrod, *The Reign of Edward III* (New Haven, CT: Yale University Press, 1990), 122–23. The scant legacy of William's mirror is traced by L. E. Boyle, "The 'Oculus Sacerdotis' and Some Other Works of William of Pagula," *Transactions of the Royal Historical Society*, 5th ser., 5 (1955): 81–110.

94. Louise Marlow, *Medieval Muslim Mirrors for Princes: An Anthology of Arabic, Persian, and Turkish Political Advice* (Cambridge: Cambridge University Press, 2023), 3. Marlow notes similarities in medieval Muslim and Christian courts. The same kind of courtly culture that led John of Salisbury, for instance, to analogize his prince to the head of an organic body led an anonymous Muslim

scholar (two centuries earlier) to extol a virtuous Indian king who offered his son this analogy: "Imagine a man, alive and standing upright: The man's head is you, O ruler; his heart is your vizier, his hands are your officials, his legs your subjects" (92). The well-being of the whole body, the ability to stand at all, depends on direction from the head, the king.

95. On al-Ghazali as "the Muslim Aquinas," see J. J. Saunders, *Muslims and Mongols*, ed. G. W. Rice (Christchurch, New Zealand: Whitcoulls for the University of Canterbury, 1977), 111.

96. *Ghazali's Book of Counsel for Kings*, 89 (al-Ghazali's authorship of part 2 has been disputed, but the book remains representative of the genre regardless).

97. *The Sea of Precious Virtues (Bahr al-Fava'id): A Medieval Islamic Mirror for Princes*, ed. and trans. Julie Scott Meisami (Salt Lake City: University of Utah Press, 1991), 56–57.

98. *Ghazali's Book of Counsel for Kings*, 89.

99. *Sea of Precious Virtues*, 294.

100. *Ghazali's Book of Counsel for Kings*, 77.

101. *Ghazali's Book of Counsel for Kings*, 45.

102. Ann K. S. Lambton, "Islamic Mirrors for Princes," *Quaderno dell'Accademia Nazionale dei Lincei* 160 (1971): 425.

103. *The Book of Government or Rules for Kings (The Siyasat-nama or Siyar al-Muluk) of Nizam al-Mulk*, trans. Hubert Darke (New Haven, CT: Yale University Press, 1960), 51.

104. *The Book of Government or Rules for Kings*, 10–11; and *Sea of Precious Virtues*, 297.

105. *Sea of Precious Virtues*, 299.

106. *Book of Government or Rules for Kings*, 133–34.

107. *Sea of Precious Virtues*, 45.

108. Neguin Yavari, "Polysemous Texts and Reductionist Readings: Women and Heresy in the Siyar al-Muluk," in *Views From the Edge*, ed. Neguin Yavari, Lawrence G. Potter, and Jean-Marc Ran Oppenheim (New York: Columbia University Press, 2004), 337.

109. *Sea of Precious Virtues*, 80–81.

110. *Book of Government or Rules for Kings*, 63. See also *Ghazali's Book of Counsel for Kings*, 19.

111. *Book of Government or Rules for Kings*, 62–63.

112. *Book of Government or Rules for Kings*, 63.

113. *Book of Government or Rules for Kings*, 62.

114. *Sea of Precious Virtues*, 215.

115. *Book of Government or Rules for Kings*, 50.

116. *Sea of Precious Virtues*, 28–29, 31, 33–34.

117. Louise Marlow, "Advice and Advice Literature," *Encyclopedia of Islam 3*, ed. Gudrun Krämer, Denis Matringe, John Nawas, and Everett Rowson (Brill Online, 2007), accessed April 27, 2015, http://referenceworks.brillonline.com.flagship.luc .edu/entries/encyclopaedia-of-islam-3/advice-and-advice-literature-COM_0026.

118. *Sea of Precious Virtues*, 224.

119. Linda T. Darling, "*Mirrors for Princes* in Europe and the Middle East: A Case of Historiographical Incommensurability," in *East Meets West in the Middle Ages and Early Modern Times*, ed. Albrecht Classen (Berlin: De Gruyter, 2013), 239.

120. Patricia Crone, *God's Rule: Government and Islam* (New York: Columbia University Press, 2004), 150, 161.

Chapter 7: Renaissance Mirrors

Epigraph: Erasmus, *The Education of a Christian Prince*, trans. Neil M. Cheshire and Michael J. Heath, ed. Lisa Jardine (Cambridge: Cambridge University Press, 1997), 47.

1. Otto of Freising quote in Quentin Skinner, *The Foundations of Modern Political Thought*, vol. 1: *The Renaissance* (Cambridge: Cambridge University Press, 1978), 4.

2. Marco Santagata, *Dante: The Story of His Life*, trans. Richard Dixon (Cambridge, MA: Belknap / Harvard University Press, 2016), 10, 11, 13, 177, 271.

3. Dante, *Monarchy*, trans. Donald Nicholl (New York: Noonday, 1954), 16, 20, 25, 26–27, 93.

4. Dante, 26, 39, 48; see also Charles T. Davis, "Dante's Vision of History," *Dante Studies* 93 (1975): 143–60.

5. Dante, Letter VI (to the Florentines), March 31, 1311; and Letter VII (to the Emperor Henry VII), April 17, 1311, both in Dante, *Monarchy*, 103–8, 109–15.

6. Morris Bishop, *Petrarch and His World* (Bloomington: Indiana University Press, 1963), 13, 25, 28, 39–40, 160–71, 372–74.

7. Francesco Petrarca [Petrarch], *How a Ruler Ought to Govern His State*, trans. Benjamin G. Kohl, in *The Earthly Republic*, ed. Benjamin G. Kohl and Ronald G. Witt (Philadelphia: University of Pennsylvania Press, 1978), 39, 41.

8. Petrarch, 42–43, 46.

9. Petrarch, 49, 52.

10. Petrarch, 55, 58.

11. Petrarch, 42, 46, 61, 76–77.

12. Petrarch, 78.

13. Petrarch, "Lament for the Loss of the Holy Land, and a Diatribe against Contemporary Popes and Princes" (*De vita solitaria* II, ix) in *Petrarch: A Humanist among Princes*, ed. and trans. David Thompson (New York: Harper & Row, 1971), 167–68; and Petrarch, *On Religious Leisure*, ed. and trans. Susan S. Schearer (New York: Italica, 2002), 1:6.

14. Petrarch, "Exhortation to the Emperor Charles IV" (*Epistolae familiares* X), in *Petrarch: A Humanist among Princes*, 1:102.

15. Petrarch, 104.

16. Petrarch, 103.

17. Petrarch, 105; see also Nancy Bisaha, "Petrarch's Vision of the Muslim and Byzantine East," *Speculum* 76 (2001): 76, 284–314.

18. Kohl, introduction to Petrarch, *How a Ruler Ought to Govern*, 25–34.

19. Martin McLaughlin, "Petrarch: Between Two Ages, between Two Languages," in *Italy's Three Crowns*, ed. Zygmunt G. Barański and Martin McLaughlin (Oxford: Bodleian Library, 2007), 25.

20. Petrarch, "Invective against a Certain Man of Great Rank but No Knowledge or Virtue," in *Petrarch: A Humanist among Princes*, 141.

21. Arpad Steiner, "Petrarch's *Optimus Princeps*," *Romanic Review* 25 (1934): 99–111.

22. Steiner, 100.

23. Christine de Pizan, *The Book of the City of Ladies*, trans. Earl Jeffrey Richards (New York: Persea, 1982), 3–4.

24. Christine de Pizan, *A Medieval Woman's Mirror of Honor: The Treasury of the City of Ladies*, trans. Charity Cannon Willard (New York: Persea / Bard Hall Press, 1989), 70–73.

25. Christine de Pizan, 76.

26. Christine de Pizan, 79, 80.

27. Christine de Pizan, 86.

28. Christine de Pizan, 95, 101, 109, 114.

29. Christine de Pizan, "Christine's Vision," in *The Writings of Christine de Pizan*, ed. Charity Cannon Willard (New York: Persea, 1994), 12, 16.

30. Charity Cannon Willard, *Christine de Pizan: Her Life and Works* (New York: Persea, 1984), 44–45, 54–56, 115, 135, 163–64, 173–77.

31. Kate Langdon Forhan, *The Political Theory of Christine de Pizan* (Aldershot, Hampshire, UK: Ashgate, 2002), 20–21, 34–38; and Christine de Pizan, *The Book of the Body Politic*, ed. and trans. Kate Langdon Forhan (Cambridge: Cambridge University Press, 1994), 4.

32. Christine de Pizan, *Book of the Body Politic*, 17, 38.

33. Christine de Pizan, 68.

34. Christine de Pizan, 92, 93, 99, 101.

35. Forhan, *Political Theory of Christine de Pizan*, 80–100.

36. Willard, *Christine de Pizan*, 179.

37. Christine de Pizan, *Book of the Body Politic*, 5, 8–10, 36–37.

38. Forhan, introduction to *Book of the Body Politic*, xxiii.

39. Kate Langdon Forhan, "Reflecting Heroes: Christine de Pizan and the Mirror Tradition," in *The City of Scholars: New Approaches to Christine de Pizan*, ed. Margarete Zimmermann and Dina De Rentiis (Berlin: Walter de Gruyter, 1994), 195.

40. Andrew Pettegree, *The Book in the Renaissance* (New Haven, CT: Yale University Press, 2010), 21, 27–43; and Martin Davies, "Juan de Carvajal and Early Printing: The 42-Line Bible and the Sweynheym and Pannartz Aquinas," *The Library*, 6th series, 18 (1996): 196.

41. Pettegree, *Book in the Renaissance*, 44, 82, 84–85.

42. Lisa Jardine, introduction to *The Education of a Christian Prince* by Erasmus, trans. Neil M. Cheshire and Michael J. Heath (Cambridge: Cambridge University

Press, 1997), vi–xxiv; and Charles Nauert, "Desiderius Erasmus," *The Stanford Encyclopedia of Philosophy (Winter 2012)*, ed. Edward N. Zalta, accessed May 15, 2015, http://plato.stanford.edu/archives/win2012/entries/ erasmus/.

43. Cecil H. Clough, "Erasmus and the Pursuit of English Royal Patronage in 1517 and 1518," *Erasmus of Rotterdam Society Yearbook* 1 (1981): 126–40; and Neil M. Cheshire and Michael J. Heath, introductory note to *Collected Works of Erasmus*, vol. 27 (*Literary and Educational Writings 5*), ed. A.H.T. Levi (Toronto: University of Toronto Press, 1986), 200–202.

44. Erasmus, *Education of a Christian Prince*, 1, 3.

45. Erasmus, 1, 66.

46. Erasmus, 25, 66.

47. Erasmus, 75–76.

48. Erasmus, 34–35, 70, 92, 101.

49. Erasmus, 93, 94, 108.

50. Erasmus, 8–9, 83.

51. Erasmus, 106, 109.

52. James D. Tracy, *Erasmus of the Low Countries* (Berkeley: University of California Press, 1996), 87, 88.

53. Erasmus, *Education of a Christian Prince*, 21, 23, 109–10.

54. Erasmus, 5, 12, 14, 72.

55. J. K. Sowards, introduction to *Collected Works of Erasmus*, vol. 25 (*Literary and Educational Writings 3*), ed. J. K. Sowards (Toronto: University of Toronto Press, 1985), xvii.

56. Erasmus, *Education of a Christian Prince*, 23–24.

57. Erasmus, 26.

58. Erasmus, 27.

59. Erika Rummel, *Erasmus* (London: Continuum, 2004), 56–57.

60. J. Kelley Sowards, *Desiderius Erasmus* (Boston: Twayne, 1975), 114, 115.

61. A.H.T. Levi, introduction to *Collected Works of Erasmus*, vol. 27 (*Literary and Educational Writings 5*), xxvii.

62. Erasmus, *Education of a Christian Prince*, 15.

63. Sir Walter Raleigh, "Preface to the History of the World" in *The Harvard Classics, Prefaces and Prologues*, ed. Charles W. Eliot (New York: Collier, 1910), 81.

64. James D. Tracy, *Emperor Charles V, Impresario of War* (Cambridge: Cambridge University Press, 2002), 1–9, 155–56; and Sowards, *Desiderius Erasmus*, 116.

65. Peter Burke, *The Fortunes of the Courtier* (University Park: Pennsylvania State University Press, 1996), 57–65, 158–62; and Frank Lovett, "The Path of the Courtier: Castiglione, Machiavelli, and the Loss of Republican Liberty," *Review of Politics* 74 (2012): 589.

66. Baldesar Castiglione, *The Book of the Courtier*, trans. Charles Singleton, ed. Daniel Javitch (New York: Norton, 2002), 10, 213–14, 222–23, 226.

67. Still, *The Courtier* was also an artful mirror for princes, as Volker Reinhardt suggests: "The fact that Castiglione's writing was as much addressed to princes as to those who served them is widely attested by its success among the powerful,

such as Charles V." Volker Reinhardt, "Refutation, Parody, Annihilation: The End of the Mirror for Princes in Machiavelli, Vettori, and Guicciardini," in *A Critical Companion to the "Mirrors for Princes" Literature*, ed. Noëlle-Laetitia Perret and Stéphane Péquignot (Leiden: Brill, 2023), 221–22.

68. Castiglione, *Book of the Courtier*, 211–12.

69. Castiglione, 210, 49, 53, 29.

70. Castiglione, 32, 22, 210.

71. Daniel Javitch, "*Il Cortegiano* and the Constraints of Despotism," in *Castiglione: The Ideal and the Real in Renaissance Culture*, ed. Robert W. Hanning and David Rosand (New Haven, CT: Yale University Press, 1983), 17–28.

72. Castiglione, *Book of the Courtier*, 213; see also Daniel Javitch, preface to Castiglione, *Book of the Courtier*, vii–xvi.

73. Francesco Guicciardini, *Ricordi*, quoted in Javitch, "*Il Cortegiano* and the Constraints of Despotism," 17.

74. Lovett, "Path of the Courtier," 591.

75. Lovett, 600. See also Omid Payrow Shabani, "To Be a Courtier in the Islamic Republic of Iran," *Political Theory* 43 (2015): 427–50; and Virginia Cox, "Castiglione and His Critics," in *The Book of the Courtier* by Baldassare Castiglione, ed. Virginia Cox (London: Everyman, 1994), 409–24.

Chapter 8: Machiavellian Mirrors

Epigraph: Niccolò Machiavelli, *History of Florence*, in *Internet Medieval Source Book*, ed. Paul Halsall (New York: Fordham University, 1998), accessed January 30, 2012, http//www.fordham.edu/halsall/source/machiavelli-histflo-lorenzo.html.

1. Niccolò Machiavelli, "Letter to Francesco Vettori; December 10, 1513," in *Niccolò Machiavelli: Selected Political Writings*, ed. and trans. David Wootton (Indianapolis: Hackett, 1994), 4.

2. Machiavelli, 2–3.

3. Machiavelli, 3.

4. Machiavelli, 3.

5. Niccolò Machiavelli, *The Prince*, in *Niccolò Machiavelli: Selected Political Writings*, ed. and trans. David Wootton (Indianapolis: Hackett, 1994), 6 (chap. 2).

6. Niccolò Machiavelli, *The Prince*, trans. and ed. Robert M. Adams, 2nd ed. (New York: Norton, 1992), 4–5 (chap. 2).

7. Machiavelli, 5 (chap. 3).

8. Machiavelli, 17 (chap. 6).

9. Machiavelli, 17 (chap. 6).

10. Machiavelli, 40–42 (chap. 14).

11. Machiavelli, 46 (chap. 17).

12. Machiavelli, 46 (chap. 17).

13. Machiavelli, 45, 50 (chap. 17, 19).

14. Machiavelli, 42–43 (chap. 15).

15. Machiavelli, 48 (chap. 18).

16. Machiavelli, 49–50 (chap. 18–19).

17. Machiavelli, 52, 58, 60, 63–64 (chap. 19–23).

18. Machiavelli, 66, 70–71 (chap. 24, 26); and Robert M. Adams, historical introduction to *The Prince* (ed. Adams), vii–xvi.

19. Niccolò Machiavelli, *The Discourses*, in *Niccolò Machiavelli: Selected Political Writings*, ed. and trans. David Wootton (Indianapolis: Hackett, 1994), 154–56, 160–61 (1.58, 2.pref.).

20. Machiavelli, 156–58, 166, 170 (1.58, 2.2).

21. Machiavelli, 125–29 (1.17, 1.18).

22. Tom Burns and G. M. Stalker, *The Management of Innovation*, 2nd ed. (London: Tavistock, 1971), 119–22, quote at viii.

23. Machiavelli, *Discourses*, 129, 199 (1.18, 3.9); and Niccolò Machiavelli, *Discourse on Florentine Affairs after the Death of Lorenzo*, in *Machiavelli: The History of Florence and Other Selections*, ed. Myron P. Gilmore, trans. Judith A. Rawson (New York: Twayne, 1970), 20.

24. Aurelio Lippo Brandolini, *Republics and Kingdoms Compared*, ed. and trans. James Hankins (Cambridge, MA: Harvard University Press, 2009), 41.

25. Machiavelli, *Discourses*, 215 (3.41).

26. Maurizio Viroli, *Niccolo's Smile: A Biography of Machiavelli*, trans. Antony Shugaar (New York: Hill and Wang, 2000), 155–56; Robert M. Adams, "The Rise, Proliferation, and Degradation of Machiavellism: An Outline," in *The Prince* (trans. Adams), 236–47; and Reginald Pole, *Apology to Charles V*, quoted in Sydney Anglo, *Machiavelli: The First Century* (Oxford: Oxford University Press, 2005), 17.

27. Jerónimo Osório, *On Civil and Christian Nobility*, quoted in Anglo, *Machiavelli*, 146; and Robert Bireley, *The Counter-Reformation Prince* (Chapel Hill: University of North Carolina Press, 1990), 14–16.

28. Victoria Kahn, "Machiavelli's Afterlife and Reputation to the Eighteenth Century," in *The Cambridge Companion to Machiavelli*, ed. John J. Najemy (Cambridge: Cambridge University Press, 2010), 245–46.

29. William Shakespeare, *Henry VI, Part 3*, 3.2.191–94.

30. Felix Raab, *The English Face of Machiavelli* (London: Routledge & Kegan Paul, 1964), 34, 52–53, 118–23, 168, 259–60; see also Kahn, "Machiavelli's Afterlife," 239–55.

31. J.G.A. Pocock, "Machiavelli, Harrington and English Political Ideologies in the Eighteenth Century," *William and Mary Quarterly*, 3rd ser. 22 (1965), 549–83; and Paul A. Rahe, ed., *Machiavelli's Liberal Republican Legacy* (Cambridge: Cambridge University Press, 2006), xix–xxvii.

32. On Machiavelli and management, see Peter J. Galie and Christopher Bopst, "Machiavelli & Modern Business: Realist Thought in Contemporary Corporate Leadership Manuals," *Journal of Business Ethics* 65 (2006): 235–50.

33. Quentin Skinner, *The Foundations of Modern Political Thought*, vol. 1: *The Renaissance* (Cambridge: Cambridge University Press, 1978), 117.

34. Adams, historical introduction to *The Prince* (ed. Adams), vii.

35. Sylvia Poggioli, "At 500, Machiavelli's 'Prince' Still Inspires Love and Fear," National Public Radio, May 27, 2013, http://www.npr.org/sections/parallels/2013 /05/27/185746692.

36. Machiavelli, *The Prince* (trans. Adams), 42 (chap. 14).

37. Allan H. Gilbert, *Machiavelli's Prince and Its Forerunners* (Durham, NC: Duke University Press, 1938), 3–15.

38. Gerald of Wales quoted in Lester Kruger Born, "The Perfect Prince: A Study in Thirteenth- and Fourteenth-Century Ideals," *Speculum* 3, no. 4 (1928): 478; Christine de Pizan, *The Book of the Body Politic*, ed. and trans. Kate Langdon Forhan (Cambridge: Cambridge University Press, 1994), 14; and Walter of Milemete, *On the Nobility, Wisdom, and Prudence of Kings*, ed. and trans. Cary J. Nederman, in *Political Thought in Early Fourteenth-Century England*, ed. Cary J. Nederman (Tempe: Arizona Center for Medieval and Renaissance Studies in collaboration with Brepols, 2002), 30.

39. Steven Pinker, *The Better Angels of Our Nature* (New York: Viking, 2011), 130.

40. Gilbert, *Machiavelli's Prince*, 234.

41. Maurizio Viroli, *Machiavelli* (Oxford: Oxford University Press, 1998), 42.

42. Viroli, 42.

43. Viroli, 49.

44. Maurizio Viroli, *From Politics to Reason of State* (Cambridge: Cambridge University Press, 1992), 132–40, 146–47.

45. George L. Mosse, "Puritanism and Reason of State in Old and New England," *William and Mary Quarterly*, 3rd ser., 9, no. 1 (1952): 68.

46. Bireley, *Counter-Reformation Prince*, 45–49. Biographical information from Italian scholars is summarized in Stephen Eastwood Bobroff, "The Earthly Structures of Divine Ideas: Influences on the Political Economy of Giovanni Botero" (master's thesis, University of Saskatchewan, 2003), http://library.usask.ca /theses/available/etd-08082005-135926/unrestricted/copyrightthesis.pdf.

47. Giovanni Botero, *The Reason of State*, trans. P. J. Waley and D. P. Waley (London: Routledge & Kegan Paul, 1956), xiii.

48. Botero, 3.

49. Botero, 7–8.

50. Botero, 13–15.

51. Botero, 15–22, 31–32.

52. Viroli, *Machiavelli*, 53.

53. Botero, *Reason of State*, 34–35.

54. Giovanni Botero, *The Reason of State, Supplement on The Reputation of the Prince*, trans. and ed. George Albert Moore, in *Practical Politics*, ed. George Albert Moore (Washington, DC: Country Dollar, 1949), 232–33.

55. Botero, *Reason of State*, 26.

56. Machiavelli, *The Prince* (trans. Wootton), 24–25 (chap. 7).

57. Botero, *Reason of State*, 26.

58. Botero, 112–13.

59. Botero, 55–58, 113–14.

60. This line of analysis is elaborated by George L. Mosse, *The Holy Pretense: A Study in Christianity and Reason of State from William Perkins to John Winthrop* (Oxford: Basil Blackwell, 1957), 33–43, 148, 153–54.

61. Botero, *Reason of State*, 63, 65, 66, 67.

62. Botero, 66, 67.

63. Botero, 67, 100, 108, 110.

64. Harro Höpfl, *Jesuit Political Thought* (Cambridge: Cambridge University Press, 2004), 94.

65. Botero, *Reason of State*, 221.

66. Bireley, *Counter-Reformation Prince*, 45, 49–50.

67. Donald W. Bleznick, "Spanish Reaction to Machiavelli in the Sixteenth and Seventeenth Centuries," *Journal of the History of Ideas* 19, no. 4 (1958): 542–50; H. Höpfl, "Orthodoxy and Reason of State," *History of Political Thought* 23, no. 2 (2002): 211–37; Mosse, "Puritanism and Reason of State," 67–80; and William F. Church, *Richelieu and Reason of State* (Princeton, NJ: Princeton University Press, 1972), 505–7.

68. Armand-Jean du Plessis duc de Richelieu, *The Political Testament of Cardinal Richelieu*, trans. Henry Bertram Hill (Madison: University of Wisconsin Press, 1961), 5, 11.

69. Richelieu, 45, 73, 78, 84.

70. Richelieu, 80, 85, 86, 87, 89, 90, 91.

71. Richelieu, 118.

72. Richelieu, 14, 15.

73. Richelieu, 31.

74. Richelieu, 75.

75. David Hackett Fischer, *Champlain's Dream* (New York: Simon & Schuster, 2008), 391.

76. Jean-Vincent Blanchard, *Éminence: Cardinal Richelieu and the Rise of France* (New York: Walker, 2011), 227.

77. Joseph Bergin, *Cardinal Richelieu and the Pursuit of Wealth* (New Haven, CT: Yale University Press, 1985), 243–49, 253.

78. Fischer, *Champlain's Dream*, 388.

79. Fischer, 404.

80. Fischer, 404.

81. Giovanni Botero, *The Greatness of Cities*, trans. Robert Peterson, in *Reason of State*, 247.

82. Andrew Fitzmaurice, "The Commercial Ideology of Colonization in Jacobean England: Robert Johnson, Giovanni Botero, and the Pursuit of Greatness," *William and Mary Quarterly*, 3rd ser., 64, no. 4 (2007): 791–820.

83. Robert Johnson, *Nova Britannia* (London, 1609), 14, in Virtual Jamestown, accessed August 16, 2012, http://etext.lib.virginia.edu/etcbin/jamestown-browse ?id=J1051.

Chapter 9: Puritan Mirrors

Epigraph: Cotton Mather, *The Way to Prosperity*, preached May 23, 1689, in *The Wall and the Garden, Selected Massachusetts Election Sermons 1670–1775*, ed. A. W. Plumstead (Minneapolis: University of Minnesota Press, 1968), 133–34, 138.

1. John Winthrop, *A Model of Christian Charity*, in *The American Puritans*, ed. Perry Miller (New York: Columbia University Press, 1956), 79–80, 83.

2. Joseph Mead quoted in Kenneth Shipps, "The 'Political Puritan,'" *Church History* 45, no. 2 (1976): 196.

3. Thomas Shepard, *The Sincere Convert*, in Thomas Shepard, *Works*, vol. 1 (Boston: Doctrinal Tract and Book Society, 1853), 28, Internet Archive, Princeton Theological Seminary, http://www.archive.org/details/worksofthomasshe01shep.

4. Shepard, 26.

5. Shepard, 29. See also Edmund S. Morgan, *The Puritan Dilemma, The Story of John Winthrop* (Boston: Little, Brown, 1958), 8–14.

6. Quoted in Edmund S. Morgan, *Visible Saints: The History of a Puritan Idea* (Ithaca, NY: Cornell University Press, 1965), 7, 8.

7. Morgan, 9.

8. Henry Smith, *The Trumpet of the Soul Sounding to Judgment*, in Everett H. Emerson, *English Puritanism from John Hooper to John Milton* (Durham, NC: Duke University Press, 1968), 129.

9. Smith, 130.

10. William Perkins, *A Treatise of the Vocations or Callings of Men*, in *Puritan Political Ideas, 1558–1794*, ed. Edmund S. Morgan (Indianapolis: Bobbs-Merrill, 1965), 39, 51.

11. Perkins, 55.

12. T. H. Breen, *The Character of the Good Ruler* (New Haven, CT: Yale University Press, 1970), 3, 23, 24.

13. William Perkins, *On Christian Equity*, in *Puritan Political Ideas, 1558–1794*, ed. Edmund S. Morgan (Indianapolis: Bobbs-Merrill, 1965), 60, 64.

14. George L. Mosse, "The Assimilation of Machiavelli in English Thought: The Casuistry of William Perkins and William Ames," *Huntington Library Quarterly* 17, no. 4 (1954): 318.

15. Darrett B. Rutman, *Winthrop's Boston* (New York: Norton, 1972), 5.

16. "The Charter of the Colony of Massachusetts Bay, 1628," in *The Charters and General Laws of the Colony and Province of Massachusetts Bay*, pub. by the General Court (Boston: Wait, 1814), 9.

17. George Lee Haskins, *Law and Authority in Early Massachusetts* (Hamden, CT: Archon, 1968), 9.

18. Nathaniel Hawthorne, *The Scarlet Letter* (London: David Bogue, 1851), 280.

19. A. W. Plumstead, ed., *The Wall and the Garden, Selected Massachusetts Election Sermons 1670–1775* (Minneapolis: University of Minnesota Press, 1968), 24; Harry S. Stout, *The New England Soul* (New York: Oxford University Press, 1986), 29–30; and Breen, *Character of the Good Ruler*, 49–51.

20. Plumstead, *Wall and the Garden*, 24. See also Stout, *New England Soul*, 70-74.

21. Lindsay Swift, *The Massachusetts Election Sermons: An Essay in Descriptive Bibliography* (Cambridge, MA: John Wilson, 1897), 8.

22. Thomas Shepard, *Election Sermon*, preached May 3, 1638, *The New-England Historical and Genealogical Register and Antiquarian Journal* 24, no. 4 (1870): 363.

23. Shepard, 361.

24. Shepard, 361–66.

25. Shepard, 363.

26. Thomas Shepard, *A Wholesome Caveat for a Time of Liberty*, in Thomas Shepard, *Works*, vol. 3 (Boston: Doctrinal Tract and Book Society, 1853), 285–360.

27. John Higginson, *The Cause of God and His People in New-England*, preached May 27, 1663, in *Election Day Sermons: Massachusetts*, ed. Sacvan Bercovitch (New York: AMS Press, 1984); William Stoughton, *New-England's True Interest; Not to Lie*, preached April 29, 1668, in Bercovitch, *Election Day Sermons*; Samuel Danforth, *A Brief Recognition of New-England's Errand into the Wilderness*, preached May 11, 1670, in Plumstead, *Wall and the Garden*, 53–77; Urian Oakes, *New-England Pleaded With*, preached May 7, 1673, in Bercovitch, *Election Day Sermons*; Samuel Willard, *The Only Sure Way to Prevent Threatened Calamity*, preached May 24, 1682, in Plumstead, *Wall and the Garden*, 85–105; William Adams, *God's Eye on the Contrite*, preached May 27, 1685, in Bercovitch, *Election Day Sermons*; Cotton Mather, *Things for a Distressed People to Think Upon*, preached May 27, 1696, in Cotton Mather, *Days of Humiliation*, ed. George Harrison Orians (Gainesville, FL: Scholars Facsimiles & Reprints, 1970), 1–76; and Nicholas Noyes, *Duty and Interest, To Be an Habitation of Justice, and Mountain of Holiness*, preached May 25, 1698, in Bercovitch, *Election Day Sermons*.

28. Higginson, *Cause of God and His People*, 10, 11, 14.

29. Stoughton, *New-England's True Interest*, 20.

30. Cotton Mather, *Things for a Distressed People*, 15, 16.

31. Mather, 9, 11, 16, 17.

32. Mather, 10.

33. Mather, 42.

34. Mather, 15, 62, 67.

35. Swift, *Massachusetts Election Sermons*, 20.

36. Cotton Mather, *Parentator*, in *Two Mather Biographies*, ed. William J. Scheick (Bethlehem, PA: Lehigh University Press, 1989), 105.

37. Increase Mather, *The Great Blessing of Primitive Counsellours*, preached May 31, 1693, in Early English Books Online, https://www.proquest.com/docview/2248550297, 21.

38. Mather, 22.

39. Mather, 15, 20.

40. Mather, 10, 12, 15.

41. Breen, *Character of the Good Ruler*, 184.

42. Alan J. Silva, "Increase Mather's 1693 Election Sermon: Rhetorical Innovation and the Reimagination of Puritan Authority," *Early American Literature* 34

(1999): 48–77; and Philip F. Gura, "Cotton Mather's *Life of Phips*: 'A Vice with the Vizard of Vertue upon It,'" *New England Quarterly* 50 (1977): 440–57.

43. Azariah Mather, *Good Rulers, A Choice Blessing*, preached May 12, 1725, in *Early American Imprints, Series I: Evans, 1639–1800* (doc. 2662), https://www.readex.com/products/early-american-imprints-series-i-evans-1639-1800.

44. Mather, 23–34.

45. Mather, 17, 18, 26.

46. Mather, 33, 34, 39.

47. Breen, *Character of the Good Ruler*, xi, 104.

48. Winthrop, *Model of Christian Charity*, 81–83.

49. Morgan, *Puritan Dilemma*, 50.

50. Bernard Bailyn, *The Barbarous Years* (New York: Knopf, 2012), 373.

51. Rutman, *Winthrop's Boston*, 22, 23.

52. Breen, *Character of the Good Ruler*, 51; and Rutman, *Winthrop's Boston*, 68.

53. Bailyn, *Barbarous Years*, 369; and Robert Emmet Wall Jr., *Massachusetts Bay: The Crucial Decade, 1640–1650* (New Haven, CT: Yale University Press, 1972), 41.

54. John Winthrop, *Defense of the Negative Vote*, in *Winthrop Papers* (Boston: Massachusetts Historical Society, 1944), 4:383.

55. John Winthrop, *Discourse on Arbitrary Government*, in *Winthrop Papers* (Boston: Massachusetts Historical Society, 1944), 4:476.

56. John Winthrop, *Speech to the General Court*, in *The American Puritans*, ed. Perry Miller (New York: Columbia University Press, 1956), 91, 93.

57. Breen, *Character of the Good Ruler*, 76.

58. Wall, *Massachusetts Bay*, 50–56.

59. Francis J. Bremer, *John Winthrop: America's Forgotten Founding Father* (New York: Oxford University Press, 2003), 353.

60. Bremer, 354.

61. Wall, *Massachusetts Bay*, 57

62. Bailyn, *Barbarous Years*, 387.

63. Edwin S. Gaustad, *Roger Williams* (New York: Oxford University Press, 2005), 9.

64. Gaustad, 10; also quoted in Daniel K. Richter, *Before the Revolution* (Cambridge, MA: Belknap / Harvard University Press, 2011), 191.

65. Gaustad, *Roger Williams*, 9.

66. Gaustad, 13.

67. "Deed of Roger Williams" (1638) in Records of the Colony of Rhode Island (Providence: Crawford Greene, 1856), 1:22.

68. Richter, *Before the Revolution*, 197.

69. Gaustad, *Roger Williams*, 122.

70. Roger Williams to Major John Mason and Governor Thomas Prence, June 22, 1670, in *The Correspondence of Roger Williams*, ed. Glenn W. LaFantasie (Providence, RI: Brown University Press / University Press of New England, 1988), 2:617.

71. Roger Williams, *The Examiner Defended in a Fair and Sober Answer* in *On Religious Liberty*, ed. James Calvin Davis (Cambridge, MA: Belknap / Harvard University Press, 2008), 240.

72. Williams, 237–38.

73. James Calvin Davis, *The Moral Theology of Roger Williams* (Louisville, KY: Westminster John Knox Press, 2004), xi, 43–45; and Edmund S. Morgan, *Roger Williams: The Church and the State* (New York: Harcourt Brace & World, 1967), 115–129.

74. Morgan, *Roger Williams*, 119.

75. Roger Williams, *The Bloody Tenent Yet More Bloody* in *On Religious Liberty*, ed. James Calvin Davis (Cambridge, MA: Belknap / Harvard University Press, 2008), 216; see also 199, 220.

76. Cotton Mather, *The Serviceable Man*, preached May 28, 1690, in *Puritan Political Ideas, 1558–1794*, ed. Edmund S. Morgan (Indianapolis: Bobbs-Merrill, 1965), 241, 243; and Cotton Mather, *Magnalia Christi Americana* (Hartford, CT: Silas Andrus, 1820), 1:109.

77. Mather, *Magnalia Christi Americana*, 2:425.

78. Mather, 2:430.

79. Mather, 1:115, 187.

80. Jill Lepore, *The Name of War: King Philip's War and the Origins of American Identity* (New York: Vintage, 1999), 44.

81. Cotton Mather, *Magnalia Christi Americana*, 1:504–5.

82. Cotton Mather, *Souldiers Counselled and Comforted*, preached September 1, 1689, in *Early American Imprints*, Series I: *Evans, 1639–1800* (doc. 488), https://www.readex.com/products/early-american-imprints-series-i-evans-1639-1800.

83. Owen Stanwood, *The Empire Reformed* (Philadelphia: University of Pennsylvania Press, 2011), 159.

84. Mather, *Magnalia Christi Americana*, 1:159; see also Jenny Hale Pulsipher, "'Dark Cloud Rising from the East': Indian Sovereignty and the Coming of King William's War in New England," *New England Quarterly* 80, no. 4 (December 2007): 588–613; and Emerson W. Baker and John G. Reid, *The New England Knight: Sir William Phips, 1651–1695* (Toronto: University of Toronto Press, 1998), xii–xiii.

85. Joseph Belcher, *The Singular Happiness of Such Heads or Rulers, as Are Able to Choose Out Their People's Way, and Will Also Endeavor Their People's Comfort*, preached May 28, 1701, in *Dedham Pulpit: Sermons by the Pastors of the First Church in Dedham* (Boston: Perkins & Marvin, 1840) [Sabin Americana, 1500–1926], 132.

86. Ralph Frasca, "Benjamin Franklin's Printing Network and the Stamp Act," *Pennsylvania History* 71 (2004): 407.

87. Arthur M. Schlesinger, "The Colonial Newspapers and the Stamp Act," *New England Quarterly* 8 (1935): 70.

88. Frasca, "Benjamin Franklin's Printing Network," 408.

89. Schlesinger, "The Colonial Newspapers," 69.

90. Stout, *New England Soul*, 266, 268.

91. William Hubbard, *The Happiness of a People in the Wisdome of Their Rulers*, preached May 3, 1676, in Bercovitch, *Election Day Sermons*, 9, 10.

92. Stout, *New England Soul*, 266, 267.

93. Samuel Cooke, sermon preached May 30, 1770, in Plumstead, *Wall and the Garden*, 328–29, 331, 344.

94. Cooke, 331, 333.

95. Cooke, 329, 334.

96. James Campbell, *Recovering Benjamin Franklin* (Chicago: Open Court, 1999), 180.

97. David Armitage, "A Patriot for Whom? The Afterlives of Bolingbroke's Patriot King," *Journal of British Studies* 36 (1997): 401.

98. H. T. Dickinson, *Bolingbroke* (London: Constable, 1970), 246.

99. Bolingbroke, *The Idea of a Patriot King* in *Bolingbroke: Political Writings*, ed. David Armitage (Cambridge: Cambridge University Press, 1997), 218–19, 220.

100. Bolingbroke, 251, 257–58.

101. Bolingbroke, 251, 294.

102. Isaac Kramnick, *Bolingbroke and His Circle* (Ithaca, NY: Cornell University Press, 1968), 169.

103. Armitage, "Patriot for Whom," 414.

104. Kramnick, *Bolingbroke and His Circle*, 1.

105. Kramnick, 168–69.

106. Kramnick, 262.

107. Kramnick, 169.

108. William D. Liddle, "A Patriot King or None: Lord Bolingbroke and the American Renunciation of George III," *Journal of American History* 65 (1979): 965.

109. Liddle, 951.

110. Liddle, 968.

111. Thomas Paine, *Common Sense*, January 1776, http://gutenberg.org/files/147/147-h/147-h.htm; and Edward Larkin, introduction to *Common Sense* by Thomas Paine (Peterborough, ON, Canada: Broadview, 2004), 7.

112. George Washington to Lieutenant Colonel Joseph Reed, January 31, 1776, Founders Online, National Archives, http://founders.archives.gov/documents/Washington/03-03-02-0163.

113. Andrew Jackson O'Shaughnessy, *The Men Who Lost America* (New Haven, CT: Yale University Press, 2013), 17; and Eric Nelson, *The Royalist Revolution* (Cambridge, MA: Belknap / Harvard University Press, 2014), 1, 192.

Chapter 10: Madison Versus Mirrors for Princes

Epigraph: George Washington, "First Inaugural Address: Final Version, 30 April 1789," Founders Online, National Archives, http://founders.archives.gov/documents/Washington/05-02-02-0130-0003.

1. Washington's inauguration is described by Douglas Southall Freeman, *George Washington: A Biography*, vol. 6 (New York: Scribner's, 1954), 185–98; and James Thomas Flexner, *George Washington and the New Nation* (Boston: Little, Brown, 1969), 182–91. The title "father of his country" was already in common use by 1789; see Richard Lim, "Father of His Country," *The Digital Encyclopedia of George Washington*, http://www.mountvernon.org/digital-encyclopedia/ article/father-of -his-country/.

2. Eliza Susan Morton Quincy, *Memoir of the Life of Eliza S. M. Quincy* (Boston: John Wilson, 1861), 51.

3. Washington's popularity and public image are discussed by Marcus Cunliffe, *George Washington: Man and Monument*, rev. ed. (New York: Mentor, 1982), 13–26; and Barry Schwartz, *George Washington: The Making of an American Symbol* (Ithaca, NY: Cornell University Press, 1987), 41. Washington Irving's attendance was reported by Rufus Wilmot Griswold in *The Republican Court, or, American Society in the Days of Washington* (New York: Appleton, 1855), 142.

4. Dorothy Twohig, ed., *The Papers of George Washington*, Presidential Series, vol. 2 (Charlottesville: University Press of Virginia, 1987), 158–73.

5. The unused first draft of Washington's inaugural address was later cut up for souvenirs. The inaugural address Washington actually delivered and additional background are provided by Charles F. Hobson and Robert A. Rutland, eds., *The Papers of James Madison*, vol. 12 (Charlottesville, VA: University Press of Virginia, 1979), 120–24.

6. For Maclay's account, see Kenneth R. Bowling and Helen E. Veit, eds., *The Diary of William Maclay and Other Notes of Senate Debates* (Baltimore: Johns Hopkins University Press, 1988), 13.

7. Hobson and Rutland, *Papers of James Madison*, 12:132–34, 141–42, 166–67.

8. Harold S. Schultz, *James Madison* (New York: Twayne, 1970), 18. See also Ralph Ketcham, *James Madison: A Biography* (Charlottesville: University Press of Virginia, 1990), 551–52.

9. William Lee Miller, *The First Liberty* (New York: Knopf, 1988), 89. Witherspoon's own philosophy was critical of "good of the whole" rhetoric, which featured prominently in mirrors for princes. Such language, he wrote in *Ecclesiastical Characteristics*, enables authorities to pretend that "an illustrious and noble end sanctifies the means of attaining it" and to condemn as selfish anyone who would question their judgment. Madison attended Witherspoon's lectures on moral philosophy at the College of New Jersey and no doubt heard his views on the elitist and intolerant potential of so-called common goals. See Thomas Miller, introduction to *The Selected Writings of John Witherspoon* (Carbondale: Southern Illinois University Press, 1990), 10–11.

10. Alan Taylor, *American Colonies* (New York: Viking, 2001), 271; and Ketcham, *James Madison*, 27.

11. James Madison to William Bradford, January 24, 1774, Founders Online, National Archives, http://founders.archives.gov/documents/Madison/01-01 -02-0029.

12. James Madison to William Bradford, April 1, 1774, Founders Online, National Archives, http://founders.archives.gov/documents/Madison/01-01 -02-0031.

13. Madison to Bradford.

14. Madison to Bradford, January 24, 1774.

15. Jack N. Rakove, *James Madison and the Creation of the American Republic*, 3rd ed. (New York: Longman, 2007), 15.

16. Irving Brant, *James Madison, The Virginia Revolutionist* (Indianapolis: Bobbs-Merrill, 1941), 247.

17. Brant, *Virginia Revolutionist*, 317; see also George Washington to Henry Laurens, December 23, 1777, Founders Online, National Archives, http://founders .archives.gov/documents/Washington/03-12-02-0628.

18. Rakove, *James Madison*, 18.

19. Brant, *Virginia Revolutionist*, 274.

20. Rhys Isaac, *The Transformation of Virginia, 1740–1790* (New York: Norton, 1988), 286.

21. Irving Brant, *James Madison, The Nationalist, 1780–1787* (Indianapolis: Bobbs-Merrill, 1948), 343.

22. Rakove, *James Madison*, 37.

23. Brant, *The Nationalist*, 343–44.

24. Brant, 343–45.

25. James Madison, "Memorial and Remonstrance Against Religious Assessments," ca. June 20, 1785, Founders Online, National Archives, http://founders .archives.gov/documents/Madison/01-08-02-0163.

26. Madison; see also Isaac, *The Transformation of Virginia*, 287–93.

27. Frederick W. Marks III, *Independence on Trial* (Baton Rouge: Louisiana State University Press, 1973), 83. See also Eli Merritt, "Sectional Conflict and Secret Compromise: the Mississippi River Question and the Unites States Constitution," *American Journal of Legal History* 35 (April 1991): 117–71; Carol Berkin, *A Brilliant Solution* (New York: Harcourt, 2002), 13–20.

28. Marks, *Independence on Trial*, 64.

29. Marion L. Starkey, *A Little Rebellion* (New York: Knopf, 1955), 14.

30. Starkey, 15.

31. Richard B. Morris, *The Forging of the Union, 1781–1789* (New York: Harper & Row, 1987), 258–66.

32. George Washington to Henry Knox, December 26, 1786, Founders Online, National Archives, http://founders.archives.gov/documents/Washington/04-04 -02-0409.

33. Brant, *The Nationalist*, 383.

34. Rakove, *James Madison*, 46.

35. James Madison, *Federalist* No. 40, January 18, 1788, Founders Online, National Archives, http://founders.archives.gov/documents/Madison/01-10-02-0236.

36. William Lee Miller, *The Business of May Next* (Charlottesville: University Press of Virginia, 1992), 14–15, 21–25.

37. James Madison, "Vices of the Political System of the United States," April 1787, Founders Online, National Archives, http://founders.archives.gov /documents/Madison/01-09-02-0187.

38. Lance Banning, *The Sacred Fire of Liberty* (Ithaca, NY: Cornell University Press, 1995), 124. See also James Madison, "Notes on Ancient and Modern Confederacies," April–June 1786, Founders Online, National Archives, http:// founders.archives.gov/documents/Madison/01-09-02-0001.

39. Madison, "Vices of the Political System."

40. James Madison to George Washington, April 16, 1787, Founders Online, National Archives, http://founders.archives.gov/documents/Washington/04-05-02 -0139. See also James Madison to Thomas Jefferson, October 24, 1787, Founders Online, National Archives, http://founders.archives.gov/documents/Jefferson/01 -12-02-0274; and Alan Gibson, "Madison's 'Great Desideratum': Impartial Admin- istration and the Extended Republic," *American Political Thought* 1 (Fall 2012): 181–207.

41. Madison to Jefferson, October 24, 1787.

42. Madison to Jefferson.

43. Madison to Washington, April 16, 1787; "The Virginia Plan," May 29, 1787, Founders Online, http://founders.archives.gov/documents/Madison/01-10 -02-0005; and Richard Beeman, *Plain, Honest Men* (New York: Random House, 2009), 54.

44. Rakove, *James Madison*, 47.

45. James Madison, *Notes of Debates in the Federal Convention* (New York: Norton, 1987), 221.

46. Beeman, *Plain, Honest Men*, 162.

47. Michael J. Klarman, *The Framers' Coup* (Oxford: Oxford University Press, 2016), 266.

48. Beeman, *Plain, Honest Men*, 153, 155.

49. Beeman, 125. Hamilton's leanings toward a philosopher-king were described long ago by Cecelia Kenton, "Alexander Hamilton: Rousseau of the Right," *Political Science Quarterly* 73 (June 1958): 175. Hamilton's monarchist speech to the Philadelphia Convention on June 18, 1787, speaks for itself; see Madison, *Notes of Debates in the Federal Convention*, 129–39.

50. Madison, *Notes of Debates in the Federal Convention*, 332–33.

51. Madison to Jefferson, October 24, 1787.

52. George Thomas, *The Founders and the Idea of a National University* (New York: Cambridge University Press, 2015), 63.

53. Max Farrand, "If James Madison Had Had a Sense of Humor," *Pennsylvania Magazine of History and Biography* 62 (April 1938): 136. See also Berkin, *Brilliant Solution*, 49.

54. Beeman, *Plain, Honest Men*, 370.

55. "Centinel," No. 1, October 5, 1787, in *The Anti-Federalist Papers and the Constitutional Convention Debates*, ed. Ralph Ketcham (New York: Mentor, 1986), 229, 231, 234, 236.

56. Pauline Maier, *Ratification* (New York, Simon & Schuster, 2010), 120, 122–23.

57. James Madison, *Federalist* No. 14, November 30, 1787, Founders Online, National Archives, http://founders.archives.gov/documents/Madison/01-10-02-0185.

58. David E. Narrett, "A Zest for Liberty: The Antifederalist Case against the Constitution in New York," *New York History* 69 (July 1988): 293.

59. "Cato," Letter III, October 25, 1787, in *The Debate on the Constitution*, vol. 1, ed. Bernard Bailyn (New York: Library of America, 1993), 214–15.

60. James Madison, *Federalist* No. 10, November 22, 1787, Founders Online, National Archives, http://founders.archives.gov/documents/Madison/01-10-02 -0178.

61. Madison, *Federalist* No. 10.

62. Madison.

63. Madison to Jefferson, October 24, 1787. This contemporaneous letter elaborates on Madison's analysis in *Federalist* No. 10.

64. Madison to Jefferson, October 24, 1787.

65. Madison to Jefferson.

66. James Madison, *Federalist* No. 51, February 6, 1788, Founders Online, National Archives, http://founders.archives.gov/documents/Hamilton/01-04 -02-0199; see also Samuel Fleischacker, "Adam Smith's Reception among the American Founders, 1776–1790," *William and Mary Quarterly* 59 (October, 2002): 897–924. On the dark side of group goal-seeking, see Michael Keeley, "The Trouble with Transformational Leadership: Toward a Federalist Ethic for Organizations," *Business Ethics Quarterly* 5 (1995): 67–96; and Lisa D. Ordóñez, Maurice E. Schweitzer, Adam D. Galinsky, and Max H. Bazerman, "Goals Gone Wild: The Systematic Side Effects of Overprescribing Goal Setting," *Academy of Management Perspectives* 23 (February 2009): 6–16.

67. Madison, *Federalist* No. 51.

68. Madison; see also Banning, *Sacred Fire of Liberty*, 296–97.

69. George Mason, "Objections to the Constitution," October 1787, in *The Debate on the Constitution*, vol. 1, ed. Bernard Bailyn (New York: Library of America, 1993), 346, 349.

70. Maier, *Ratification*, 216.

71. Maier, 226. See also Beeman, *Plain, Honest Men*, 372.

72. Henry Mayer, *A Son of Thunder* (New York: Grove, 1991), 85.

73. Bernard Bailyn, ed., *The Debate on the Constitution*, vol. 2 (New York: Library of America, 1993), 1140.

74. John P. Kaminski and Gaspare J. Saladino, eds., *The Documentary History of the Ratification of the Constitution* (Madison: State Historical Society of Wisconsin, 1990), 9:929–31.

75. Maier, *Ratification*, 267.

76. Kaminski and Saladino, *Documentary History of the Ratification*, 9:989, 995; 10:1499.

77. Kaminski and Saladino, 9:914.

78. Kaminski and Saladino, 9:960–61, 962–63, 1046, 1055–56, 1057, 1059, 1060, 1063.

79. Kaminski and Saladino, 9:1031, 1033, 1145; 10:1502. See also Irving Brant, *James Madison: Father of the Constitution, 1787–1800* (Indianapolis: Bobbs-Merrill, 1950), 212–19.

80. Kaminski and Saladino, 9:959. See also 9:991, 1038; 10:1499, 1501–2.

81. Beeman, *Plain, Honest Men*, 400. See also James Madison to Thomas Jefferson, October 17, 1788, Founders Online, National Archives, http://founders .archives.gov/documents/Jefferson/01-14-02-0018; and Kaminski and Saladino, *Documentary History of the Ratification*, 10:1500, 1540–41. It turned out that Virginia did not act in time to cast the deciding ninth vote for ratification. As the delegates left Richmond for home, they learned that New Hampshire had ratified the Constitution on June 21, creating the new Union. Still, "although New Hampshire technically made it official, Virginia made it real," notes historian Lorri Glover in *The Fate of the Revolution* (Baltimore: Johns Hopkins University Press, 2016), 150.

82. Brant, *Father of the Constitution*, 241–42.

83. Ketcham, *James Madison*, 278.

84. John C. Miller, *The Federalist Era* (New York: Harper & Row, 1960), 109. See also Coleen A. Sheehan, *James Madison and the Spirit of Republican Self-Government* (Cambridge: Cambridge University Press, 2009), 6–11, 17.

85. Madison to Jefferson, October 24, 1787.

86. Madison, *Federalist* No. 10.

87. James Madison, speech to U.S. House of Representatives, *The Congressional Register*, June 8, 1789, in *Creating the Bill of Rights: The Documentary Record from the First Federal Congress*, ed. Helen E. Veit, Kenneth R. Bowling, and Charlene Bangs Bickford (Baltimore: Johns Hopkins University Press, 1991), 83.

88. Carol Berkin, *The Bill of Rights* (New York: Simon & Schuster, 2015), 147.

89. Berkin, 56; Jack N. Rakove, "James Madison and the Bill of Rights: A Broader Context," *Presidential Studies Quarterly* 22 (Fall 1992): 668; and Michael P. Zuckert, Madison's Consistency on the Bill of Rights," *National Affairs*, No. 51 (Spring 2022): 158–59.

90. *The Congressional Register*, June 8, 1789; and August 17, 1789, in *Creating the Bill of Rights*, 13, 81, 83, 85, 188–89. "Freedom of speech" was added to Madison's original amendment in the House.

91. James Madison, "Detached Memoranda: Monopolies, Perpetuities, Corporations, Ecclesiastical Endowments," ca. January 31, 1820, Founders Online, National Archives, http://founders.archives.gov/documents/Madison/04-01-02-0549.

92. Madison.

93. For more historical background, see Bray Hammond, *Banks and Politics in America from the Revolution to the Civil War* (Princeton, NJ: Princeton University Press, 1957), 145, 453; and Tamara Plakins Thornton, "'A Great Machine' or a 'Beast of Prey': A Boston Corporation and Its Rural Debtors in an Age of Capitalist Transformation," *Journal of the Early Republic* 27 (Winter 2007): 567–97.

94. Madison, "Detached Memoranda."

95. Madison.

96. Madison, *Federalist* No. 51.

97. Niccolò Machiavelli, *The Prince*, in *Machiavelli: Selected Political Writings*, ed. and trans. David Wootton (Indianapolis: Hackett, 1994), 69, 70 (chap. 21).

98. John Rawls's famous principles of justice are (1) "Each person has an equal right to a fully adequate scheme of equal basic rights and liberties, which scheme is compatible with a similar scheme for all"; and (2) "Social and economic inequalities are to satisfy two conditions; first, they must be attached to offices and positions open to all under conditions of fair equality of opportunity; and second, they must be to the greatest benefit of the least advantaged members of society." John Rawls, "Justice as Fairness: Political Not Metaphysical," *Philosophy & Public Affairs* 14 (Summer 1985): 227.

99. Alexander Hamilton, "Report on Public Credit," January 9, 1790, in *Alexander Hamilton: Writings*, ed., Joanne B. Freeman (New York: Library of America, 2001), 532, 534, 544, 549–50; see also Miller, *Federalist Era*, 38–39.

100. James Madison to Alexander Hamilton, November 19, 1789, Founders Online, National Archives, http://founders.archives.gov/documents/Hamilton /01-05-02-0325.

101. James Madison, "Discrimination between Present and Original Holders of the Public Debt," February 18, 1790, Founders Online, National Archives, http:// founders.archives.gov/documents/Madison/01-13-02-0040.

102. James Madison to Thomas Jefferson, January 24, 1790, Founders Online, National Archives, http://founders.archives.gov/documents/Madison/01-13-02-0005.

103. Madison, "Discrimination between Present and Original Holders."

104. Madison.

105. Madison.

106. James Madison to Edmund Randolph, July 26, 1785, Founders Online, National Archives, http://founders.archives.gov/documents/Madison/01-08 -02-0175.

107. Elizabeth Dowling Taylor, *A Slave in the White House* (New York: Palgrave Macmillan, 2012), 6.

108. Taylor, 23.

109. James Madison, "Instructions for the Montpelier Overseer and Laborers," [ca. 8] November 1790, Founders Online, National Archives, http://founders .archives.gov/documents/Madison/01-13-02-0222.

110. Taylor, *Slave in the White House*, 23.

111. Ketcham, *James Madison*, 374.

112. Madison, *Notes of Debates in the Federal Convention*, 77.

113. Drew R. McCoy, *Last of the Fathers: James Madison and the Republican Legacy* (Cambridge: Cambridge University Press, 1989), 260–61.

114. Edward Coles to James Madison, January 8, 1832, Founders Online, National Archives, http://founders.archives.gov/documents/Madison/99-02 -02-2506.

115. Coles to Madison.

116. James Madison, "Original Will [April 15, 1835] and Codicil of April 19, 1835," Founders Online, National Archives, http://founders.archives.gov /documents/ Madison/99-02-02-3114; Holly C. Shulman, "Madison v. Madison: Dolley Payne Madison and Her Inheritance of the Montpelier Estate, 1836–38," *Virginia Magazine of History and Biography* 119 (2011): 354; and Taylor, *Slave in the White House*, 112. The claim that Madison could not afford to free his slaves is repeated, for example, in Noah Feldman, *The Three Lives of James Madison* (New York: Random House, 2017), 621.

117. Jonathan Capehart, "Telling the Full History of a Founding Father's Plantation," conversation with James French, chair of the Montpelier Descendants Committee, *Washington Post*, April 19, 2022.

118. Madison, *Federalist* No. 51.

Chapter 11: Toward Mirrors for Managers

Epigraph: Harry Howells Horton, "The Only Salvation for Man," lecture delivered September 16, 1838 (Manchester: A. Heywood, 1838), 1.

1. Robert Allen Rutland, *James Madison: The Founding Father* (New York: Macmillan, 1987), 247.

2. Robert Owen, "A Discourse on a New System of Society," (first) address delivered in the Hall of Representatives of the United States, February 25, 1825, in *Robert Owen in the United States*, ed. Oakley C. Johnson (New York: Humanities Press, 1970), 25.

3. Owen, 27, 32, 34, 35, 36.

4. Owen, 23, 29.

5. Owen, 32.

6. Robert Owen, "A Discourse on a New System of Society," (second) address delivered in the Hall of Representatives of the United States, March 7, 1825, in *Robert Owen in the United States*, 51.

7. Frank Podmore, *Robert Owen* (London: Hutchinson, 1906), 1:291; see also Arthur Bestor, *Backwoods Utopias*, 2nd ed. (Philadelphia: University of Pennsylvania Press, 1970), 101–10.

8. William Hazlitt, "On People with One Idea," in *Table-Talk* (London: John Warren, 1821), 151.

9. James Madison to Nicholas P. Trist, April 1827, Founders Online, National Archives, https://founders.archives.gov/documents/Madison/04-04-02-0347. See also Drew R. McCoy, *The Last of the Fathers* (Cambridge: Cambridge University Press, 1989), 205–6.

10. William Hazlitt, "A New View of Society," in *Political Essays* (London: William Hone, 1819), 97–98.

11. Robert Owen, *A New View of Society and Other Writings*, ed. Gregory Claeys (London: Penguin, 1991), 10.

12. Owen, 27.

13. Owen, (second) "Discourse on a New System of Society," 53.

14. Owen, (first) "Discourse on a New System of Society," 23, 32.

15. Owen, *New View of Society*, 28–31.

16. Owen, 61, 143–44.

17. Hazlitt, "New View of Society," 98, 103.

18. James Madison to Nicholas P. Trist, April 1827.

19. Robert Owen, "Address in the Hall of New Harmony, April 27, 1825," *New-Harmony Gazette* 1, no. 1 (October 1, 1825).

20. James Madison, *Federalist* No. 10, November 22, 1787, Founders Online, National Archives, http://founders.archives.gov/documents/Madison/01-10-02-0178.

21. Bestor, *Backwoods Utopias*, 115–16.

22. Bestor, 168.

23. Bestor, 162–64; see also Karl John Richard Arndt, "The Indiana Decade of George Rapp's Harmony Society: 1814–1824," *Proceedings of the American Antiquarian Society* 80 (October 1970): 306–9; and Rowland Hill Harvey, *Robert Owen* (Berkeley: University of California Press, 1949), 97–98.

24. Podmore, *Robert Owen*, 1:292.

25. Bestor, *Backwoods Utopias*, 160–196.

26. Bestor, 164.

27. William Owen to Robert Owen, December 16, 1825, New Harmony Working Men's Institute, Branigin Archive, Indiana University Libraries, http://purl.dlib.indiana.edu/iudl/workingmens/branigin/VAA4026-0163.

28. Robert Owen, Address in the Hall of New Harmony, April 27, 1825.

29. Bestor, *Backwoods Utopias*, 160.

30. Bestor, 133–34.

31. "Constitution of the New-Harmony Community of Equality," *New-Harmony Gazette* 1, no. 21, February 15, 1826.

32. Bernhard, Duke of Saxe-Weimar-Eisenach, *Travels through North America, During the Years 1825 and 1826* (Philadelphia: Carey, Lea & Carey, 1828), 2:117.

33. Marie Duclos Fretageot to William Maclure, March 2, 1827, in *Education and Reform at New Harmony*, ed. Arthur E. Bestor, Jr. (Indianapolis: Indiana Historical Society, 1948), 390–91.

34. Carol A. Kolmerten, *Women in Utopia* (Syracuse, NY: Syracuse University Press, 1998), 90, 92–93.

35. Sarah Pears to Benjamin Bakewell, March 4, 1826, in *New Harmony, An Adventure in Happiness: Papers of Thomas and Sarah Pears*, ed. Thomas Clinton Pears Jr. (Indianapolis: Indiana Historical Society, 1933), 69.

36. Robert Owen, "Continuation of Mr. Owen's Lecture, and the Conversation, of Sunday Evening the 20th," *New-Harmony Gazette* 1, no. 49, August 30, 1826.

37. Kolmerten, *Women in Utopia*, 75.

38. Bestor, *Backwoods Utopias*, 176.

39. Kolmerten, *Women in Utopia*, 75, 91, 96–97; and Bestor, *Backwoods Utopias*, 176–77.

40. Owen, *New View of Society*, 16.

41. Bestor, *Backwoods Utopias*, 141.

42. Bestor, 149.

43. Charles Burgess, "The Boatload of Trouble: William Maclure and Robert Owen Revisited," *Indiana Magazine of History* 94 (June 1998): 138–50; and Kolmerten, *Women in Utopia*, 72.

44. Robert Owen, "New-Harmony Sunday Meeting for Instruction in the New-System, August 6, 1826," *New-Harmony Gazette* 1, no. 46 (August 9, 1826).

45. William Maclure to Marie Fretageot, August 21, 1826 (2 letters), in *Education and Reform at New Harmony*, 357, 358–59.

46. Robert Owen, "New-Harmony Sunday Meeting for Instruction in the New-System, August 13, 1826," *New-Harmony Gazette* 1, no. 47 (August 16, 1826).

47. William Maclure to Marie Fretageot, August 29, 1826, August 30, 1826, September 19, 1826, September 25, 1826, *Education and Reform at New Harmony*, 361–63, 365–68, 370. Owen's early education program at New Lanark had a clear business rationale; by enrolling children from one year of age, both parents were available for millwork (increasing the labor supply in rural New Lanark) and Owen could pay each of them less: "In fact wage levels at New Lanark were lower *per capita* than elsewhere, but not per family," according to John Butt, "Robert Owen as a Businessman," in *Robert Owen: Aspects of His Life and Work*, ed. John Butt (New York: Humanities Press, 1971), 190.

48. George B. Lockwood, *The New Harmony Movement* (New York: Dover, 1971), 166–69; and Bestor, *Education and Reform at New Harmony*, 398–400, 406.

49. Lydia E. Eveleth to Sarah Pears, March 29, 1827, in *Adventure in Happiness*, 87.

50. An Inhabitant of New Harmony to Thomas Pears, February 2, 1827, in *Adventure in Happiness*, 89.

51. Sarah Pears to Benjamin Bakewell, September 29, 1825, in *Adventure in Happiness*, 40.

52. Lydia E. Eveleth to Sarah Pears, March 29, 1827, 87.

53. The distinctiveness of persons as a critique of utilitarianism is from John Rawls, *A Theory of Justice* (Cambridge, MA: Harvard University Press, 1971), 27.

54. James Madison, "Memorial and Remonstrance Against Religious Assessments," ca. June 20, 1785, Founders Online, National Archives, http://founders .archives.gov/documents/Madison/01-08-02-0163.

55. Owen, *New View of Society*, 4–6. At New Lanark, Owen treated even the schoolchildren as living machines; see Cornelia Lambert, "'Living Machines': Performance and Pedagogy at Robert Owen's Institute for the Formation of Character, New Lanark, 1816–1828," *Journal of the History of Childhood and Youth* 4 (Fall 2011): 419–33.

56. Robert Owen, "An Address to the Working Classes," March 29, 1819, in *A New View of Society and Other Writings*, ed. Gregory Claeys (London: Penguin, 1991), 248.

57. Hazlitt, "New View of Society," 100.

58. Robert Dale Owen, *To Holland and to New Harmony*, ed. Josephine M. Elliott (Indianapolis: Indiana Historical Society, 1969), 257–59.

59. Sarah Pears to Mrs. Bakewell, March 19, 1826, in *Adventure in Happiness*, 74.

60. Ian Donnachie, *Robert Owen: Social Visionary* (Edinburgh: John Donald, 2005), 250–62.

61. James O'Toole, *Leading Change* (San Francisco, CA: Jossey-Bass, 1995), 201, 202, 204.

62. Favorable assessments of Owen include Francis J. O'Hagan, "Robert Owen and Education," in *Robert Owen and his Legacy*, ed. Noel Thompson and Chris Williams (Cardiff, Wales: University of Wales Press, 2011), 88; and Tim Hatcher, "Robert Owen: A Historiographic Study of a Pioneer of Human Resource Development," *European Journal of Training and Development* 37, no. 4 (2013): 414.

63. Frederick Winslow Taylor, "Shop Management," in *Scientific Management* (New York: Harper & Brothers, 1947), 32–33, 35.

64. For "Schmidt's" story, see Frederick Taylor, "The Principles of Scientific Management," in *Scientific Management*, 43–47.

65. Hugh G. J. Aitken, *Taylorism at Watertown Arsenal* (Cambridge, MA: Harvard University Press, 1960), 150.

66. Frederick Winslow Taylor, testimony before the Special Committee of the House of Representatives to Investigate the Taylor and Other Systems of Shop Management, January 25, 1912, in *Scientific Management* (New York: Harper & Brothers, 1947), 26–27. See also the testimony of workers in *Hearings before the Special Committee*, vol. 3 (Washington: Government Printing Office, 1912), 1886–1911.

67. Taylor, testimony before the Special Committee, 29–30.

68. Taylor, "Shop Management," 21.

69. Taylor, 137; see also Robert Kanigel, *The One Best Way* (New York: Penguin, 1997), 373.

70. Charles D. Wrege and Ronald G. Greenwood, *Frederick W. Taylor, the Father of Scientific Management* (Homewood, IL: Irwin, 1991), 207.

71. Kanigel, *One Best Way*, 510.

72. Wrege and Greenwood, *Frederick W. Taylor*, 207.

73. Kanigel, *One Best Way*, 562–63.

74. Leo Troy, "Trade Union Membership, 1898–1962," National Bureau of Economic Research (1965), https://www.nber.org/chapters/c1707.pdf.

Chapter 12: Classic Mirrors for Managers

Epigraph: Peter F. Drucker, *The Future of Industrial Man: A Conservative Approach* (New York: John Day, 1942), 99.

1. Michael A. Janson and Christopher S. Yoo, "The Wires Go to War: The US Experiment with Government Ownership of the Telephone System during World War I," *Texas Law Review* 91 (April 2013): 993.

2. Richard Gillespie, *Manufacturing Knowledge* (Cambridge: Cambridge University Press, 1991), 18–19; and "The Hawthorne Club," employee booklet, Western Electric Company, accessed January 25, 2019, http://www.westernelectric.com/library/corporate-history.html.

3. Gillespie, *Manufacturing Knowledge*, 38–40.

4. Gillespie, 48–51, 61–64, 68–70, 96, 234–38.

5. Richard C. S. Trahair, *The Humanist Temper* (New Brunswick, NJ: Transaction, 1984), 25, 93, 103–5.

6. Elton Mayo, *Democracy and Freedom* (Melbourne: Macmillan, 1919), 4, 5, 71, 72.

7. Mayo, 48, 50, 51, 54, 55, 58.

8. Mayo, 73.

9. Elton Mayo, "Industrial Autonomy," *Queensland University Magazine* 6, no. 8 (August 1919): 5.

10. Trahair, *Humanist Temper*, 143–51; and David O'Donald Cullen, "A New Way of Statecraft: The Career of Elton Mayo and the Development of the Social Sciences in America, 1920–1940" (PhD diss., University of North Texas, 1992), 95, 98–99, 143.

11. Elton Mayo, "The Irrational Factor in Human Behavior: The 'Night-Mind,' in Industry," *Annals of the American Academy of Political and Social Science* 110 (November 1923): 125.

12. Elton Mayo, "The Great Stupidity," *Harper's Magazine* 151 (July 1925): 227.

13. Elton Mayo, "A New Way of Statecraft" (1924), Laura Spelman Rockefeller Memorial records (FA061), Series 3.6, Box 53, Folder 572: 7, Rockefeller Archive Center, Sleepy Hollow, New York.

14. Mayo, "The Irrational Factor in Human Behavior," 130.

15. Gillespie, *Manufacturing Knowledge*, 103, 119; Kyle Bruce and Chris Nyland, "Elton Mayo and the Deification of Human Relations," *Organization Studies* 32, no. 3 (March 2011): 395–96; and US Senate Committee on Education and Labor, *Violations of Free Speech and Rights of Labor*: Hearings, pt. 45 "The Special Conference Committee," 76th Cong, 1st sess. (Washington, DC: US Government Printing Office, 1939), 16781, 16785.

16. Gillespie, *Manufacturing Knowledge*, 89.

17. Elton Mayo, *The Human Problems of an Industrial Civilization* (1933; repr., New York: Viking, 1960), 67–69.

18. Mayo, 70–71, 87, 175.

19. Mayo, 124, 144–45, 170, 176–77. Chapters of the book, published in 1933, were first delivered as Lowell lectures at Harvard in 1932.

20. Elton Mayo, "A Supplement to 'The Great Stupidity,'" *Bulletin of the Taylor Society* 10, no. 5 (October 1925): 225.

21. Jason Oakes, "Alliances in Human Biology: The Harvard Committee on Industrial Physiology, 1929–1939," *Journal of the History of Biology* 48 (Fall 2015): 366.

22. Mayo, "A Supplement to 'The Great Stupidity,'" 225; see also Mayo, "The Great Stupidity," 226–27; and Mayo, "A New Way of Statecraft," 1–8.

23. Ellen O'Connor, "Minding the Workers: The Meaning of 'Human' and 'Human Relations' in Elton Mayo," *Organization* 6, no. 2 (May 1999): 229, 231.

24. A similar point was made by an early observer of Mayo and his team's work, sociologist Mary Gilson, who suggested "that their research simply told the company what it wanted to hear." See Joanne B. Ciulla, *The Working Life* (New York: Times Books, 2000), 103.

25. Editorial, *The Iron Age*, March 7, 1918.

26. Charles M. Schwab, "Human Engineering," *Law and Labor* 10 (January 1928): 14.

27. Schwab, "Human Engineering," 16; see also David Brody, *Workers in Industrial America*, 2nd ed. (New York: Oxford University Press, 1993), 51–56.

28. Brody, *Workers in Industrial America*, 55–56, 57.

29. James Madison to Thomas Jefferson, October 17, 1788, Founders Online, National Archives, http://founders.archives.gov/documents/Jefferson/01-14-02-0018.

30. John N. Schacht, *The Making of Telephone Unionism, 1920–1947* (New Brunswick, NJ: Rutgers University Press, 1985), 42.

31. Schacht, 14–15.

32. E. K. Hall, "The Spirit of Cooperation Between Employer and Employee," *Law and Labor* 11 (March 1929): 52, 53.

33. F. J. Roethlisberger and William J. Dickson, *Management and the Worker* (Cambridge, MA: Harvard University Press, 1939), 569.

34. Roethlisberger and Dickson, 598–99. Company training materials derived from *Management and the Worker* are more revealing about how counselors got workers to take responsibility for their problems. For instance, "workers who complained about the lack of opportunity for advancement were shown that their complaints stemmed not from the job hierarchy of the company, but rather from the unrealistic demands placed on them by their families": Gillespie, *Manufacturing Knowledge*, 219.

35. R. S. Meriam, "Employee Interviewing and Employee Representation," *Personnel Journal* 10 (August 1931): 98–99.

36. F. J. Roethlisberger, *Management and Morale* (Cambridge, MA: Harvard University Press, 1941), 25.

37. Stephen Meyer, *Manhood on the Line* (Urbana: University of Illinois Press, 2016), 150.

38. Gerald Markowitz and David Rosner, eds., *"Slaves of the Depression": Workers' Letters about Life on the Job* (Ithaca, NY: Cornell University Press, 1987), 35, 40, 42, 43, 49, 61.

39. Robert F. Wagner, "Speech on the National Labor Relations Act," February 21, 1935, *Congressional Record*, 74th Cong., 1st sess., vol. 72: 2371–72.

40. Franklin D. Roosevelt, "Statement on Signing the National Labor Relations Act," July 5, 1935, in Gerhard Peters and John T. Woolley, The American Presidency Project, https://www.presidency.ucsb.edu/node/208893.

41. Trahair, *Humanist Temper*, 287.

42. Franklin D. Roosevelt, "Address of the President on the Occasion of His Acceptance of the Unanimous Nomination of the Democratic Party," Philadelphia, Pennsylvania, June 27, 1936, Roosevelt Presidential Library & Museum, National Archives, http://www.fdrlibrary.marist.edu/archives/collections/franklin /index.php?p=collections/findingaid&id=582.

43. Joshua L. Rosenbloom, "Labor Unions," in *Historical Statistics of the United States*, millennial ed. online, ed. Susan B. Carter, Scott Sigmund Gartner, Michael R. Haines, Alan L. Olmstead, Richard Sutch, and Gavin Wright (Cambridge: Cambridge University Press, 2006), https://hsus.cambridge.org /HSUSWeb/HSUSEntryServlet; Gillespie, *Manufacturing Knowledge*, 221–22; and Trahair, *Humanist Temper*, 287.

44. Elton Mayo, *The Social Problems of an Industrial Civilization* (Boston: Harvard University Graduate School of Business Administration, 1945), 44–45, 49, 50.

45. J. H. Smith, "The Significance of Elton Mayo," foreword to the 1975 edition of *The Social Problems of an Industrial Civilization* by Elton Mayo (Abingdon, UK: Routledge, 1975), ix.

46. Wilbert E. Moore, "Review of *The Human Problems of an Industrial Civilization*, 2nd ed., by Elton Mayo; *The Social Problems of an Industrial Civilization*, by Elton Mayo; *Industry and Society*, ed. by William F. Whyte," American Sociological Review 12 (February 1947): 123.

47. Moore, 123.

48. Wilbert E. Moore, "Current Issues in Industrial Sociology," *American Sociological Review* 12 (December 1947): 654.

49. Moore, 654.

50. Daniel Bell, "Adjusting Men to Machines," Commentary 3 (January 1947): 88.

51. Walter Kiechel III, "The Management Century," *Harvard Business Review* 90 (November 2012): 66.

52. Raymond E. Miles, "Human Relations or Human Resources?" *Harvard Business Review* 43 (July 1965): 148–57; Douglas McGregor, *The Human Side of Enterprise* (New York: McGraw-Hill, 1960), 45–57; Frederick Herzberg, "One More Time: How Do You Motivate Employees?" *Harvard Business Review* 46 (January 1968): 53–62; and Peter F. Drucker, *The Practice of Management* (New York: Harper, 1954), 121–36.

53. Drucker, *Practice of Management*, 121.

54. Drucker, 122.

55. Drucker, 112.

56. Peter F. Drucker, *Concept of the Corporation* (New Brunswick, NJ: Transaction, 1993), 206.

57. Peter F. Drucker, *The New Society* (New York: Harper & Brothers, 1950), 283; and Drucker, *Concept of the Corporation*, 198.

58. Drucker, *Practice of Management*, 268.

59. Drucker, *The New Society*, 283.

60. Peter F. Drucker, *Managing in the Next Society* (New York: St. Martin's, 2002), 116–17.

61. Drucker, *Managing in the Next Society*, 111.

62. Kate Conger and Noam Scheiber, "California Bill Makes App-Based Companies Treat Workers as Employees," *New York Times*, September 11, 2019.

63. Peter F. Drucker, *The Essential Drucker* (New York: HarperCollins, 2001), 11.

64. Drucker, 11, 23.

65. Drucker, *Practice of Management*, 7, 3.

66. Drucker, *Managing in the Next Society*, 291.

67. Zack Cooper, Fiona Scott Morton, and Nathan Shekita, "Surprise! Out-of-Network Billing for Emergency Care in the United States," National Bureau of Economic Research, Working Paper No. 23623, July 2017, rev. January 2019, http://www.nber.org/papers/w23623; Julie Creswell, Reed Abelson, and Margot Sanger-Katz, "The Company Behind Many Surprise Emergency Room Bills," *New York Times*, July 24, 2017; and Margot Sanger-Katz, "A New Ban on Surprise Medical Bills Starts This Week," *New York Times*, December 30, 2021.

68. Drucker, *New Society*, 292–93.

69. Drucker, 118–19, 123, 139–40, 146, 337, 338, 345; see also Drucker, *Concept of the Corporation*, 201.

70. Drucker, *New Society*, 297.

71. David Halpern and Stephen Osofsky, "A Dissenting View of MBO," *Public Personnel Management* 19 (Fall 1990): 321–30; and Charles D. Pringle and Justin G. Longnecker, "The Ethics of MBO," *Academy of Management Review* 7 (April 1982): 305–12.

72. Peter F. Drucker, *Management: Tasks, Responsibilities, Practices* (New York: HarperCollins, 1985), 325.

73. Drucker, *Future of Industrial Man*, 92, 99, 275.

74. Michael Hiltzik, "Peter Drucker's Revolutionary Teachings Decades Old but Still Fresh," *Los Angeles Times*, December 31, 2009.

75. Clarence E. Bonnett, *Employers' Associations in the United States: A Study of Typical Associations* (New York: Macmillan, 1922), 295, 306–7, 337, 351–52.

76. William E. Leuchtenburg, *Franklin D. Roosevelt and the New Deal* (New York: Harper & Row, 1963), 19, 21, 23; and Stuart Ewen, *PR!* (New York: Basic Books, 1996), 234–35.

77. Ewen, *PR!*, 303, 304.

78. Richard S. Tedlow, "The National Association of Manufacturers and Public Relations during the New Deal," *Business History Review* 1 (Spring 1976): 33, 34, 36.

79. Kevin M. Kruse, *One Nation Under God* (New York: Basic Books, 2015), 6, 8–9. See also Elizabeth Fones-Wolf and Ken Fones-Wolf, "Managers and Ministers: Instilling Christian Free Enterprise in the Postwar Workplace," *Business History Review* 89 (Spring 2015): 99–100.

80. Charles R. Hook, "What Does Capitalism Want for Itself and America?," Address before the Annual Convention of the Missouri State Teachers

Association, St. Louis, November 16, 1939 (New York: Division of Publications, National Association of Manufacturers, 1939), 7, 8, 9, 15, 16, 18, 20, 21, 22, 23.

81. Colleen A. Moore, "The National Association of Manufacturers: The Voice of Industry and the Free Enterprise Campaign in the Schools, 1929–1949" (PhD diss., University of Akron, 1985), 606.

82. National Association of Manufacturers, *The American Way*, "You and Industry," booklet No. 1, rev. ed. (New York: National Association of Manufacturers, 1940), 21.

83. National Association of Manufacturers, 11.

84. National Association of Manufacturers, *Employer-Employee Cooperation*, "You and Industry," New Series (New York: National Association of Manufacturers, 1942), 8, 31, 32, 35.

85. National Association of Manufacturers, 43.

86. National Association of Manufacturers, *Our Material Progress*, "You and Industry," New Series (New York: National Association of Manufacturers, 1941), 32.

87. National Association of Manufacturers, *Employer-Employee Cooperation*, 57, 58.

88. National Association of Manufacturers, 44.

89. National Association of Manufacturers, *The Profession of Management*, "You and Industry," New Series (New York: National Association of Manufacturers, 1942), 11.

90. National Association of Manufacturers, 35.

91. National Association of Manufacturers, *Study Guide*, "You and Industry," New Series (New York: National Association of Manufacturers, 1942), 34, 39, 41.

92. Burton St. John III and Robert Arnett, "The National Association of Manufacturers' Community Relations Short Film *Your Town*: Parable, Propaganda, and Big Individualism," *Journal of Public Relations Research* 26 (March 2014): 110.

93. Senate Committee on Education and Labor, *Violations of Free Speech and Rights of Labor*, report no. 6, part 6 ("Labor Policies of Employers' Associations," part 3, "The National Association of Manufacturers"), 76th Cong., 1st sess., August 14, 1939 (Washington, DC: US Government Printing Office, 1939), 154, 173, 174, 175, 221; see also Jerold S. Auerbach, "The La Follette Committee and the CIO," *Wisconsin Magazine of History* 48 (Autumn 1964): 4. Critical studies of NAM's American Way campaign and similar propaganda efforts include Elizabeth A. Fones-Wolf, *Selling Free Enterprise* (Urbana: University of Illinois Press, 1994), 39–44; Ewen, *PR!*, 303-21; and Wendy Wall, *Inventing the "American Way"* (New York: Oxford University Press, 2008).

94. Senate Committee on Education and Labor, *Violations of Free Speech and Rights of Labor*, report no. 6, part 6, 178.

95. Subcommittee on Economic Progress of the Joint Economic Committee, *Economic Education*, vol. 2 ("Related Materials": "The Economic World of the

Child," by Lawrence Senesh), 90th Cong., 1st sess., April 17, 1967 (Washington, DC: US Government Printing Office, 1967), 148.

96. "The Admonitions of Ipu-Wer and The Prophecy of Neferti," in *Ancient Near Eastern Texts*, ed. James B. Prichard, 3rd ed. (Princeton, NJ: Princeton University Press, 1969), 441–46; "Instruction for King Merikare," in *Ancient Near Eastern Texts*, 414–18; Ronald J. Williams, "Literature as a Medium of Political Propaganda in Ancient Egypt," in *The Seed of Wisdom*, ed., W. S. McCullough (Toronto: University of Toronto Press, 1964), 20; "The Instructions of Kagemni," quoted in Christopher A. Faraone and Emily Teeter, "Egyptian Maat and Hesiodic Metis," *Mnemosyne* 57, 4th ser., fasc. 2 (2004): 187; and "The Teaching of Ani," in *Writings from Ancient Egypt*, trans. Toby Wilkinson (London: Penguin, 2016), 304, 305, 309.

97. Juan Carlos Moreno García, *The State in Ancient Egypt* (London: Bloomsbury, 2020), 139.

98. Drucker, *Practice of Management*, 158, 159.

99. Philip Stadter, "Fictional Narrative in the *Cyropaideia*," in *Xenophon (Oxford Readings in Classical Studies)*, ed. Vivienne J. Gray (Oxford: Oxford University Press, 2010), 369.

100. Christopher Nadon, *Xenophon's Prince: Republic and Empire in the Cyropaedia* (Berkeley: University of California Press, 2001), 6.

101. Melina Tamiolaki, "Xenophon's *Cyropaedia*: Tentative Answers to an Enigma," in *The Cambridge Companion to Xenophon*, ed. Michael A. Flower (Cambridge: Cambridge University Press, 2017), 192.

102. King James VI and I, *Political Writings*, ed. Johann P. Sommerville (Cambridge: Cambridge University Press, 1994), 12.

Chapter 13: Beyond Mirrors for Leaders

This chapter builds on points first made in Michael Keeley, *A Social-Contract Theory of Organizations* (Notre Dame, IN: University of Notre Dame Press, 1988); and Michael Keeley, "The Trouble with Transformational Leadership: Toward a Federalist Ethic for Organizations," *Business Ethics Quarterly* 5 (January 1995): 67–96.

1. Business Roundtable, "Business Roundtable Redefines the Purpose of a Corporation to Promote 'An Economy That Serves All Americans,'" press release, August 19, 2019, https://www.businessroundtable.org/business-roundtable -redefines-the-purpose-of-a-corporation-to-promote-an-economy-that-serves -all-americans.

2. Jeffrey S. Harrison, Robert A. Phillips, and R. Edward Freeman, "On the 2019 Business Roundtable 'Statement on the Purpose of a Corporation,'" *Journal of Management* 46 (September 2020): 1224.

3. Luigi Zingales, "Don't Trust CEOs Who Say They Don't Care about Shareholder Value Anymore," *Washington Post*, August 20, 2019.

4. Robert Reich, "The Biggest Business Con of 2019: Fleecing Workers While Bosses Get Rich," *Guardian*, December 29, 2019.

5. David Lazarus, "CEOs Say They Care about Customers and Workers. Propaganda Experts Are Unimpressed," *Los Angeles Times*, August 21, 2019.

6. Business Roundtable, "Purpose of a Corporation."

7. Nell Minow, "Six Reasons We Don't Trust the New 'Stakeholder' Promise from the Business Roundtable," Harvard Law School Forum on Corporate Governance, September 2, 2019, https://corpgov.law.harvard.edu/2019/09/02/six-reasons-we-dont-trust-the-new-stakeholder-promise-from-the-business-roundtable/.

8. Reich, "Biggest Business Con." Similar points were made long ago by a founding father of business ethics: Howard R. Bowen, *Social Responsibilities of the Businessman* (1953; repr. Iowa City: University of Iowa Press, 2013), 42.

9. Harrison, Phillips, and Freeman, "On the 2019 Business Roundtable 'Statement,'" 1233; and Kristin Bresnahan, "Back to the '80s: Business Roundtable's 'Purpose' Statement Redux," *Directors & Boards* 43, no. 5 (September 2019): 22.

10. James Madison to Thomas Jefferson, October 24, 1787, Founders Online, National Archives, http://founders.archives.gov/documents/Jefferson/01-12-02-0274.

11. Harold Koontz, "The Management Theory Jungle," *Journal of the Academy of Management* 4 (December 1961): 174.

12. Petro Georgiou, "The Goal Paradigm and Notes towards a Counter Paradigm," *Administrative Science Quarterly* 18 (September 1973): 291.

13. Georgiou, 291, 299.

14. Aristotle, *The Politics* (Jowett/Barnes trans.), ed. Stephen Everson (Cambridge: Cambridge University Press, 1996), 2.1, 3.9, 8.1.

15. Robert C. Solomon, *Ethics and Excellence* (New York: Oxford University Press, 1993), 131.

16. Andrew M. Carton, Chad Murphy, and Jonathan R. Clark, "A (Blurry) Vision of the Future: How Leader Rhetoric about Ultimate Goals Influences Performance," *Academy of Management Journal* 57 (December 2014): 1545.

17. James MacGregor Burns, *Presidential Government* (Boston: Houghton Mifflin, 1973), 195.

18. James MacGregor Burns, *Leadership* (New York: Harper & Row, 1978), 20, 258, 425.

19. Burns, 3.

20. Bernard M. Bass, *Leadership and Performance Beyond Expectations* (New York: Free Press, 1985), 4, 30.

21. Bass, 187.

22. Daan van Knippenberg and Sim B. Sitkin, "A Critical Assessment of Charismatic-Transformational Leadership Research: Back to the Drawing Board?," *Academy of Management Annals* 7, no. 1 (2013): 2, 39, 43, 49–50.

23. Bernard M. Bass, "From Transactional to Transformational Leadership: Learning to Share the Vision," *Organizational Dynamics* 18 (Winter 1990): 25, 26–27.

24. Bass, 20.

25. Burns, *Leadership*, 405.

26. James MacGregor Burns, *The Deadlock of Democracy* (Englewood Cliffs, NJ: Prentice-Hall, 1963), 6.

27. William D. Liddle, "A Patriot King or None: Lord Bolingbroke and the American Renunciation of George III," *Journal of American History* 65 (1979): 956.

28. Samuel Eliot Morison, *The Oxford History of the American People* (New York: Oxford University Press, 1965), 230.

29. James Thomas Flexner, *George Washington in the American Revolution* (Boston: Little, Brown, 1967), 542–43. Compare Flexner's description of George Washington with the ideal characteristics of organizational leadership outlined by Jay A. Conger and Rabindra N. Kanungo in their chapter "Behavioral Dimensions of Charismatic Leadership," in *Charismatic Leadership: The Elusive Factor in Organizational Effectiveness*, 78–97 (San Francisco: Jossey-Bass, 1988): Charismatic-transformational leaders set bold (even utopian) goals. They employ unconventional or countercultural tactics. They build enthusiasm for their vision through symbols, rhetoric, and other forms of impression management. Finally, they set examples by performing heroic deeds involving personal risk and self-sacrifice, such as serving without salary.

30. Bolingbroke, *The Idea of a Patriot King* in *Bolingbroke: Political Writings*, ed. David Armitage (Cambridge: Cambridge University Press, 1997), 251, 272.

31. Madison to Jefferson, October 24, 1787.

32. James Madison, *Federalist* No. 10, November 22, 1787, Founders Online, National Archives, http://founders.archives.gov/documents/Madison/01-10-02-0178.

33. James Madison to Nicholas P. Trist, February 15, 1830, Founders Online, National Archives, http://founders.archives.gov/ documents/Madison/99-02-02-1982.

34. "Jefferson's 'Original Rough Draught' of the Declaration of Independence, 11 June–4 July 1776," Founders Online, National Archives, https://founders.archives.gov/documents/Jefferson/01-01-02-0176-0004; and Mark Hulliung, *The Social Contract in America* (Lawrence: University Press of Kansas, 2007), 11–22.

35. "What the President Said," *Daily Milwaukee News*, September 23, 1862 (with credit for updated language to tech journalist William Machrone). The Emancipation Proclamation, January 1, 1863, National Archives, https://www.archives.gov/exhibits/featured-documents/emancipation-proclamation. Lincoln's proclamation acknowledged that actual emancipation depended on military victory by the Union.

36. Jeremy Waldron, "John Locke: Social Contract versus Political Anthropology," *Review of Politics* 51 (Winter 1989): 3–28; and John Locke, *The Second Treatise of Government* in *John Locke: Two Treatises of Government*, ed. Peter Laslett, rev. ed. (New York: New American Library, 1965), 361 (2.6.76).

37. Locke, *Second Treatise*, 369, 370, 372 (2.7.90, 2.7.91, 2.7.93).

38. Waldron, "John Locke," 18.

39. Hulliung, *Social Contract*, 13; and Declaration of Independence, July 4, 1776, National Archives, https://www.archives.gov/founding-docs/declaration -transcript.

40. Margaret Jane Radin, "Response: Boilerplate in Theory and Practice," *Canadian Business Law Journal* 54 (September 2013): 294.

41. Karl N. Llewellyn, "What Price Contract?—An Essay in Perspective," *Yale Law Journal* 40 (March 1931): 731–32

42. Wayne Norman, "Rawls on Markets and Corporate Governance," *Business Ethics Quarterly* 25 (January 2015): 52.

43. David Steingard and William Clark, "The Benefit Corporation as an Exemplar of Integrative Corporate Purpose (ICP): Delivering Maximal Social and Environmental Impact with a New Corporate Form," *Business & Professional Ethics Journal* 35, no. 1 (Spring 2016): 73.

44. Daryl Koehn, "Why the New Benefit Corporations May Not Prove to Be Truly Socially Beneficial," *Business & Professional Ethics Journal* 35, no. 1 (Spring 2016): 41.

45. Koehn, 24, 41.

46. Steingard and Clark, "The Benefit Corporation," 89.

47. Willem Buiter quoted in Kathryn C. Lavelle, *Money and Banks in the American Political System* (Cambridge: Cambridge University Press, 2013), 1. For more failures of self-regulation, see Jukka Mäkinen and Eero Kasanen, "Boundaries between Business and Politics: A Study on the Division of Moral Labor," *Journal of Business Ethics* 134 (March 2016): 110–11.

48. Robert Birnbaum, *How Academic Leadership Works: Understanding Success and Failure in the College Presidency* (San Francisco: Jossey-Bass, 1992), 29.

Afterword

1. John Rawls, *A Theory of Justice* (Cambridge, MA: Harvard University Press, 1971), 302. Compare, e.g., Amartya Sen, *The Idea of Justice* (Cambridge, MA: Harvard University Press, 2009), 10–12.

2. Use of the organic social model in utilitarianism is described by Scott Gordon, *Welfare, Justice, and Freedom* (New York: Columbia University Press, 1980), 40, 57.

3. Rawls, *Theory of Justice*, 29.

4. Rawls, vii–viii, 190–91.

5. Rawls, 182–83. Influential post-Rawlsian works include Elizabeth Anderson, "Expanding the Egalitarian Toolbox: Equality and Bureaucracy," *Proceedings of the Aristotelian Society*, Supplementary Volume, 82 (June 2008): 139–60.

6. R. Edward Freeman, "The Politics of Stakeholder Theory: Some Future Directions," *Business Ethics Quarterly* 4 (October 1994): 416.

7. Nien-hê Hsieh, "Rawlsian Justice and Workplace Republicanism," *Social Theory and Practice* 31 (January 2005): 121, 132.

8. Magali Fia and Lorenzo Sacconi, "Justice and Corporate Governance: New Insights from Rawlsian Social Contract and Sen's Capabilities Approach," *Journal of Business Ethics* 160 (December 2019): 955.

9. Thomas Donaldson and Thomas W. Dunfee, *Ties That Bind: A Social Contract Approach to Business Ethics* (Boston: Harvard Business School Press, 1999), 19, 41–43, 102, 49. Calls for more specificity include Edward Soule, "Managerial Moral Strategies: In Search of a Few Good Principles," *Academy of Management Review* 27 (January 2002): 119.

10. Richard Marens, "Speaking Platitudes to Power: Observing American Business Ethics in an Age of Declining Hegemony," *Journal of Business Ethics* 94, supplement no. 2 (August 2010): 243–46.

11. "Abuse of superior bargaining position" is regulated by law in Austria, France, Germany, Italy, Japan, Korea, the Slovak Republic, and Taiwan. See Albert A. Foer, "Abuse of Superior Bargaining Position (ASBP): What Can We Learn from Our Trading Partners?" Federal Trade Commission Hearings on Competition and Consumer Protection in the 21st Century, Fall 2018, https://www.ftc.gov/system/files/documents/public_comments/2018/08/ftc-2018-0054-d-0007-151038.pdf.

12. Robert Owen, "A Discourse on a New System of Society," addresses delivered in the Hall of Representatives of the United States, February 25, 1825, and March 7, 1825, in *Robert Owen in the United States*, ed. Oakley C. Johnson (New York: Humanities Press, 1970), 23, 32, 53.

13. Rawls, *Theory of Justice*, 180–83.

14. Lisa D. Ordóñez, Maurice E. Schweitzer, Adam D. Galinsky, and Max H. Bazerman, "Goals Gone Wild: The Systematic Side Effects of Overprescribing Goal Setting," *Academy of Management Perspectives* 23 (February 2009): 6–16.

15. David Effelsberg, Marc Solga, and Jochen Gurt, "Transformational Leadership and Follower's Unethical Behavior for the Benefit of the Company: A Two-Study Investigation," *Journal of Business Ethics* 120 (March 2014): 81–93.

16. Guillermo J. Grenier, *Inhuman Relations* (Philadelphia: Temple University Press, 1988), 98–115, 158.

17. John Boatright, *Ethics and the Conduct of Business*, 7th ed. (Upper Saddle River, NJ: Prentice-Hall, 2012), 6.

18. Pierre-Yves Néron, "Rethinking the Very Idea of Egalitarian Markets and Corporations: Why Relationships Might Matter More than Distribution," *Business Ethics Quarterly* 25 (January 2015): 103–4.

19. Axel V. Werder, "Corporate Governance and Stakeholder Opportunism," *Organization Science* 22 (September–October 2011): 1347.

20. Chester I. Barnard, *The Functions of the Executive* (1938; repr. Cambridge, MA: Harvard University Press, 1968), 168, 233.

21. Barnard, 284.

22. Christopher McMahon, "Comments on Hsieh, Moriarty and Oosterhout," *Journal of Business Ethics* 71 (April 2007): 374, 377–78; and Eyal Press, "The Moral Crisis of America's Doctors," *New York Times Magazine*, June 15, 2023.

23. R. H. Coase, "The Nature of the Firm," *Economica* 4 (November 1937): 391. Coase is careful to qualify his statement that workers contract "to obey the directions of an entrepreneur *within certain limits*." But he implies that such limits are somehow negotiated in the employment contract, which is usually not the case; see Elizabeth Anderson, *Private Government* (Princeton, NJ: Princeton University Press, 2017), 52–53. Business ethicists who argue from Coasian theories are not usually so careful; see, for example, John Boatright, "*Public Capitalism: The Political Authority of Corporate Executives*, by Christopher McMahon" (book review), *Business Ethics Quarterly* 23 (July 2013): 477–80.

24. Peter W. Bardaglio, *Reconstructing the Household: Families, Sex, and the Law in the Nineteenth-Century South* (Chapel Hill: University of North Carolina Press, 1995), 27.

25. Anderson, *Private Government*, 61.

26. Anderson, xix, 49, 133.

27. "FDR and the Wagner Act," Franklin D. Roosevelt Presidential Library and Museum, National Archives, accessed January 13, 2021, https://www.fdrlibrary.org/wagner-act; Justin McCarthy, "U.S. Approval of Labor Unions at Highest Point Since 1965," Gallup, August 30, 2022, https://news.gallup.com/poll/398303/approval-labor-unions-highest-point-1965.aspx; and Thomas A. Kochan, Duanyi Yang, William T. Kimball, and Erin L. Kelly, "Worker Voice in America: Is There a Gap between What Workers Expect and What They Experience?" *ILR Review* 72 (January 2019): 19–20.

28. Lawrence Mishel, Lynn Rhinehart, and Lane Windham, "Explaining the Erosion of Private-Sector Unions," Economic Policy Institute, November 18, 2020, https://www.epi.org/unequalpower/publications/private-sector-unions-corporate-legal-erosion/, 16.

29. Mishel, Rhinehart, and Windham, 15, 16, 17, 19; and Celine McNicholas, Margaret Poydock, Julia Wolfe, Ben Zipperer, Gordon Lafer, and Lola Loustaunau, "Unlawful: U.S. Employers Are Charged with Violating Federal Law in 41.5% of All Union Election Campaigns," Economic Policy Institute, December 11, 2019, https://www.epi.org/publication/unlawful-employer-opposition-to-union-election-campaigns/, 2.

30. Steven Greenhouse, *Beaten Down, Worked Up* (New York: Knopf, 2019), 153–54; and Communication Workers of America, "Truth to Power: Fired T-Mobile Worker Questions CEO about Its U.S. Labor Practices," *CWA News*, May 22, 2014.

31. Kate Bronfenbrenner, "No Holds Barred: The Intensification of Employer Opposition to Organizing," Economic Policy Institute, May 20, 2009, https://www.epi.org/publication/bp235/, 2, 3, 12, 13, 14.

32. Greenhouse, *Beaten Down*, 154.

33. Jane McAlevey, *A Collective Bargain* (New York: HarperCollins, 2020), 28–35; and Patty Murray, "Senator Murray, Top Democrats Introduce Bill to Protect Workers' Right to Organize and Make our Economy Work for

Everyone [Protecting the Right to Organize (PRO) Act fact sheet]," news release, February 4, 2021, https://www.murray.senate.gov/public/index.cfm /mobile/newsreleases?ID=C0506ABD-D3D7-4C88-B297-EC452646D03D.

34. Karl N. Llewellyn, "What Price Contract?—An Essay in Perspective," *Yale Law Journal* 40 (March 1931): 731–32.

35. Rebecca Smith, David Bensman, and Paul Alexander Marvy, *The Big Rig: Poverty, Pollution, and the Misclassification of Truck Driver's at America's Ports* (New York: National Employment Law Project, 2010).

36. On the "ABC" test and alternatives to regulate gig companies, see Samantha J. Prince, "The Shoe Is about to Drop for the Platform Economy: Understanding the Current Worker Classification Landscape in Preparation for a Changed World," *University of Memphis Law Review* 52 (Spring 2022): 627–702.

37. Ratna Sinroja, Sarah Thomason, and Ken Jacobs, "Misclassification in California: A Snapshot of the Janitorial Services, Construction, and Trucking Industries," UC Berkeley Labor Center, March 11, 2019, https://laborcenter .berkeley.edu/misclassification-in-california-a-snapshot-of-the-janitorial -services-construction-and-trucking-industries/; and Margaret Jane Radin, *Boilerplate* (Princeton, NJ: Princeton University Press, 2013), 130–35.

38. Katherine V. W. Stone and Alexander J. S. Colvin, "The Arbitration Epidemic: Mandatory Arbitration Deprives Workers and Consumers of Their Rights," Economic Policy Institute, December 15, 2015, https://www.epi.org /publication/the-arbitration-epidemic/#epi-toc-13, 20–21.

39. Alexander J. S. Colvin, "The Growing Use of Mandatory Arbitration," Economic Policy Institute, September 27, 2017, https://www.epi.org/publication /the-growing-use-of-mandatory-arbitration/, 4, 5.

40. Emily Kadens, "Cheating Pays," *Columbia Law Review* 119 (March 2019): 587.

41. Hugh Baran and Elisabeth Campbell, "Forced Arbitration Enabled Employers to Steal $12.6 Billion From Workers in Low Paid Jobs in 2019," National Employment Law Project, June 7, 2020, https://www.nelp.org/publication/forced -arbitration-cost-workers-in-low-paid-jobs-12-6-billion-in-stolen-wages-in-2019/.

42. Myriam Gilles, "The Politics of Access: Examining Concerted State/Private Enforcement Solutions to Class Action Bans," *Fordham Law Review* 86 (2018): 2228.

43. Gretchen Carlson, "Forced Arbitration Enables Harassers," *Fortune*, July 1, 2018, 5.

44. Michael S. Barr, "Mandatory Arbitration in Consumer Finance and Investor Contracts," *New York University Journal of Law & Business* 11 (Special Issue 2015): 806–8, 812.

45. Emily Flitter, "The Price of Wells Fargo's Fake Account Scandal Grows by $3 Billion," *New York Times*, February 21, 2020.

46. Flitter.

47. Michael Hiltzik, "How Wells Fargo Exploited a Binding Arbitration Clause to Deflect Customers' Fraud Allegations," *Los Angeles Times*, September 26, 2016.

48. Andrea Cann Chandrasekher and David Horton, "Arbitration Nation: Data from Four Providers," *California Law Review* 107 (February 2019): 57.

49. Michael Corkery and Stacy Cowley, "Wells Fargo Killing Sham Account Suits by Using Arbitration," *New York Times*, December 6, 2016. See also Heidi Shierholz, "Forced Arbitration Is Bad for Consumers," Economic Policy Institute, October 2, 2017, https://www.epi.org/publication/forced-arbitration-is-bad-for -consumers/.

50. David Horton, "Infinite Arbitration Clauses," *University of Pennsylvania Law Review* 168 (February 2020): 657, 658, 659.

51. Forced Arbitration Injustice Repeal Act, HR 1423, 116th Cong., 1st sess., Cong. Rec. 165, no. 152, daily ed. (September 20, 2019): H7849. A relevant history of mandatory arbitration at work is provided by Sarah Staszak, "Privatizing Employment Law: The Expansion of Mandatory Arbitration in the Workplace," *Studies in American Political Development* 34 (October 2020): 239–68.

52. Forced Arbitration Injustice Repeal Act.

SELECTED BIBLIOGRAPHY

Alcuin. *The Rhetoric of Alcuin and Charlemagne.* Translated by Wilbur Samuel Howell. Princeton, NJ: Princeton University Press, 1941.

Aquinas, Thomas. *On Kingship.* In *St. Thomas Aquinas: Political Writings*, edited and translated by R. W. Dyson, 5–51. Cambridge: Cambridge University Press, 2002.

Aristotle. *Aristotle:* The Politics *and* The Constitution of Athens. Edited by Stephen Everson, trans. Jonathan Barnes and J. M. Moore. Cambridge: Cambridge University Press, 1996.

Bercovitch, Sacvan, ed. *Election Day Sermons: Massachusetts.* New York: AMS Press, 1984.

Bolingbroke, Henry St. John. *The Idea of a Patriot King.* In *Bolingbroke: Political Writings*, edited by David Armitage, 217–94. Cambridge: Cambridge University Press, 1997.

The Book of Government or Rules for Kings (The Siyasat-nama or Siyar al-Muluk) of Nizam al-Mulk. Translated by Hubert Darke. New Haven, CT: Yale University Press, 1960.

Born, Lester Kruger. "The Perfect Prince: A Study in Thirteenth and Fourteenth-Century Ideals." *Speculum* 3 (October 1928): 470–504.

Botero, Giovanni. *The Reason of State.* Translated by P. J. Waley and D. P. Waley. London: Routledge & Kegan Paul, 1956.

Brandolini, Aurelio Lippo. *Republics and Kingdoms Compared.* Edited and translated by James Hankins. Cambridge, MA: Harvard University Press, 2009.

Breen, T. H. *The Character of the Good Ruler.* New Haven, CT: Yale University Press, 1970.

Burns, James MacGregor. *Leadership.* New York: Harper & Row, 1978.

Castiglione, Baldesar. *The Book of the Courtier.* Translated by Charles Singleton, edited by Daniel Javitch. New York: Norton, 2002.

Christine De Pizan. *The Book of the Body Politic.* Edited and translated by Kate Langdon Forhan. Cambridge: Cambridge University Press, 1994.

———. *The Book of the City of Ladies.* Translated by Earl Jeffrey Richards. New York: Persea, 1982.

————. *A Medieval Woman's Mirror of Honor: The Treasury of the City of Ladies.* Translated by Charity Cannon Willard. New York: Persea / Bard Hall Press, 1989.

Cicero. *De Re Publica.* Translated by Clinton Walker Keyes. Loeb Classical Library *Cicero* Vol. 16. Cambridge, MA: Harvard University Press, 1928.

————. *On Duties.* Edited by M. T. Griffin and E. M. Atkins. Cambridge: Cambridge University Press, 1991.

Dante Alighieri. *Monarchy.* Translated by Donald Nicholl. New York: Noonday Press, 1954.

The Debate on the Constitution. Edited by Bernard Bailyn. 2 vols. New York: Library of America, 1993.

Dosher, Harry Randall. "The Concept of the Ideal Prince in French Political Thought, 800–1760." PhD diss., University of North Carolina at Chapel Hill, 1969.

Drucker, Peter F. *Managing in the Next Society.* New York: St. Martin's, 2002.

————. *The New Society.* New York: Harper & Brothers, 1950.

————. *The Practice of Management.* New York: Harper & Row, 1954.

Erasmus. *The Education of a Christian Prince.* Translated by Neil M. Cheshire and Michael J. Heath. Edited by Lisa Jardine. Cambridge: Cambridge University Press, 1997.

Gerald of Wales [Giraldus Cambrensis]. *Concerning the Instruction of Princes.* Translated by Joseph Stevenson. In *The Church Historians of England.* Vol. 5. Part 1. London: Seeleys, 1858.

————. *The Conquest of Ireland.* Edited and translated by A. B. Scott and F. X. Martin. Dublin: Royal Irish Academy, 1978.

Ghazali's Book of Counsel for Kings (Nasihat al-Muluk). Translated by F. R. C. Bagley. London: Oxford University Press, 1964.

Gilbert, Allan H. *Machiavelli's Prince and Its Forerunners.* Durham, NC: Duke University Press, 1938.

Giles of Rome. *On the Rule of Princes.* Translated by Matthew Kempshall. In *The Cambridge Translations of Medieval Philosophical Texts,* edited by Arthur Stephen McGrade, John Kilcullen, and Matthew Kempshall. Vol. 2, 200–215. Cambridge: Cambridge University Press, 2001.

Hexter, J. H. *The Vision of Politics on the Eve of the Reformation.* New York: Basic Books, 1973.

Isocrates. *To Nicocles; Nicocles.* Translated by George Norlin. Loeb Classical Library *Isocrates* Vol. 1. Cambridge, MA: Harvard University Press, 1991.

John of Salisbury. *Policraticus.* Edited and translated by Cary J. Nederman. Cambridge: Cambridge University Press, 1990.

Johnson, Oakley C. *Robert Owen in the United States.* New York: Humanities Press, 1970.

Jonas of Orleans. *De Institutione Regia.* Translated by R. W. Dyson. Smithtown, NY: Exposition Press, 1983.

Lichtheim, Miriam, ed. *Ancient Egyptian Literature: A Book of Readings*. Vol. 1 and 3. Berkeley: University of California Press, 1975, 1980.

Locke, John. *The Second Treatise of Government*. In *John Locke: Two Treatises of Government*, edited by Peter Laslett. Rev. ed. New York: New American Library, 1965.

Lucian. *Apology for the "Salaried Posts in Great Houses."* Translated by K. Kilburn. Loeb Classical Library *Lucian* Vol. 6. Cambridge, MA: Harvard University Press, 1959.

———. *On Salaried Posts in Great Houses*. Translated by A. M. Harmon. Loeb Classical Library *Lucian* Vol. 3. Cambridge, MA: Harvard University Press, 1960.

———. *Selected Satires of Lucian*. Edited and translated by Lionel Casson. New York: Norton, 1968.

Machiavelli, Niccolò. *The Discourses*. In *Niccolò Machiavelli: Selected Political Writings*, edited and translated by David Wootton, 81–217. Indianapolis: Hackett, 1994.

———. *The Prince*. Translated and edited by Robert M. Adams. 2nd ed. New York: Norton, 1992.

Madison, James. *Notes of Debates in the Federal Convention of 1787*. New York: Norton, 1987.

———. *Writings*. Edited by Jack N. Rakove. New York: Library of America, 1999.

Map, Walter. *De Nugis Curialium: Courtiers' Trifles*. Edited and translated by M. R. James. Revised by C. N. L. Brooke and R. A. B. Mynors. Oxford: Clarendon, 1983.

Marie de France. *The Fables of Marie de France*. Translated by Mary Lou Martin. Birmingham, AL: Summa, 1984.

Marlow, Louise. *Medieval Muslim Mirrors for Princes*. Cambridge: Cambridge University Press, 2023.

Mayo, Elton. *Democracy and Freedom*. Melbourne: Macmillan, 1919.

———. *The Human Problems of an Industrial Civilization*. New York: Macmillan, 1933. Reprint, New York: Viking, 1960.

———. *The Social Problems of an Industrial Civilization*. Boston: Harvard University Graduate School of Business Administration, 1945.

Morgan, Edmund S., ed. *Puritan Political Ideas, 1558–1794*. Indianapolis: Bobbs-Merrill, 1965.

Owen, Robert. *A New View of Society and Other Writings*. Edited by Gregory Claeys. London: Penguin, 1991.

Pañcatantra. Translated by Patrick Olivelle. Oxford: Oxford University Press, 1997.

Perret, Noëlle-Laetitia, and Stéphane Péquignot, eds. *A Critical Companion to the 'Mirror for Princes' Literature*. Leiden: Brill, 2023.

Petrarch (Francesco Petrarca). *How a Ruler Ought to Govern His State*. Translated by Benjamin G. Kohl. In *The Earthly Republic*, edited by Benjamin G. Kohl and Ronald G. Witt, 25–80. Philadelphia: University of Pennsylvania Press, 1978.

Plumstead, A. W., ed. *The Wall and the Garden: Selected Massachusetts Election Sermons 1670–1775*. Minneapolis: University of Minnesota Press, 1968.

Pritchard, James B., ed. *Ancient Near Eastern Texts*. 3rd ed. Princeton, NJ: Princeton University Press, 1969.

Rawls, John. *A Theory of Justice*. Cambridge, MA: Harvard University Press, 1971.

Richelieu, Armand-Jean du Plessis duc de. *The Political Testament of Cardinal Richelieu*. Translated by Henry Bertram Hill. Madison: University of Wisconsin Press, 1961.

The Sea of Precious Virtues (Bahr al-Fava'id): A Medieval Islamic Mirror for Princes. Edited and translated by Julie Scott Meisami. Salt Lake City: University of Utah Press, 1991.

Secretum Secretorum. Edited by Robert Steele. *Opera Hactenus Inedita Rogeri Baconi*, fasc. 5. London: Oxford University Press, 1920.

Seneca. *Moral Essays*. Translated by John W. Basore. Loeb Classical Library *Seneca* Vol. 1. Cambridge, MA: Harvard University Press, 1958.

——. *Moral and Political Essays*. Edited and translated by John Cooper and J. F. Procopé. Cambridge: Cambridge University Press, 1995.

Sheehan, Colleen A. *The Mind of James Madison*. Cambridge: Cambridge University Press, 2015.

Skinner, Quentin. *The Foundations of Modern Political Thought*. Vol. 1: *The Renaissance*. Cambridge: Cambridge University Press, 1978.

Stout, Harry S. *The New England Soul*. New York: Oxford University Press, 1986.

Taylor, Frederick Winslow. *Scientific Management*. New York: Harper & Brothers, 1947.

Wallace-Hadrill, J. M. "The *Via Regia* of the Carolingian Age." In *Trends in Medieval Political Thought*, edited by Beryl Smalley, 22–41. Oxford: Basil Blackwell, 1965.

William of Pagula. *Mirror of King Edward III*. In *Political Thought in Early Fourteenth-Century England*, edited and translated by Cary J. Nederman. Tempe: Arizona Center for Medieval and Renaissance Studies/Brepols, 2002.

Williams, Stephen J. *The Secret of Secrets*. Ann Arbor: University of Michigan Press, 2003.

Xenophon, *The Education of Cyrus*. Translated by H. G. Dakyns. London: Dent, 1992.

INDEX

mirrors for princes: formula, 4, 36–37, 80, 97, 107–8, 116, 132, 153, 244, 257; general audience for, 2, 11, 57, 95–96, 125, 291; mirror metaphor, 1, 24, 118, 136, 180; mirrors for managers, 241, 244, 257, 263, 267, 270, 275, 277, 279, 281, 291, 305, 319, 321; moral education of rulers, 13, 19, 62, 80, 98–99, 110, 127, 133–34, 136, 177; as motivational books, 15, 24, 62, 96, 121; New England sermons as, 4, 172–73, 181–82, 184, 191, 193; for patronage, 3, 112, 117, 125, 127, 129, 196, 303; powers from God, 43, 49–50, 70, 85, 108, 126, 134, 160, 179, 193; satires of, 4, 31, 35–36, 74–75; social responsibilities, 25, 45, 50, 52, 70–71, 91, 93, 127, 172, 290; "tips for tyrants," 3, 18, 42, 119, 145–46, 154, 160–64, 177, 259; vision propagation, 4, 9, 12, 14, 29, 37, 43, 84, 111, 121, 132–33, 197, 257, 264, 279. *See also specific authors and titles*
monarchy: ancient views, 12, 14, 18, 20, 30, 290–292; medieval views, 66, 73, 90–93, 97–99; modern views, 195, 197–200, 212–13; renaissance views, 116, 133–34, 143, 148–50, 156, 162, 164
Moore, Wilbert, 276
Moreno García, Juan Carlos, 291
Morgan, Edmund, 182
Morison, Samuel Eliot, 303
Mosse, George, 171
Murphy, Chad, 298

National Association of Manufacturers (NAM), 283–84, 290; American Way campaign, 284–89, 294; "You and Industry," 286–89
National Labor Relations Act, 271–73, 275, 284, 286, 288, 324, 326; National Labor Relations Board, 273, 324–26
Native Americans, 12, 16, 166, 187, 194, 215, 299, 306; Cotton Mather on, 167, 176, 189–91
Nederman, Cary, 105–6
Nelson, Janet, 46

Nero (emperor), 27–29, 54, 70, 118
Néron, Pierre-Yves, 320
New Deal, 272–75, 284–86, 294, 330; La Follette Committee, 288–90
New Harmony, Indiana, 243, 246–47, 254, 290; Boatload of Knowledge, 249–50; governance, 248–250, 252–54, 256–57; "woman problem," 250–51, 279
Nithard, 39
Nizam al-Mulk, 108: *Book of Government*, 108–11

O'Connor, Ellen, 268
organic metaphor, 51, 170, 194, 209, 267, 280, 282, 297, 308–9, 322; in mirrors for princes, 4–5, 65–68, 125, 134, 155, 184, 296, 305, 315, 349n94
Orme, Nicholas, 102
O'Toole, James, 257
Otto of Freising, 115
Owen, Robert, 241, 258, 262–63, 278–79, 287, 327; critics of, 243, 245–46, 250–54, 276; as educator, 249, 251–53, 290, 319, 371n47; as manager, 242, 244–45, 248, 252, 255–57; *New View of Society*, 243–45, 255. *See also* New Harmony
Owen, Robert Dale, 248, 256
Owen, William, 247–48

Paine, Thomas, 199
Pañcatantra, 79
Pears, Sarah, 251, 254–56
Perkins, William, 169–71
Petrarch (Francesco Petrarca), 27, 115, 117, 121–22, 125, 127; *How a Ruler Ought to Govern*, 117–120
Pettegree, Andrew, 128
Philip the Fair (king), 73, 95, 99–102
Philip of Macedon, 15, 19, 26
Phips, Sir William, 179, 191, 193
Pinker, Steven, 153
Plumstead, A. W., 172
Portenar, Abraham Jacob, 259–60
Providence, Rhode Island, 187–88

ABOUT THE AUTHOR

Michael Keeley is Emeritus Professor of Management at Loyola University Chicago. His research involves the intellectual history of organizational theory. He has published in top-tier journals in both management (*Administrative Science Quarterly, Academy of Management Journal, Academy of Management Review*) and business ethics (*Business Ethics Quarterly, Journal of Business Ethics*). His articles focus on the application of political philosophy to organizations. His book *A Social-Contract Theory of Organizations* (University Notre Dame Press, 1988) was influential in introducing classical social-contract ideas to the study of management. He has served on the editorial board of *Business Ethics Quarterly* and has earned multiple awards for teaching at Loyola University Chicago. He earned his PhD from Northwestern University.